Joseph Corbett

The Reformers

Lectures delivered in St. James' Church, Paisley

Joseph Corbett

The Reformers

Lectures delivered in St. James' Church, Paisley

ISBN/EAN: 9783337412760

Printed in Europe, USA, Canada, Australia, Japan

Cover: Foto ©Lupo / pixelio.de

More available books at **www.hansebooks.com**

THE REFORMERS:

LECTURES DELIVERED IN ST. JAMES' CHURCH,

PAISLEY,

BY

MINISTERS OF THE UNITED PRESBYTERIAN CHURCH,
GRADUATES OF THE UNIVERSITY OF GLASGOW.

GLASGOW:
JAMES MACLEHOSE & SONS,
Publishers to the University.
1885.

Preface.

THESE Lectures have, in substance, been delivered on Sabbath evenings from a provincial pulpit by Lecturers who are ministers of the same branch of our Scottish Church, and graduates of the same University. It was deemed seasonable, as the five hundredth anniversary of the death of Wyclif was approaching, thus to commemorate the service which he and his successors rendered to spiritual Christianity, and to the cause of civil and religious liberty.

The selection made from among the Reformers was determined by the desire to trace the general history of the Reformation, from its distant beginnings in Wyclif and Hus, down to its accomplishment by Luther and its formulation by Calvin, taking account by the way of kindred upheavals as represented by Savonarola, and of the influence of the Renaissance as represented by Erasmus; and then to sketch the peculiar history of the Scottish Reformation from its earlier and later precursors, through its two most illustrious martyrs, to its consummation under John Knox.

Each Lecturer, in dealing with the subject assigned to him, has been left free to select his standpoint and method of treatment, and is responsible only for his own lecture.

St. James' Manse,
Paisley, 8th December, 1884.

Contents.

		PAGE
I.	*WYCLIF*,	1
	By JOSEPH CORBETT, D.D., Glasgow.	
II.	*HUS*,	49
	By DANIEL M'LEAN, B.D., Alloa.	
III.	*SAVONAROLA*,	91
	By JOHN P. MITCHELL, M.A., Cupar-Fife.	
IV.	*ERASMUS*,	142
	By JOHN MEIKLEJOHN, M.A., Kirkmuirhill.	
V.	*LUTHER*,	191
	By MATTHEW MUIR DICKIE, B.D., Haddington.	
VI.	*CALVIN*,	241
	By JAMES ORR, B.D., Hawick.	

CONTENTS.

               PAGE

VII. LOLLARDS OF KYLE AND OTHER PRECURSORS OF THE SCOTTISH REFORMATION, . 296
   By WILLIAM DICKIE, M.A., Perth.

VIII. PATRICK HAMILTON AND GEORGE WISHART, 344
   By JAMES KIDD, B.D., St. Andrews.

IX. JOHN KNOX, ... 412
   By JAMES BROWN, D.D., Paisley.

THE REFORMERS.

John Wyclif.

HE would be a bold man, though hardly a wise one, who should undertake to say exactly when and where that momentous movement originated which, in the sixteenth century, startled the whole civilized world of Europe, and shook to its very foundation the time-honoured ecclesiastical fabric of the Papacy. The Reformation was a series of events of so complex a character as to bid defiance to the most resolute endeavours made to trace its history back to its fountain-head. It was the resultant of well-nigh numberless forces, political and religious, many of which had been in operation even for ages before their effects took shape in the revolution with which the names of Luther and Melanchthon, Calvin and Zwingli are identified. In periods and localities far apart from each other, the surface of society had been again and again disturbed by phenomena that witnessed to undercurrents of thought which, flowing along various channels, were all converging to the one sure issue, and foretelling, with no uncertain voice, of a determined, victorious revolt from intellectual and spiritual despotism. It would betray, therefore, an utter lack of historic sense, a complete misunderstanding of the spirit and significance of the movement were we to claim for any country or for any man the honour of having really begun the work of which it was the completion, and, certainly, we have no wish to interpret in this absolute sense the title so often given to John Wyclif, as "The morning star of the Reformation." For even he had his predecessors both abroad and at home.

To confine our view to our own country, his was not the first English voice to make itself heard in eloquent protest against the arrogant usurpations of Rome. As near as may be a century and a half before Wyclif's birth, the famous Robert Grosseteste had been born at the little village of Stradbrook, and of his character and work Matthew Paris gives this summary: "He was a manifest confuter of the Pope and the King, the blamer of prelates, the corrector of monks, the director of priests, the instructor of clerks, the support of scholars, the preacher to the people, the persecutor of the incontinent, the sedulous student of all Scripture, the hammer and the despiser of the Romans."[1] In Wyclif's eyes it was one of the many crimes of the Papacy that it had no honours of saintship to bestow on a man whose fervent zeal for the purity of the Church compelled him to denounce the sins that were eating away its strength and poisoning its influence, and were still, in his own day, as virulent as before. Not fifty years had elapsed after Grosseteste's death before another English hamlet had given to the world the boy who subsequently be-

[1] Quoted in H. Morley's English Writers, book i. chapter 22.

came the "invincible doctor," the "dear Master Ockham" of Martin Luther, a paragon of philosophical acumen, and, at the same time, a doughty champion of national independence as opposed to the political supremacy of the Pope. To him, as to Wyclif after him, the doctrine of the Papal infallibility was a delusion only to be laughed at by reasonable men, nor was it beyond the bounds of possibility that the Roman Pontiff might be the veriest heretic under the sun, as he shrewdly suspected was actually the case in the person of his particular enemy, John XXII. Much about the same time, at Hartfield in Sussex, Thomas Bradwardin was born, destined to be known as the "doctor profundus," who was himself what he describes the great Augustin as having been, a "splendid and strenuous champion of grace," and affirmed the all-sufficiency of that divine principle with an uncompromising effectiveness and eloquence on a par with those of Luther himself. In these and others like them the very spirit moved that asserted itself with more commanding power still in the greater Englishman whom his continental followers did not scruple to designate the fifth evangelist, and who is the subject of the present lecture.

Born, not later than 1324, in quiet Teesdale, Wyclif spent his childhood and early youth amid scenes whose natural loveliness is enhanced to the modern visitor because of the glamour cast over them by the wizard hand of Sir Walter Scott, who, in his romance of Rokeby, celebrates the very hills and streams frequented by our young Reformer. The family he belonged to owed their name to the peculiar features of the locality in the heart of which the ancestral mansion stands overlooking the river, and there may still be seen the little, simple church, within whose walls, with boyish faith yet undisturbed, Wyclif was wont to kneel. Little is told us, practically nothing indeed, of the home in which he was reared. We search in vain through his writings for such reminiscences of early days as abound in Luther's works, nor do the family records throw any light upon the domestic influences by which the man was "fashioned in his youth." No echoes can we catch of the sounds either of merriment or trouble that issued from his childish lips, nor any signs of the inevitable pains that accompanied his first attempts to pluck the fruit of the tree of knowledge. Whether he gave early indications of the sceptical spirit that, in later years, drove him so far away from the traditional Christianity of his family, or showed himself a loyal and unquestioning son of the Church till he went forth to breathe the perilous air of Oxford, we have no means of deciding. This only appears to be tolerably certain, that he came of a stock marked by a jealous conservatism of the staunchest and most orthodox type. The fact is a noticeable one that Romanism has always held its own in that secluded Yorkshire parish, and that no other member of the Wyclif family seems to have regarded with aught but utter repugnance the revolutionary tenets of their greatest representative. There is, indeed, one passage in his writings which reads like a page out of his own experience, and may imply that his assaults upon the established order of things had alienated from him the affection and good-will of those nearest to him. It occurs in a wise and pithy tract entitled "Of wedded men and wives, and of their children also,"[1] and reads

[1] Select English Works of Wyclif (Edit. Arnold.) vol. 3, p. 188.

thus—wedded men and women often say " that if their child draw him to meekness and poverty, and flee covetousness and pride, for dread of sin and for to please God, he shall never be man, and never cost them penny, and curse him, if he live well and teach other men God's law, to save men's souls. For by this doing, the child getteth many enemies to his elders, and they say that he slandereth all their noble kin that ever were held true men and worshipful." Even this unique reference to his own circumstances, if such it is, is too meagre to permit any biographer, however cunning, to weave out of it a narrative of the early joys and sorrows of young Wyclif, and we must be content to leave his boyhood in the obscurity that has hitherto enveloped it.

Some compensation for this misfortune is to be found in the fact that it is not impossible to form a fairly satisfactory idea of the social conditions that prevailed in the country whilst Wyclif was advancing towards manhood. The England to which he belonged was that which still lives and moves before us in Chaucer's bright, unfading page. In the ordinary society of the day were to be found in abundance representatives of all the characters delineated with such infinite grace and skill by the father of English poetry. The travelled knight who, meek as he is brave, has fought on every field of battle where a strong arm and a stout heart can be of service; the gentle squire who has not yet lost youth's predilection for a dainty coat; the nut-headed, short-haired yeoman, who is skilled in the use of the weapon that wrought such havoc at Cressy and Poitiers; the solid merchant whose well-to-do comfort shines out in his costly raiment and his solemn speech; the weather-beaten sailor, better able to handle a ship than to ride a horse; the sage doctor, learned in astronomy and fond of gold; and the ready lawyer, full, like Shakespeare's Justice, of "wise saws and modern instances," all figure on Chaucer's stage, only because they were every day playing their part on the English soil trodden by John Wyclif's feet. How women dressed and gossiped in their pithy mother-tongue or the French of Stratford-le-Bowe; how goat-voiced pardoners exhibited their relics to gaping, superstitious crowds; how threadbare students spent their little all on the purchase of their meagre store of books; how jolly friars lisped and sang and harped the money out of people's pockets, may all be seen on the rich canvas painted for us by the author of the Canterbury Tales. The subtle spirit of that wonderful poem, too, reveals better far than any prosaic history the temper of the time. There is a strange lack of earnestness and true sobriety. As has been well remarked, it is the life rather of children than of men and women that we are spectators of. The gaiety that loves bright surfaces, however thin, and hates a preacher with all its small apology for a soul, is the common characteristic of the actors in the panoramic drama. In almost equally distinct relief the extravagance stands out which contemporary annals delineate with hardly less force of language, and which was not to be repressed even by the sumptuary laws that forbade a third course at dinner or the use of furs for trimming. It is, indeed, not too much to say that there was prevalent a "desire to make life one long holiday, dividing it between tournaments and the dalliance of courts of love, or between archery meetings (skilfully substituted by royal command for less useful exercises) and the seductive company of "tumblers," "fruiterers," and "waferers."[1]

To take a somewhat deeper and broader view than is furnished by the poet, Wyclif's lot was cast in times of singular interest and importance. But a few years after his birth, Edward III., a prince of fourteen, was proclaimed king, and began a reign in the course of which good and evil, honour and shame, were almost equally distributed. While Wyclif was yet a boy there broke out the disastrous conflict with France which "dragged its slow length along" for a weary hundred years. Vast changes were passing over the social conditions of the people. Serfdom was giving token of very speedily becoming a thing only of the past. The question of the poor, which ever since has so severely taxed the wisdom alike of statesmanship and philanthropy, was beginning to force itself imperiously upon the thoughts of men. The stern conflict between capital and labour, which rages so fiercely still, was entering upon its earliest stages and provoking attempts at pacification that, like many later ones, were pregnant alike with good intentions and evil consequences. Vagabondage and mendicancy were assuming dimensions ominous of disaster. The rapid dissolution of those restraints on freedom of movement that were inseparable from feudalism, was being followed, on the part especially of the poorer classes, by a restlessness quite new in English history. The tongue of the common people was at last triumphantly asserting itself against the foreign language that had hitherto been regarded as the only honourable medium of intercourse, and the

[1] Ward's Chaucer, in English Men of Letters, p. 42.

real birthday both of English poetry and English prose is to be found in this epoch, in the chronicles of which the names of Geoffrey Chaucer and John Wyclif stand side by side. So far, indeed, as regards the strong, solid framework of the national life, the England of this fourteenth century was essentially modern rather than mediæval, despite unglazed windows and unchimneyed houses, narrow and filthy streets, rough and perilous roads, rush-strewn floors and morning-dinners, and despite the lack of forks and the plethora of priests.

This last feature was singularly characteristic of Wyclif's age as compared with our own. Ecclesiastics were ubiquitous. There was, on the average, one priest for every eighty of the population. Monks and friars, abbots and bishops swarmed like bees. They crowded about the steps of the throne and clutched greedily at offices of state, and they crept into the hovels of the poor, and cajoled or threatened them out of their scanty earnings. They were of every type and character. There were black friars and grey; there were summoners, limitors and pardoners; there were priests that played the mountebank, and priests that played the tyrant; there were priests that feigned a poverty to which they were utter strangers, and priests that made no attempt to hide their predilection for horses and hounds, for furs and jewellery, for good fellowship and dainty fare. Others, certainly, there were of nobler mould, and the poet has not neglected to adorn his canvas with the figure of the poor parson of the town, who was "rich of holy thought and work," who failed

> "Not for either rain or thunder
> In sickness nor mischance to visit all—

The furthest in his parish, great and small,
Upon his feet, and in his hand a staff.

. . . .

He put not out his benefice on hire,
And left his sheep encumbered in the mire,
And ran to London unto Saintë Paul's,
To seek himself a chantery for souls,
Or maintenance with a brotherhood to hold,
But dwelt at home, and keptë well his fold ; "

while, to all his other virtues, he added this, that he would " sharply snub at once " any " obstinate " person either of " high or low estate." This, however, was all too surely a comparatively rare type of ecclesiastic, and it is not improbable that the exquisite figure would not have been found at all in Chaucer's gallery had Wyclif not been among his contemporaries.

With many of these features of the period our young Yorkshire scholar may have been little familiar whilst he still lingered in remote, secluded Teesdale, but his removal to Oxford, when he was, in all likelihood, about fifteen or sixteen years of age, would vastly enlarge his horizon, and would necessarily bring him face to face with characters and movements full of interest and novelty to his quick, observant intellect. An almost bewildering change it would be from the quiet country home to the thronged, restless university town, with its six or seven thousand students, for many of whom there was but scanty, uncleanly accommodation. Of the five colleges that then existed, one had a special interest for Wyclif, as it had been founded in 1269 by the widow of Sir John de Balliol of Barnard Castle, a lordly mansion only five miles distant from our student's native parish ; and there can be little doubt that it was to this college he attached himself on his arrival at Oxford.

It was a troubled and tumultuous world into which he now entered, not by any means distinguished by the calm, dignified repose popularly associated with the idea of intellectual and philosophical pursuits. The air of Oxford was full of the spirit of strife. There was rivalry and contention, sometimes fierce and deadly, between the Australes and the Boreales, the southerns and the northerns, as the two nations were called into which the students were divided. There was war still, even after long ages of battle, between the Realists and the Nominalists, whose contests, marked by a vehemence strangely disproportioned to the intrinsic insignificance of the questions discussed, recall the poet's question, "Dwells such dire wrath in minds divine?" And there were conflicts between gown and town, to use modern phraseology, where the combatants were counted by thousands, and in one of which, occurring in Wyclif's own time, no fewer than forty students were killed. Notwithstanding these elements of unrest Oxford was, "during the fourteenth century, by far the greatest theological and philosophical university in Europe,"[1] and the young Yorkshire student was destined to add not a little to the lustre already belonging to her famous schools.

For the first four years of his curriculum he would attend lectures on logic, rhetoric, grammar and arithmetic, and would then attain his Bachelor's degree, provided he passed with *éclat* through a nine days' ordeal, in the course of which he was expected to settle all manner of subtle dialectical conundrums flung at him in a *vivâ voce* examination. Three years more, spent in mastering geometry, astronomy, and philosophy,

[1] Creasy's History of England, vol. ii. chap 5.

would prepare him for the higher degree that secured the right of lecturing, of which at a later date, at all events, Wyclif largely availed himself.[1] It is impossible, unfortunately, to follow his career with any minuteness throughout the greater portion of his student life, and he must have been at the university for some sixteen years or more before the occurrence of a change in his position which witnesses to the reputation he had then achieved.

In the interval, however, occurred one terrible incident which must have left its impress upon a man of Wyclif's temperament as it certainly did upon the history of the nation as a whole; I refer to the first of the four epidemics of the black death that occurred during his lifetime. For fourteen years rumours had reached England of a fell plague that was raging in Central Asia, and in 1347 it made its appearance at Constantinople. Before a few months had gone it burst upon Avignon, and carried off no fewer than 60,000, for whom burial could be secured only in the Rhone, which was duly consecrated for that purpose by the Pope. In August, 1348, it swooped down on Dorsetshire, and thence spread over the length and breadth of the land, working appalling desolation and ruin wherever it came, and utterly disorganizing the whole fabric of society. In Norwich, where seven out of every ten were carried off, no fewer than " 15,374 died besides religious and beggars, and twenty churches fell into ruins"; and in Bristol "grass grew several inches high on the High Street and Broad Street."[2]

[1] Canon Pennington's John Wyclif, chap. 2
[2] Longman's Life and Times of Edward III., vol. i. p. 305. Hecker's Epidemics of the Middle Ages. Seebohm, *Fortnightly Review*, vol. i.

In the West Riding of Yorkshire two-thirds of the priests fell victims to its power. In London, after all the existing burial places had been filled, 50,000 corpses were laid in a graveyard specially provided by Sir Walter Manny, and at least half the population of the country was swept away in the course of a few months. The rural districts were as fiercely scourged as the towns, and there were whole villages in which no sound of life was to be heard either from man or beast. This, too, was but a specimen of what was taking place over the entire continent of Europe, where it is calculated that the enormous number of twenty-five millions were destroyed. It is impossible that Wyclif learnt nothing from a calamity so overwhelming. His was not the ear to be deaf to, nor was his the heart to be proof against the lessons that were being imparted in this visitation by a higher teacher than any whose scholastic disquisitions were to be heard in Oxford's lecture-halls. We can hardly be wrong in thinking that to this agony of distress something was due of the passionate earnestness of the man, and of the vivid sense he had of the supreme importance of spiritual realities.

The first distinct discoverable token of the high place Wyclif occupied in the esteem of the university is the occurrence of his name in 1356 as one of the Fellows of Merton College, to which both Ockham and Bradwardin had belonged. The significance of this fact is all the greater that Merton and Balliol were, in some respects, antagonistic, and the election of Wyclif to this office cannot well be explained except on the ground of his acknowledged preeminence. Four years afterwards he appears as the Master of Balliol, a position he held only for a short time, and the last honour of this kind bestowed upon him was the Wardenship of the new Canterbury Hall with which he was invested at the close of 1365. From this he was dismissed by Archbishop Langham on grounds it is unnecessary to specify, but which were of such a nature that Wyclif appealed to the Pope, though without effect.¹ These dignities bestowed upon him witness to the fact that his learning and power were such as to make him one of the very foremost men of the university, if, indeed, there were any at all to be put in the same rank. "He made his great aim," says an opponent who lived in his own day, "with learned subtlety, and by the profundity of his genius, to surpass the genius of other men," and he is constrained to allow that "as a theologian Wyclif was the most eminent in the day, as a philosopher second ton one, and as a schoolman incomparable."² A similar judgment is passed upon him by Professor Shirley, who assigns to Wyclif a place with Duns Scotus, Ockham, and Bradwardin as the "four great schoolmen of the fourteenth century."³

It has, indeed, become the fashion to laugh at the representatives of scholasticism as though they were little better than earnest quibblers who spent their strength in splitting hairs and spinning cobwebs. "They constructed monstrous books," writes one brilliant critic, "in great numbers, cathedrals of syllogism of unheard-of

---

¹ The doubts raised by the late Professor Shirley as to the identity of the Fellow of Merton and the Warden of Canterbury with the Reformer appear to be dispelled by later researches; *vide*, Pennington's John Wiclif, Warburton's Edward III., and an able article in the *Church Quarterly*, October, 1877.

² Vaughan's John de Wycliffe, ch. 7.

³ Fasciculi Zizaniorum, Introduction, p. 51.

architecture, of prodigious finish, heightened in effect by intensity of intellectual power, which the whole sum of human labour has only twice been able to match. These young and valiant minds thought they had found the temple of truth, they rushed at it headlong, in legions, breaking in the doors, clambering over the walls, leaping into the interior, and so found themselves at the bottom of a moat. Three centuries of labour at the bottom of this moat added not one idea to the human mind. Each one in turn mechanically traversed the petty region of threadbare cavils, scratched himself in the briars of quibbles, and burdened himself with his bundles of texts, nothing more."[1] A higher and truer estimate of the schoolmen than M. Taine's will be formed by all who are not oblivious of the simple fact that the philosophy of which they are the exponents was "the philosophy which created the universities of Europe,"[2] an achievement which a whole army of sparkling critics could neither appreciate nor accomplish, though their glib pens should run on till doomsday. There is doubtless much in the aims and methods of scholasticism that strikes the modern student with utter amazement, so plainly does it carry in itself the doom of barrenness and failure. Numberless questions are discussed the very mention of which provokes a smile and brands them as mere ingenious but absolutely impractical speculations. But there is at the same time a most impressive grandeur about the earnestness and hungry zeal with which the mighty intellects of the schoolmen press forward to the furthest verge of the

[1] Taine's English Literature, translated by Von Laun, book i. ch. 3.
[2] Shirley's Scholasticism, p. 9.

only world of thought they felt at liberty to explore, and there are names associated with this stage of philosophy which will bear an untarnished glory so long as the world sets any value on sublety, acuteness, and accuracy of thought. Nor can we fail to see that, even whilst indulging in these wild, fanciful speculations, the intellect was but passing laboriously across the wilderness in unconscious search of a rich land of promise, and was there undergoing the very discipline necessary to fit it for the conquest and enjoyment of a worthier heritage. Many of the qualities developed in the arid soil and in the dry air of scholasticism were to stand humanity in good stead when once a breach had been made in the stone boundary-walls beyond which it was, for centuries, counted heresy to peep.

It is not, therefore, to be regretted that Wyclif passed with such signal success through this scholastic discipline, and it may well be doubted whether he would ever have been so resolute and so incisive a reformer had he not first achieved fame as a prince among the schoolmen. When he had taken his degree of Doctor of Theology, he was at liberty to expound not merely the "Sacred Page," as the Bible was called in academical circles, but also the great university text-book of the age, "The Sentences of Peter the Lombard," a "series of extracts from the Latin Fathers and the Popes, so tesselated together as to construct a system of theology out of the most unsystematic of all possible materials."[1] In all probability, however, Wyclif did not take this degree till after his removal from the Wardenship of Canterbury Hall, and after the occurrence of a crisis in his career which brought him to the very front

[1] Shirley's Scholasticism, p. 21.

of the national life and committed him virtually to the path he pursued throughout his subsequent history.

This happened in 1366, when Pope Urban V. demanded from Edward payment of arrears of an annual tribute of 1000 marks which, promised by King John, had not been transmitted to the papal treasury for the last thirty years. There were many circumstances that made this demand peculiarly offensive and exasperating. Very shortly before, statutes had been framed and enacted asserting most emphatically the independence of the empire, and imposing severe penalties upon all who should affirm the supremacy of the Pope in any such way as infringed the rights of the people or the King. Urban's insolent demand, therefore, was ominously like an intentional defiance, and a formal declaration that all such enactments would be treated by him as null and void. The claim, too, came not from Rome but from Avignon, where the head of the Church was bearing his share of what was termed the "second Babylonian captivity." He was himself a Frenchman and a slave of the French monarch, and it was quite reasonably suspected that the money was needed, not to meet the wants of the Church, but to swell the resources of the nation's rival and enable him to carry on the war with this country. If ever England might have been expected to play a part so suicidal as that the Pope enjoined upon her, it was not like an infallible Pontiff to ask her to do so when just at the zenith of her power, and when she had won victory after victory in the open field.

It might have been conjectured beforehand how Parliament would deal with the foolish and impertinent demand when the matter was referred to them by

Edward. With one voice, Lords spiritual and temporal, as well as the members of the lower chamber, indignantly denied the obligation, and with no " bated breath or whispered humbleness" let it be known after what fashion they would shape their reply, were any attempt made to enforce the claim. Challenged by an anonymous monk to vindicate the attitude of the King and Parliament, Wyclif, not without manifest delight in the work, published a most vigorous statement, professedly reproducing the arguments used by certain of the Lords. " Let the Pope get the money if he can; England is not afraid," says one. " Christ was no civil governor," affirms another, " neither should the Pope be if he is Christ's follower." " Wages are for work," argues a third, " but popes and cardinals do us no good either in body or soul, therefore, give them no pay, say I." " If King John undertook to pay in silver and gold for spiritual blessings," another insists, " the King was a fool and the Pope a simonist." " If, as is maintained, the Pope gave the King this country of England, then," a fifth declares, " the Pope either gave what was not his and so could not have been given, or he gave what was his only for the Church, and so should not have been given." Thus with strong, sturdy strokes, the reply is shaped into a form there could be no mistake about, and which pretty well settled the matter for all time to come. Speaking in his own name, Wyclif emphatically repudiates the opinion that the State has no right to touch or meddle with ecclesiastical persons and possessions, though, whilst broaching this most pernicious heresy, he claims to be " a lowly and obedient son of the Roman Church," and to " assert nothing that may appear unjust towards the said Church, or that may reasonably offend pious ears."

The next important step in Wyclif's career was the publication in 1367 or 1368 of his treatise on "Divine Dominion," the preface to which is regarded by Professor Shirley as "the true epoch of the beginning of the English Reformation."[1] The fundamental principle of the work is that all dominion belongs to God alone, and that others—popes, priests, emperors, kings, and individual men—hold whatever authority they possess only and directly from Him on condition of loyal service and obedience, and that to Him each is immediately responsible. Into any examination of this striking theory it is impossible to enter here, but it is evident that this one simple principle struck at the very root of sacerdotal supremacy, and must have provoked the ire of the ecclesiastical world, apart altogether from Wyclif's assertion of the startling paradox, at which his adversaries clutched with jubilant avidity, that "God must obey the devil."

Another opportunity for the affirmation of his bold radicalism with regard to the relative power of Church and State arose out of the national disgrace and humiliation which followed so swiftly upon the noon-day of England's glory. After a period of almost uninterrupted successes, there came a time when disaster after disaster robbed the kingdom of all the fruits of her toil, bravery, and sacrifice. "It was a time of shame and suffering such as England had never known. Her conquests were lost, her shores insulted, her fleets annihilated, her commerce swept from the sea; while within she was exhausted by the long and costly war, as well

[1] Fasc. Ziz., Introd. p. 40.

as by the ravages of the pestilence."[1] The interests of the country demanded that most strenuous efforts should be made to utilize all her resources for the maintenance of her integrity. The community in general were already overburdened, but there was one organization that still rolled in riches and whose members managed to keep themselves well out of the straits in which all besides were pressed; that organization was the Church. Hitherto its representatives had been allowed to tax themselves, and, being human, and especially ecclesiastically human, they had not made too severe demands upon their exchequer. Now, however, the hour was come for them to bear a heavier yoke, and no sooner was it proposed that taxes should be levied upon livings hitherto exempt, and that the Church should bleed a little for the nation's good, than the clergy were up in arms. The thought of such sacrilege stung their noble souls to the quick, and the Archbishop of Canterbury fainted, either from pious horror or physical exhaustion, whilst denouncing the enormity from the pulpit of St. Paul's Cathedral. A nobler voice than the Archbishop's championed the cause of the patriot as against the ecclesiastic, and in his work on Civil Dominion, published probably in 1371, Wyclif quotes, with marked approval, a fable ascribed to a certain peer who argued that the temporalities should be taken from the clergy, as being the property of the realm, and so the kingdom should be wisely defended with its own possessions.

The appearance of a Papal emissary called Garnier kept the fire burning in Wyclif's soul. He came, of course, to gather funds, travelled in great style, with

[1] Green's Short History of the English People, chap. 5, sec. 3.

a large retinue, netted a considerable amount of ill-spared gold, and, after two years and a half of pleasant harvesting, withdrew to Rome resolved in a few months to return for fresh spoil. This new illustration of Papal greed called forth from Wyclif a tractate in which he demonstrates the falsehood of this rapacious foreigner, who had secured permission to prosecute his work in England only by taking an oath of which his whole procedure was a violation. For he had sworn to do nothing hurtful to the interests of the kingdom when his very mission was to rob it of resources most urgently required for its own necessities. Such procedure should be withstood, Wyclif insists, by every true patriot, even though sanctioned by the Head of the Church himself, for even our Lord Pope, he dares to say, is "sufficiently peccable." Evidently he is moving fast, and not without the sympathy and approval of some at least who are high in power. Of this proof is given in the appointment of Wyclif to act on a Commission sent to Bruges in 1374, to confer with representatives of the Pope about questions of procedure and jurisdiction. The meeting was productive of little good, and a curious illustration of the subtle power of the Church is furnished in the anomaly that a reward for his services was given to the chief of the English commissioners, the Bishop of Bangor, not by the King, but by the Pope.

This visit to Bruges, however, was not without result, as it would appear to have brought our Reformer into close relationship with the famous John of Gaunt, who was in the city at the same time on a political mission. "Time-honoured Lancaster" had no love for the grasping, ambitious ecclesiastics that kept so firm a hold upon the highest offices of State, and was as eagerly desirous to humble the Church as Wyclif was to exalt it. Strangely enough, though apparently antagonistic, these aims were, so the two men thought, to be fulfilled by pursuing one single path. Hence, whilst no actors in the eventful history could be more unlike in spirit, they were drawn together, and were, to some extent, sympathetic. The alliance was not of much real benefit to Wyclif. John of Gaunt had, by his anti-ecclesiastical policy, incurred the bitter enmity of Courtenay, the Bishop of London, who had his revenge in an accusation of heresy he brought against Wyclif, Lancaster's friend and ally. The patience of the clergy was by this time fairly exhausted, and their desire to silence the Reformer's voice was intensified by the action of "The Good Parliament," which made it patent to all that the leaven of his principles was working effectively in the popular mind. Wyclif, therefore, was summoned to answer for himself before the Archbishop, and appeared accompanied on one side by John of Gaunt, and on the other by Lord Percy, the Earl Marshal. An unseemly squabble between Lancaster and Courtenay opened the proceedings, which terminated in something like a riot, Wyclif standing calmly by and needing not even to unclose his lips.

But higher dignitaries than Courtenay were now alarmed, and, three months after this memorable fiasco, the Pope himself issued no fewer than five separate bulls, in which the Archbishop of Canterbury, the Bishop of London, the University of Oxford, and even the King himself were all enjoined to take immediate steps to muzzle the heretic of Lutterworth. After some delay, occasioned by the death of Edward and the accession of Richard II., Wyclif received another summons, and appeared before another tribunal in the early spring of 1378. He had laid upon him the formidable duty of vindicating or repudiating nineteen different errors which he was alleged to have propounded in his writings; but, though he handed in to his judges a written defence of his teaching, this fresh attempt to arrest his influence ended in a manner as pointless as the preceding one. The King's mother forbade the prosecution of the case, and the people of London assumed a threatening attitude, whereupon, in Walsingham's angry and scornful language, the champions of orthodoxy were "like reeds shaken with the wind, and their words were softer than oil." They retained only courage enough to give the vexatious Reformer a caution, to which he paid practically no attention.

Almost immediately after this, Pope Gregory XI. died, and then occurred the great schism in the Church, and the edifying spectacle was presented to the world of two rival Pontiffs, each claiming to be the vicegerent of Christ, the one at Rome thundering forth anathemas against his brother at Avignon, and the other at Avignon proving himself quite as good at hating and cursing as his brother at Rome. At first Wyclif was in hopes that Urban VI., the Italian Pope, would introduce beneficial changes and prove himself in sympathy with the spirit of the gospel. But he was doomed to disappointment, and as, from his peaceful home at Lutterworth, he watched the progress of the wretched quarrel he came to the common-sense conclusion that the Church would not lose much even if it lost both its heads.

A few months more, and our Reformer, less and less

able to rest content with a system so utterly disorganized, found himself compelled to take a great step forward, and to surrender the doctrine of transubstantiation, which is of the very essence of the Papacy. To his repudiation of this dogma he gave formal expression in a series of twelve theses, which he undertook to defend against all comers. This bold utterance set even Oxford on fire, reluctant as its authorities had been to take action against their ablest and most influential graduate. The Chancellor of the university called together instantly a judicial committee, largely composed of monks, who branded Wyclif's statements as erroneous and heretical. On the basis of this decision, an ordinance was published prohibiting all students from listening to such revolutionary teaching, and forbidding Wyclif from any further academical promulgation of his opinions. This injunction, which practically terminated his connection with the university, was brought to the Reformer whilst lecturing to his students on the very doctrine in dispute, and evoked from him the immediate declaration that neither the Chancellor nor any similar authority could make him alter his opinion.

There were other methods of promulgating the truth than that from which he was thus debarred, and whilst for scholars he published a treatise on the sacrament of the altar, written in his not too classical Latin, he sent forth for the people generally his famous tract entitled "The Wicket," of which the English is full as usual of nervous force. His adversaries, however, were not done with him, and his old antagonist Courtenay, now Archbishop of Canterbury, summoned a large council consisting of ten bishops, sixteen doctors of law, thirty doctors of divinity, thirteen bachelors of theology, and four bachelors of law, reliable men all of them, and of unimpeachable orthodoxy, who would not find it hard to agree upon a verdict. They assembled in the Dominican Chapter House at Blackfriars, but hardly had they begun their deliberations when an earthquake startled them, and made them dubious as to the wisdom of their action. Courtenay was not, however, to be thus baffled, and interpreted the omen as a sign of Heaven's approval, and an indication that, following the trembling earth's example, the Church must purge herself of the evil humours that were distressing her. After this ingenious piece of exegesis, things moved on comfortably, and a most satisfactory issue was reached. A long catalogue of damnable errors and heresies was drawn up, some twenty-four in all, and these were duly condemned. A mandate was sent to Oxford ordering that steps should be taken to prevent the dissemination of these obnoxious tenets. An imposing penitential procession of barefooted priests and others paraded the streets of London, and a Carmelite monk wound up the demonstration with a sermon denouncing the heresies of Wyclif, and threatening with severe ecclesiastical penalties all who might teach them or adopt them. The authorities at Oxford resented the interference with their right of self-government, but, after a little restiveness, they found themselves under the necessity of virtually pronouncing sentence of exile upon their famous "Doctor Evangelicus."

So only Lutterworth remains to him as the sphere of his labours, and thither he finally withdrew, but two or three years before his death, with health already shattered by incessant toil. Retirement, however, was not rest. Message after message he sent out into the world, whilst diligently fulfilling his duty to the parishioners he loved most truly. What his idea of a clergyman's life was we may gather from a passage in " A Short Rule of Life," one of his English writings. " If thou be a priest," he says, " live thou holily, passing others in holy prayer and holy desire and thinking, in holy speaking, counselling, and true teaching, and ever that God's commands and His gospel be in thy mouth, and ever despise sin, to draw men therefrom. And that thy deeds be so rightful that no man shall blame them with reason, but thine open deeds be a true book to all subjects, and lead men to serve God and do His commands thereby. For example of God, and open and lasting, stirreth rude men more than true preaching by naked word. And waste not thy goods in great feasts of rich men, but live a mean life of poor men's alms and goods, both in meat and drink and clothes ; and the remnant give truly to poor men that have nought of their own, and may not labour for feebleness or sickness, and then shalt thou be a true priest both to God and man." A beautiful picture fitted to stand alongside of Chaucer's, to which reference has been already made, and the first of a notable series of similar portraits of the ideal English clergyman with which our literature has been enriched. Nor was Wyclif's only a fancy sketch, but rather a model he did his best to realize in his several parishes of Fylingham, Ludgershall, and Lutterworth, though it was impossible for him to confine his work to the comparatively little sphere of the quiet Lincolnshire village.

Even after his withdrawal to its retirement, he was not left alone by those who imagined they could silence his fearless voice. He was again cited to appear before an imposing array of bishops in November, 1382, at a time when he was sorely discouraged by the cowardly retractations of more than one of his most intimate associates, and in 1383 he was ordered to betake himself to Rome to answer before the Pope himself for the heresies he had so persistently propounded. Whether he actually responded to the former summons is a matter involved in considerable uncertainty, but his reply to the last citation, which he did not obey, is still extant. Pleading his inability to take so long a journey, he uses the opportunity for a renewed and impressive assertion of some of the convictions he had already reiterated in many forms. Before this incident took place, moreover, his fierce indignation had been enkindled by the proceedings of Spencer, Bishop of Norwich, who headed a crusade and went forth to wage war in the interests of Pope Urban, and against those of Pope Clement. Every kind of spiritual bribe was held out to induce people to join the army by which this holy war was to be prosecuted, and Wyclif, burning with wrath as he heard of the blasphemous allurements, denounced in keen, uncompromising words the guilt incurred by such gross departure from the law of Christ.

The most absorbing and momentous work of these last few years was, however, beyond all question, that of preparing, completing, and revising the first Bible ever issued in our mother tongue, and, indeed, the first, by a century, in any living European language.[1] It was the grandest work of his life, a most fitting close to his splendid service, and when once that priceless

---

[1] Wyclif's Place in History, by Prof. Burrows, p. 20.

gift had been bestowed upon his country, it might well seem that there was little left for him to do but die, and enter into rest. No premature summons, therefore, was that which came to him while attending service in his church at Lutterworth, and was obeyed when, two days after, on 31st December, 1384, he "fell asleep in Jesus." "Requiescat in pace" was, we may be sure, the tender prayer breathed by many as they took farewell of a master and a friend who had endeared himself to them, not more by his untiring zeal than by the purity and grace of his personal character. The loving wish was vain, indeed, so far as the poor mortal dust of him was concerned. For forty years it lay undisturbed beneath the stones of Lutterworth Church; but then, in obedience to one of the countless irrational and inhuman decrees of which Church Courts have been guilty, the innocent bones were rudely disinterred, borne to the village bridge, burned to ashes, and flung in contemptuous triumph into the waters of the Swift. And there was an end of Wyclif—at least, so some men thought.

A very meagre sketch this is of the life of one of the grandest Englishmen that ever breathed. The outline needs filling up as it cannot be filled up here. The years over which we have run so swiftly were packed to the uttermost with diligent toil. "Man is born to work," Wyclif says in one passage, "as the bird for flight," and the principle is one to which he rendered most constant homage. His writings are a library in themselves, numbering, according to different methods of estimating them, from 150 to 200 separate compositions. The larger proportion of them are in Latin, and the others, in English, belong, most of them to the last few years of his life, when he made his appeal directly to the people, one of those daring, original, and patriotic acts that threw great light upon his character and spirit, and elicited the bitter animadversion of his opponents. In 1410 two hundred volumes of his works were burned by order of the Archbishop of Prague, and there are still extant some four hundred of his sermons.[1] Of the theologico-philosophical system expounded in his writings no survey can be attempted in this lecture, and it will be hardly possible to do more than indicate even his fundamental positions as a Reformer.

One fact to be constantly borne in mind, if our estimate of his character is to be fair and intelligent, is that Wyclif's was eminently a progressive life. He has been often charged with inconsistency, and the accusation was plausible enough so long as no attempt had been made to discover the sequence of his writings. It is now manifest that the inconsistency is only such as is inseparable from growth. He declares honestly that he has changed, and that he is ready to change again should that be necessitated by loyalty to truth and conscience. He was not the man to see any beauty in the metallic immobility that, with so many, passes current for faithfulness, when it is nothing better than an amalgam of indolence and cowardice.

Another point with reference to which censure has been passed upon him is the part he took in the politics of his day. Milner laments that " a political spirit deeply infects Wyclif's conduct," and for that and other reasons he cannot " rank him among the highest worthies of the Church," and a greater critic than Milner

[1] Shirley's Catalogue of Wyclif's Works.

has spoken of politics as the rock on which Wyclif split. Such a judgment is possible only when a mere fragment of his work is kept in view, and when there has been an entire failure to appreciate the spirit that animated him when bearing his part in the settlement of national problems. Happily, he was not ashamed to be a patriot. He had enough of the old prophet's faith in him to be convinced that a man is little likely to do any divine work in the world who is so exceedingly cosmopolitan that his fatherland is no more to him than any other country on the face of the earth. He was jealous, with a godly jealousy, for the honour and welfare of the nation. There was nothing in him of the sickly other-worldliness that surrenders the reins of civic and political government into any hands, however dirty, and regards such matters as too secular to have any claim upon the attention of a pious soul. All honour to his memory, that any attempt to trample on the independence of England provoked him to passionate protest and resistance, and that his very faith in God made it simply impossible for him to sit tamely by, "a dumb dog," whilst the people were being wronged by foreign usurpation or domestic injustice. Wyclif was, to his praise be it said, an Englishman, every inch of him, not unworthy of a place in the very front rank of those whose names, "familiar in our ears as household words," suggest the memory of glorious battles fought and won in the cause of Britain's liberties. Besides, it was impossible that Wyclif could steer clear of politics if he were to be a Reformer at all. The Church itself was more political than anything else. It claimed to be the supreme civil power in Europe.

It arrogated to itself the right to dethrone kings and instruct parliaments. Its dignitaries were at the bottom of every intrigue that sought to arrest the nation's march to freedom. If, therefore, Wyclif was political, the fault lay not with the Reformer but with the system he laboured to reform; if he wrote much about Church and State, it was only because the former was intent upon devouring the latter, or degrading it into a mere puppet of ecclesiastic ambition.

What, essentially, Wyclif's aim was, there can be little doubt about. It was just to bring back Christianity to its original character as portrayed in the New Testament. He was a reformer because he was, first and above everything else, a student of the "Sacred Page." The early Apostolic records he had pored over year after year, until the one fact that, more than any other, bulked largely in his intellectual horizon, was the absolute disparity between the Christianity of the first and that of the fourteenth century. "Back to the Bible," the so-called formal principle of the sixteenth century movement, was the scroll he blazoned on his banner from the outset, and in the elevation of this principle, as has been truly said, he is without a compeer throughout the history of the English Reformation.[1] Authority which, with the Church, meant the whole heterogeneous mass of ecclesiastical tradition, meant, with Wyclif, simply and alone the Word of God. That constituted, he maintained, the sole tribunal whose verdict was final and without appeal in matters of doctrine, worship, and practice. "If there were a hundred popes, and all the monks were to be

[1] Boehringer's Vorreformatoren, Johannes v. Wykliffe, p. 3.

transformed into cardinals, we ought not," he said, " to ascribe to their opinion in matters of faith any other value than they have as founded on the Scriptures." His convictions as regards the supreme glory and excellency of the Bible were intense. It is "the immutable Testament of God the Father." " God and His Word is all one and they may not be separated." " To be ignorant of the Scriptures is to be ignorant of Christ," Who, in these writings, " has given a law sufficient for the government of the whole militant Church,"[1] the one Magna Charta of the kingdom of God.

This single principle once adopted, all else, in Wyclif's procedure as a reformer, followed by natural and necessary sequence. In Apostolic days he could find nothing answering to the haughty, grasping priesthood. " These brokers of the city of Rome," as they are styled in the Complaint of the " Good Parliament," who sold benefices to the highest bidder, whose income was as large again as the royal revenue, who had turned the Church into a huge banking concern, and who haggled and bargained about the very grace of God as if it were an ox or an ass, these were no successors of the men who had said, " Silver and gold have we none." Wretched " penny priests " they were who bartered to the devil the souls Christ had redeemed by His precious blood.[2] " Ah, Lord God, where is there reason," he exclaims in a Petition to King and Parliament, " to constrain the poor people to find a worldly priest, sometimes unable both of life and cunning, in pomp and pride, covetous-

[1] Johann v. Wicklif (Lechler), Buch 2, Kap. 7.
[2] Cf. Boehringer, l.c. p. 445.

ness and envy, gluttony and drunkenness and lechery, in simony and heresy, with fat horse, and jolly and gay saddles, and bridles ringing by the way, and himself in costly clothes and furs, and to suffer their wives and children and their poor neighbours perish for hunger, thirst, and cold, and other mischiefs of the world."[1] And the case was in no way better that at the head of this priesthood was a Pope who, in life and teaching, was "most contrary to Christ," not Peter's successor but Christ's enemy, "poison under colour of holiness," the "root and ground of all the misgoverning of the Church,"[2] and nothing else, indeed, than Antichrist, and if a vicar at all, then a vicar only of Satan. As Wyclif scanned the features of the organization represented by this priesthood he could discover there no resemblance to the "Church of poor confessors" described in the New Testament. There was clamant need of reform, and the measures he advocates are sufficiently drastic. He is a champion of the principles of "Thorough." His plea is for a "root and branch" re-organization. He does not hesitate to cry out even for disendowment, strange as such a method may appear amid the old-fashioned manners and customs of the fourteenth century. The Church is being suffocated by its wealth, he argues, and the State should restore to it its original poverty, undeterred by any denunciations of sacrilege and spoliation, or any predictions of calamity and retribution. Wyclif even appeals to the clergy themselves, with what success need hardly be said, to forego their riches and return to the wholesome use-and-wont of earlier days. He quotes with emphatic approval St. Bernard's famous

[1] English Works (Arnold), iii. 519. [2] *Ib.* p 278.

saying, " Whatsoever thou takest to thee of tithes and offerings besides simple livelihood and straight clothing, it is not thine, it is theft, ravine, and sacrilege"; and argues that all priests of whatsoever rank should live " of alms, freely and wilfully given."[1] There you have a reformer indeed, and one who approaches very near the furthest extremes even of voluntaryism itself.

We have already seen how absolutely he denies the right of Pope or priest to possess temporal lordship or to be independent of civil authority. The State must assert its rule, he avers, over all citizens alike without distinction of class or person. This he holds to be indispensable to the welfare both of the nation and the Church, and, curious, unaccountable soul that he is, he lets it be plainly seen that he has little faith in the ecclesiastical administration of justice, and that, if he had to be tried at all, he would prefer, as his judges, a bench of civil magistrates to a bevy of tonsured priests.[2]

With equal emphasis did he challenge the Pope's supremacy in spiritual things. The "power of the keys" was a figment of sacerdotal assumption. Excommunication he did indeed believe in as a terrible reality, but not one in the control of any but God Himself, Who is alone able to discern the true character of men. Hence he affirmed that "no man could be excommunicated at all who had not first and chiefly excommunicated himself";[3] and that "man's curse harmeth nothing, neither interdicting, nor any censures

---

[1] English Works (Arnold), III. 518.
[2] Boehringer, l.c. 494.
[3] Fasc. Ziz. p. 250.

that Satan may feign."[1] Just as little could the Pope grant remission of sins, and indulgences he brands as worthless and wicked mockeries, " a subtle merchandise of Antichrist's clerks," which tempt men to wallow in sin like hogs.[2] Christ, and Christ alone, is the true custodier of heavenly grace.

Whilst Wyclif condemns so unsparingly the wealth and luxury of the clergy, he is not less vehement in his denunciation of the mendicant orders who professed to have adopted poverty as their rule of life. His assault upon the friars was not, as has often been supposed, one of the earliest exhibitions of his zeal as a reformer, though even in his Oxford days he must have grown suspicious of the Franciscans, who exercised a pernicious influence over the youthful students at the university. As he approached the close of his career, however, his wrath boiled over, and he scourges, with overwhelming scorn, these able-bodied and strong-handed beggars who were robbers alike of the rich who willingly gave and of the poor who had need to receive. He tramples upon their appeal to the example of Christ, Who, he indignantly protests, was no mendicant, as they affirmed, even though (to refer to the incidents they founded on) He had asked a drink of the woman of Samaria, cast Himself upon the hospitality of Zacchæus, and borrowed the ass on which He rode into Jerusalem.[3] He accumulates proof upon proof of their falsehood, dishonesty, and blasphemy, and never, in the whole history of the Church, has so conclusive a demonstration been given of the utter cor-

[1] English Works (Arnold), iii. 218.
[2] "Of Prelates," quoted by Pennington, John Wiclif, p. 262.
[3] Boehringer, l.c. 542.

ruption of the orders that began their career in a spirit of holy enthusiasm and magnificent promise.

The wrath enkindled by his assault upon the friars grew into white heat when Wyclif repudiated the dogma of Transubstantiation, of which they especially were the acknowledged champions. In defence of his position on this matter (which, as already seen, was absolutely antagonistic to that of the Church), he appealed to Scripture, to the testimony of the senses, to the axioms of philosophy, and even the poor church-mouse is called into court as an unprejudiced witness whose testimony is more to be depended on than that of any number of bigoted bishops and popes. The orthodox doctrine, he insisted, cast an unpardonable slur upon the truthfulness of the evangelists and apostles, and even of Christ Himself; it involved the blasphemy of believing that a creature can create its Creator; it imposed upon men the necessity of discrediting and contradicting the clearest evidence of the faculties of taste and touch; and it posited the utterly impossible absurdity of "accident without subject," qualities without an underlying substance, "the most heresy that God suffered to come to His Church."[1] It is not easy to gather from Wyclif's writings an altogether satisfactory idea of his position with regard to this matter, his language not appearing quite self-consistent, and lacking the clear-cut precision which is desirable in theological and philosophical formulæ. He certainly does not adopt the somewhat baldly emblematic interpretation that subsequently found favour with Zwingli, and has come to be the popular doctrine in our Presbyterian Churches. The bread was with

[1] English Works, iii. 502.

him something more than a mere figure of the body of Christ. That body itself is there, though only spiritually and sacramentally, not essentially, substantially, or corporeally. At the same time his departure from the idea of any change answering to the phrase "transubstantiation" is absolute and final, and there is no sufficient ground for ascribing to him any such compromise as that with which Luther was satisfied. His position is rather Calvinistic than Lutheran, though it cannot fairly be identified with the interpretation put upon the sacrament either by the German or the French reformer.[1] He believed, however, that by his assault upon this dogma he had done much to emancipate the people from a pernicious superstition, and to wrest from the hands of the clergy a weapon by the use of which they had too long enslaved and tyrannized over a credulous Church.

For Wyclif's battle was, all through, in the interests of the people. It was no mere strife of theological opinion or for speculative victory. His concern was, pre-eminently, for the men and women who had for ages been denied their rights and privileges, and, very especially, had been kept in ignorance of the truth of God. How intensely he pursued this aim appears from the methods he adopted for the dissemination of his principles. He was not content to proclaim his faith to amazed students in the Oxford lecture-rooms, nor satisfied either with his enunciation of them in the pulpit. He did preach with all the effectiveness of a

---

[1] Cf. "The Wicket," The "Confessio Magistri Johannis Wyclif," Fasc. Ziz. 115. Two Short Papers "Concerning the Eucharist," English Works, iii. 499-503; and many passages in the Sermons, English Works, i.

man who believes strongly in the power of a living voice proclaiming living convictions. His faith in this method of influencing men was very firm, as it certainly could not have been had not his idea of preaching been widely different from that illustrated by the great mass of sermons to which people listened in those days. Very pungently he ridicules the pitiable maunderings that, passing current as sermons, might make idiots laugh, but could only make wise men weep. No patience had he with the long-robed quacks who served up to their hearers, instead of the simple truth of God, a despicable medley of pagan mythologies and hagiological incredibilities. Hardly a greater sinner could he conceive of than the preacher whose whole aim, as often happened, was to amuse his audience and put them into so good a humour that they would be willing to pay liberally for the spicy entertainment. Wyclif resolutely set himself to redeem this ordinance from the desecration to which it had been subjected, and his sermons, though many of them are but outlines, throb still, as we read them, with the earnestness, directness, passion, and spirituality of the preacher. There is a boldness and simplicity about them that at once explain the influence his eloquence had not only over the residents of Lutterworth but also over the citizens of London.

But his single voice was an instrument by no means adequate to the results he was anxious to achieve, and hence an institution in which he anticipated a method adopted, with signal success, by John Wesley, in modern times. Wyclif's "poor priests," as he styled them, were men whom he had drawn to himself, probably during his Oxford days, and whom, after special training, he sent out to proclaim, in simple language, the good tidings of the grace of God. There is no reason to suppose he meant to originate a permanent order, or to supersede the parochial system and replace it by a ministry of itinerant and unendowed evangelists. These "true men" were rather a temporary expedient, suited to the present need and designed only to awaken in the people an interest in spiritual realities, and to secure their co-operation in the work of reform. As they wandered about the country in pilgrim guise, bare of foot and with staff in hand, clad in long russet robes, their appearance excited alternately the ire and the ridicule of the clergy. Whether, however, priests laughed or raged, despised or persecuted, these evangelists, ordained and unordained, held upon their way preaching anywhere and everywhere, and not without result. The statement that before long every second man in the country was a Lollard is manifestly an exaggeration, but it witnesses to the sagacity of the Reformer in originating the institution, and to the attention these "poor priests" excited and the acceptance they secured.

A yet more startling appeal to the people was that made by Wyclif in his translation of the Bible into the common tongue, which, as we have seen, was the splendid culmination of his career. The attempt has been made to rob our Reformer of the crown of honour that belongs to him in this respect, and even a man so learned as Sir Thomas More maintained that the Scriptures had been translated into English before Wyclif's day. It has, however, been conclusively proved that his statement rests upon a manifest blunder, and the fact may be accepted as established that "down to

1360 the Psalter was the only book of Scripture which had been entirely rendered into English." But "within less than twenty-five years from that date a prose version of the whole Bible, including as well the Apocryphal as the Canonical books, had been completed, and was in circulation among the people. For this invaluable gift England is indebted to John Wyclife."[1] Not that the actual work of translation was all done by our Reformer. He was assisted, to a very considerable extent, by Nicholas Hereford, though the rendering of the New Testament appears to be all his own. As was to be expected, the first edition was not quite satisfactory, and before Wyclif's death a revision was begun which was carried on by John Purvey and published about 1388. The work was rapidly disseminated, as is demonstrated by the large number of manuscript copies, some 150, that are still extant, and that were issued within a very short period after the first publication. This bold adventure was, of course, the rankest heresy in the eyes of the ecclesiastical authorities. How they regarded the matter may be inferred from Knyghton's often-quoted language—" This Master John Wycliffe translated it out of Latin into the Anglican, not the angelic tongue, and thus laid it more open to the laity and to women who could read than it had formerly been to the most learned of the clergy, or even to those of them that had the best understanding. And in this way the Gospel pearl is cast abroad and trodden under foot of swine, that which was before precious both to clergy and laity is rendered as it were the common jest of both. The jewel of the Church is turned into the common sport of the people, and what was hitherto the

---

[3] Forshall and Madden's Preface to Wycliffe's Bible, p. 6.

principal gift of the clergy and divines is made for ever common to the laity."[1] A reluctant but most emphatic testimony on the part of his antagonists to the wisdom displayed and the success achieved by Wyclif in the use of these sacred weapons.

And yet the fact must be conceded that, despite his choice of the aptest methods and the most effective instruments, this great man did not accomplish the Reformation for which he worked with such unsparing diligence. The yoke was not broken for more than a whole century which he strove so hard to destroy, and the question has often suggested itself, Was Wyclif's life a failure? Certainly no such results followed upon his labour as crowned with almost immediate success the kindred toil of Martin Luther. The light he kindled, instead of steadily spreading and deepening till the whole horizon was filled with its beauty, speedily faded into almost utter darkness, and the ecclesiastical powers he had sought to overthrow scarcely lost aught of their supremacy, and, before long, appeared to have attained to more absolute and tyrannic rule than before. To account for this apparent futility of Wyclif's labours, we must remember how great were the disadvantages under which he laboured as compared with his great German successor. Wyclif stood practically alone against the world and the Church. His few political allies deserted him so soon as he assailed the fundamental doctrinal positions of the Papacy. He had no colleagues of intellectual calibre approaching his own to aid him with their weapons. He lacked the invaluable help of the press, and was able to publish his writings only by the slow and limited processes of the

[1] Eadie's English Bible, vol. 1, ch. 4.

amanuensis. He was accused, especially in connection with the Revolt of the Peasants, of fostering and promulgating wild revolutionary tenets, and of advocating a policy of rebellion, and the mere suspicion of such purposes was enough to imperil and wreck his cause; and his followers, thanks partly to their own extravagance, were combated with the dread instruments of persecution, and among these, the monstrous statute concerning the burning of heretics, which "asserted the orthodoxy of the Faith of the Church of England." In fact, it is one of the distinctions of Wyclif that his work suffered from the very grandeur of his personality. He was not really a man of his age, but rather a man full a century and more in advance of his time. England was not ready for him, and the under-currents of thought and feeling that in the sixteenth century had gathered the force necessary to carry forward the vessel of the Reformation, were, in Wyclif's day, too sluggish and too isolated to serve his cause. In some aspects, indeed, despite the antique garb in which his thoughts are arrayed, Wyclif strikes the student of his history as being the most modern of all the Reformers, really touching our nineteenth century life more directly than any of his successors, and this very peculiarity explains, in some measure, the fact that the immediate effects produced by him were not larger and more permanent.

We must not, however, exaggerate this apparent failure. His work told at home to a much greater degree than is generally recognised. It is not my place to trace the history of Lollardism, but its representatives survived all down the fifteenth century, and were to be found in every class of the community, developing at last, on the less extreme side, into "the Reformed Church of the age of Elizabeth," and, on the more extreme side, "into the Puritanical party of the same period."[1] The obnoxious tenets of Wyclif lingered on at Oxford, too, for many a long year, notwithstanding repeated attempts to extirpate the heresy; and if the followers of the Reformer, the "Lollard Bible-men," did nothing else, they did certainly not a little to disseminate among the people a knowledge of, and love for, the sacred Scriptures,[2] and so to perpetuate the work of their great Master. This was done, too, on a larger scale and with vaster results, on Continental soil, where the Bohemian movement was, beyond all question, largely inspired and fashioned by the influence of our English Reformer. Whether this was a mere "echo" of Wyclif, as has been maintained by a German historian,[3] is a question the settlement of which belongs to my successor in this lectureship, but Hus himself made no secret of the impulse and instruction he had received from his English predecessor. Thus Wyclif, dead, yet speaking, contributed not a little to the great European movement of the sixteenth century, prepared the way for Luther's work, and helped to make it the success which so remarkably fulfilled a prophetic dream in which he had indulged. For even in the midst of his fierce conflict with the Friars he cherished the conviction that, in days to come, there would arise among them men who would,

---

[1] Mr. Babington's Introduction to Peacock's "Repressor," cited by Canon Pennington.

[2] Professor Lindsay's "Lollards," Encycl. Brit.

[3] Boehringer, l.c. Einleitung; cf. also, Loserth's Wiclif and Hus.

by their service, atone for the evil with which the mendicant Orders were chargeable, return freely to the original religion of Christ, and then build up the Church as the Apostle Paul had done.[1] The great German monk, in whom this anticipation was realized, did, indeed, but little justice to Wyclif, whom, strangely enough, he charges with bringing too much logic and too little grammar to bear upon his interpretations, and with having attacked the life rather than the doctrine of the Papacy.[2] Luther's acquaintance with the English Reformer could only have been meagre and, probably, second-hand, otherwise he would have done frank homage to one of the healthiest, noblest natures that ever did battle for God and the world.

For such, indeed, we hold Wyclif to have been. Our hurried and fragmentary review of his doctrinal position and his methods of reform must have been a sheer failure if it has not presented him as a man of transcendent originality. Give all the credit that is due to those who preceded him in opposing the Papal claims, and the fact still remains that there is a comprehensive sweep in Wyclif's assault, a massive majesty in his grasp of the questions involved, and a keen, subtle discernment of the root principles requiring to be affirmed, to which we find no parallel at all in all the previous history of England, and which give him some right to be called the first of the Reformers. This originality is nowhere more signally displayed than in his bold, unprecedented appeal to the common people to bear their part in casting off the oppressive yoke of the clergy. It was a new thing that the laity should be credited with a right to think and act in-

[1] Lechler, l.c. Buch. ii. Kap. 7. [2] Boehringer, l.c. 605.

dependently in ecclesiastical and spiritual affairs, and greatly must they have marvelled at the intrepid eccentricity of a priest who thus trusted ordinary men and women, and flung himself with confidence upon their sympathy. It was a grand conception that of flooding the country with his short, telling, pungent tracts, and originating a method of influencing the national thought, which has since proven a mighty power in England's political and religious history. And the most daring act of all was performed by this first of pamphleteers when he put into the people's hands his noble translation of the Bible and bade them read it for themselves, and fashion their own creed and their own conception of life and duty. Therein, certainly, he was a true Protestant, and affirmed a principle which, for many an age, was branded only as rankest blasphemy. It was the inevitable penalty of this originality that throughout the chief part of his life "his soul was like a star, and dwelt apart." There is something approaching sublimity in the loneliness of the man. Hus had his Jerome, and Luther his Melanchthon, but Wyclif had no such equal and sympathetic nature to walk by his side. The comparatively very feeble voices that echo his utterances are only the echo, and nothing more. The mine he works is one within whose dark galleries he is cheered by the presence of no fellow-labourer with indomitable will and iron arm like his own. At best those nearest him are content to wait till he brings to bank the treasures he has toiled for on bended knee and with aching brain, and to bid him God-speed as he betakes himself again to his solitary labour. In his heart, too, all the while was a vivid sense of the risk he ran, and of the possibility there was of his being overtaken by some terrible calamity. It was not given him, indeed, to wear the martyr's crown, but within the tall, spare frame there burned the martyr spirit, and through the clear eye there shone the dauntless soul, all whose care was—

> "To stand approved in sight of God, though worlds
> Judged him perverse."

That there are deficiencies in his doctrinal statements cannot be denied, and it is well known that Melanchthon maintained Wyclif had no conception of the crucial truth of justification by faith. The assertion need not be vehemently disputed, if it means that he failed to apprehend and formulate that doctrine with the precision of the later Reformers. There was something left for them to do in recovering the Pauline conception, and restoring it in a worthy form to the conscious possession of Christendom. But the essence of the truth is enshrined unmistakeably in Wyclif's teaching, and no language has ever affirmed more emphatically than his, the sinner's absolute dependence upon the grace of God, and the undivided prerogative and glory of Christ as the Saviour of men. "Christ," he affirms, "is all manner of meat and drink";[1] He is "our Patron"; He is "the Prior of all His religion, the Abbot of the best order that can be";[2] He is "the highest Pope,"[3] "our ever august Cæsar, and the saint of saints, who is at once priest and prophet, law-giver and king."[4] It is true, indeed, that Wyclif frequently presents evangelical truth in somewhat legal phraseology. He designates Christ as

[1] English Works (Edit. Arnold), vol. i. 4.
[2] Ib. pp. 28, 77.   [3] Ib. p. 283.   [4] Lechler, l.c. Buch. ii. Kap. 7.

our Legifer, our Law-bringer, and he habitually speaks of the Gospel as the law of Christ. But this is neither surprising nor inexcusable. In an age when, even in ecclesiastical circles, religion was to so large an extent divorced from even common decency and morality, Christianity divested of its ethical significance and degraded into mere ceremonial conformity, it was urgently necessary to enforce this special side of truth, to insist upon the fact that "faith without works is dead," and that Christianity means nothing if it does not mean holiness of life.

It would have been little short of a miracle had none of the old dross been found adhering to the rich gold which Wyclif made his own and the world's, but its existence is hardly to be spoken of in presence of the fact that " to Wyclif we owe, more than to any one person who can be mentioned, our English language, our English Bible, and our reformed religion." It was honour enough for one man to win and service enough for one man to render, that he fought the battle of his country's freedom with a power, persistency, and courage never surpassed and seldom equalled; that he broke the might of huge superstitions that, for almost untold ages, had lain like a nightmare on immortal souls; that he taught men to repudiate the disastrous, paralysing delusion that the clergy are the Church, and lords of the human conscience; and that, securing for himself the foremost place in the long heroic succession of the Reformers, he won also, for his country and ours, the honour of serving as the advanced guard of the noble army whose efforts resulted at last in the triumph of truth over error, of

[1] Professor Montagu Burrow's Wyclif's Place in History, p. 6.

light over darkness, of freedom over slavery, and of humanity over priestcraft. And his right to our fervent admiration and thankfulness is all the greater that, despite the terrible fierceness of the battle, his fair fame is untarnished by aught in life or character unworthy of the cause in which he fought. As has been already remarked, indeed, we do not get into any close intimacy with his personal experience. We cannot follow him into the humble homes in which he spent his days, unblest by either wife or children, those " hostages to fortune " and " impediments to great enterprises," as Bacon terms them. We seldom catch the smile upon his face, for his humour, at its best, is somewhat stern and grim, and we are not permitted to see him on those rare occasions when he was able to unstring his bow and forget the hard conditions of his service. Now and again we are privileged to hear the prayers that burst from his burdened heart, and which, breathing the spirit of a beautiful humility, reveal the deep sense he had of the risk he ran of being betrayed into unholy passion and unseemly speech ; but these are only rare occasions. But one fact speaks most eloquently for the purity and nobleness of his personal character. Though his years were spent in the blaze of a light as fierce as that

> " Which beats upon a throne,
> And blackens every blot,"

no word of blame issued from the lips of his bitterest antagonists. They pelt him with abundance of hard names, but there is never even so much as an insinuation that he did not wear

> " The white flower of a blameless life."

Among his friends he had the reputation of being "a perfect liver," and his enemies had grace enough not to challenge his right to praise so rare.[1] A negative, it is said, proves nothing, but the silence of such angry critics as watched Wyclif's course is worth more, a thousand times, as a testimony to his character than the most elaborate eulogium of interested admirers. "It was," says Professor Burrows, "the goodness of the man that made him formidable," and there can be no question that one real secret of his power is to be found in the fair illustration he gave, in his own life, of the earnestness and simplicity of his faith, the sanctifying strength and sincerity of his convictions. This, taken with all besides, makes it the more amazing that England has been so strangely ignorant of, and indifferent to, the man whom Milton styles "the divine and admirable Wyclif," and that we have to go to Germany to find scholars, such as Lechler, Boehringer, Buddensieg and Loserth, eager to render full justice to our great Reformer, and, in works distinguished for their Teutonic thoroughness, vindicating for him the high place he is entitled to. He was a true prophet, meeting with the prophetic fate, but, happily, undisturbed by anticipations of neglect, able to keep alive within his heart the prophetic fire, and to impart to the world the divine impulse the force of which has never been arrested and never will die out until Wyclif's confident expectation is fulfilled, and the truth of God has won its final triumph, and proved its inherent, invincible omnipotence.

[1] Eadie's English Bible, vol. i. p. 57.

Hus.

LIKE a picture set in a framework of hills, Bohemia lies on the north-west frontier of Austria, and may generally be described as the basin of the Elbe, with Prague as the centre of its converging streams. As a nation, Bohemia emerges from pre-historic times in a struggle between the Boii and a branch of the Slavonic race; but it comes distinctly on the horizon of history as a Slav province, speaking the Czech language.

During the ninth century, Christianity was introduced into Bohemia. Its upland valleys felt the touch of that missionary age, as the inlets of the sea respond to the tidal wave. Yet they showed their insular character by a stubborn resistance to ecclesiastical uniformity; for, while accepting the leading doctrines of the Church of Rome, they refused to adopt the Latin language in the liturgy, and were allowed to retain their mother tongue. Through the dark ages, therefore, the Czesko-Slavonic fire burned on their altar and hearth; and the native dialect—like our Gaelic and Welsh—became in the hands of the preachers the mesmeric touch of patriotic brotherhood. Gradually, however, the astute leaders at Rome were able to introduce the Latin liturgy, as well as other details of order; still the true-born Czechs protested against the use of a foreign tongue in their religious service; and this was one of the burning questions in the time of Hus.

But, throughout the centuries, the Papal genius was working on more ambitious lines of policy. The bold determination of Hildebrand to rescue the Church from feudal power, was carried out with marvellous persistence by his successors, until the Papal chair was erected on the top of the world,[1] and the kings of Europe crouched before the Sovereign Pontiff of Rome. Then, apparently on the principle of making the most of both worlds, purgatory was annexed to the Papal dominions, and the Church reached the giddy height of absolute temporal and spiritual power.

But her success was won at great cost. As the apotheosis of Cæsar marked the decline of pagan Rome, so this self-deification became the *caput mortuum* of Papal Rome and the back stroke of the two-edged sword fatally wounded the life of the Church. "The fish rots from the head downwards." The avaricious example of the Popes was soon imitated by the priests; and the rate of progress in degeneracy among the lower orders of the clergy increased by the natural law of acceleration. The prostration of moral and spiritual energy was followed by various kinds of corruption, until the unblushing shamelessness of the priesthood shocked the more thoughtful friends of the Church. The monastics arose in alarm at the prevailing abuses, and a stern protest was uttered from the Alpine valleys; but the noise of the Simonists in their unhallowed

[1] Roger Bacon.

traffic, and of the Sensualists in the haunts of vice, completely drowned the voice of the mystic brotherhoods and the warning of the Waldenses. Samson slept in the lap of Delilah, and awoke at last, shorn of strength, to become the slave of the Philistine.

The crisis came with a rude suddenness at the beginning of the fourteenth century. Philip the Fair of France resented the imperious claims of Boniface VIII. on his kingdom, and the contest ended in the defeat of the Pope, with the transference of the Papal seat to Avignon (1305-76). Petrarch called this "The Babylonish Captivity." It may also be regarded as one of those historic satires on human ambition which illustrate the action of a moral principle in the government of the universe. "Whom the gods wish to destroy they first make mad."

During this period of Papal conquest and captivity, Bohemia was developing qualities of character well suited to give her weight in the councils of Europe Her mountains were a barrier against envious neighbours and avaricious priests, and also a cohesive girdle round the native energy. She was less affected by the numbing touch of Rome than most other countries, and was left free to develop her national resources according to her own genius. Hence, she rose to a first place among the nations, about the middle of the fourteenth century, when Charles IV. was created Roman Emperor. He was the Augustus of Bohemia, and his reign is the golden age of progress and prosperity. He was the founder of the University of Prague (1348), the defender of religious liberty, and the patron of the Czech language and literature. He is, therefore, justly regarded as the father of Bohemia, and as one of the brightest ornaments among the crowned heads of Europe. He died in 1378, and was succeeded by his son Wenzel the Lazy, in whose hands the kingdom fell into disorder, and lost its prestige among the nations. His whole reign was a fruitless effort to gain the crown of the Roman Empire; it is not otherwise distinguished in "the equilibrium of weakness"[1] among the leading powers of Europe. There was neither statesmanship nor steadfastness of purpose in the domestic policy of Wenzel, and his accession to the throne is chiefly remembered for the schism in the Papacy, and the rise of a new power in the government of the Church.

This split in the Popedom forms one of the great epochs in ecclesiastical history. It arose out of a dispute about the true seat of Papal power. The Italian cardinals insisted on restoring the ancient glory of Rome,—the French cardinals had a natural preference for Avignon; and out of this contention came the Papal schism, in which the outward unity of the Church was sacrificed to the self-interest of two parties in the hierarchy. The rival Popes, Urban VI. and Clement VII., hurled their anathemas at each other with great violence, and disorders of every kind swept in full tide through the gap between Avignon and Rome. "The chair of St. Peter was like to be broken by two sitting down on it at once,"[2] and Charles IV., the one man able to reconcile the difference, died in the year of the rupture. This state of self-contradiction lasted for forty years—it practically covered the active life of Hus—and it suggested the deeper controversy about the true headship of the Church, which issued in an appeal to sacred Scripture.

[1] Palacky.   [2] Fuller.

At this juncture, the Universities appear as a third power in the public life of Europe. From their free constitution, as so far independent of both civil and ecclesiastical jurisdiction, and also as the nurseries of the best thought of their age, they were well qualified to act the part of umpire in this contest, and to gain the respect of both claimants to the Papal throne. Gerson, the Chancellor of Paris University, proposed to bridge the gulf by a general council, at which the whole case should be discussed. As a preliminary measure, it was agreed to ask the two Popes to resign in favour of "a new single, supreme head of the Church," —and it was a great gain for freedom when both sides consented to accept the decision of the Council. Hallam calls this the inauguration of a Whig policy in the Papacy, by which an absolute became a limited monarchy, subject to review and reform.[1] The Council met at Pisa (1409), and, although it failed in its immediate object of healing the breach, and even increased the confusion by the election of a third Pope, it nevertheless put the balance of power theoretically on a broader representative basis than either kings or cardinals, and it also asserted the right of the Church in council to reform abuses in its head and members. Gerson was a reformer on constitutional principles, who wished to restore discipline without disturbing doctrine, but the vested interests of the clergy were too strong for abstract theories of morality, and more drastic measures were required to cleanse the life of the Church.

In Oxford a more radical idea of reform had taken root through the teaching of Wyclif. He went back to

[1] Hallam's Middle Ages, 4th edition, p. 394.

the original charter for the principles of doctrine and duty. He brought from the teaching of Christ and his Apostles the ethics of religious life, and applied the truth of God with unflinching logic to the expulsion of error and corruption. The Excalibur of England flashed in the eye of France, where feudal tendencies were strongest, and excited in Gerson the fear of revolution; but, notwithstanding his timidity, the genius of history has owned the method of Wyclif in the progress of reform, rather than the negative theory of the merely critical school. Both currents of reform united in the movement identified with Hus, and it is easy to recognise, in the progress of his work, traces of mental conflict between the principles of Gerson and Wyclif; indeed, Hus never seemed consciously to realize that his plea for intelligent faith was fatal to blind authority

But, long before his day, the same symptoms were evident in the religious life of Bohemia, and earnest minds were engaged in efforts to stem the tide of wickedness in society and in the Church. This spirit of renaissance expressed itself in two main directions, —in a revived interest in the mother tongue, and in an assertion of religious freedom. In the retirement of the University of Prague, Aldbertus Ranconis (1360) was engaged in the attempt to mould his native speech into more flexible forms of expression in sympathy with the new thought. He was a renowned scholar of Paris, the most distinguished Bohemian of his day, and a great friend of national education. He founded a travelling scholarship for gifted Czechs, at Paris or Oxford University, and left his library to native students at Prague. Ranconis represents the scientific and literary side of Bohemian reform. Stitny—called "the prose Chaucer of Bohemia"—was also labouring in the same field with great success; hence, at the beginning of the fifteenth century, the language of the land of Hus was, next to Italian, the best literary medium in Europe. Bohemia had the greater portion of the Scriptures in the vernacular even before England, and some of the germs of reformation-thought were sown by unseen hands among its hills before the soil of the Saxon race was ploughed.

On the more direct side of Church reform, the immediate precursors of Hus are distinguished by the same patriotic feeling; and the native dialect is the magic charm for reaching the heart of the people. Konrad found it a powerful weapon in his crusade against vice in Prague, and his popular discourses in the Czechian speech glowed with the warmth of practical piety and the robust force of sanctified commonsense. Militz the Moravian acquired the vernacular in order to reach the national conscience, and ultimately became the centre of a school of itinerant preachers like the Lollards, who transformed the hot-beds of vice in Prague into the nurseries of virtue.

Konrad died in the birth-year of Hus, Militz five years afterwards; but the work of reform was carried forward into fuller statement by Matthew of Janow. He is said to have been the most profound Bohemian thinker of his time, and, without knowledge of Wyclif, to have thought out the leading doctrines of the new theology. He rejected the clay-mould type of uniformity; he advocated the unity of difference as the richest result of a living faith; he taught the priesthood of believers with or without orders; and based the whole idea of the Church on the revelation of the Scriptures. He also revived the old controversy in Bohemia about the use of the cup in the sacrament of the altar, and insisted on the right of all to both kinds in the supper. He was forced to retract on this subject; still, though perhaps wanting in moral courage, his spiritual insight and his efforts to restore a better tone to the life of the clergy, undoubtedly lift him into the front rank of Reformers before the Reformation. He died in 1389, lamenting the state of religious degeneracy, regretting his recantation, and predicting a brighter dawn for Bohemia, without being aware that already the hour and the man were near who should fulfil the prediction.

John Hus was born at Husinetz in 1369. His parents called him John, but, according to the custom of that age, he afterwards adopted the surname Hus, from the place of his birth. He was the child of simple peasants. Like Luther, he was educated as a choir-boy, and was evidently familiar with the pease porridge of the convent school. He thus refers to it in later life,—"When I was a poor scholar I used to make a spoon of a piece of bread till I had done eating my pease porridge, and then I ate the spoon."[1] The plain fare of Scotland was once supposed to account for the mental and moral vigour of our students. So perhaps the severe discipline of youth helped to develop the manly virtues which fitted Hus for the duties of after-life. Before his education was finished his father died, but his mother spared no sacrifice in assisting him towards the profession of the priesthood, for which, by early choice and home

[1] Wratislaw, p. 67.

consent, he was destined. His personal motive at first was rather a boyish envy of the luxury and laziness of the clergy, than any love for the work of the ministry; and at a later date he somewhat severely judged the irreverence of his service in the choir. Strong lights cast deep shadows, intense earnestness is apt to exaggerate defects, so possibly these reflections on his former conduct at the close of life are largely due to the keener vision reached through conflict. "The remembrance of youth is a sigh."[1]

Hus matriculated at the University of Prague at the age of twenty-one; he became Bachelor of Divinity at twenty-five; and obtained priest's orders about thirty-one. Little is known of his earlier student days except his "loss of time in playing chess";[2] but there is evidence at least of a fair knowledge of classics and scholastic philosophy. His intellect was of a practical cast, with little taste for abstract speculations or logical puzzles, and therefore, throughout his arts curriculum he does not seem to have attained to any great distinction. During his divinity course, however, the touch of the Oxford thought opened his eyes to the value of philosophy in theology, and transformed him into an earnest student of Realism. His ability was recognised in the university by an appointment as examiner in philosophy, then as a lecturer, and last of all as Dean of the Faculty of Arts. In theology, he attracted the notice of Stanislas, and retained his friendship until the charge of heresy alarmed his old teacher and drove him into an attitude of opposition. These

[1] Sayings of Ali.
[2] Letter to Martin from Constance.

facts prove that John of Husinetz was above an average student, and left his university with some reputation for ability and eminence in study.

But the great era of his history opened in his ordination to the priesthood, and through direct contact with the people in preaching. He set himself earnestly to acquire the art of popular discourse, and soon found in the pulpit a congenial sphere for all his latent talent. His inherited sympathies drew him towards the native population, and his fame as a Czech preacher so rapidly rose, that in two years after taking orders, he was one of the leading spiritual forces in the city of Prague. Through this distinction as a popular teacher Hus was unconsciously led into the great arena of Bohemian reform.

About 1390 a merchant named Kreuz or Cross, a friend of Ranconis, resolved to found a chapel for purely native preaching, to be consecrated to the Innocents and called Bethlehem. Through the influence at Court of John of Milheim, a royal charter was obtained from Wenzel, granting certain privileges to the rector and congregation. The high renown of Hus as a preacher attracted the attention of the founder of Bethlehem Chapel, who invited him to become its rector, within three years after his ordination. The chapel was founded in the year Hus entered the university, but its renown dates from the time he began his work within its walls. Brought face to face with the practical duties of his office, the mind of the young preacher began to recoil from the indifference of the parochial clergy, and he determined to discharge his sacerdotal function conscientiously to society and the Church. As in the early dawn of the Christian era a star guided the Magi to the cradle of the greatest Reformer in the history of the world, so, in less degree and over a smaller area, a new attractive force drew the wise men of the age to this chapel, named after the birthplace of Christ—a voice, as from heaven, was heard by the faithful shepherds watching their flocks in the midst of darkness, and a strange excitement pervaded society, which terrified the Herod-hierarchy into measures for the suppression or slaughter of the innocents, But Hus was charged with a divine message, and could not be diverted from declaring it; so he continued to preach the gospel of truth and righteousness in the calm consciousness of duty. Crowds came to Bethlehem Chapel—even Queen Sophia was fascinated by the eloquence of the preacher, and made him her private chaplain; but neither popular applause nor Court favour turned him aside from the serious purpose of his ministry. Balbinus the Jesuit said— " Hus was even more remarkable for his acuteness than his eloquence; but the modesty and severity of his conduct, . . . his pale and melancholy features, his gentleness and affability, persuaded more than the greatest eloquence."[1] Through conflict with error and superstition, a strong element of puritan earnestness was developed in his character, which gave edge to his preaching. He had no language too severe for " the shepherds who sheared the sheep,"[2] caring more for the fleece than the flock; and he was specially indignant at the mendicant friars who peddled their pardons from house to house, concealing avarice under the garb of sanctity. Chaucer's pen and ink portraits of

[1] Reformers before the Reformation, Bonnechose, p. 71.
[2] Letter to Zawyssius.

these fraternities easily explain the invective of Hus, " It is not the stole that makes the priest."

By the regular and secular clergy a strong remonstrance was uttered against these attacks of Hus, and an appeal for protection was presented to the Archbishop, who either thought the case too glaring for defence or was afraid to interfere. He died without taking notice of the complaint; and his successor, Zybnek, was evidently at first in sympathy with the earnest priest of Bethlehem Chapel. Zybnek (1403) consulted Hus on the best means of restoring discipline in the diocese, and invited him to examine a reputed discovery of the real blood of Christ in a ruined church in the neighbourhood. Hus denied the reputed miracle in a tract on " The glorified blood of Christ," in which he urged a more faithful preaching of the truth of God as the best cure for traffic in relics, for pilgrimages to sainted shrines, and for the whole machinery of superstition. His pamphlet checked the excitement in one direction, but awoke it in another. The priests were mad with rage at the prohibition of their lucrative trade. Even the Archbishop was alarmed at the commotion; and, for politic reasons, withdrew from the extreme position of Hus, while still retaining some admiration for his heroic defence of religious morality. But the preacher in Bethlehem Chapel was undaunted by the clamour of these religious monopolists, and became still more aggressive in attack upon the sacrilegious tendency among the authorities of the Church. Hence another memorial was sent to the Archbishop, charging Hus with slanderous attacks in the vulgar tongue against the clergy, " which were undermining their influence" and threatening untold evils in the diocese. Zybnek was as reluctant as his predecessor to take up the case; so the complaint was forwarded to Rome, with the result that instructions were sent down "to use all diligence in the extirpation of heresy and disorder." In view of this Papal edict, forty-five articles were extracted from the writings of Wyclif for the judgment of the diocesan synod. By the condemnation of these as heretical, it was intended to strike a blow at Hus, whose chapel was beginning to be called the Wyclif Cave. It was also gradually becoming the Kaabah of Bohemian reform.

Zybnek, in this emergency, asked the advice of the university, which, from this point, became an important factor in the history of reform. The University of Prague was founded on the model of the University of Paris, and was intended by Charles IV. to rival it as a centre of culture. It was divided into four nations in voting on any public or constitutional question, and the vote of the majority of nations was the decision of the university. At first Bohemia held three of these votes, but, in the course of time, the German influence gained the ascendency, and absorbed three votes, leaving only one to the Czechs. There was nothing unjust in this arrangement on the principle of proportion, but it was a constant source of irritation to the Slavonic minority, because it virtually silenced their voice in the government of a native institution. The ancient feud between the Teuton and the Slav (which is not yet dead) appeared in this seat of learning on every debated question. The solid vote of the Germans was given in favour of Nominalism and Papal absolutism; whereas the one vote of the Bohemians went in the direction of Realism and reform. This swamping of their opinions in philosophy and theology was a standing grievance to the Czechs. Such a dividing line was certainly injurious to truth and freedom, and it declared itself most clearly in this case of reference on the doctrines of Wyclif.

Stanislas, the teacher of Hus, and Paletz, his fellow-student, argued a general defence of the writings of Wyclif, and refused to accept the forty-five extracts as a true statement of his position; nevertheless, even without argument, the mechanical majority voted down the heretic, and decreed that all such teaching should be forbidden in the university or diocese. Zybnek issued an edict to this effect. However, the condemnation only increased the interest in the study of Wyclif, and intensified the enthusiasm of Hus in the defence of the Oxford Doctor, whom he was accustomed to call "the master of deep thoughts."

By the broad movements of history, and the more subtle affinities of learning, England and Bohemia had been drawn very close together. In 1382, Anne, the sister of Wenzel, was married to Richard II., and students passed between Oxford and Prague in the prosecution of their studies, so that the two nations united by marriage also clasped hands in thought. It is impossible to examine the numerous traditions about the introduction of Wyclif literature into Bohemia, and perhaps the story of English students exhibiting a cartoon of Christ and of the Pope as Antichrist in their lodgings at Prague, or of their carrying a forged certificate of Wyclif's university attesting his orthodoxy, may be set aside in view of the undoubted facts that Jerome was a student in Oxford, and that an interchange of students had gone on for many years. Such a leavening as existed at this time must have been the work of various agencies, and cannot with any safety be associated with a name or any single incident. While the thought of Wyclif was in process of incubation in Bohemia, it attracted no special attention; it was when in the act of taking wing it caused anxiety, and all efforts to kill the dangerous brood at this stage only succeeded in enlarging the area of flight. The spent shot fell harmless in the region of truth and conscience.

The controversy about the doctrines of Wyclif went on with increasing virulence after their condemnation, and stirred up a strong antagonism in the university between the Teuton and the Slav sections. At first the Archbishop leaned to the side of Hus, and selected him as the synod preacher in 1405 and 1407. This preference offended the other dignitaries of the diocese, who secretly conveyed the information to Rome that heresy was becoming defiant in Prague, under a too mild episcopal rule, and that strong measures were needed for its suppression. Innocent VII. at once issued a bull calling upon Zybnek to use energetic means for the wiping-out of all schism and heresy. The Archbishop recognised in this edict the intriguing spirit of the offended prelates, and, in resentment at their action, left the edict unfulfilled in its strictest reading. An instruction was published on the sacrament of the altar, which touched the central doctrine of Wyclif, without in any way affecting the modified position of Hus on that subject. A conference was held with the Bohemian nation in the university, at which all that was heretical in Wyclif was unanimously disallowed, without any real definition being given of heresy. This open verdict greatly displeased the aggrieved prelates and the German party in the theological faculty; so, on the accession of the new Pope, Gregory XII., much more stringent injunctions were laid upon the Archbishop, to protect the clergy from abusive attacks, and to root out the revolt from Church authority. The fear of the Pope now overcame the fear of the King in the mind of Zybnek, and forced him to more severe methods of action against Hus. He forbade all references to the evil lives of the clergy in sermons to the people; he forbade all preaching in the diocese without episcopal sanction, and ordered those in possession of Wyclif books to give them up immediately. Both the prohibitive and preventive instructions were generally ignored by the reform party, while, to the great consternation of the clergy, Hus became even more bold in lashing the vices rampant among the dignitaries of the Church.

The year 1409 brought this movement to a crisis. The Council was about to meet at Pisa to accept the resignation of the rival Popes Gregory XII. and Benedict XIII., and the King agreed to assist Gerson in the attempt to heal the schism in the Papacy, by the election of "a single, supreme head of the Church." Wenzel invited the University and Archbishop of Prague to support him in this decision—in which he was looking mainly to his own imperial prospects; but the Bohemian nation alone sustained his position, while the three German nations and Zybnek resolved to cling to Gregory as the duly elected Pope. This opposition awoke the resentment of the Court, and offered a great opportunity to Hus for reversing the voting power in the university, and for gaining the protection of the King in the growing struggle with the local authorities in the Church. Jerome, the literary genius of reform, assisted Hus in this attempt to make the native influence ascendant in the national school. Home rule was the party cry; it stirred the memory of the old feud, and unseated the more sober judgment of its advocates; for it lost sight of the advantages of federation, and sacrificed imperial to parochial views of education. The German majority were indignant at the attempted coercion, and at the threat of being deprived of their ascendency, and they resolved, in the event of the movement being successful, to leave Prague in a body. Through the Court influence of Hus, the constitution of the university was restored to its original idea, giving three votes to Bohemia, and one to foreign residents. Thereupon an exodus of German professors and students took place, carrying with it the intellectual glory of Prague. This disruption caused a great commotion in the city, and raised among the shopmen and citizens, dependent on the university, a reaction against the movement of reform. Besides, the Bohemians, hitherto held together by their standing grievance, soon began to show signs of dissension among themselves, and the University never regained the influence of its former days. Hus was elected rector under the new regime, but he nowhere appears less worthy of admiration than in the rectorial chair of a narrow Slavonic school. The right that ignores duty is intolerance; the patriotism that forgets justice outrages the sanctities of human freedom; and the spirit that would crush conviction into weak concurrence contradicts the first principle of the Gospel. Hus undoubtedly made a mistake in this matter, and Nemesis avenges mistakes as well as misdemeanours.

The breach with the Archbishop occurred in the same year. One cause of alienation was the refusal of Zybnek to support the policy of the King in relation to the Council of Pisa ; but there was a deeper reason in the defiant attitude maintained by Hus in his exposure of clerical abuses, and in his bold remonstrance against certain judicial acts in the episcopal function of the Archbishop. The temper of Zybnek quite broke down under such interference, and he was roused into fury by a citation to Rome through the combined influence of Wenzel and Hus. Therefore, he at once gave in his adherence to the new Pope, sent a serious counter-charge to the Papal Court, and asked increased powers to deal effectively with the rising revolution. Immediately on his submission, the benediction of the Pisan Pope (Alex. V.) was conferred on the Archbishop in a bull of 20th Dec., 1408, authorizing him " to remove the writings of Wyclif from the eyes of the faithful, and to forbid all preaching except in cathedral, conventual, or parish churches, and to proceed in its execution without the right of appeal." Hus protested against this attempt to silence him at Bethlehem Chapel, and, on the ground of its free charter, continued to preach as before to even larger audiences. He denied the imputation of heresy, and called on the excited people to sustain him in the determination to stand by the truth of God even to the death. The process of crushing was generating dangerous heat, and symptoms of explosion were very soon evident.

The Papal edict was at once put into force against the writings of Wyclif. All in possession of these writings were ordered to surrender them under severe pains and penalties, and about two hundred volumes of manuscript were delivered up to the Archbishop. When it became known that these books were to be burned, a strong representation was made by the University and by the King; but, although Zybnek promised to do nothing without consulting Wenzel, the glare of the burning in the palace yard at the cathedral soon intimated to all concerned the arbitrary destruction of the forfeited writings. Like a prairie fire, the popular excitement ran beyond all control. It expressed itself in satirical ballads, howled by long processions in the streets, and it greatly helped to recover the popularity lost to reform by the University schism. Hus said of it—" I call the burning of books a poor business. Such burning never yet removed a single sin from the hearts of men, but only . . . . multiplied among the people disturbances."[1] The King, as the guardian of the public peace, forbade all social disorder under pain of death. At the same time he was greatly enraged at the duplicity of Zybnek, in casting such a stigma on the kingdom, and thus spoiling his imperial prospects at Rome. He therefore wrote to the newly elected Pope, Belthassar Cossa (John XXIII.), denying the existence of heresy in Bohemia, and inviting him either to investigate the case or remove the gratuitous charge. Hus also appealed against the infringement of the charter of Bethlehem Chapel, and in defence of the rights of the University so seriously injured in the burning of its books; but the only answer to such representations was a more furious bull against prevailing heresy, and a direct citation of Hus to appear at the Papal Court. The king protested; the queen interceded; Hus

[1] Neander, vol. ix. p. 356.

petitioned to be released from personally appearing before the Pope, and even sent a deputy to plead his case; nevertheless, the cruel Cossa was inexorable, and, in due course, a sentence of excommunication was published against the Reformer. The court and cathedral, long in a state of tension, now fell into open rupture, and the King made reprisals on the temporalities of the Church, to recoup the loss caused by the burning of the books, and to recover some of the property for his own exchequer.

The university interposed in favour of compromise between the temporal and spiritual rulers. A council of arbitration was appointed, and, during its deliberations, the interdict on Hus was removed; but no final decision was reached, as in the midst of this strife and confusion the Archbishop died on 28th September, 1411.

Up to this point, Hus had no idea of leaving the Church or of founding a new sect. He was rather bent on reforming abuses, and on rousing the conscience of the priesthood to a truer sense of moral obligation; still, while he protested his freedom from Wyclif heresy in all good faith, it is easy to see the influence of the more doctrinal aspects of Oxford teaching on his mind, as the movement continued to widen, and as the conflict with Rome deepened. We come now to a stage in the struggle where the controversy is less about Wyclif heresy than papal authority, and where the battle is fought with weapons directly borrowed from the armoury of Lutterworth.

At the installation of Albik (1412), the successor of Zybnek, the Papal legate preached a crusade against the King of Naples for protecting Gregory XII., one of the Popes deposed at Pisa. Indulgence was offered to all assisting in this holy war, by personal service or money contributions. The treasury of the saints was opened to all comers, and the drum of the pardon-monger everywhere called the faithful to buy in the Church bazaars. Hus was roused by this profane traffic, and at once declared war to the death with the wicked invention of Hildebrand. He assailed the doctrinal principle of indulgence, as subversive of the divine prerogative and of social morality, and declared that he "would resist it though the stake were staring him in the face." He announced a public disputation in the university, which the authorities in vain tried to prevent.

His old allies Stanislas and Paletz began to feel the danger of being further identified with his views, and they retired into the safer position of obedience, on the plea of honouring the will of the Pope who had issued the bull, and the wish of the King, who had sanctioned its promulgation. Hus greatly regretted this retrograde action, and compared his old professor and friend to crabwalkers, who, afraid of the Pope, were willing to renounce conscience. "Paletz is my friend, truth is my friend; and both being my friends, it is my sacred duty to give the first honour to truth."[1]

This rupture in the reform party is an important landmark in the history of Hus. It accelerated the speed of the impact and recoil, and gave a tone of bitterness to his further assaults on Papal authority; besides, it brings into view his greatest enemies in the future development of the movement. Jerome, the brilliant Uhlan of reform, skirmishing on the outer margin of the area of conflict, came to the assistance of Hus in this crisis, and made a defence of his position

[1] Reply to Paletz: "Retrocedens sicut cancer."

with so great power on the popular mind, that a public ovation by the students and citizens was given him on leaving the university hall His intellectual and oratorical triumph set the whole population in a blaze; and, a few days afterwards, the excited mob of Prague burned the Papal bull, in answer to the bonfire of Wyclif's writings, and in defiance of Papal authority. The logic of enthusiasm is rarely a syllogism—reason and order seldom rule the action of a panic-stricken crowd, and there was undoubtedly much in this riotous outbreak that it would be difficult soberly to defend. Hus behaved with studied moderation, evidently awed by the popular excitement, and anxious to restrain his followers from conflict with another proclamation of the King, just issued, threatening death to disturbers of the peace. In spite of his moderation, three youths attempted to stop the sale of indulgences by force in one of the churches, and came under the lash of the law. Hus interposed in their favour, and obtained a promise of their release; but a few hours thereafter they were executed at the instigation of the German party in the city council. This first blood was the consecration of the cause of reform—it placed the wreath of martyrdom on the brow of its victims—it welded the rising force into stubborn resistance, and transformed Bethlehem Chapel into the "church of the three saints." [1]

As soon as the news of the action of Hus with regard to indulgences reached Rome, it roused the wrath of the Pope, and immediately the heaviest artillery of the Church was levelled at him. A bull of the greater excommunication was published in 1412, forbidding all intercourse with the arch-heretic, ordering the demoli-

[1] Abbot of Dola.

tion of the chapel, and interdicting all religious service in the place of his residence, unless he submitted to Papal authority within twenty days.

There was a solemn pause in the battle after this edict was read at Prague. Both sides held their breath to hear the reply of Hus. He threw his scabbard in the face of the foe, and, refusing to surrender, appealed from the Pope to Christ, as the only true head of the Church. This defiant attitude greatly pleased the local priesthood; for, besides enjoying a happy holiday during the ban on Prague, they saw, in this burning of the boats and cutting of the bridge, the inevitable capitulation of their inveterate enemy. On the expiration of the days of grace, the arrest of Hus was ordered, with all the fulminations of apostolic wrath; and the necessity arose of considering whether to fight for freedom to the bitter end or retire into seclusion. After consultation with his friends, Hus agreed, at their request, to leave the scene of his labours for a time, and disappoint the immediate hopes of the elated clergy.

This period of exile opens the last chapter in the life of Hus, as it also brings into view the more literary side of his work. Hitherto, the exigencies of duty were fatal to any serious efforts at writing, beyond his Bohemian discourses on current questions, and a few pamphlets on special aspects of the controversy in which he was involved; but now, from his retreat among his native hills, and in view of the wider bearing of the question at issue, he endeavoured to consolidate his position by a more systematic statement of its main contentions. His letters—some personal, some pastoral—offered an outlet for his large-hearted affection, and revealed one of the great secrets of his power over the congregation at Bethlehem Chapel. Luther was greatly charmed with these exile and prison letters, and published an edition of them in Latin, as evidence to his age of how a noble, heroic soul could suffer for conscience and truth. It would be as impossible to convey an idea of "the inflexible sweetness" of this correspondence by analysis, as to present the fragrance of a flower in a dissection chart. The letters present a picture from within of the various stages in the development of the closing chapter of the Reformer's history. His mental conflict is expressed to Martin—"My soul is sad, for I know not what to resolve on;" his calm faith to the rector of the university—"I have never felt myself overwhelmed by persecution;" and his counsel to the congregation—"Be not shaken in your faith, and regard not those, who, having placed only an uncertain foot in the path, have turned aside elsewhere, and have become the most violent enemies of God and of his disciples."[1]

His principal controversial writings also belong to this season of retirement, as well as the greatest of all his works, the Latin treatise on "The Church." This was the Novum Organum of reform, first conceived by the master mind of Wyclif, then adopted in the main by Hus, and more or less borrowed by later reformers. Its principles are drawn directly from Scripture, with variations in application according to circumstances, and its essential idea is that which has found expression in the accepted summaries of the various Protestant Churches. It was an answer to an attempt at compromise between the Papal authorities of the Church and the representatives of Bethlehem Chapel; and it

[1] Luther's edition. Translated by Bonnechose.

was most conclusive, for its first principles and whole spirit are such as to show quite clearly that Hus was outside the then received idea of the Church.

During this exile, Sigismund, brother of Wenzel, was created Roman Emperor; and, with the assistance of Gerson, urged the Pope to call another General Council, to close the state of triangular tension in the Papacy, to reform the Church, and to put down heresy. John XXIII. had sufficient reason to dread such a threatened infringement of his absolute power, or any inquiry about the uses he had made of his authority; and, with the casuistry of an expert, evaded any decision, until, under severe pressure, he was at last compelled to summon a Council at Constance on 1st November, 1414.

With a good deal of diplomatic adroitness, Sigismund also prevailed on Hus, under promise of a safe conduct, to appear at this Council for the purpose of explaining his principles before the best minds of the Church. Confiding in the promise, and confident in the justice of his cause, Hus consented to appear, in the belief that he would gain a victory for truth. Some of his friends shook their heads, others openly predicted danger; yet they failed to alter his determination to defend his faith before the highest ecclesiastical tribunal of the day. Under a vague presentiment of death, he left in the hands of one of his disciples a valedictory address to his followers, including a disposition of his little property. He began his preparations for the Council by getting a certificate of orthodoxy from the local inquisitor, and a similar document from the Archbishop, on the plea that he had never been convicted of heresy. The documents were readily granted, because his opponents were playing a subtle game, and did not wish to discourage his hopes in the Council, in which they saw the best means of finally crushing this revolt from the authority of the Church.

In complete ignorance of their scheme, Hus started for Constance, leaving Jerome in charge of Bethlehem Chapel. Everywhere on the journey he was well received by sympathizers with religious freedom, and wrote to his friends that "his worst enemies were Bohemians." On 3rd Nov. he reached Constance, a few days after the entry of the Pope; and the interdict, already a dead letter, was formally removed. Before his arrival, however, Paletz was busy among the leading members of this greatest of all Councils, endeavouring to prejudice their minds against Hus, on the grounds of heresy, contumacy, and revolutionary action. The French Nominalists were urged to suppress this Realist; the Germans were incited to avenge the insult offered to their nation in their expulsion from the University of Prague; the English were instigated to crush the disciple of Wyclif; and the Italians were advised to stand by the authority of their Pope. The treatise on "The Church" was also put in process, and every agency was set in operation calculated to rouse the passions of the priesthood. Several ingenious attempts were made to settle the case "in camera" before the arrival of the Emperor; but these were successfully resisted on the plea of the safe conduct, with its promise of a fair hearing in the open Council. But, under pretence of a conference with a commission appointed by the Pope, Hus was taken into custody, and, a week after, was sent as a prisoner to the Blackfriars' Convent on the side of the lake. By whose orders he was arrested has never been determined; yet the fact remains that he was a prisoner in a Dominican monastery when the Emperor came to Constance on Christmas-day. Sigismund professed to be greatly displeased at this breach of honour, and severely assailed the Pope for his violence, and accompanied his reproof with a threat that if Hus were not liberated he would leave the Council. He was soon pacified by the cardinals on the assurance that "no promise made to a heretic was binding in law or conscience," and, to his indelible disgrace, the Emperor left Hus to the mercy of an assembly, who began by prejudging the case, and putting out of court the elementary principles of justice. From this point the fate of the Bohemian was practically sealed, though a long series of formal investigations took place, the prisoner meantime undergoing a process of slow poisoning in his unwholesome cell. The letters of his prison life shed a lurid light on these dark proceedings, and reveal the inner history of an indomitable spirit undergoing martyrdom. At one time, like an untamed bird, dashing against the bars of its cage, his heart rebels against injustice and imprisonment. At another time, like a domestic fowl, as he says, playing on his name,[1] his soul is resigned to the will of heaven; but never once in the most extreme suffering does he lose sight of the interests of truth. His prison letters are a manifesto of faith worth all the creeds. They show the secret of his heroic courage, and sweeten the tragic surroundings of his death with the sunshine of God.

[1] The word Hus means goose.

The programme of the Council was drawn on a plan which had the condemnation of Hus for its culminating point, and all its acts were grouped on this principle. The first public decision directly affected the Popes. The two absent pretenders were formally deposed; and, as the peace of the Church was more important than the interests of an individual, John was called on to resign. He resisted for a time without improving his case, and at last, under threats of prosecution for immorality, the infamous Cossa thought it wise to abscond and thus escape from being deposed. Hus, as the prisoner of the Pope, was now taken over into the custody of the Council and was transferred to the castle of Gottlieben to endure the exquisite pain of starvation in fetters.

The second stage of procedure was the examination of the writings of Wyclif, which were condemned again with all the anathemas of the Church, and given over to the public executioner to be burned. This was a foregone conclusion; it was now intensified by the further instruction to exhume his bones and remove them by fire from the dust of the faithful. This settled the question of principle, and the severity of the sentence was a bad omen for the cause of Hus. News of these cruelties created great excitement in Bohemia, and a strong remonstrance was sent to Sigismund, with the result of arousing the wrath of the Council, and of hastening the activity of Paletz in preparing the accusation against Hus.

The trial more resembled a gladiatorial show than a judicial proceeding, and reflected little credit on the accusers and judges; for it was only in the hands of Gerson and D'Ailly that it rose above the level of a farce.

The charge against Hus was based on extracts from his own writings in Latin, which in their constructive form he repudiated as garbled; and also on acts of his life which were greatly misrepresented; still there can be little doubt that, from the standpoint of the cardinals, Hus was the direct antithesis of orthodoxy. He professed himself a true son of the Church, seeking to free it from abuses, and desiring to be instructed in any truth on which he might seem to have erred; but the Council was bent on suppressing discussion and laughed at the idea of debate. It was a conflict between rational freedom and slavish submission to authority.

On 5th June, 1415, Hus was called before the open Council to hear the libel read, on which already the draft of his sentence was prepared. His exceptions to the various points were hissed down, and, on persisting in his defence, the tumult became so great that an adjournment was made to allow the disorder to subside. This clamour forced Hus to exclaim—" I thought there was to be found in this Council more decency, more piety, and more discipline."[1]

On 7th June began the second sederunt. The writings of Wyclif, specially the defence of the forty-five articles, were made the ground of the charge of heresy. It was contended by D'Ailly that a Realist could not accept the doctrine of the sacrament in the Church sense, but this was a point on which Hus never could follow Wyclif, although it is somewhat difficult to grasp his modified position. He denied that he supported any error of Wyclif, and insisted that his defence of the forty-five articles was based on

[1] Letters from Constance.

the wholesale character of the condemnation, and not on agreement with each in detail. His work in Bethlehem Chapel was also charged with revolutionary tendencies. To this he replied with an affirmation of loyalty to the throne, to the best interests of social morality, and to the Church as based on Apostolic truth. His appeal to conscience and revelation was ridiculed, and a general finding was come to in the line of the charge.

On 8th June the conflict gathered round his treatise on "The Church" along with his other polemical pamphlets—and Paletz was the principal accuser. Gerson held that the teaching of this treatise was subversive of all Church order, and averred, that while anxious for reform, he could see nothing but revolution in the doctrine of Hus. There are worse things than revolution, as this good man lived to know; in the meantime, however, he could recommend nothing but recantation as a safe course out of the difficulty. Hus appealed to Apostolic principles in vain, even urged that the Church without a Pope was an argument for the true headship, but the Council refused to listen to his pleadings for liberty. So he at last gave up the unequal contest in a prayer for his persecutors.

A solemn charge was then read, offering Hus the alternative of an unqualified recantation of heresy, with a full surrender to the mercy of the Council ; or, the unanimous condemnation of the Church. Ecclesiastical law and ethical principle were thus in antagonism, and to the mind of Hus the authority of conscience left him no choice. Death was the only escape, and he resolved to die rather than deny the truth. With less equanimity did the Emperor and Council look on the result of the trial, and several efforts were made to induce Hus to yield. Friends urged him; even Paletz pleaded with tears, and several deputations were sent to argue down his doubts; but the love of truth was stronger than the love of life, and he preferred death to dishonour. The letters to Prague at this supreme moment are full of calm resolution, and urge a similar faithfulness on those still left in the field of struggle.

On 6th July, the Council met in full court. The shadow of death was over it, and the last scene of the tragedy was opened with solemn mass. The sentence of degradation from the priesthood, with death, was pronounced on Hus; his tonsure was disfigured, his official robes were removed, then his soul was handed over to the devil and his body to the flames.

His Latin and Bohemian writings were already burning as he passed to the place of execution. The faggots were lighted as he breathed his prayer for all his enemies and friends, and the smoke choked his utterance as he commended his soul to God. Thus, in a chariot of fire, the Elijah spirit of Bohemia was translated to heaven, leaving his mantle to Jerome and a consecrated memory to his country. Hus died a martyr's death—contending for a rational faith, a pure conscience, a Scriptural Church—exposing the fallacy of force in religious life, as exemplified in the Cross, in the Catacombs, and in the Inquisition; and lifting into view again the old saying of Tertullian—" The blood of the martyrs is the seed of the Church."

The fire that was intended to burn out heresy only burned it more deeply into the heart of Bohemia. On 30th May, 1416, Jerome, having recovered from his temporary eclipse in the conflict with material force, also stood at the stake to witness for the truth in death, and passed across the stage of Constance in another blaze of light. Hus and Jerome—united in life and death—remind us of Latimer and Ridley, the twin martyrs of England. One was the moral fibre, the other the intellect and culture of the Bohemian revival in the fifteenth century; and their immortality on the page of history proves beyond dispute, that great ideas in moral or mental life cannot be destroyed by any material weapon. "Truth, like a torch, the more it's shook it shines." The voice of Antigone,[1] which is the voice of Conscience, is heard in Hus and Jerome—

> "Nor did I deem thy heralding so mighty
> That thou, a mortal man, could'st trample on
> The unwritten and unchanging laws of heaven.
> They are not of to-day nor yesterday,
> But ever live, and no one knows their birth-tide.
> These, from the dread of any human anger,
> I was not minded to annul, and so
> Incur the punishment which heaven enacts."

In the afterglow of these fires of martyrdom, a weird lament rose from the native heart of Bohemia; it penetrated into the upland valleys like the coronach of a Highland funeral, and it crept in a subdued wail into the most distant households among the hills. The Czech spirit for the moment was stunned—wounded in its patriotism and in its religious freedom—and took some time to recover the blow thus struck at its chiefs. The issue of the edict of the Council to suppress the Hussite cause awoke a deep resentment in reforming circles, and acted like oil on the smouldering fire of rebellion. Their nobles were ordered to restore all property taken from the Church, their leaders in re-

[1] Sophocles (Dr. Donaldson's translation).

form were cited to Rome, and all adherents of Hus were required to openly abjure the principles of his teaching. Clamour greeted this proclamation on all sides; it rose into a wild shriek in some quarters, and a general movement began among the nobles to resist this invasion of popular rights. It was as if the fiery cross had been sent among the hillmen. Watchfires were lighted in all directions, and the scattered forces of reform gathered into solid mass. The weak King was placed in a serious dilemma—with the Emperor and Pope on one side, with signs of social revolution on the other—and his habitual indolence increased the difficulty of decision until the opportunity was gone.

The advent of the Papal legate to enforce the decision of the Council roused the cry of revenge, which drove him out of Prague with all his inquisitorial apparatus. The Emperor then brought pressure to bear on his brother, which still further increased the confusion, for it drove Ziska from the Court of Wenzel, and made him the head of the Hussites. The personal dignity and military genius of Ziska gave cohesion to the undisciplined army of reform; and, like Cromwell, he was soon surrounded by Ironsides whom nothing could resist. The old question of the cup in communion had been revived during the prison life of Hus, and had gained his sanction on scriptural grounds. This, therefore, was made a leading doctrine of the party. Their watchword was "Ziska of the cup," their standard bore a chalice as its symbol, and one of the features of the ninth century Church of Bohemia was again restored.

Ziska set up his standard at Tabor, a few miles from Prague, quite in the spirit of Deborah and Barak, and began to drill the rustic soldiers to the use of their primitive weapons, for the defence of the ancient liberties of Bohemia. Very soon they swept the country with fire and sword, crying vengeance on the priests and on the German domination. They even attacked the palace of the vacillating king and threw him into a fit of apoplexy, from which he died. They also, in wild fanaticism, sacked the cathedral palace and drew the Archbishop (Konrad) over to their side. An intense republican feeling then laid hold of Ziska's followers, feebly opposed by the nobles, and social disintegration threatened to ruin both Church and State, when the Emperor and Pope joined in a crusade against the revolutionists. Signs of internal dissension already beginning to appear among the Hussites were at once lost sight of in this crisis, and the again united ranks of Ziska defeated and routed the forces of Sigismund. Ziska lost both eyes in the conflict, but his intrepid spirit could not be broken by blindness. He still led on in an unbroken series of victories. The Emperor tried to buy him over with the promise of his being made lieutenant-governor, and had so far succeeded when the veteran was stricken with the plague and died in 1424. On an altar near his tomb, on which Hus and Ziska are represented, is found this scroll—" O Hus, here reposes John Ziska, thy avenger, and the Emperor himself has quailed before him."[1]

The Hussites were called "The Orphans" after the death of Ziska, and soon fell into family feud—one section more moderate, the other more extreme in it demands for concessions from the authorities of the

[1] Bonnechose, vol. ii. p. 311.

Church, while both were loyal to the principle of communion in both kinds. The Taborites, as distinct from the chalice men, rejected all outward ceremonial in worship, denied the doctrine of the real presence in the sacrament, and refused to acknowledge a hierarchy. This sectarian tendency increased in the after-history of the movement; yet these sporadic germs, thrown off at different times, had all the living principle of truth within them, and borne on the breeze to various parts of Central Europe, they took root and grew into seed, which, sown again by other causes, gradually ripened into a more glorious harvest.

Luther said, on his way to Worms, "They could burn Hus but they could not burn the truth." A century after the death of Hus another illustration was given of the truth of his saying, "Pharisee, pontiff, and priest have formerly condemned the Truth and buried it, but it has risen from the tomb and vanquished them all";[1] or perhaps Luther is the historical reading of the prophecy of Hus—"The cackle of the goose will awake the eagle"; for, on the strong wing of the far-seeing monk of Erfurt, the work of Wyclif and Hus was lifted into a clearer atmosphere before the eye of Europe, in the greater Reformation of the sixteenth century.

This review of the life and work of Hus has already so far indicated his relation to Wyclif; yet, as that relation has excited a good deal of discussion, it may be well, in conclusion, to offer a broad, general statement of the controversy.

The natural desire to discover the origin of life, or the beginning of great movements of thought, is like

[1] Letter to the believers in Prague.

the ancient sigh of Egypt, to gaze upon the fountains of the Nile, or to solve the riddle of the Sphinx. History is a divine plan unfolding through human experience, with a distinct law of continuity, with an equally evident variety in its forms of manifestation, and, working on large areas, and through long periods of time, it brings into view phases of thought which defy analysis. The spirit of an age is an inspiration, not an invention, and the historian comes too late into the field to discover the subtle relation of its motive powers. Still, there are great epochs, with clearly marked characteristics, and one of these is represented by Wyclif and Hus, when the chrysalis of the middle ages was breaking into the winged life of modern history by the natural development of inherent vitality.

The very success of the Papacy, in its struggle against the temporal powers, awakened in the Church the spirit of freedom, which showed itself in religious questionings and social upheavals. The moral law is constant, and wherever it comes into antagonism with error and corruption in the Church, struggle is inevitable; and more or less of resemblance will be discernible among those who lead the conflict. Froude says—"A man is great as he contends best with the circumstances of his age, and those who fight best with the same circumstances, of course grow like each other."[1] Similar plants are found under the same conditions of soil and climate in the most distant zones; volcanic disturbance moves in magnetic circuit over wide areas, and throws up signs of its action in places far separated, yet in sympathy with each other; so also in mental and moral life, similar causes working under like conditions will produce

[1] Short Studies, vol. i. p. 582.

corresponding effects. " Nature is full of a sublime family likeness throughout her works; and delights in startling us with resemblances in the most unexpected quarters."[1]

Thus, England and Bohemia, outlying provinces of the Roman Empire, with an inborn love of independence, were most sensitive to this spirit of freedom, therefore, they rose with spontaneous impulse to the leading place in reform, and presented many features of likeness in their general history, and also in their outstanding figures.

The spirit of independence among the Czechs had never quite submitted to the rule of papal uniformity, and its protest was at least as early as that of England; but the mind of the Saxon took a deeper grasp of the positive side of reform than the Slav, and it was this constructive principle that gave it permanence. Absolute originality belonged to neither Wyclif nor Hus; they were comparatively late workers in the field of remonstrance, but the Oxford Doctor was not content with jeremiads on the state of the Church, he suggested curative treatment through doctrinal reform. This undoubtedly made him a greater dynamic force in the movement, and this also gave him influence over the practical mind of Hus. The teaching of Wyclif found Hus in the University entangled in the intricacies of the schoolmen; it gave him the clue with which to thread the labyrinth, so the grateful student followed the philosopher into the region of theology, and increasingly found him " the master of deep thoughts." This is the principle on which schools are founded, and it is this affinity of complementary natures which

[1] Emerson's Essay on History.

really explains the relation between the two early Reformers. No teacher or system of education will give insight to a superficial mind; the faculty to recognise profound statements of truth is near akin to the power that originates them, just as the next thing to being great is the ability to admire greatness. "The mute, inglorious Miltons," the artistic instinct even without technical skill, the appreciative sense of qualities not our own, are beautiful traits of character; and we do not admire Wyclif the less but Hus the more for this unity of difference. It is no fair objection to the moon that it is not the sun.

Stokes, an English priest, accused Hus at Prague in 1411 of direct plagiarism from Wyclif. The answer is a frank confession of indebtedness, running into a noble panegyric of the great master, towards whom he had been drawn by instinct and conviction.[1] If Carlyle can so justly refute the imposture theory as an explanation of the work of Mohammed and the forging of the sword of Islam, it becomes easy to feel that the fanaticism of Ziska was not warmed at a painted fire, nor his sword unsheathed to defend the fame of a professional tragedian. Nothing less than a great moral force in society will cover the facts of the Hussite rebellion, and the cause must be equal to the effect. The spirit of the life of Hus refutes the charge of pious fraud, and in the fire at Constance the insult is consumed.

Milton, in the Areopagitica, says, "Had it not been the obstinate perverseness of our prelates against the divine and admirable spirit of Wycliffe, to suppress him as a schismatic and innovator, perhaps neither the Bo-

[1] Neander, ix. p. 329.

hemian Husse and Jerome, no, nor the name of Luther or of Calvin had ever been known. The glory of reforming all our neighbours had been completely ours."[1]

The laws of human history are not concerned with the glory of a nation so much as the good of the world, and Milton's regret is simply an admission that Hus was necessary to Wyclif in the evolution of events. A second Wyclif would have been less powerful than Hus, who, instead of attempting to rival the thinker of Oxford, set himself to carry out his theory into a practical result, until he had made Wyclif more powerful on the Continent than at home. Through the life and work of Hus, Wyclif was called the fifth evangelist in Bohemia. History, therefore, has not lost in any degree by the admission that more than one man was required for the reformation of Europe.

On the Continent the keenest controversy has raged around this subject in more recent times, and the efforts of some to minimize the work of Hus almost suggest the current of feeling against the Slav which still permeates Austro-German minds. At the one extreme, Neander urges a heroic defence of the independence of Hus, and calls him the direct offspring of Bohemian reform. The law of heredity is very apparent on the patriotic side. It explains to some extent the points of difference between Wyclif and Hus on the doctrine of transubstantiation, and on the value of tradition; as also the pathetic clinging of Hus to the hope of reforming without leaving the Church. Still, in view of his own admission, and his undoubted leaning to the side of Wyclif, such a claim for Hus cannot be fairly maintained. At the opposite extreme Böhringer calls Hus an

[1] Milton's Prose Works, Bohn's edition, vol. ii. p. 91.

"echo" of Wyclif, and Loserth endeavours to establish this charge by direct quotation.[1] It is possible that the very choice of such a task unconsciously assists in its performance, as it is easy to select extracts from writers, on the same theme, about the same time, of similar tenour or diction, which, while true in detail, may be misleading in their general impression. The points of divergence in method and thought may be unduly left in the background, and thus a tone of special pleading given to the argument.

It is granted that Bohemian reform in the earlier days of Hus was associated with the name of Wyclif; it is also true that the name of Hus came more to the front in the later stages, as his personal courage transformed doctrinal belief into moral energy. It is also admitted that the Latin tracts bear strong evidence of borrowing largely from Wyclif; and, if this is not acknowledged by their author, it is not therefore necessary to accept the charge of plagiarism. Even Shakspeare would suffer if the same tests were applied to his historical plays.

But Hus was less a school divine than a native preacher; and it has never been shown, scarcely even suggested, that in his regular sermons there was anything more than a general likeness to Wyclif, such as any disciple would bear to an admired master. The life of active labour laid upon Hus so soon, was fatal to leisured thought; the voices that visit the solitudes and whisper to meditative minds were little heard by him in the over-pressure of pastoral duty and prelatic debate. Like the average Presbyterian minister, his whole capacity required to be concentrated on duty

[1] Loserth's Wyclif and Hus. 1884.

lying to hand, and his literary talent was given up to the feeding of his flock. Besides, Hus died in his forty-sixth year, about the age when ripe fruit generally begins to fall for the benefit of thinking men, and, like a wise man, he was content to leave his immortality to the test of practical work. His expositions in Czech of the Church service, his homilies on the Commandments, the Creed, the Lord's Prayer, and the Scripture lessons, are full of spiritual insight and moral earnestness; while his letters unite the qualities of a Boanerges and Barnabas in a true Pauline combination. If, therefore, a thing is the sum of its relations, an era the resultant of its forces, and a man the equivalent of all his thoughts and deeds, then it may be allowed to claim for Hus, in the work of reform, a place scarcely less honourable than his more renowned and greater predecessor.

A fair statement of the case seems to be something like this. The thought of the great theologian found and educated the great preacher—the prophet of England inspired the patriot of Bohemia, who, thinking less of literary fame than of the cause of truth, used the instruments already provided with the skill of a successful workman. Hus is a man lost in his work, oblivious of the ambitions of self-conscious men, and totally removed from the jealous rivalry of the partizan. Wyclif is like Moses on Pisgah sketching the plan of conquest, Hus is like Joshua carrying it out into practical effect, while both are really one in the spirit of the enterprise. The one had mental power, the other moral courage; and, just as Calvin was a greater theologian than Luther, yet vastly his inferior as a religious reformer, so the intellectual thought of England, polarized into the moral energy of Bohemia, produced its greatest result on the Continent of Europe. Wyclif and Hus are twin stars of different magnitude shining in the dawn; they are the reason and conscience of mediæval times breaking into the spiritual freedom of modern history, and they represent the revolt from blind authority to the inherent right of private judgment. The real contribution of Hus to the advent of the Reformation was moral or spiritual more than intellectual; and after all, it is character transfigured by conscious communion with God that is the strongest force in moral and religious regeneration. Hus is an example of ordinary ability under extraordinary conviction, and even his weaknesses reveal the intense earnestness of his purpose. He was before all things a Christian patriot, he bore to the stake a stainless reputation, and he died in the heroic effort to restore revelation, reason, and conscience to the throne of religious life. An echo will not explain that commotion at Bethlehem Chapel; an inspiration is needful to account for his courage—an inspiration which is more than verbal likeness or dogmatic agreement, and which comes from a source beyond Wyclif. That crown of martyrdom at Constance has lifted Hus into the sacred galaxy of heroic men who have fought the battles of humanity in the name of God; and in letters of fire this confession may for ever be read in his name, " God alone is Lord of the conscience."

Savonarola.

This man has been denounced as a demagogue, sneered at as a fanatic, cursed as a heretic. On the other hand, he has been extolled for his patriotism, reverenced for his earnestness, and deemed worthy of a place in the calendar of the Church of Rome. Finally, he has been claimed as a precursor of the Reformation. Sympathy with this last estimate has, it appears to us, solid enough foundation on which to rest.

He stands somewhat apart. There is an evident bond between Hus and Wyclif. The Bohemian was obviously a disciple of the English Reformer; and if he did not make an advance upon the stand taken by his master such as would have brought him nearer to the position which Luther was urged eventually to assume, if it be even admitted that, while later in time, his work was not so far forward in tendency, yet the fact is incontestable that the labours of Hus cannot be studied without explicit reference to the teaching of Wyclif. Externally, however, Savonarola is related to neither of these. We have found no indication of acquaintance on his part with their lives, nor is there any trace of his having been consciously influenced by their labours. His work, the result in measure of like forces bearing upon a man in whom there was kinship of soul, is as independent as it is unique.

We are brought to the latter half of the fifteenth century, a period of history pregnant with interest to every student of the progress of humanity. Essentially an era of transition, an age of becoming, it is the morning-dawn of the modern world. Long ere this, it is true, there had been signs of restlessness under the yoke of authority, dogma, and scholasticism, and already the spirit of freedom was stirring to its resurrection. As it is impossible to trace the religious movement back to its first beginning, so it is futile to attempt to fix any date as the origin of the intellectual unrest without which the Reformation could not have been. Still, it cannot be denied that while the events which occurred in this epoch did not call into existence the new life, they gave such an impulse to its development as that it seemed like a fresh creation. In no previous age was growth so signal, so great, so general. Gutenberg had invented printing five years before this half-century began; four years before it closed, Columbus discovered America; and in its third year Mahomet II. captured Constantinople. The moment of these three events as forces acting on thought becoming conscious of its liberty, there can be no danger of exaggerating, and it is not without reason that the era on which they wrought so mightily is distinguished as that of the Renaissance.

With the import of the last of these we are here most immediately concerned. From one point of view the capture of Constantinople can be regarded only as a dire disaster whose baleful results remain till this day. It meant the downfall of Christian rule in the East, and the substitution of an empire based on a religious system of whose falsity the fruits are at least one telling testimony. On its occurrence, however, the catastrophe involved nearer consequences of another kind. In one direction the Western world gained by the loss which the Eastern world suffered. For the monasteries in the East were rich in classic lore, and the scholars there were imbued with the learning of the past. Exiled, they crossed the Adriatic seeking an asylum in Italy. All the principal Courts of Europe extended a welcome to the refugees, but nowhere could the welcome have been warmer than in the land on which the majority of them first set foot. Italy was ready with a deeper sympathy than that which feels for distress. Petrarch in the past had sung of the beauties of the olden time and had wistfully sighed for the repose of the antique culture; Boccaccio had bidden men see life to be sunny and free; and before them both, Dante had awakened his countrymen to think of things that widen thought. The study of Plato, too, giving movement to speculation and quickening aspiration for knowledge, had been revived, and in some centres bade fair to rival devotion to the rigid logic of Aristotle. And this spirit was fostered by the patronage of enlightened princes who, Mæcenas-like, were glad to place their palaces and wealth at the disposal of scholars and teachers, poets and philosophers, painters and sculptors, that they might pursue their labours free from too much care. In these circumstances the advent of so many exponents of the old-world literature and art was hailed with almost rapturous delight. The classic revival set in with full tide. Its energy was intensified to passion which dominated wherever it took hold. Blind old

Bardo di Bardi, taxing the patience of his gentle daughter in the library, and greeting Tito Melema with eagerness when he learned of the country whence he came and of the dispositions he professed to cherish,[1] may well enough be believed to represent hundreds of his day and spirit over whom the fascination of the Renaissance had cast its spell.

At the same time it has to be borne in mind that the very nature of the mental culture of this period did nothing to stem the flood of its moral corruption. It is on all hands admitted that iniquity never so abounded as at the time of the revival of the humanities—that, far from tending to pureness, the learning of the Renaissance served only to add an outward polish to the license that prevailed and which had infected all political and social life. The historians are unanimous in their witness, "neither public nor private morality in our sense of the word existed."[2] The most refined classic tone was quite compatible with the coarsest vices, their coarseness only covered by the haze of a corrupt æstheticism. The abominations of Paganism were side by side with its elegancies. Popes, princes, prelates, priests, people, were all unrestrained in their courses of incest, murder, falsehood, gambling, and every conceivable form of wickedness, which has led to a comparison of this age with the days of Nero. As to the relation in which it stood to Christianity, perhaps no more suggestive illustrations can be adduced than the counsel of Cardinal Bembo to his friend Sadolet not to read the Epistles of St. Paul, whose barbarous style might corrupt his taste, and the fact that when on his

---

[1] Romola, chap. v. vi.
[2] J. A. Symonds. Renaissance in Italy, vol. i.

return from Mantua, after a vain endeavour to raise a crusade against the infidels, Pius II. stepped ashore from his galley at Ferrara, the landing-place was adorned in honour of his Holiness by statues of the gods.

It can easily be anticipated that in such a condition of society the man fitted to do a religious work must be one who breathed freely the spirit of its culture, so that he might commend himself to its intelligence; who loathed utterly the atmosphere of its sin, so that without suspicion he might denounce its corruption; who had a firm faith in the truth which was travestied or treated with neglect; a fearlessness of any personal consequence for his genuine devotion, and in whose nature, for consecration to God and man, self must nowhere be. There was such a man, and it is of his heroic endeavour, his almost incredible but short-lived success, his most touching failure, that it falls to us now to speak.

Girolamo Savonarola was born at Ferrara on the 21st of September, 1452.[1] His family was originally of Padua, but on the invitation of Nicolas III., Marquis d'Este, Michele Savonarola, a celebrated physician, and author of several works on medicine, had come from his native city to add lustre to his patron's Court. He was still alive when his grandson was born, and during the first ten years of his life the boy, designated from infancy for his profession, enjoyed a large measure of the old man's regard. Of his father, Niccolo, but little is known. It would appear that he was not without good parts, inasmuch as on the death of Michele he

[1] The principal authority followed is the work of Villari. Quotations are taken from the French translation by Gustave Gruyer, Paris, 1874.

was able to superintend the studies of his son in scholastic science, a subject then considered necessary as a preliminary to any professional calling. Beyond this, however, he was for the most part a hanger-on at the palace, and succeeded in dissipating a not inconsiderable patrimony in the festivities of the Court. The memory of his mother, Elena di Buonacorsi, Savonarola cherished with the tenderest affection. To her he wrote amid the heavy trials of after-life as to his only confidant, and in terms which prove how pure and noble he knew her to be. He was the third of seven children, but of them all he alone lives in history.

Life in Ferrara was of the gayest for all who could afford to be gay, and for those who were poor, if bread was not provided of charity to keep them from starving, entertainments were furnished to give for the hour a sense of excitement. Borso, who swayed the city during the youth of Savonarola, held its people in subjection by his very munificence. To see the town *en fête* one would have thought that if there was anywhere where sorrow was not it was here. Had he gone to the homes of the poor, or into the cells of the fortress, he would have speedily recognized the vastness of the misery which lay concealed from sight. None that was clothed in sackcloth might enter the King's gate. There was no gentle sensibility, no fellow-feeling, no generousness in Ferrara, where there was splendour so lavish and luxury so ample. And there were occasions when extravagance really deceived those who shared in it and made them forget their constant woes. One such occasion fell when Savonarola was but six years old. It was incident to that mission of Pius II. to which allusion has already been made. Going and returning the Pope rested in the city of the Estés. Never was spectacle more gorgeous, never emperor was more royally received, never were balls merrier and *festas* more brilliant and carousals cheerier than while the vicar of Christ tarried in the town! What matter the lavish outlay if there was a sufficient impression of grandeur made; what matter a debauch for a week if the people were pleased and cried " *Viva il Duco !* " Perhaps that child saw the cavalcades from a window, and, as he looked, his face perhaps beamed with glee. We do not know how it was with him then, but this is certain, that scenes such as this were indelibly graven on his heart, and that the memory of them made him sorrowful. As evidence of the revulsion of his soul from all such, we have it that having once been taken by his father to a great Court festival, instead of being dazzled he vowed he would never again cross the threshold of the palace, and that at the age of twenty he had never walked on the fashionable promenade of Ferrara, which was on the citadel where the dungeons were down below.

It was early evident that the purpose of his parents as to his career was alien to his disposition. When he ought to have been giving the energies of his mind to the study of medicine, he was deep in thought upon St. Thomas Aquinas and Aristotle. Soon as the fixed hours of study were over (and amongst his fellows he approved himself a careful, competent scholar) he betook himself to the paths by the river side to read and muse alone. The writings of the "Angelic Doctor" specially won his soul, and so thoroughly did he imbibe his teaching that in one of his sermons, long after he had joined the order of the great schoolman, he can say: "I am almost nothing, and even that little which I am I possess because I have kept within the influence of his doctrine. He was truly profound, and when I want to become small in my own eyes I read his works, and then it appears to me that he is a giant and I nothing." Not that he confined himself to metaphysic and theology. "He read with eagerness the ancient authors, wrote verses, studied drawing and music."[1] Devout, too, he prayed much in secret, and learnt by heart passage after passage of the Scriptures, a practice which he continued to follow in after-days until, as several of his biographers attest, he had committed almost the whole Latin Bible to memory. Little, however, can be said of the inward development of mind which marked his youth. The true history of that period of any great life reduces itself to hidden thoughts, secret impressions, unutterable struggles of the spirit which we can never know. Only what we do see is a quiet, serious, meditative man, melancholy as he surveys his surroundings, but laying, in his learning and his moral tone, the basis of force for a work to which a higher Will than that of his parents has appointed him.

There was a gleam of sunshine shot athwart the solemn sadness of these days—only a gleam. The daughter of Filippo Strozzi surely forgot not only that she was an exile in Ferrara, but that her mother had not been her father's wife, when she haughtily spurned the generous advances of young Girolamo. Poor, proud flutterer, in thy disdaining of so pure a love! Yet methinks that thou wert even used by God to give thy noble lover to his immortality.

[1] Villari, i. 34.

Savonarola felt keenly the unexpected rejection of his suit, but the manner of refusal only revealed to him more clearly than ever the lack of true-heartedness which he discerned everywhere in the world, and renewed more strongly the inclination, which had only been weakened for the little while, to seek elsewhere than in its intercourse a rest, which to him it could not give. That tendency grew as he was cast back upon himself. The line of the poet began to seem as though it was a voice to him,

"Heu! fuge crudeles terras, fuge litus avarum."[1]

and as he repeated the words he prayed the prayer of another poet—

Domine, notam fac mihi viam in quâ ambulem,
Quia ad Te levavi animam meam.[2]

It was at Faenza, sometime in the year 1474, that he heard the answer to the cry of his heart. Listening to a sermon preached by a dissolute monk of the order of St. Augustine, he caught a word—a word which he never spoke to another—but which fixed his resolve. Not till the year following did he feel ready to take the way revealed. Sitting one evening alone with his mother, he played a plaintive melody upon his lute. The strain stirred a strange presentiment. She looked up from her work at the face so calm and yet so sad, and said, "My son, that is a sign of parting." Girolamo coloured, controlled himself, but did not answer. The next day, the 24th of April, 1475, Savonarola left home whilst all the family were taking part in the festival of St. George, and was received into the monastery of the Dominicans at Bologna.

[1] Virg. Æn., iii. 44.   [2] Ps. cxliii. 8.

Enough has probably been said to indicate that this step was taken under no spasmodic impulse. It was the decision of a full and mature deliberation. Were it possible to question this, any doubt is set at rest by a letter of apology which he wrote to his father two days after his admission to the convent. That letter gives the reasons for the choice he had made. "The motives which determine me are these: the great misery of the world, the iniquity of men, the rapes, the adulteries, the robberies, the pride, idolatry and awful blasphemy. The age is so depraved that good is nowhere. . . . From one end of Italy to the other I saw virtue in contempt, vice in honour."[1] Similar sentiments found expression in a short poem which bears the title "*De Ruinâ Mundi*," and the date of the previous year.

From the very outset, however, he seems to have had another conviction than that of the terrible degradation of his native land—to have had, indeed, a measure of the prophetic consciousness which became the very inspiration of his future life. In that same letter he tells his father that in a spot near the window of his room he will find some papers upon which he has written the record of his thoughts. One of these closes thus—"The righteous are oppressed, and the Italians are become like the Egyptians, who kept in bondage the people of God. Already dearths, floods, plagues and many other signs forebode evils to come, announce the wrath of God. Open, O Lord, open anew the waters of the Red Sea and gulf the godless in the waves of Thine anger."

Thus, then, at the age of twenty-three, recoiling from

[1] Villari, ii. 447, Appendix.

the scandalous wickedness of the world, not a mere moody misanthrope, but a hater only of men's sin, a man with discernment of the signs of the times, a man of good intellectual calibre, of unblemished moral character, of a profoundly religious disposition, enters upon his noviciate, and little more than twelve months from the day of his coming to the cloisters vows to be poor, chaste, and obedient.

It can scarcely have been in ignorance of the corruptions of the Church that Savonarola sought this rest from the evil of the world. Or if it was so, that he hoped to find holiness here, the delusion must have been soon dispelled. For very shortly after he took on him monastic vows he told out his horror of the abysm of moral depravity in which it was sunk. The verses *De Ruinâ Ecclesiae* are cast in the form of a dialogue. The poet demands of a chaste virgin—the Church—where be the saints, the teachers, the love, the learning of days bygone? The maiden takes him by the hand, leads him to a cave, and speaks: "When I saw pride and ambition get to Rome's heart, soiling all, I distanced far, and shut me here that I may pass my life in weeping." Then she shows him the scars and bruises on her breast, and after further colloquy concerning the proud harlot who has so disfigured her, Savonarola utters an apostrophe so suggestive, when read in the reflected light of his later labour: "O God, could these great wings be broken!" "Weep and be silent, for this is best," bids the maiden. Weep the monk might; silent he could not always remain, though for a time he must.

If such were the emotions of the young friar they must have been made yet more intense by an event of the year 1478. We refer to the Pazzi conspiracy. Of its causes nothing need here be said. The facts are briefly those: Death was decreed for the brothers Medici. At *mass* in Santa Maria del Fiore in Florence Giuliano was stabbed. Lorenzo escaped, wounded, to the sacristy, for the stiletto which the *priest* was to plunge to his heart did not go home. It was a *cardinal* who had planned the assassination. It was *Pope* Sixtus IV. who, in the hope of advancing his family interests, had more than sanctioned the sacrilege. Lorenzo took a terrible revenge. More than two hundred conspirators, actual and suspected, were executed. The Archbishop of Pisa swung in his clerical robes from a window in the Palazzo Vecchio. Then the Pope replied by hurling his anathema against the city where his scheme of nepotism had failed. The tidings of all this sped throughout Italy, and one can conceive how they must have affected a man who already knew and felt the iniquity of those evil times as he pondered in his cell. Savonarola, however, was not yet prepared for his endeavour. His convent life in Bologna extends over a period of seven years—years of sustained study in Aristotle and Plato and the Bible—years during which he wrote several of those treatises on science and philosophy which disclose the grasp and subtilty of his intellect—during which, too, he covered the margin of his copies of the Scriptures with notes in a hand so cramped and in contractions so illegible, that for the most part they bear a dumb witness to his devotion, but which also, so far as they can be deciphered, evince a fine union of critical faculty with spiritual feeling. They were years, also, during which, for that his superiors were quick to discern his fitness, he taught the novices, discharging so ably the functions of "lettore" as to command the respect of his pupils for his genius, and to win their affection by his gentleness. He began, too, to preach on occasions during this period, only, however, to pass through a not isolated experience of a fire burning within, while no warmth seemed to glow in kindled utterance. The mountain had not yet been touched that it might smoke.[1] For the rest, it must suffice to say that he kept faithfully the vows he had taken on him, and that not from the outward restraint of their imposition, but from the inward imperative of his moral nature. Physically he was constitutionally delicate and suffered from his asceticism; not a stain of impurity was contracted; his submission was worthy of better superiors than those to whom it was implicitly rendered. He had conceived a high ideal of the true son of the Church, the servant of Christ, and, even though he saw the miserable contradiction of it in others who professed to cherish it, his aim was that for himself he might realize it ever more fully, as, when afterwards he acquired his influence, he strove to raise all over whom he was set to a like consistency.

It was not in sombre Bologna that Fra Girolamo was destined to fulfil his mission, but in the bright capital of Tuscany, beyond the Apennines. He came to Florence for the first time in 1482. It was the only kingdom in the north of Italy in which there was then no political embroilment, for, while Venice, Ferrara, Genoa, and Milan were in arms, Florence, thanks to the prudent policy of her prince, was able to maintain an honourable neutrality. Hither, then,

[1] Psalm cxliv. 5.

for personal safety, Savonarola was sent, warmly commended by the Dominicans of Bologna to their brethren in San Marco. The commendation, indeed, was not needed except as a formal introduction of one whose name was already well esteemed as that of an ornament of the order.

The monastery, from whose inmates he received cordial greeting, was famous. Given to the Dominicans by the illustrious Cosimo de' Medici, it had been designed by Michelozzi, one of the most celebrated architects of his day. The valuable collection of MSS. made by Niccolo Niccoli had been purchased by the same prince, and retaining some of these for himself, he made over the larger number to the convent, thus entitling it to the claim of possessing the first public library in the land, and in the age of the Renaissance attracting to its cloisters the foremost scholars of the time. San Marco had been dignified, also, by the piety of Antonino, its first prior, a man who with his early disciples approached very near to the ideal of monastic life which Padre Marchese had expressed in his words: "What is the use of the cloister in the midst of society if it is not a focus and centre of morality and religion, diffusing and planting deep in the hearts of the people ideas of honesty, justice and virtue, in order to temper and hold in balance the brutal force of the passions which threaten continually to absorb all the thoughts and affections of men?" It is to this good prior that Florence owes the institution of the "Good Men of S. Martin," who to this day gather the offertories at the street-corners and distribute the charity amongst the city poor. There was another noble name early identified with the monastery—the name of Fra Angelico. His marvellous frescoes are not yet too faded to speak their silent eloquence of the sufferings and triumphs of the God-man, and when Savonarola first came they were all in their early freshness.

Coming from the gloomier environments of Bologna to take up his abode in this Athens of Italy—from the drearier precincts of the monastery there to the bright cloisters of this convent—from the society of ruder monks to intercourse with the brethren who were students of letters, and who in their converse revered the memory of holy Antonino—Savonarola, we are told, was charmed. As he came to know Florence and San Marco better the charm was dispelled. His new home was soon to be his field of conflict, of victory, and of defeat.

All that has already been said regarding the condition of Italy in general, and of Ferrara in particular, applies with special force to Florence. We are not called upon to trace the steps of her history as the freest of all the old Italian republics, Venice only excepted, walked into a willing bondage so thorough that she submitted to the despotism of one house for three generations, so wonderful that she was all the while unconscious of her loss of liberty. It was by the lavish use of his wealth that Cosimo de' Medici forged the fetters with which he bound her to his sway—a sway albeit wise and righteous. For although he gradually secured the monopoly of every appointment to civil office which had formerly lain with the citizens convened in "Parlamento," it may freely be allowed that his judgment was quite as politic for conserving the interests of the State as his ambition was resolute to secure the supremacy of his family. It was not possible, however, to pursue political ambition after the fashion of liberal patronage without depraving those whose subjection was solicited; and the result, if not so apparent in the days of the founder of the tyranny, had become terribly evident when Lorenzo "the Magnificent," in the third generation, was able as though by hereditary right to assume the despotism without a whisper of dissent. Of his character, it can only be said that it combined the best and worst features of his time. The partiality of his English biographer[1] has led him to pronounce a panegyric which cannot stand the criticism of history. With very much of it no fault can be found. Of Lorenzo's sagacity as a statesman there is no doubt; the peace and prosperity of his princedom in an era when constant feuds were elsewhere prevalent, were in large measure due to his clear-sighted policy. Himself a scholar (trained in early days under Ficino, the exponent of Platonism in the Florentine Academy), he did all that wealth and sympathy could do to encourage learning. A fine artistic taste set him to secure the services of the best painters and sculptors of the age to enrich his halls and gardens. All this and much more in like direction can be admitted. But that does not complete the true portrait of the man. There are ample grounds upon which the following description can be demonstrated as not more vivid by its few strokes than correct in its general tenor: "A man of superb health and physical power, who can give himself up to debauch all night without interfering with his power of working all day, and whose mind is so versatile that he can sack a town one morning and discourse upon the beauties of Plato the next, and weave joyous

---

[1] Roscoe, Life of Lorenzo de Medici.

ballads through both occupations."[1] We venture to add: who can write a letter full of pious counsels to his son in the morning, and at nightfall head a band of boon revellers through the streets of Florence, and who is probably quite as conscientious when he does the former as he is abandoned when he does the latter. It is quite necessary to insist upon this, for Roscoe's estimate of Savonarola is darkened in hue just in proportion to the brilliancy of colour with which he paints Lorenzo de' Medici. The testimony is convincing that, with no lack of culture, with a true perception of the beautiful in art, with a certain magnanimity, with a cautious faculty of control, with even a tinge of emotionalism, he was destitute of all steadfast moral principle, not to say of religious faith. One needs only to read some of the lewd *Canti Carnaleschi* which he wrote, to be shocked at the prostitution of his genius. And if it be held to be too grave a charge to prefer against him that he was directly responsible for the degradation of his subjects, for their gross sensualism, their unblushing profligacy, their sheer disregard of moral sanctions, their rusted infidelity beneath the smooth enamel of refined religionism, still it must be a valid indictment that not only did he in nowise use the influence at his command to keep the flood within barriers closer than had respect to political security, but that his personal countenance of iniquity was a force to the popular license, which it is hard to call other than an encouragement. The fact at least is established that, under his rule, Florence, not merely intellectually and æsthetically, but not less morally, was paganized.

[1] Mrs Oliphant, The Makers of Florence.

Savonarola's first pulpit appearances in the gay metropolis were disappointing to the Dominicans and disheartening to himself. Little more than a score of hearers were found willing to listen to him in San Lorenzo, while San Spirito could not accommodate the crowds that flocked to hear Fra Mariano, a clerical "browser in the Medicean Park."[1] The polished style of the Court preacher, as he treated with all the aids of studied oratory some theme as far removed from men's consciences as possible, who sympathized with the conception of preaching as one of the fine arts, and was careful beyond all else to avoid giving offence to delicate sensibilities, pleased the *élite*, and those who aped the tone of the *élite* followed the fashion. Fra Girolamo's ponderous expositions, spoken with harsh voice and ungainly gesture, loaded, too, at this time with a burden of scholastic "fivefold sense," fell flat upon the cultured society of Florence; for still the inspiration tarried that should make his words penetrate the crust of complacency to reach the passions of the heart.

For the moment Savonarola seems to have questioned his call and to have been so crushed by his failure that he resolved to confine himself to the work of teaching, in which he had achieved conspicuous success. The consciousness of a mission, however, could not be repressed. It strengthened while he kept vigils, fasted, prayed, and, concentrating the forces of his soul upon the Bible, waited for the vision.

It came at last. Rumours reached Florence of a revival of religion in San Gemigniano and Brescia and other villages and towns where the less sophisticated mountaineers and the more impressionable provincials

---

[1] Romola, c. vii.

were being moved by the fervent predictions of the brother of San Marco, who declared that, as God had of old dealt sore chastisement upon His people for their wickedness, His judgments upon Italy were near at hand. Then Giovanni Pico della Mirandola, that "prodigy of intelligence," "Phœnix of geniuses,"[1] a man who, at the age of twenty-three, had mastered not only Latin and Greek, but several of the Eastern languages, and whose name for learning was acknowledged beyond the bounds of Tuscany, came from Reggio to tell Lorenzo that at a chapter there he had heard a monk whose words had stirred strange springs of thought in him, and to beg the Prince to bid the friar's return.

That Dominican chapter at Reggio is virtually the turning-point in Savonarola's career. It is interesting to learn of the part he took in the deliberations. While dogma was discussed his lips were sealed. To him doctrinal precision was not the clamant need of the age. But when the debate turned on discipline he rose. "His voice trembled, and, like thunder, terrified the auditors, silent and spell-bound. He stigmatized the corruption of the clergy, and so let himself be carried away by the impetuosity of his words that he had difficulty in coming to a close. Everyone gazed on him as an extraordinary man, animated by a higher spirit."[2]

Nor is it less interesting to think of the significance of the impression made upon Pico, an impression which deepened as intimacy became closer, and which was so real that only a premature death prevented the scholar from becoming a monk. For " it was, so to speak, the

---

[1] Villari, i. 116.   [2] Villari, i. 120.

first point at which the Frate had touched the men of the new learning."[1] And to the last Savonarola had friends like him who were able to appreciate the union of religious enthusiasm and intellectual culture in the man they admired.

For the present, however, as we trace the course of external events, the importance of this crisis lies in this, that it prepared the way for a favourable reception to Savonarola, invited by Lorenzo, and esteemed by Pico.

This was in 1486, and there is a gap in the history containing the record of no events of much moment. It extends over four years, during which he seems to have been almost entirely absent from the monastery. It is impossible that these years can have been other than amongst the most fruitful of force to himself, but we can read anything of their secrets only in the light of the work that was done after they closed.

In 1490 he returned to San Marco, only, however, at first to resume his lectures within its walls. Pressed to open his prelections to others than the inmates, he found ere many weeks had passed that the room in which he taught was much too small for his increasing audience, and, under a damask rose-tree in the garden of the convent, he began his exposition of the Apocalypse to a circle of hearers, who stood or sat round him riveted by the teacher's power. They implored him to preach, and, at length, overcoming a diffidence, due, probably, to the memory of the past, he yielded to their entreaties. At the close of lecture on the first Saturday in August he intimated simply, "To-morrow we shall speak in the church; our discourse will be at once a lesson and a sermon."

[1] Prebendary Clark, Savonarola, His Life and Times, p. 75.

The next day the capacity of the convent church was taxed to the utmost to contain the crowd. The motives, doubtless, were various. Many were already, as we have seen, devotedly attached to the *lettore*—more, perhaps, were urged by curiosity to see and hear the man that Mirandola had praised; some, perhaps, were prompted by the tidings of the provincial revival, and were desirous to learn, like the Athenians, what new doctrine was disturbing men's tranquillity. Conjecture is easy when the mobile temper of the Florentines is considered. Be this as it may, none who came that morning could ever forget the scene or the sermon.

What like was the preacher? Not tall, but erect; finely-limbed, but not robust; sallow and wan with years of anxious waiting. But it is a wonderful face. The forehead would be high but for the furrows; the lashes are long and dark; the deep-set blue eyes are large, like windows of a great, pure soul; the nose is heavy, and like that of the sons of Israel; and the wide mouth, with its broad lips, silently tells of power. When the massive features are in repose there seems the *soupçon* of a smile about them.[1] But when the lips part and the eyes gleam and the thin transparent hand points its long tapering fingers, one could imagine that it was as though they were piercing an entrance for the words and looks into the hearers' conscience. Effort after oratorical effect there was no more now than there was years ago, but there was the free eloquence of a man possessed by his theme commanding the submission which no rhetoric without conviction can secure.

Savonarola's sermon on that day insisted upon

[1] See the portrait in The Makers of Florence, p. 243.

three propositions, the earnest enforcement of which had been the cause of his success in the highlands of Tuscany and elsewhere during his preaching tours, and which were at the foundation of all his future achievements in Florence. They were as follows:—

1. The Church is to be renewed in our time.
2. God will bring a great scourge on Italy before this renewal.
3. Both these things will happen very soon.

That was the burden of his message to Italy, and when Florence first heard it in 1490 she began already to believe it. Villari says of the immediate effect: "The success was complete. In every circle Florentine society spoke only of Savonarola; the learned as in an instant abandoned Plato, to discuss the merits of the Christian preacher." These last words indicate the nature of this initial complete success. Fra Girolamo had awakened interest and criticism. It remained to win moral consent.

As he had had to pass from the lecture-room to the garden, from the garden to the church, so now he was soon compelled by the popular excitement to pass to the cathedral. There, beneath Brunelleschi's splendid dome, which one of his hearers and afterwards one of his most ardent followers declared to be as noble, if not so large, as the vastest in the world which he himself designed,[1] Savonarola, fired with prophetic certainty, cried aloud to Florence, "The kingdom is at hand; repent, repent, repent!" And as he exposed the vices of the land and pictured in language all aglow with

[1] Michel Angelo's comparison of the dome of S. Peter's at Rome with that of the Duomo of Florence: "Piu grande, ma non piu bello."

passion the advent of Divine purifying vengeance, Florence was fascinated in anxiety. The audiences in San Spirito dwindled when the elegant Mariano aired his sermonizing talents, the Duomo was densely packed as the earnest monk denounced luxury and sin, preached righteousness and temperance and judgment, and then, softening his sharp tones, with tearful tenderness commended the love of Christ.

In endeavouring to account for this quickening of interest it has to be kept in mind that iniquity had assumed startling proportions in the last years of the century. We have not space to enlarge on the fact, but one incident is worth volumes of platitude. Innocent VIII. filled the Pontifical chair, and he was no purist. Yet even he was forced to think of reform. And this is the reform he attempted. He revived an edict of Pius II. forbidding "priests to keep taverns, playhouses or brothels, or to act as paid agents of courtesans." Men were sunken, indeed, but when evil had gone lengths like that, it would be strange if, when it was laid bare, there should be no fear, however vague. Beyond this it must be noticed that Savonarola proclaimed the imminence of the cleansing judgments. He was not the first to lift a warning voice. Vincent Ferrier, Bernardino of Siena, Bussolari, Capistrano and others had preached crusades against sin in various parts of Italy, and had predicted disaster as sure to befal. Fra Girolamo, however, lifted foreboding out of the mist of indefiniteness. The catastrophe and the cure were both to happen "very soon" "in our time," and thus by declaring the nearness of these he wielded a power which their indistinct assertions lacked. Just when evil was at its worst his words proclaimed that doom was at the door, adding to the force of fear the influence of hope that when the storm was over there would be the wreck only of corruption.

Moreover, we cannot join hands with those who seek to minimize the claim which Savonarola advanced to have received revelations from God. No doubt many special predictions have been attributed to him which are obviously to be discredited and relegated to the category of legend. No doubt, also, he did not at the very outset of his career explicitly maintain the certainty of his three assertions as other than conclusions from his study of Bible history and the exercise of his reason. But that these three propositions were believed by him to be God-given, that as he continued to unfold and illustrate them he in the most unqualified language so averred, no one can deny. And to place that fact in the background is to deprive us of one aid to the explanation alike of his success and his failure. It has only to be added that while cynicism must perforce write down one who makes such a claim a fanatic,[1] the evidence of Savonarola's work is to the end that it was consistent with the most rational views of human life, and the most practical endeavours for the good of men.

When in 1491 the Prior of San Marco died, the brethren with one consent chose Fra Girolamo to be their Superior. This election at once brought him into contact with Lorenzo, who, as some say, had already evinced some uneasiness at the hold which the preacher was obtaining on the people. The evidence of this, however, is not sufficiently clear, and, as seems

[1] Bayle, Critical Dictionary.

confirmed by all that follows, it is at least quite as probable that "The Magnificent" had even conceived an incipient respect for the learned and interesting friar.

It had been the custom of all former priors to go to court on their election to office to do obeisance. Savonarola, on being reminded of his duty by the elders of the order, bluntly replied, "I owe my election to God; to Him alone shall I promise submission." Lorenzo, learning of the refusal, said to some of his courtiers in a half-amused tone which covered his chagrin, "See, a stranger has come to my house and does not deign even to visit me." The vexation, nevertheless, was due not so much to a feeling of insult as to a sense of disappointment, and to the credit of Lorenzo it must be said that instead of thinking of retaliation he was prompted to seek acquaintance with the monk who had so set use and wont at defiance. He went to mass at San Marco and then after service hovered about the gardens of the monastery. Savonarola, informed of the fact, inquired, "Has he asked for me?" "No." "Then let him enjoy his walk." The convent coffers began to glitter with golden pieces. The prior sent the Prince's presents to the "good men" to be given to the poor. And all the while that Lorenzo was thus devising to win regard, the preacher preached, hurling his invectives with uncompromising plainness of utterance against the immoralities of court and clergy, not in wild aimless declamation, but with definite exposure of individual vices, and with a directness of reference which not unreasonably excited alarm. Still Lorenzo was not minded to declare war. A deputation was commissioned, cautioned to conceal whence they came. It was composed of five noble citizens of Florence, who, having sought and obtained audience, begged Savonarola as he cared for the peace of the city to moderate his tone, insinuating that by so doing he would consult also his personal safety. They failed to deceive his perception. "I fear not your threats. Go, tell Lorenzo that though I be a stranger in the town, while he is its chief citizen I must stay; he must go."

In spite of this dauntless attitude with regard to personal peril it is worthy to be noticed that Savonarola at this point calmly reviewed the position to which his outspokenness was surely leading, and did so with a momentary misgiving as to the issue. He even considered with himself whether he might not remain true to his mission, while in some measure he yielded to the request which had been preferred. He told the people, in a sermon, preached about this time, that he had endeavoured to persuade himself to this effect, but that even as he prayed he seemed to hear the rebuke: "Fool! dost thou not see that God wills thee to follow the same path?" Such an incident deserves to have a place given to it in any testimony which enables us to determine our verdict as to the sobriety of judgment which characterized his intense enthusiasm.

Foiled in this effort, with the same denunciations of wickedness ringing in his ears, and aware of the increasing ascendancy of the preacher, Lorenzo took action in another direction which was not noble. Fra Mariano was ordered to combat Savonarola's teaching in the pulpit of San Gallo. Nothing loth to make an attempt for the resuscitation of his waning popularity, the Franciscan complied. The fact was soon known, and the church was full. Taking as his text the words, "It is not for you to know the times or the seasons," he attacked the doctrine of the three propositions, but with so much acrimony, such evident personal animus, such palpable misrepresentation, that even the partizans of the Medici were disgusted, and numbers who had cherished some suspicion of Savonarola's integrity were induced to espouse his cause. It only required that the Prior should discourse upon the same text to convert what was designed to be a crushing humiliation into a signal victory. Mariano, smarting under defeat, invited Savonarola to celebrate mass with him. The celebration took place, but soon afterwards Mariano left Florence for Rome, and there restlessly wrought to compass the ruin of the man he hated with fiendish spite, and whom he did not hesitate to call an agent of the devil.

There is but one more scene between the Prior and the Prince of which to tell. Lorenzo knows that he is dying. The gem-potion of Lazzaro da Ficino cannot stay the disease; the philosophic comfort of Poliziano cannot calm his fears; no cleric sycophant can shrive to give him peace. "Send for the prior of San Marco; he is the only true monk I know." So whispering, as he lay on his death-bed, Lorenzo de' Medici reveals the real esteem which for months he had silently cherished for the man who had challenged his wickedness. Having been assured of the good faith of a summons he could scarcely credit, Savonarola came to the splendid villa of Careggi and into the richly furnished chamber of death. Lorenzo confessed, and asked absolution for the sack of Volterra, the confiscation of the funds banked to provide dowries for the poorer girls of Florence, and the massacre of the innocent with the guilty in the revenge which followed the Pazzi conspiracy. Savonarola demanded three things of the penitent—First, faith in the infinite mercy of God; Lorenzo avowed his utter confidence. Second, the restitution of all ill-gotten gains; after a pause, the prince consented. "Savonarola raised himself to his full height, and, while the dying man cowered trembling on his couch, the austere Dominican added, 'Lastly, liberty must be restored to Florence.'" Lorenzo turned his back to the confessor and was silent. Savonarola left without bestowing the boon. Soon after he left "The Magnificent" was no more.[1]

The attitude of Savonarola seems harsh and unfeeling. But full account must be made of the fact that he held the despotism which Lorenzo had exercised to be not only a political wrong but a moral injury. And we have already indicated our sympathy with that estimate. He read the history of Florence during the past years as it told not of the usurpation of a people's civil rights alone, but as it showed also the wreck of religious sentiment. In his view the two were indissolubly joined, and he could not have been true to his deepest convictions had he given the faintest semblance of countenance to the continuance of a tyranny which sapped the foundations of pure social life, and which so long as it existed presented an insurmountable barrier to the salvation of men's souls. Ere this course of lectures closes, the story will be told of

[1] This account is preferred after sifting of evidence. See Villari's note, i. 205.

another reformer who would not bend before a beautiful but imperious Queen. If a parallel in more familiar history to this less known intercourse of the Florentine Prior and Prince may be suggested, let some features of such be sought in the relations of John Knox to Mary Queen of Scots.

Our space forbids more than a few sentences recounting the events in the history of Florence which led to the utmost of Savonarola's success. Lorenzo died in 1492. He was succeeded by his son Piero, as incompetent to govern as his father had been capable, as imprudent as he had been cautious, as vacillating as he had been firm, and with all the love of dominion, all the longing for display, all the passion for self-indulgence which had marked Lorenzo's character. The citizens became conscious of a despotism they had not felt before, while the sermons of Fra Girolamo, daily more pointed and fervid in the interests of righteousness and freedom, gained to their own inherent power from the sense of oppression and the spectacle of the tyrant's sin. The visitation of God was drawing nigh, and as he proclaimed its advent, the people began eagerly to look for its coming. Two years of endurance, and then Savonarola declared that the instrument of divine anger was Charles VIII. of France. He had crossed the Alps to undertake that famous expedition in furtherance of his title, as a scion of the house of Anjou, to the throne of Naples, that "excursion" of which one wishes that the historian of the "Decline and Fall of the Roman Empire" had been spared to write. Piero had at first resolved to side with the claims of Arragon, but on the approach of the French army he changed his mind and hastened to the camp to surrender five of the fortresses of Tuscany that Florence might be spared. On receipt of the tidings of these terms the smouldering passions of the citizens burst. In a few days Piero de' Medici was hissed out of the town, saved from a worse fate by the counsels of Savonarola, who assuaged the popular fury by reminding the people that the hand of God was in the mission of the monarch.

Piero Capponi had spoken bravely the will of Florence when he had declared for the deposition of the traitor-tyrant, and now he spoke their will again when, recommending an embassy to Charles, he added, "And above all things let us not fail to send along with the other ambassadors Father Girolamo Savonarola, who now possesses the entire affection of the people." That counsel was followed, and the preacher solemnly charged the king to be faithful to the divine commission with which he was entrusted. So profound was the impression made by the earnest appeal, that Charles pledged himself not only to pass through Florence in peace, but on his return to restore to her her own—a pledge the latter portion of which he never redeemed. Then when, having entered the city, the invader seemed loth to leave, when he threatened to exact harder conditions, and if they were not acceded to, to "sound his trumpets," Capponi fairly cowed the little blusterer by his immortal retort, "And we will ring our bells"; but it was the persuasion of Savonarola that induced the God-sent man to depart.

And so the crisis passed. The strong despotism of more than sixty years was at an end; the danger of conquest by France was averted; Florence was free, and not a drop of blood, Medicean, French, or Florentine, had been shed. Nor can it be denied that all this had been mainly accomplished by the patriotism, the intrepidity, the calmness, the religious force of the Dominican monk.

Much, however, remained to be done. A new constitution had to be established. Of what kind should it be? A limited democracy, said the voice in the cathedral pulpit, and the vast majority concurred. A Christocracy! cried Savonarola, and Jesus Christ was proclaimed King of Florence. This last beautiful idealism must not be confounded with any thought of ecclesiastical domination. To the mind of the man who expressed it, civil authority did not belong to the Church to seek. In one passage he speaks in language altogether remarkable. "That which has so thoroughly corrupted the Church is the temporal power. When the Church was poor she was holy; when the temporal power was given to her the spiritual power crumbled away."[1]

Nor, again, was it at all inconsistent with quiet, practical sagacity in the direction of affairs of the State. Four principles of the new Republic were propounded by the preacher—first, the fear of God and the reformation of manners; second, the care of the public weal rather than of private interests; third, an amnesty for all political offenders; fourth, a General Council on the model of that of Venice, without a Doge, consisting, however, only of those whose ancestors had filled some civil office. Then a law of appeal in capital cases was enacted, an equitable system of taxation was introduced, measures prohibiting vice were passed, work was provided for the poor—everything, indeed, was done that

[1] Sermon xvi.

was possible to protect the liberty that had been secured and to conserve purity in the free city. And for a time the history of the palmy days of the past seemed to be repeated in the experience of the people, and they reverenced the great, good man who had broken their chains. For in all Savonarola did it was not of himself he thought; not for pay or power did he labour, but only for Florence. Never did he even come to a meeting of the Signoria except his presence was requested; he did all by the power of his preaching, and prompted alone by the ambition to see the citizens living purely and peaceably. We feel safe in affirming that Savonarola was absolutely unselfish in his patriotism. A demagogue, if you will, but only in the sense that he had the cause of the people at heart, and by his wise counsel sought to win them to the adoption of an order of government, which he deemed the best to promote their well-being, anxious, above all, that political conditions might be such as to advance the kingdom of Christ in the hearts of men.

Meanwhile the monastery had undergone a thorough reform. In the year 1492 Savonarola succeeded in securing a brief which separated the Dominican congregations in Tuscany from those in Lombardy, to whose Vicar-General they had hitherto been subject. This severance, accompanied by his election to be Vicar of the Florentine congregation, placed the Prior of San Marco in a position of authority, which enabled him to correct the abuses that prevailed. So gently did he deal with the brethren, and with earnestness so single that they obeyed under the constraint of love. His own monastery was his first care. It had amassed considerable wealth, and though the words of Antonino were inscribed on its walls, "May my curse and that of God fall on him who shall bring possessions into this order," the monastic vow of poverty had come to be regarded as a mere form of initiation. Property had fostered luxury, luxury bred indolence and vanity and declining spirituality. In a letter to his mother, which bears date 10th September, 1493, Savonarola speaks of the reformation which was in progress, and tells her of the general inconsistencies which call for reform. It is no innovation the monks of San Marco are making. "What is a novelty is for men making profession of beggary to rear convents, which with their pillars and their marbles resemble palaces, to have rooms fit for lords, to possess goods contrary to the rules of the Order, because they have no confidence in this word of Jesus Christ, 'Seek first the kingdom of God and the rest will be added to you.' It is a novelty to clothe oneself not in the usual common stuffs but in the finest and most choice, to pray little, to gad about, to be willing to be poor without wanting anything," etc. It was with such abuses that Savonarola set himself to deal. The superfluous wealth was surrendered, and they who insist on this monk's iconoclasm must face the fact that the treasures were devoted in part to the purchase of the remainder of the MSS. of Niccoli which Cosimo de' Medici had reserved for his own library, and which, after the banishment of Piero, the Signoria proposed to bring to the hammer. Then, the example always set by the Prior himself, a rigid *régime* was appointed. Plain fare, simple dress, and profitable work for the maintenance of the always necessary, but never lavish, expenses of the institution marked the routine. The study of the Scriptures was revived, the classic authors were read, the monks painted and carved, copied MSS. and illuminated them. They became devout and charitable. For recreation they desired nothing better than to walk with their Prior and enjoy discourse of reason. Savonarola had this joy at least of seeing piety at home, and of finding that San Marco became a centre of influence which extended to all the convents under his control. If true, useful, cultured monks were anywhere they were in the Dominican monasteries upon whose Vicar the mantle of Antonino had fallen.

As for Florence, this is in brief the testimony. For nearly three years there was a revival of religion and morals. The aspect of the whole city seemed to be changed. Indulgence gave place to simplicity. Hymns were heard instead of lewd bacchanalian songs. Workmen read the Bible at meal times. Public worship was regular. Almsgiving was generous and ready. Usury seemed an extortion of the commercial past. And when Savonarola sent his little army of children (to whose instruction he gave himself with kindly heart, when he must not preach because of the order of the Pope) to beg the citizens to give up their "vanities" for a carnival bonfire, there was forthcoming such a *mélange* of wigs, and obscene tapestries, and boxes of face powder, and bad pictures, etc., etc., that never was there a finer blaze. For it was only evil things that Fra Girolamo would wish to be burned.

During these years he preached not to Florence only but to Italy. He proclaimed unfalteringly that God had sent him, that God spoke to him, and that what he spoke he spoke as having received it from God. There was no scholasticism in his sermons now. He had steeped his soul in the Bible. He had stood in idea with Noah before the Flood, with Amos and Haggai and Malachi in face of the iniquity of Israel, with John in Patmos, and the voices and the visions had been heard and seen by him to tell to the priests and people of his age. With increasing vehemence, in which caustic sarcasm was blended with fierce invective, both combined with searching appeal, he kept depicting the abominations of the Church which demanded the Divine scourge that it might be roused to righteousness. His message never varied. " Repent, lest ye perish " was its sum. " Behold the anger of God and return to holiness."

> Before the days of change, still is it so :
> By a Divine instinct, men's minds mistrust
> Ensuing danger ; as by proof we see
> The waters swell before a boisterous storm.[1]

This was the consciousness of Savonarola even when at the height of his success. In several of his sermons in which he exhorts Florence to remain free and pure he strikes the chord of sad foreboding. " Before my eyes I see tribulation and tempests appearing ; behind me the harbour is lost, and the wind drives me forth into the deep." That is but one sentence, spoken shortly after his reform had been achieved, representative of many utterances of an ever-present anxiety. He had cause indeed from the beginning to be fearful. It was impossible that so radical a revolution, political and moral, could be effected without awakening some hostility. There were factions from the first. Even when the character which the new constitution should assume had been openly discussed, Vespucci had com-

[1] Richard III. act 3, sc. 4.

mended an oligarchy, and with him many of the upper classes naturally sympathized. They retained their sympathy despite their defeat, and formed the party of the *Arrabiati*. Then at the opposite extreme were the *Bianchi*, impatient of the restriction which excluded them from the Grand Council. The amnesty permitted partizans of the Medici, like old Bernardo del Nero, Giannozzo Pucci, Lorenzo Tornabuoni, Niccolo Ridolfi, and Giovanni Cambi to remain in Florence secretly plotting with Piero for his restoration. There were still "fast" youths— Dolfo Spini and his *Compagnacci*—who were impatient of the restraint put upon their revelry. There is always a class of indifferents—*Tepidi*—who keep aloof from any study of principles. And that the *Frateschi*, the followers of Savonarola, could be nick-named *Piagnoni* (weepers) is proof that, though far the most numerous, they were not omnipotent. It is easy to see that a combination of all these parties and a defection from the ranks of the loyal might avail to secure a hostile majority in the annually elected Signoria. Besides, the commercial interests of perruquiers, and tavern-keepers, and purveyors suffered by the abolition, or at least the diminution, of masquerades, and debaucheries, and banquets. Beyond Florence, too, princes could not regard with equanimity such a change as had been wrought. And Mariano was at Rome, and so was Piero de' Medici, while, to crown all, the Spaniard Rodrigo Borgia had purchased his election to the Papal throne. The death of Innocent VIII., one who, like most of the Popes of the Renaissance, was a disgrace to humanity, not to say to the Christian Church, fell but a fortnight after the death of Lorenzo. "Then, as he disappears, a din of fiends is heard, and a triumphal chariot drawn by the seven deadly sins leads Belial himself upon the stage. Murder and Treachery and Fraud and Fear, and all the shapes of Death and Lust, are dancing round this car. At the side of Belial smile his two children—his daughter Incest, white as leprosy, and his son Fratricide, subtle-featured, smooth and tortuous as a snake. That is Alexander VI."[1] Let that not too strong figurative language stand in room of plain details of the monster's crimes. No sophistry can serve to drag the Borgia from the nadir of inhuman cruelty and brutish sensualism in which he lay.

Such a Pope was not one to remain indifferent to the scathing criticism of ecclesiastical corruption which was thundering forth from Florence, and, when some of Savonarola's sermons exposing the enormity of sins of which he was consciously guilty came into his hands, it hardly needed the falsehoods of the malicious Franciscan and the solicitations of the exiled Prince to determine the doom of the man who wielded so mighty an influence.

While Charles VIII. remained in Italy, however, no action could safely be taken. It was well known that the King held the friar high in favour, and that Florence of all the Italian states had alone refused to join the league against him. But when the monarch quitted Naples on being warned of the gathering peril, when he left Florence, having even taken Piero de' Medici to its gates, and having fulfilled not one of his promises, then though Savonarola spoke his condemnation of such perfidy to his very face and once more averted danger, his influence received a check, for

[1] Symonds' Renaissance in Italy.

his predictions of ultimate good to the Republic were unrealized. Capponi fell before Pisa. The five conspirators were executed, and some said that if Savonarola had not sanctioned the penalty exacted from Bernardo del Nero, who had done service to the State and whose white hairs moved compassion, his refusal to interfere on behalf of him and his comrades in the plot was virtually to approve the severity of the sentence. These and other incidents, well enough known at Rome, gave encouragement to the course of injustice which the Pope pursued to the bitter end. To follow the narration of that course is out of the question here. The main points are these. Inhibitions to preach Savonarola at first obeyed. Vague charges of heresy he boldly repelled by reference to his written works, and a Papal commission failed to detect any deviation from Catholic dogma which could give colour to the indictment. Bribed by the offer of a Cardinal's hat, he indignantly declined, declaring that the only red hat he desired was the red hat of martyrdom; commanded to reform the tie between the Tuscan and Lombard congregations, he positively refused; excommunicated at length in 1497, he kept silence for six months, and then, implored by the Signoria, he returned to the pulpit, declared the Pope illegally elected, and the excommunication to be null and void. The ground of his apology was that of his own entire harmony with Catholic dogma and the notorious character of the man who assumed the prerogative of the Vicar of Christ. He avowed his readiness to submit to any decision of the Church, but he would not submit to the iniquitous decree of this son of perdition.

The briefs, however, had a disastrous effect upon Savonarola's influence with the people of Florence. During the intervals of his silence Fra Dominico had taken his place in the pulpit, but he could not command the force of his superior's personality, and in his comparative seclusion Fra Girolamo heard, with feelings almost of despair, that all the good he had accomplished was slowly being undone. The *Arrabiati* and the *Compaynacci* took full advantage of his withdrawal, and not only succeeded in corrupting the populace, but in gaining the majority in the Signoria. An outbreak of the plague at a time when the Prior was helpless under ban to discharge his priestly functions, and the political intrigues of other States during the same period aided their determined endeavours. We cannot enlarge upon these points. It must be sufficient to say that when Savonarola was prohibited to preach by the civil government on the 17th of March, 1498, he could count upon comparatively few devoted followers beyond the walls of San Marco.

He had one hope. The Council of Constance had deposed John XXIII., why might not a General Council dethrone Alexander VI.? It was an open secret that Charles of France had even expressed to the Cardinal of San Pietro in Vincola his readiness to support such a project, and it was believed that not in Italy only but in other parts of Europe the wickedness of Borgia was causing unrest. So Savonarola wrote his memorable "Letter to the Princes," addressed to Charles VIII., Maximilian of Germany, Ferdinand and Isabella of Spain, and Henry VII. of England, telling them that the Church was full of abominations and chiding them for worshipping "the cause of evil which is undermining her. I tell you that this Alexander is not Pope, nor can he be retained as such. For not to speak of his most heinous sin of simony by which he bought the Holy See, and the fact that he sells to bidders the benefices of the Church, not to speak of his other flagrant vices, I affirm that he is not a Christian, that he does not believe in God, and that he has passed the summit of infidelity."[1]

But in the life of men there is sometimes an hour when the course of events is rolled back by a secret, irresistible force. That hour had struck for Savonarola. It is useless to conjecture what might have resulted had the Council been convened. It never met. A preliminary note despatched to the French King fell into the hands of the Duke of Milan, who promptly forwarded it to Rome.

Meanwhile incidents happened in Florence to precipitate the impending issue. We must content ourselves by referring to the historical romance for a graphic account of the "Ordeal."[2] The factions filled the square eager to see two men walk along the platform between the walls of fire. Florence was fond of spectacles, and this contest of the flames between the champion of the Dominicans, implicit believer in the Divine mission of his great superior, and him of the Franciscans who had challenged that mission to the test of miracle, seemed one which would not only settle the question, but which, however it ended, would be a splendid scene. Savonarola was there with Fra Dominico, who was to risk his

[1] The whole letter is quoted by Villari, ii. 312.
[2] Romola, lxv.

life to vindicate his master, and the brethren of San Marco were there with hopeful hearts. Savonarola had done what he could to dissuade his brother from the trial, but, when the Signoria appointed it, he could not but acquiesce and pray. They waited for the Franciscan, but he came not. Pretext after pretext prolonged delay. The feverish impatience of the mob rose to frenzy, and they clamoured that Dominico should pass through the fire alone. Savonarola forbade. Then the rain fell, and at length came a mandate from the Signoria to prevent the ordeal, which it had never intended to take place. Full well had foes gauged the mood of the Florentines. The rabble howled in fury, baulked of the sating they had been urged to expect, deceived by the prophet who would not prove his claims, and as the monks of San Marco came down from their gallery, the populace, spurred by the gibes and angry cries that rent the air, surged round Marcuccio Salviati's gallant little escort that slowly took them to the convent. While Savonarola knelt in his cell in sorrowful prayer he could hear the vengeful shrieking of the crowd that filled the piazza.

The attack was made upon San Marco the following day. Every entreaty to arm the brethren the Prior refused. The church was soon forced. Francesco Valori went to rouse the *Frateschi*. He was stabbed before the eyes of his wife, and she was shot as she saw her husband slain. The soldiers of the Republic came to help the assailants. Savonarola retired to the library to prepare for the end. Gathering round him those of the brotherhood who could respond to his summons he addressed them thus: "My children, before God, before the sacred host, at this hour when our enemies have made entrance to the convent, I affirm anew the truth of my doctrine. What I have spoken is what God has revealed to me, and he is my witness in heaven that I lie not. I did not know that all the city was so soon to turn against me; but the will of the Lord be done. This is my last counsel: let faith, patience, and prayer be your armour. I leave you in anguish to give me to mine enemies. I know not if they will take my life, but sure I am that, dead, I shall be able to help you more in heaven than, living, I have been able to do on earth. Be brave, clasp trustingly the Cross, and by it you shall reach the haven of salvation."

The demand of the Signoria was that Fra Dominico, Fra Salvaestro, and Fra Girolamo should be surrendered. There was a Judas, called Malatesta, and he whispered, "Should not the shepherd give his life for the sheep?" Savonarola kissed the traitor and the other brethren, and then he and Fra Dominico, amid hooting and jeering, were led away to prison. Fra Salvaestro was in hiding, but the next day he too was in a cell; Malatesta told the soldiers where he was.

If the joy of the Pope, on being informed of what had transpired, was great, other tidings not less welcome must have enlarged it beyond measure. On the very day of the ordeal Charles VIII. died at Amboise.

The trial (?) was protracted for six weeks. The one charge which the Signoria resolved to formulate was that Savonarola was an impostor. To establish this they had recourse to the most awful tortures with the view of eliciting from him a confession of deceit. At the same time they hired a notary, Ser Ceccone, to fabricate a process that might be circulated in the city. There seems no room to doubt that physical agony wrung some ambiguous utterances from his lips, but it is certain that the only true confession he made was to this effect—"Now hear me, magistrates of Florence. I have denied my light through fear of torture. If I have to suffer, I seek to suffer for the truth. That which I have spoken I have received from God." The concoction of Ceccone, however, deftly substituted for another scroll, upon which were written the prisoner's answers to his inquisitors, was signed by Savonarola, and the Dominicans believed that their prior had admitted the falseness of his claims. It was cowardly of them to crave absolution for having put faith in him—an absolution accorded at once on their disowning "the head of the whole error, Fra Girolamo Savonarola."

There was one voice raised in the Signoria in noble protest against a capital sentence. "Do not," pled Agnolo Pandolfini, "inflict an irreparable loss on the world by putting to death a man so remarkable that one scarce sees his like in a century. This man might not only restore faith on the point of perishing, but might render the greatest services to the sciences which he has cultivated with success so signal. Keep him in prison, then, if you will, only I counsel you to spare his life and to give him the means of writing that the world may not lose the fruits of his genius." That manly appeal, a magnificent witness to the impression which Savonarola had made upon the culture of his day, was greeted with the coarse rejoinder, "A dead enemy makes no war."

The Papal commissioners, Romolino and Turriano, arrived in Florence on the 19th of May, armed with instructions to expedite the sentence, even though Savonarola were John the Baptist. Another examination was held, another false process was penned, and then judgment was pronounced. On the 23rd of May, 1498, in the Piazza of the Palazzo Vecchio, the three martyrs finished their course. Pronouncing the formal sentence of anathema against Savonarola, the Bishop of Vasona in his confusion made an addition to the formula. He said—"*Separo te ab Ecclesia militante atque triumphante.*" Calmly the martyr corrected him—"*Militante, non triumphante, hoc enim tuum non est.*" The fire soon finished the hangman's work, and when it was dark they carted away the ashes and tumbled them into the Arno.

Such is the plain story of the life of Girolamo Savonarola. He was a patriot and his people killed him. He did a prophet's work and he met a prophet's end. He was a pure man and the wicked slew him. There is an exquisite pathos in these simple words spoken in his adieu to San Marco—"I did not know that all the city was so soon to turn against me." They breathe the melancholy of disappointed hope, the sad consciousness of ill-requited sacrifice, the plaint of fell ingratitude. Yet, as he speaks them, we can almost believe that that noble, disinterested soul was crushed in sorrow far more for the ruin which Florence had chosen for herself than for the destruction she was dealing upon him. He would have saved her, but she would not have the salvation for which with passionate love he had laboured to the last.

In the course of the centuries he has received his due,

which the men of his own day denied him. "Even in the city of Dante no greater figure has its dwelling. The shadow of him still lies across those sunny squares and the streets through which in triumph and in agony he went upon his lofty way, and consecrates alike the little cell in San Marco, and the little prison in the tower, and the great hall built for his great Council, which in a beautiful poetical justice received the first Italian Parliament, a greater Council still. Thus, only four hundred years too late, his noble patriotism had its reward."[1]

Savonarola's relation to the progressive culture of the Renaissance was one of cordial sympathy. That has been more than once indicated in our sketch of his career. With all that was pure in art he was in full consent, and, not to cite the testimony of his writings, let the devotion of Michel Angelo to his memory be sufficient witness. For that devotion was determined not only by regard for his wisdom in politics and his earnestness in religion, but also by his instruction on the true principles of beauty, expressed in a treatise which the great sculptor used often to read in his old age. The same holds good of his esteem for heathen writers. There is something touching in the advice he gave, that in school boys should read only the authors who were "clean," and that "Jupiter" or "Zeus" should always by them be translated "God." Restrictions such as these were the outcome of his single aim, that learning should go hand in hand with purity. But in this matter Savonarola's attitude recalls very strikingly the position of Origen, as it anticipates remarkably the bearing of Erasmus. Christianity was no foe to

[1] The Makers of Florence, pp. 327-8.

liberal culture, but should find a handmaid in all learning. We submit only one quotation taken from his work, "The Triumph of the Cross"—a work in which Savonarola undertakes to demonstrate the truth of Christianity by arguments from reason. "Despise no good works nor reasonable laws of pagan peoples, of philosophers, and emperors. In their doctrines and in their books gather what is true and good, affirming that all which is true and good comes from God and has been given specially for His elect."[1]

We are more immediately concerned in this lecture, however, with his relations to the reform of the Church. And, here, while conceding willingly the warrant which the Church of Rome of to-day has in claiming Savonarola as a faithful son, we not the less claim to regard him as in many respects deserving well to be ranked as unconsciously but really preparing for the work of Luther.

We have seen the impression which ecclesiastical corruptions made upon him at the very outset of his career, and we have alluded in general terms to his uncompromising antagonism to these iniquities. But, when we read such of his sermons as have been edited, then we feel that not even Wyclif was severer in his censures. Hear him on the prelates—"They speak against pride and ambition, in which they are themselves plunged up to the eyes; they preach chastity and keep concubines."[2] "With their rich chasubles and their brocaded copes they chant vespers and admirable masses before the altar, and they seem full of solemnity and holiness." "See him, this priest, who struts along so spruce, with his fine locks, his

[1] Triumphus Crucis, iii. 13.   [2] Sermon iii. p. 209.

purse, and his perfumes. Go to his house, you will find his table laden with plate, his chambers garnished with tapestries. They have so many dogs, so many mules, so many horses, so many ornaments, so much silk, so many servants. Think ye that these fine lords will open to you the kingdom of God?"[1] The sarcasm of this is inimitable. "Hear what I say. In the primitive Church the chalices were of wood and the prelates were of gold. To-day the Church has golden chalices and wooden prelates."[2] These are samples of the doughty flail-blows with which Fra Girolamo lashed the clerical chaff of his famished age.

Again, Savonarola recognized the clamant evil of a soulless externalism which was fostered. He scoffs at the summons, "Come from this side and that; cover with kisses Saint Peter and Saint Paul, such and such a saint. Come, come, ring bells, deck altars, garnish churches."[3] "O preachers and monks," he cries, "ye have buried this people in the sepulchre of ceremonies. I tell you this sepulchre must be broken, for Christ wishes the resurrection of His Church to spiritual life."[4] Countless such citations can be adduced in which the dead ritualism of the Church is exposed without sparing.

But Fra Girolamo was not content with denunciation of abuse. He proclaimed the remedy, and that he declared to consist in the preaching and reviving of Bible truth. He was himself a priest, and he does not discountenance the right observance of ceremony. But it belongs to him in that era of empty formalism to have given to the pulpit its true place and to have

[1] Sermon xvii., p. 545. [2] Sermon xvii., p. 540.
[3] Lent Sermon. [4] Sermon xxii.

asserted for the Word of God its place in the pulpit. "I shall preach the Scripture," he maintains, and the most cursory perusal of his sermons testifies how true he was to that resolve. True, the Old Testament prophecies have, from the very character of his genius, by far the largest space; but there are expositions of the Gospels and of the Epistles of St. John which are full of the very spirit of the evangel. Few sermons in any age can excel in eloquence and solemn appeal that on the visit of the Magi to the cradle of Christ, in which he contrasts the self-denial of the Eastern sages hastening from their distant homes that they might do homage to the child Jesus with the chill indifference of the men and women of the fifteenth century to the worship of a glorified Redeemer. Often words seem to fail him when he would utter all his thoughts of the love of God in Christ. "O pity! O charity! O infinite love! I have grievously sinned, and Thou, Jesu, wert the sufferer. I have been Thine enemy, and Thou, Jesu, for my sake wast nailed to the Cross." To our mind it is beyond question that Savonarola based all his hope of moral reform upon a return to Christian faith. Granted that in so far as distinctive dogma is concerned he was, as he himself averred, in perfect accord with the Church of Rome, still it is as obvious that it was to the exhibition of the fundamental doctrines of a common Christianity that he always turned for moral power. Personal holiness through the knowledge and love of God gained by devout obedience to the precepts of the Word was the imperative which he ceaselessly uttered from the pulpit. "Justification by faith" or "Justification by works" was not an alternative which occurred to him to consider. That a

Christian must be true and pure was the essential of his teaching, a doctrine which had been utterly lost sight of in the pedantic sermonizing of the age.

His conflict with the Pope was ultimately à l'outrance. When first he learned of the charges brought against him, he could not bring himself to believe that they were conceived by his Holiness. With a generosity which is quite pathetic, he attributes them all to the machinations of his enemies. Even when he has cause to suspect that in this he has erred, he writes a letter of condolence to Alexander upon the occasion of the murder of his eldest son, the Duke of Candia. Then, when suspicion becomes certainty, he discusses the question of infallibility, and avers that he cannot submit to the injustice which is prompted by hate. This is the position he defends—"It must be maintained that the Pope *quâ* Pope cannot be deceived .... because his very function preserves him from error: but when he is deceived, he is not Pope, and if he commands injustice, he does not command it *quâ* Pope, but *quâ* man."[1] It has then to be reckoned that it was with the *man*, not with the *office*, that Savonarola did battle. He says: "When the power ecclesiastical is utterly corrupted, one must address himself to Christ, who is the first cause, and say, 'Thou art my Confessor, my Bishop, my Pope. See Thy church which is falling to ruins, begin to avenge Thyself.' But, my brother, thou dost weaken the power ecclesiastical. That is not true. I have always submitted, and I submit to-day to the correction of the Roman Church; far from weakening it, I strengthen it. Only I am not willing to obey the power infernal,

[1] Sermon xi. on Exodus.

and all power which is against goodness comes not from God, but from the devil."[1] To the idea of the outward unity of the Church under the authority of a successor of St. Peter he was conscientiously loyal, while at the same time he could as conscientiously obey his conscience rather than bow to a decree of Alexander VI. We have not a word to say against his sincerity, though the casuistry which seems to straightforward common-sense to surround the Catholic principle renders it rationally somewhat incomprehensible. It must be left, too, to the decision of the theologians of the Church of Rome to say whether, in view of the enunciation of the dogma of Pio Nono, Savonarola, condemned *ex cathedrâ*, can consistently be declared orthodox. One thing, however, is clear, that protests such as he and others before him raised against the supremacy of bad men were altogether in the line of tendency to schism from the system which bad men continued to dominate.

Perhaps, however, on the whole, the surest ground we can take in support of our claim is the failure of so nobly desperate an endeavour to achieve a reform. The reasons of that failure we have striven to indicate. Certainly his close identification with Florentine politics had not a little to do with it, inasmuch as it not only brought ultimate disaster to himself, but, from its very nature, isolated him from the wider sphere. The Church was more than Florence, and though Savonarola might seek to revive the Church, it could only too easily find an apology for refusing to hear him in the determination to regard the Republican rather than the Reformer. His claim to inspiration, likewise,

[1] Savonarola's Farewell Sermon.

while it gave force to his predictive preaching, could not prevail when several of his principal predictions were unrealized. Nor has it to be forgotten that Italy, politically dismembered though it was, felt some pride in that it had within itself the centre of Christendom, and that some scion of almost every ducal house was officially connected with the Roman See. On the other hand, beyond Florence and Italy, rulers and people were becoming sensible of the corruption which had reached such fearful magnitude, and they could not be in ignorance of the endeavour which the stern, stainless monk was making for reform. When he failed accordingly, his failure was to the world a witness that effort, to be successful, must find some more decided method. Matters could not rest as they were. And as reform of the Church from within had been so convincingly shown to be hopeless, it remained for one with a clearer perception of the doctrinal roots of the moral evil and a freer individualism in face of its ecclesiastical countenance, with external conditions also in every way more favourable, but with no more earnest desire for the accomplishment of the end, to take the way that must be taken. And it will be allowed us to say that the Church of Rome, by all the witness of history, owes the magnanimous estimate which she has set upon Girolamo Savonarola in no small measure to the work of Martin Luther.

It is not altogether without interest to reflect, as furnishing slender links of external connection, that Leo X. was a son of Lorenzo de' Medici; that Tetzel and Cajetano were both of the order of St. Dominic; and that the indulgences they pressed for sale were offered to procure funds to finish the work of Michel Angelo.

Erasmus.

ERASMUS, though not usually ranked amongst the Reformers, and not regarding himself as one of them, rightly enough finds a place in a course of lectures dealing with those whose life and work influenced the great ecclesiastical and religious movement of the sixteenth century.

That event, like some others in history involving interests numerous and varied, and issuing in results momentous and far reaching, was due less to the circumstances of the time in which it took place, and less to the influence of those whose names have become associated with it, than is perhaps generally supposed. In that sphere of human action which forms the province of civil and religious history, as among phenomena of a material kind, causes are oftentimes long at work before they reveal themselves in the effects that follow them. For days before the electric force discharges itself in fire the thunderstorm has been gathering; and it is not until the moon is on the wane that the tidal wave reaches high-water mark along our shores. And that convulsion that ruptured the Roman Church and sent a wave of blessing over the face of so many nations, was the result of the co-operation of many causes, some of which, at least, had been long at work. One of these causes was undoubtedly the intellectual movement that specially characterized the sixteenth century, and found at the time of the Reformation its brightest ornament in Erasmus.

To show how this movement originated, grew, and, as represented by Erasmus, helped to fulfil those conditions without which the cause in which Wyclif laboured and Hus perished, could not but fall short of its aim, is the duty that has been specially assigned me in connection with your course of lectures.

To say, indeed, when the movement began is not easy, any more than it is easy to say when night breaks into day, or self-conscious life awakens in the child. Far back in what are called the Middle Ages there are manifest tokens of an awakened intellectual activity, and of a renewed interest in learning. As the Church has never been so corrupt as to be without those in whose hearts the Gospel shone with something of its pristine purity—pious souls that realized that religion was something else and something higher than a mere observance of outward forms—men and women who, like Anna the prophetess or Simeon the aged, mourned the desolation that had come upon Israel, and longed for the advent of a better time, so no age has been so dark as to be without those who sought knowledge for its own sake, and found the deepest satisfaction in its possession. Even in the darkest of those ages that have, through comparison with some that went before and all that have come after, been designated the Dark Ages, truth of an intellectual kind—as distinguished from that which is theological — has shone; and from a period as remote at least as the eleventh century this light became more diffused. But though the ignorance which brooded over the nations of Christendom began at this time to get dispelled, the interest in intellectual pursuits which this implied did not grow, like the breaking day, steadily and uniformly, but fluctuated, rose and fell, and as in the flowing tide, the advancing wave reached the shores of different countries only at different times.

Though the revivals of learning which took place between the eleventh and fourteenth centuries were but partial, they were not unproductive of a good that was permanent. During this time the modern languages of Europe began to be formed, and a literature that embodied them to accumulate. The study of Roman law revived, and schools and universities were founded. And in this way preparation was made for the special movement to which we have referred — a movement so deep and wide-spread, so steady and continuous, so distinct from any that went before, that it has been designated by a special name — the "Renaissance" it has been called, as indicating a time of renewing — the awakening of the European mind to a consciousness of its own nature and capacities, and the value of that intellectual inheritance which had been treasured up in ages and in countries the glory of which had for ever passed away.

The country to which we have to look as that in which this movement took its rise is Italy — beautiful then as now in its skies and the tideless seas that sweep its shores; in its fertile plains, and the lakes that lie embosomed among its mighty hills; but far from being beautiful at the time of which we speak by the moral corruption and political disorder that characterized it. And yet even its political state, its foreign wars, and internal troubles; its dissensions and its dismemberment; its despotisms and city-republics, could not in some respects prove otherwise than favourable to the growth of the new movement. The strength which springs from self-reliance, the activity which comes from jealousy and mutual conflict, could not but help to make this Queen of countries all the fitter for becoming the nursing mother of the child of the new intellectual era.

The time which those who have studied this movement regard as that in which it took its rise, is nearly the same as that which gave birth to Wyclf; and in so far as it was helpful to the Reformation, the men who took part in it, though separated from him not only by geographical distance, but by intellectual character and moral aims, may be said to have been fellow-labourers with him.

> "The old order changeth, yielding place to new,
> And God fulfils Himself in many ways,
> Lest one good custom should corrupt the world."

The individual to whom we are asked to look as the one who furnished the motive power that gave this new movement birth and direction is the poet Petrarch. And in so far as a movement which was so genial to the intellectual life of man, and for which so much had been done by others that helped to prepare the way, could be said to take its rise in any single mind, it is to him rather than to any other to whom we have to look. What seems clear is that if he was not the first who tried to awaken a general interest in the works of those who had lived in a classic age, he was at least the first to succeed in doing so. A poet born, and schooled by a greater master of poetry than himself, he was able to appreciate "the best that had been thought and written" by those whose works, through the indolence and indifference of some who had every opportunity of obtaining a knowledge of them, and a mistaken notion on the part of others whose minds were active and inquiring, as to the place which that learning that goes by the name of secular has in furthering man's development and promoting man's chief end, were allowed to lie in all but utter neglect. Of a knowledge of Greek literature, or even of the Greek language, in which we have to remember, in considering this subject, were written not merely the poems of Homer and the philosophy of Plato, but the story of the Evangelists and the letters of Paul, there was throughout Western Europe, at this time, according to those who can speak with authority on the subject, hardly any trace. With Latin indeed it was different. Latin was the language used in the service of the Church, and ecclesiastics, for the sake of a knowledge of the language, if for no other end, could not fail to make some acquaintance with Latin authors. And yet so little was Virgil known in the Middle Ages, so little heed was given to the thought and melodious words with which "the Prince of Latin poets" could charm the men of his own time, and awaken so general an interest in ours; that Dante, writing before the dawn of the new era, speaks in the opening canto of the *Inferno* of him who was his "master and his guide" as "by long silence dumb." But this could no longer be said after the time of

Petrarch. Partly through his labours, partly through the labours of those on whom his influence made itself felt, a passionate desire was awakened in the minds of many of the educated sons of Italy to understand the thought and imitate the style of those who, possessed of genius, had long ago spoken and written in the languages of Greece and Rome. Not to produce what was new, but to imitate what was old; to resuscitate an age that was thought to be golden, and reflect the light that glowed in the spirits of the men who lived in it, became the ambition of the scholars of the time. In their eagerness to come into the possession of a treasure which men who had long been dead had bequeathed to the world, and that at the time of which we speak found no better repository than the cell, or sometimes the dungeon of a monastery, scholars travelled over sea and land, and the recovery of a manuscript written by one whose name was believed to shed a lustre on the age in which he lived was welcomed by the members of the literary fraternity more than the spoils of war or than the news of the discovery of an unknown land.

The movement thus begun deepened and widened. Scholars multiplied, and princes, and even popes—little conscious at the time how great an influence the work in which the men of letters were engaged was calculated to exercise in undermining their authority and shaking their throne—patronized them and shared their labours.

In that strange intermingling of causes we see so often in human experience, and of which history furnishes us with so many examples, in which the circumstances of the time seem to develop the means which are needful for its exigencies, two events occurred in the middle of the fifteenth century which greatly furthered the new intellectual movement. One of these was the fall of the Byzantine Empire in 1453. Before that event, indeed, "wise men" had come from the East carrying with them treasures in the form of Greek manuscripts, and a knowledge of the language in which they were written, the value of which the scholars of Italy were learning to appreciate, and the possession of which they were eager to secure. But on the downfall of Constantinople, many more Greek-speaking refugees sought the hospitality which the educated sons of Italy were so willing to afford in return for the educational services that could be rendered them.

The other event was the invention of printing, the influence of which, in promoting the cause of literature and preparing the way for the Reformation, it would be difficult to estimate, and perhaps be hardly possible to exaggerate. By it copies of books were more rapidly made and their prices greatly reduced. By it not only was a previously existing demand more readily met, but as in the introduction to a civilized country of a root, or fruit, good for food and pleasant to the taste, the supply helped to create the demand. By it the inner shrine of knowledge was opened, so that not only the high priests of literature could enter, but so too could those whose approach had been barred by poverty and ignorance.

It was not in Italy, however, this invention was made, but in Germany; and this fact is itself an evidence that the light which had now been shining so long among the Italians was beginning to make its influence felt elsewhere. When Gutenberg indeed established his press at Mentz, and consecrated it and all its produce by issuing somewhere between 1452 and 1455, as the first book printed from its types, the Mazarin Bible, the prevailing condition in his own country, as in other countries on this side the Alps, was one of ignorance and superstition. The study of physical science could hardly be said to have begun, and classical learning was possessed only by the few. In Germany and the Low Countries, it is true, schools had been established about the beginning of the fifteenth century, where Latin was taught to bands of peasant youths, who formed a kind of religious brotherhood and supported themselves mainly by the labours of their hands. These, combined with others of a more public kind that were founded shortly afterwards, became the source whence emanated ere many years had gone much of the light that enlightened Germany. Scholars issuing from them, inflamed with a desire to learn more than any in their own land could teach them, went to Italy that they might sit at the feet of some of those whose fame was spreading throughout the whole of Christendom. Returning with the instruction they received, and with a zeal which those with whom they came into contact could enkindle in minds already possessed of a desire to learn, they laboured hard to redeem their country from the ignorance and barbarism with which in comparison with Italy they felt it could be reproached. The hardy Teutonic mind, with its steadiness and patience, its industry and earnestness, formed a soil more favourable for the growth of knowledge than the Italian; and the seeds which these scholars of the fifteenth century sowed upon it yielded fruit more valuable and more enduring than any of which Italy could boast.

Of those on this side the Alps whose spirits caught fire from the light that shone beyond them, there was none stimulated to the same degree of earnestness, or accomplished through his labour the same measure of good, as he of whom we wish specially to speak.

Erasmus indeed was not a German, but a native of Rotterdam, though for few biographies is the country to which their subjects belonged a matter of as little moment. If it be true, as has been said, "that Greece or Rome never produced a great man but only a great Greek or a great Roman," that is not true of Holland. Of anything peculiarly Dutch there was nothing retained by Erasmus—hardly even a knowledge of the language; for in after years we find him apologizing to a friend for writing to him in Latin, on the ground of his being unable to do so freely in his own tongue. His Dutch name, Gerard, too was dropped, and the Latin and Greek languages—after the fashion of the time—furnished him with the one by which we best know him—Desiderius Erasmus. The languages of the classics were regarded as those which are best suited to man as man, and in so far as they are so, there was a special fitness in naming young Gerard by words found in them; for of all that was specially characteristic of humanity there was much in Erasmus. Great he was not in having in any pre-eminent degree that which is best in men—moral force or earnestness—but his spirit was broad and human—many-sided, and saw truth in aspects to which greater men were blind. Whatever concerned man as an intellectual or spiritual being afforded him the deepest interest; and those of any nation who devoted themselves to literary pursuits were regarded by him as his friends. He claimed no country as his own, but found a home, as he said, "wherever he had his books." In the wandering life he led he could say, like Dante in his exile—"The whole world is my kingdom."

In his career there is nothing to record of tragic incident or heroic suffering for righteousness' sake - none of the elements which give to the lives of the others who have found a place in your syllabus of lectures much of the interest that belongs to them— and we shall deal with that career only in so far as it may help us to understand the nature and the measure of the influence Erasmus exercised on the Reformation movement.

Like others whose names are more closely associated with that event than his own, he grew up a baptized son of the Church; and one of the first views we get of him from his biographers is when he is four years of age, and in the year 1471, singing as a chorister in the cathedral at Utrecht. In the school to which he afterwards went, despite the disadvantages which the Latin language presented to learners at the time, through the imperfect helps that were then in use, he took so readily to his lessons and progressed so rapidly in them that at the age of thirteen, we are told, he had the whole of the poems of Horace on his memory. About this time his parents died, and he was left in the hands of guardians, who, in so far as they interested themselves in him, seem to have done so specially for the sake of his small patrimony. To dispossess him of his claim, and get his portion into their own hands, they tried to induce him to devote himself to the Church. And notwithstanding a resistance which showed a measure of wisdom unusual in one of his years, through threats and entreaties he was persuaded at the age of fifteen to enter a monastery of the Augustinian order. Though he remained here for eight or nine years, he did so involuntarily, and it was only in his helplessness he in course of time took the vows of a monk.

Very different was the experience of Erasmus as a monk from that of another of the same order who was born into the world sixteen years after him, and for whose work he did so much to prepare the way. Of that darkness and unrest, of that long and earnest struggle through which the soul of Luther passed, Erasmus never knew anything, and he never felt accordingly as Luther did with regard to those conceptions of truth in which he found light and peace. Different, too, was the life of Erasmus as a monk from that of those with whom he was associated in the house of Steyn. For a time, indeed, he seems not to have been altogether untainted by their vice, but he had little sympathy with them in their habits of idleness, immoral ways, or religious practices. Even as a monk he was studious, and found more interest in his Horace and Terence than in his psalter or missal.

Though in this house he breathed an atmosphere he found neither genial nor wholesome; though he had duties to perform and company to associate with he could not find agreeable, the time seems to have been spent not altogether unpleasantly. Having a nature in which there was much natural buoyancy, and an element of mischievous trickery, he lightened by its indulgence time that might otherwise have been dull.

Nor was it altogether unprofitable; for he here not only acquired that intimate knowledge of monks and monkery that helped to lead him in after years into so direct antagonism to them, and give point to the missiles he so vigorously discharged against them; but, despite the disadvantages, such a place could not but afford for the acquisition of learning; through reading, and essays in composition, he laid the foundation of that vast erudition and acquired the elements of that literary skill for which he became so famous.

Though the monastery seems to have provided the young scholar with plenty of books, yet a house whose numerous inmates almost without exception had no interest themselves in literature, and held all in suspicion who had, and where, as one of his biographers has said, "one could get drunk quite openly, but had to carry on study in secret," could not at any time afford him much satisfaction; and he very readily took advantage of the first favourable opportunity that was given him of leaving it. This he had when he was twenty-four years of age through the Bishop of Cambray offering to appoint him, on the reputation of his scholarship, as his secretary. The Bishop had intended taking him to Italy—whither Erasmus had the strongest desire to go,—but he changed his mind, and sent him, after he had been ordained as priest, to the University at Paris. The funds with which his master and patron provided him were too limited to enable him to keep himself with comfort, and he had to take up his abode in one of the colleges that were intended for the poorer class of students.

Of the kind of life led here, Erasmus in one of the famous dialogues in his "Familiar Colloquies," gives what has usually been regarded as a description; but he makes fun of it, and probably exaggerates its hardship. If it is to be trusted as giving in any measure a faithful account of his experience, however unpleasant his life at the house of Steyn had been, it must have been more so at the College of Montague—" Vinegar College " as he nicknames it. Through false notions prevalent at the time, and heartily imbibed and acted on by the rector or president under whose supervision Erasmus found himself, as to the best way of practising self-denial, and the manner in which it stands related to the development of spiritual life, the students were subjected to the severest discipline. They had hard beds to sleep on, and menial work to do. The drink was unwholesome, and " rotten eggs " furnished part of their meals. There were " unmerciful whippings, too, even of innocent persons"; though, he says, he mentions these things not " out of any ill-will to the College," but to give a warning lest the young and inexperienced should be injured " through severity being practised in the name of religion." The treatment Erasmus underwent in this, his first trial of college life, was too much for his health—which at all times was delicate—and he returned to the Bishop, taking back nothing with him, he says, but " disease in his body and vermin in his clothes."

But there was another reason for Erasmus disliking this College of the " Scotists," which, if we would understand him and his relation to the Reformation movement, it is needful we look at with some care. And that was, that the studies in which he had now so much interest were held in little favour there. Though Paris had one of the most famous universities in Europe, it was only within recent years it gave the slightest evidence of being influenced by the literary movement that had been so long at work in Italy. Here, as in most other seats of learning, subject to the authority of the Church, Scholasticism was dominant, and with Scholasticism Erasmus had, even at this period of his life, but little sympathy, and had still less as time went on. And it could not be otherwise, for with its method and aims the movement which was now carrying Erasmus along with it had nothing in common. To its assumption that the truth of the Creed was to be received on the authority of the Church, and that other truth had value as it stood related to that Creed, the spirit of the Renaissance was entirely opposed. And though sharp disputes arose, and rival schools were formed by those who sought, in fulfilment of the end of Scholasticism, to systematize the doctrines of the Church and vindicate them at the bar of reason; though questions in endless number were put, and conflicting answers returned; though different leaders viewed the relation in which faith stands to reason in different lights; though Anselm differed from Abelard, and Duns Scotus from both, they were all agreed that the truth of the doctrines of the Church was unquestionable, and that all things else had value only as they stood related to them. Philosophy, it was supposed, had its value, but only as "the handmaid of Faith"; Logic had its use, but only as its formulas and categories could be pressed into the service of truth of a different kind.

This system, which for centuries engaged the attention and exercised the ingenuity of the ablest minds in

Europe, was not altogether a wasteful or profitless expenditure of thought; for not only did it keep alive an intellectual interest in the Church, but though opposed to the "New Learning," it helped to prepare the way for it. In trying to make clear to the understanding what had previously been received by faith;[1] in seeking to rationalize the dogma, it prepared the way for that freer movement of mind which attaches value to and finds interest in everything that is rational—everything, that is to say, that bears in itself the evidence of being the expression of mind or reason, whether human or divine, in nature or the Bible, in art or science, in literature or politics —and that is the spirit of the Renaissance—a spirit which finds its legitimate issue in our own time in the twin processes of criticism and physical science— a spirit which, though opposed to Scholasticism and that ecclesiasticism which found its development in the Roman Catholic Church, as the history of science in relation to the action of the Church so clearly shows, is not opposed to that religion we have been taught by Christ, which affords not only a controlling principle for the conduct of life, but seeks, too, to hallow all human knowledge by leading the mind to regard its increase as an evidence and manifestation of the growth of human intelligence, and a widening of human thought by a further participation in that Divine wisdom which underlies and gives unity to all the varied phenomena of the universe.

Of this general movement of mind it will be seen the Revival of Letters was but a phase. Art, like literature, had suffered through being subjected to

[1] "Credo ut intelligam."—Anselm.

scholastic methods. The activity of mind which the pursuit of art implies had been trammeled through another end being sought than that which art seeks for itself. The importance was attached to the object and not in the least to the form in which it was presented. The less the form diverted the attention from the saint or virgin, or whatever other object possessing the element of sacredness, was pictured, the more completely it was supposed it had fulfilled its end. But in the new impulse under which the mind was working, the beautiful was sought for its own sake, and its search thought to be justified by the satisfaction which its conception or realization could afford. And it was in that bygone age of which we have been speaking that the educated mind of Europe found beauty and truth expressed as they had not been during the centuries that intervened. Believing, too, they saw in it the human spirit in its richest development, the interest in them, and the influence over them, the knowledge of it was capable of exercising, were regarded as being of a very human kind. And there was a special appropriateness accordingly in the name of "Humanist" which those concerned in this movement both took and received. Very terrible indeed was "Humanism" in its moral consequences. Nearly all of those who were carried away by the movement as it developed itself in Italy sought to mingle, as had been done centuries before, Christianity and Greek Philosophy; and in seeking to lay hold of both they missed what was best in each. Ficino, the head of the Platonic Academy in Florence, was said [1] to keep a lamp burning before the shrine of

[1] Seebohm's Oxford Reformers, p. 10.

the Virgin, and one before the bust of Plato; but in thus seeking to pay adoration to the old and the new, to combine the lights issuing from two diverse systems, as in a process known in physical science as the intervention of waves, the result was darkness—moral disorder and confusion. Heathen vice was practised without any of the restraints which many of the heathen knew. This immorality—the selfishness and worldliness which characterized the lives of so many of the Humanists, and stirred up noble hearts like that of Savonarola to a fierce and holy antagonism—made Erasmus, in after years, fear "lest, under the pretence of a revival of ancient literature, paganism should again rear its head." But the immorality to which the Renaissance led in so many cases was not an essential feature of it, and it was in the end to which Erasmus and those who acted like him made it subservient, it found its justification. The Humanists for the most part sought to live in the past, and finding Christianity rather a barrier in the way, took from it only what was considered to be compatible with thought which had received expression before Christianity began. But Erasmus sought to lay hold of what in itself was good in the past, and make it helpful in supplying the intellectual and moral needs of man in the present. And how he did so we shall see by looking further at the life he led and the work he did.

Unable at the time to go to Italy through want of money and enfeebled health, Erasmus returned to Paris, and spent there the most part of several years in hard and congenial labour. Books afforded him not only work but pastime. "At dinner," he wrote to a friend, as quoted by one of his biographers, " we talk of nothing but books; and our suppers are made palatable with literature. When we go to walk our conversation is still about books, and even in our games we cannot quite forget them. We converse about them till sleep steals over us, and then our dreams are learned. When we waken in the morning we begin the day with letters." And the habits of industry and interest in learning to which this bears witness continued with Erasmus throughout his life. Already was he sufficiently well known for his scholarly acquirements to make his services as tutor solicited by students who had been drawn from other countries to Paris through the fame of its university; and it was through the emoluments he received in teaching some of these he was able at this time to maintain himself. One of these pupils—an Englishman, named Lord Mountjoy—helped him in after years freely with money, and remained throughout life his friend. Through his influence, and in his company, Erasmus, now thirty-one years of age, set foot on English soil.

His fame had gone before him; and there may be truth in the story so often repeated, that on meeting with Sir Thomas More—who was some years younger than himself—at the dinner-table of the Lord Mayor, or ex-Lord Mayor, of London, and getting into friendly discussion with him, each was so much struck with the ability of the other, that Erasmus, who had heard of his antagonist, but had not been introduced to him, exclaimed: "Either thou art Sir Thomas More, or nobody;" on which Sir Thomas replied: "Either thou art Erasmus, or the devil." Whatever truth there may be in this, the famous Lord Chancellor, with his great intellectual gifts, combined with a disposition sweetened, as we know from Erasmus' own account of him, by great gentleness and strong affection, quickened in Erasmus, as he did in many others who became acquainted with him, a feeling of the keenest interest and warmest attachment. But there were others besides him whom Erasmus got to know on this visit to England whose friendship was, throughout life, helpful to him and a source of the greatest satisfaction. These he found at Oxford. Though the University there, like that of Paris, was still under the control of the Scholastics, there were men in it who had gone to Italy, and were teaching—though with little favour from those in authority—the Greek they had learned there.

Among the scholars with whom Erasmus became acquainted at Oxford, there was one who perhaps exercised in course of time a greater influence upon him than any other. A man—according to all we are told of him—of deep and fervent piety; of unselfish ways and religious earnestness; of great ability and varied learning; and one who did more perhaps than any other, since the days of Wyclif, to prepare the way for the Reformation in England. That was John Colet—afterwards the Dean of St Paul's. He, too, had been in Italy, and may in Florence have heard Savonarola pour out the fiery eloquence that quickened new life and new interest in many hearts that were satiated and deadened through worldliness and unbelief; and on his return to Oxford, Colet showed the influence the New Learning had exercised over himself, in a way that was not only novel, but calculated to excite opposition on the part of those in authority, and who were still regarding the Greek language—the language of "pagans and heretics"—with the greatest suspicion, and were affording even less freedom for the study of the Scriptures than had been enjoyed in days before Wyclif began his work. Despite the danger he ran, Colet began to lecture on the Epistle of Paul to the Romans; and in doing so, rejected the Scholastic method of treating the Bible as an armoury of texts, in which those possessed of logical skill might find weapons either for offending each other or defending the dogmas they held in common; and in the use of which they were led in their interpretation of Scripture to meanings that were fanciful and absurd. To Colet, the Bible was a book of vital truth—of truth that stood in the closest relation to the hearts and welfare of men. To him the Christ of the Epistles was real, and the apostle in writing about Him was rational. To him, as much perhaps as to Luther, " Paul's words were not dead words, but living creatures that have both hands and feet"; and in so treating the book, he was led, and led others, into direct opposition not only to the corruption that characterized the Roman Church, but to much that was regarded as an essential part of the system it had reared. From this man, it would appear, Erasmus got not a little of that material which in after years he fashioned with so much skill into those shafts he levelled at the abuses of the Church; and which, pointed as they were with a wit and raillery peculiarly his own, did so much to injure it.

Erasmus was not only charmed with Colet, Colet was charmed with Erasmus, and finding in him one who not only shared his tastes and aims, but an apt pupil who was already prepared to receive his views, Colet had hope of finding in Erasmus a fellow-labourer at

Oxford; and on seeking to realize that hope urged him to deal with some book or part of the Old Testament in the way in which he himself had been dealing with the New. But Erasmus, now and always, was unsettled in his views and restless in his habits; not without ambition either, and looking perhaps at the time elsewhere and in other ways for rewards such as Oxford had not then in its power to bestow upon him. That was not the reason, however, he gave to his friend for refusing his appeal. This he found in his imperfect knowledge of Greek, and in the fact that though he approved of Colet's opposition to the Schoolmen, he did not believe that he himself " had strength of mind sufficient to enable him to sustain the ill-will of so many men stoutly maintaining their own ground."

From Oxford Erasmus went to London, where, unrestrained by any of the Puritanic notions that gave to the life of his friend Colet a serious earnestness, he lived merrily, yet, so far as evidence goes, also morally. His scholarly reputation gave him free access to the best society, and his affable ways and ready wit made him a favourite with all. Of those away from Oxford to whom he was introduced there was none whose acquaintance was regarded by him with the same measure of interest, or held as so great an honour, as that of a lad of nine years into whose presence his friend Sir Thomas More brought him in a quite unexpected way. This was Prince Henry, afterwards Henry VIII. of England.

Gratified by this and other introductions, and delighted with England and the scholarly men he had met—of whom he specially mentions Grocyn and Linacre, Colet and More, he returned to the Continent, where for some years, partly through want of money and partly through want of health, life pressed somewhat heavily upon him ; and there is a touch of pathos in this earnest student, though not actually poverty-stricken, crying out for money, and declaring that as soon as he gets some " he will buy first Greek books and then clothes." Poor he really was not, but he liked to live comfortably, and believed that the delicate state of his health required him to be more than ordinarily careful with regard to his food and drink, and whatever else may be thought to furnish an external condition of human comfort. To attain this end he dunned his friends for money and presents ; and though he always did so in the best of humour, yet he did it in terms so plain and direct that it would be difficult to understand how one so sensitive as he was could write as he did, if we forgot that he had been, and was still, a monk, and that begging and beggary were in a monk if not a virtue, at least no disgrace.

But we shall not seek to follow this little fair-haired man—as he was painted by his contemporary and friend Holbein—with his delicate health and restless brain, with his sparkling eye and subtle mind, as he wanders from place to place, shunning the plague or seeking intercourse with the learned ; editing old books or producing new ones ; composing as he rides and writing when he rests ; penning the cleverest letters, and sometimes, in after-life at least, as many as forty in a day. It is enough for our purpose to notice that during these years Erasmus carried out his long-cherished desire of going to Italy and seeing the capital of the western world.

Very different was the manner in which Erasmus entered Rome from that of Luther, who went there a year or two after him. The Monk of Erfurt, in the company of another, goes on foot depending for board and lodging upon the charity shown him at the various religious houses that lie in the way. Erasmus rides, is clothed comfortably—having received a dispensation to abandon his monkish dress—and lives on the best that money can command. Different, too, were the feelings which possessed the hearts of these two men, who were afterwards so closely related in their work, as they approach the same destination. To Luther, Rome was interesting, specially as the city where the blood of so many martyrs had been shed; to Erasmus, as the city where so many men of genius had lived. Here poets had sung and orators had spoken, whose very names excited in the breast of the scholar of Rotterdam feelings of admiration and even affection; and did so, because he was able to say with regard to them, as he wrote years afterwards in his colloquies:[1] "I find some things said by some of them"—among whom he specially mentions Cicero—"so chastely, so holily, and so divinely, that I cannot persuade myself but that when they wrote they were divinely inspired, and perhaps the Spirit of Christ diffuses itself further than we imagine, and that there are more saints than we have in our calendar."

The interest Erasmus felt in the writers of a classic age was shared by some of those he met in Rome, and to whose society he found a ready entrance. But in Rome—the citadel of the Church, as throughout Italy the Renaissance was not developing as it was in some

[1] Colloquies. The Religious Treat.

other countries through transforming and assimilating the thought of the time, and already was its strength all but exhausted. The Pope, Julius II., though a patron of men of letters, had, according to Ranke, "as the ruling passion of his life" an "innate love of war and conquest"; and Erasmus found him, as he wrote, " warring, conquering, triumphing, and openly acting the Cæsar"; and of war Erasmus had throughout his life the greatest horror, and again and again denounced it in the strongest language. "I often wonder," he says on one occasion, "what it is that urges, I will not say Christians, but men to such a pitch of madness, that they will make every effort, incur any expense, and meet the greatest dangers for their mutual destruction . . . . Can we who glory in the name of Christ, whose precepts and example taught us only gentleness, we who are members of one body, who are one flesh and grow up by the same Spirit, who are nourished by the same Sacraments, attached to the same Head, and called to the same immortality, and who hope for that highest Communion, that as Christ and the Father are one, so we may be also one in Him,—can we, I say, think anything in this world of such value that it should provoke us to war?—a thing so ruinous, so hateful, that even when it is most just no truly good man can approve of it."

Though Erasmus found much in his experience at Rome that tempted him to remain; though he was received with favour by those whose acquaintance he was most anxious to make; though prospects of high ecclesiastical preferment were held out to him by those who had influence enough to secure it; and an honourable position in his court was actually offered him by the Pope, after a few months' stay in Rome he left it at the invitation of friends in England.

To ecclesiastical preferment, or honours in Church or State; to the friendship of popes and princes and the worldly advantage that might bring, Erasmus was far from being indifferent; and the prospect of reaping reward more speedily in England than in Rome would seem from his own account of the matter to have had something to do with his going there. There he had many friends, and amongst them one at least who had it in his power to do him service—Henry VIII., who had shortly before this time succeeded to the throne. And though the King conferred no special favour upon Erasmus, he believed he had ground for the expectation he entertained in the fact that before his accession the King, with his own royal fingers, had penned a most friendly letter to him.

Of this letter, as of others he received from those who were high in authority in Church and State, Erasmus was proud and inclined to boast. And yet we should mistake the character of the man if we supposed he did so through that "puerile vanity" with which he was so freely charged in his own day, and by D'Aubigne at least in ours. The impulse under which he acted in speaking or writing as he did, of some of the letters sent him and honours bestowed upon him, was not that feeling which so often leads a man to affect the possession of gifts, or ostentatiously display those he has, for the supposed advantage this may secure. Erasmus had at no time an exaggerated feeling of his own importance, or immoderate desire for the applause of his fellows. He was not, it is true, altogether insensible to his own merits, or without a feeling of gratification in their receiving acknowledgment from those in high places. Possessed of a nature that was quick and sensitive, and that felt praise and blame as men of coarser mould do not, this poor scholar of Rotterdam, who was by the sheer force of his own exertions quickly raising himself to the foremost place among the men of letters, found no little gratification in the testimony that was borne to his merits and influence in the notice taken of him and the favours bestowed upon him by those, around whose names worldly greatness had thrown a halo of glory; and with that frankness that characterized him and led him to open his heart to all the world, and make everyone who would a partaker of its secrets, he readily gave expression to it. A truer estimate indeed of himself and of the influence he exercised, a clearer perception of the value of his work and the principles that were guiding him in it, would have made him less anxious for the applause of popes and princes, and afforded him the satisfaction of knowing that his name had a lustre which their favour could not increase, and would yet shine with a splendour such as theirs would never have.

Ambitious, too, Erasmus was, as his conduct on this and other occasions, and his letters with regard to them, clearly show, and yet his ambition was not of that ignoble kind which finds its end in mere self-gratification. Wisdom he placed above wealth, and all the honours of the world he thought were not to be compared in value with the culture which learning brings; and though he found and felt the highest satisfaction in excellence of an intellectual kind, yet his pursuit of literature had not merely that as its end, but the promotion of a general good to be attained through the diffusion of a knowledge in the benefits of which all might share.

Of his desire to further useful ends, through the application of the knowledge he had been acquiring during years of hard and continuous work, he had already, before this visit to England, given abundant proof. Besides other books he had published, there was issued in 1500 the first edition of his "Adages"—a collection of "the wise and witty sayings" of those who in former days had written in the languages of Greece and Rome. To this he appended notes, explanatory and practical, which are interesting —if for nothing else—as showing that the age of mere collecting and editing had gone, and that one of criticism and exposition had begun. In subsequent editions we are informed by the accounts we get of the book, not only was the number of the Proverbs greatly increased, but Erasmus took advantage of some of them when explaining and applying the principle they contained, to attack many of the abuses of the time in Church and State, and as exemplified in the conduct of popes and princes, priests and monks.

But another book Erasmus published shortly after his first edition of the "Adages," though less interesting in a literary point of view, is more so for our present purpose, as giving us a clearer indication of the relation in which he stood to the Romish Church, and the views he held of religious truth in its application to daily conduct. The occasion of the book is interesting and is worth mentioning.

A lady whom Erasmus met at the Castle of Tornenhens, though herself manifesting a spirit of true piety and religious earnestness, had as a husband a soldier of licentious life. Concerned about him, and anxious to do him good, she asked Erasmus to write a few thoughts on the subject of religion, such as he supposed were calculated to effect the end she had in view. Erasmus complied, afterwards expanded his notes, and published them under the title of "Enchiridion," or the "Christian Soldier's Dagger," or "Manual."

Though Ignatius Loyola, in his consuming zeal, found, we are told, no "unction" in the treatise, and forbade his Order to read it, ere many years had gone it became a favourite with the Reformers. Of much in the book, bearing more particularly on the subjects of human depravity and the relation of faith to works, they could not approve; but they liked it because of the manner in which it condemned the superstitions of the Church, and commended a piety that was practical. "The most acceptable worship," he wrote, "which you can offer to the Virgin Mary is to endeavour to imitate her humility." "If you must adore the bones of Paul locked up in a casket, adore also the spirit of Paul which shines forth from his writings." "You gaze with mute wonder on a tunic or handkerchief which is said to have belonged to Christ, and yet when you read the oracles of Christ your eyes droop with sleep."

But with monks and monkery, and the abuses generally which in the course of centuries had grown up in the Christian Church and marred its beauty, Erasmus dealt in a different manner, and with more effect, in a book published in 1510, and shortly after he arrived in England from Italy. Sitting in the house of his friend Sir Thomas More, ill, and waiting for his books, he beguiled his leisure by writing from notes he had made on his travels, his "Praise of Folly"—or "Encoinium Moriæ"—suggested to him, he tells us in its dedication, by the fact that his wise friend had a name whose literal meaning was "Folly." In the book, Folly is represented as mounting the rostrum, and, as in Holbein's illustration, with cap and bells, speaking in terms of the highest self-laudation. This she finds ground for doing in the conviction that all men are more or less under her influence, and it is because they are so happiness is so generally enjoyed. In a vein of the richest satire, men of all classes are attacked, and abuses of all kinds exposed. The value so many in his time ascribed to shrines and relics, fasts and pilgrimages, pardons and indulgences, is freely ridiculed; and kings and princes, popes and cardinals, schoolmen and divines, priests and monks are freely chastised, and chastised all the more severely that raillery and banter give directness and force to the serious purpose the writer has in view. "Erasmus," it has been said, "injured the Pope more by joking than Luther by scolding."

Of the Popes, amongst much more, he says: "They think to satisfy the Master they pretend to serve, our Lord and Saviour, with the great state and magnificence, with the ceremonies of instalments, with the titles of reverence and holiness, and with exercising their episcopal function only in blessing and cursing. . . . . Their only weapons ought to be those of the spirit; and of these indeed they are mighty liberal, as of their interdicts, their suspensions, their denunciations, their aggravations, their greater and lesser excommunications, and their roaring bulls whomever they are thundered against; and these most holy fathers never issue them more frequently than against those who at the instigation of the devil, and not having the fear of God before their eyes, do feloniously and maliciously attempt to lessen and impair St. Peter's patrimony; and though that Apostle tells our Saviour in the gospel in the name of all the other disciples, we have left all and followed thee, yet they challenge as his inheritance, fields, towns, treasures, and large dominions; for the defending whereof, inflamed with a holy zeal, they fight with fire and sword, to the great loss and effusion of Christian blood; thinking they are apostolical maintainers of Christ's spouse, the Church, when they have murdered all such as they call her enemies; though indeed the Church has no enemies more bloody and tyrannical than such bloody popes, who give dispensations for the not preaching of Christ; evacuate the main design and effect of our redemption by their pecuniary bribes and sales; adulterate the gospel by their forced interpretations and undermining traditions; and, lastly, by their lusts and wickedness grieve the Holy Spirit and make their Saviour's wounds to bleed anew."

Of the monks, amongst other things, he says: "Most of them place their greatest stress for salvation on a strict conformity to their foppish ceremonies, and a belief of their legendary traditions: wherein they fancy to have acquitted themselves with so much supererogation, that one heaven can never be a condign reward for their meritorious life; little thinking that the Judge of all the earth at the last day shall put them off with a—Who hath required these things at your hands? and call them to account only for the stewardship of his legacy, which was the precept of love and charity. It will be pretty to hear their pleas before the great tribunal: one will brag how he mortified his carnal appetite by feeding only upon fish; another will urge that he spent most of his time in the divine exercise of singing psalms; a third will tell how many days he fasted, and what severe penance he imposed on himself for the bringing the body into subjection; another will produce in his own behalf as many ceremonies as would load a fleet of merchantmen; a fifth will plead that in three score years he never so much as touched a piece of money, except he fingered it through a thick pair of gloves; the next that comes to answer for himself shall plead that for fifty years together he had lived like a sponge upon the same place, and was content never to change his habitation. But amidst all their fine excuses our Saviour shall interrupt them with this answer: Woe unto you, scribes and Pharisees, hypocrites, verily I know you not: I left you but one precept of loving one another, which I do not hear any plead he has faithfully discharged; I told you plainly in my gospel, without any parable, that my Father's kingdom was prepared, not for such as should lay claim to it by austerities, prayers, or fastings, but for those who should render themselves worthy of it by the exercise of faith and the offices of charity; I cannot own such as depend on their own merits without a reliance upon my mercy; as many of you therefore as trust to the broken reeds of your own deserts, may even go search out a new heaven, for you shall never enter into that which from the foundation of the world was prepared only for such as are true of heart."

Seven years before Luther publicly attacked the sale of indulgences, Erasmus wrote: "What shall I say of such as cry up and maintain the cheat of pardons and indulgencies that by these compute the time of each soul's residence in purgatory, and assign them a longer or shorter continuance according as they purchase more or fewer of these paltry pardons and saleable exemptions. . . . . By this easy way of purchasing pardon, any notorious highwayman, any plundering soldier, or any bribe-taking judge shall disburse some part of their unjust gains, and so think all their grossest impieties sufficiently atoned for; so many perjuries, lusts, drunkennesses, quarrels, bloodsheds, cheats, treacheries, and all sorts of debaucheries, shall all be, as it were, struck a bargain for, and such a contract made as if they paid off all arrears and might now begin a new score."

A book, much of which is written after this manner, circulating rapidly and widely—and no less than seven editions, we are told, were sold out in a few months of its first publication—could not but prove an effectual means of preparing the way for those who in virtue of the definiteness of their aim, and the success that attended their work, have by special emphasis been named the Reformers.

It is not merely, however, through his publication of the Praise of Folly we see the relation in which he at this time stood to the Church. Paying a visit one day to the shrine of "Our Lady of Walsingham," and being shown a gate in the churchyard wall so small that one had to stoop to enter, through which, he was assured, a knight on horseback pursued by an enemy, on recommending himself to the Holy Virgin, managed to go; a huge joint, which he was told belonged to the finger of St. Peter; some of the Virgin's milk, and other curiosities, he expressed his scepticism so freely that the "shewer of relics" got indignant, and was only pacified by the bestowal of a small sum of money.

From the same dialogue in which, after his humorous way, he records a description of this visit we learn that in the company of his friend Colet he paid a visit to the shrine of St. Thomas à Becket at Canterbury. Through the favour of Archbishop Wareham, with whom Erasmus was on terms of friendship, and to whom he dedicated one of his greatest works—his edition of St. Jerome—there was not a little shown them that was regarded as too sacred, or too precious, for ordinary eyes to see; and on Colet suggesting that much of the wealth they saw in the form of jewels and gold might be devoted to the good of the poor, and that one who was kind to them in his lifetime was more likely to be gratified by its being put to that use than allowed to lie where it was, "the shewer of relics," Erasmus says, got angry, and but for the Archbishop's recommendation "would have taken them by the shoulders and turned them out of the Church."

During the period in which these and other excursions were made, Erasmus was engaged part of the year teaching Greek at the University of Cambridge; and nothing he did helped the Reformation movement so much as his labours in connection with this language. As early as 1505 he had edited and published some annotations on the New Testament by Laurentius Valla, and in doing so prefaced the book with a letter in which he publicly vindicated "the right and necessity of a free criticism, as in many passages the Vulgate was manifestly at fault, was a bad rendering of the original Greek, or had been corrupted." But Erasmus took a step in advance of this, and believed in doing so he was doing, as he said, "a work acceptable to the Lord, and necessary to the cause of Christ," when as the fruit of a labour so great that he was able to say of it: "If I told you how much sweat it cost me you would not believe me." He superintended in 1516 at the famous printing press at Basle the issuing of his "Novum Instrumentum," or "Greek New Testament with a new Latin Translation," a book the importance of which we shall acknowledge all the more readily as we recognize as a main element of the principle involved in the Reformation movement the assertion of the right of the individual conscience to be brought into direct contact with the Eternal, or any manifestation He may have made of Himself.

Not only did the Church put itself between the heart of man and the Bible, but it was by no means careful to see that the truth it received was in the purest form attainable. For centuries the Vulgate, or Latin translation of the Scriptures, had been the only one in use, and, imperfect as it was, the Church of Erasmus' time received it as having an authority that was absolute. And all the translations that had been made of the Bible into the vernacular tongues of Europe, Wyclif's included, had been made from this.

Though not a few translations had been made, to the great bulk of the people the Bible was an unknown book, and many ecclesiastics knew nothing more of it than was contained in the church service. But the work Erasmus did, put the New Testament into the hands of scholars in the language in which it was written, and stimulated men like Tyndale in our own land to put the truth, as they found it at its source, into the hands of the people in the tongue they spoke. So much did D'Aubigne think the Reformation in England was due to this that he was led to say: "The principle of the Reformation at Oxford, Cambridge, and London was the Greek New Testament published by Erasmus."

That Erasmus contemplated in the work he was doing not merely the good of scholars but that of others as well, is manifest from much that was said in the lengthy and remarkable preface with which the book was issued. "The sun itself," he says," is not more common to all than the teaching of Christ. For I utterly dissent from those who are unwilling that the Scriptures should be read by the unlearned translated into their vulgar tongue, as though Christ had such subtleties that they can scarcely be understood even by a few theologians, or as though the strength of the Christian religion consisted in men's ignorance of it. The mysteries of kings it may be safe to conceal, but Christ wished his mysteries to be published as openly as possible. I wish that even the weakest woman should read the Gospel—should read the Epistles of Paul. And I wish these were translated into all languages, so that they might be read and understood, not only by Scots and Irishmen, but also by Turks and Saracens. To make them understood is surely the first step. It may be that they might be ridiculed by many, but some would take them to heart. I long that the husbandman should sing portions of them to himself as he follows the plough, that the weaver should hum them to the tune of his shuttle, that the traveller should beguile with their stories the tedium of his journey."

These words are not only interesting as showing the feeling with which Erasmus regarded the truth of the Bible, but remarkable as being expressed and published at a time when the Church was in no way favourable to the general and indiscriminate reading and teaching of the Scriptures. While, however, Erasmus had a good end in view in the publication of this book, he liked, at the same time, it has to be said, to be on the safe side, and took the precaution in this case of dedicating his scholarly work to the scholarly man who was then at the head of the Church, Pope Leo X.

The introduction to this New Testament is not, however, the only feature of it that is remarkable, and that makes it worth while for our present purpose to notice it. Several of the books and many of the passages that had hitherto been received without question on the authority of the Vulgate were challenged, and handled in a spirit that was free and critical. The Epistle to the Hebrews, *e.g.*, he maintains, was not written by Paul; and he questions the genuineness of the 2nd Epistle of Peter. The famous passage of the three witnesses in the 1st Epistle of John, which our Revised Version omits, was rejected by him on the authority of the MSS. he collated. Even the Pope's authority had doubts thrown upon it, or at least found to have no good ground in the celebrated passage, now done in purple and gold in six-feet letters on the interior of the dome of St. Peter's at Rome: "Thou art Peter, and upon this rock will I build my Church."

The critical work, indeed, of Erasmus in this book has been superseded by the labours of others, and is held by scholars to be of no value. But not only was its publication a bold step for this man with his nervous shrinking from opposition to take, but it was one that was not without value, and that not merely in preparing the way for those who would follow up his work, but as affording, too, a protest against an authority that was external and traditional.

What Copernicus did not many years afterwards in a different sphere of thought, Erasmus may be said to have done in the sphere of Biblical criticism. The labours of Copernicus were not perfect, and ere long had to give way to those of Kepler. But in shattering the cycles and epi-cycles of an older theory, and taking his stand on the sun as the centre of the solar system, his protest was no less strong against that view of things which the Church maintained had an authority that was divine. And Erasmus, in carrying out his work in the spirit he did, and writing as he wrote, showed he believed that truth was greater than the Church, and the spirit of man endowed with an authority which to him who was faithful to it was superior to that of Pope and Council. "He who is spiritual, as Paul says," he wrote in closing his New Testament, "judgeth all things, and is judged by no one." And thus, may we not say, in the spirit of the Renaissance, as that had manifested itself in Erasmus, and more particularly in his labours in connection with the New Testament, the sacred and the secular, which the Church in the Middle Ages had kept so far apart, "had met together"; intellectual enlightenment and truth divine "had kissed each other."

Erasmus, indeed, did not break away from the Church or shake off its authority, and felt all the less inclined to do so as time went on and the Reformation movement developed. It was not given him to see the full drift and value of the principles he had been so usefully applying, any more than those who first applied steam as a motive power or electricity to the practical purposes of life saw how rich the discovery was in the issues to which in its development it would lead. Erasmus believed that the Church had an origin that was divine, and, corrupt though it was, the Pope was still its head. "I am not so impious," he wrote, when the Reformation had really begun, "as to dissent from the Catholic Church nor so ungrateful as to differ from Leo, from whom I have experienced no common favour and kindness." "If the corrupt manners of the Roman Court call for some great and immediate remedy, certainly it is not for me, or the like of me, to usurp this office."

And it was through such work as that in which he had been so long and so earnestly engaged—through disseminating literature and attacking the abuses that prevailed in the Church, that he hoped to be helpful in purifying and strengthening it. But not only was the disease too serious, too deeply rooted and of too long standing thus to be cured, but the principle of the movement which had been carrying Erasmus along with it demanded in its application to the Church a reconstruction of its form. "No man putteth a piece of new cloth unto an old garment . . . Neither do men put new wine into old bottles." But this was what Erasmus was seeking to do. The seed he planted had its natural outcome in liberty—in a measure of freedom of thought that is incompatible with the authority exercised by the Roman Catholic Church, and to that authority he continued to bow.

To shake it off, indeed, and seek the reformation of

the system that asserted it, needed a different kind of man from Erasmus—one of intenser conviction and stronger self-assertion; one who feared death less, and loved truth more; one who could not only influence the learned, but move the hearts of the people; one who would not sacrifice principle for peace, and dared answer Rome's thunder with thunder. And such a one was at hand girding on his armour and all but ready for the fray. The year after Erasmus published the first edition of his New Testament, Luther nailed his famous propositions to the church door at Wittenberg—a deed which may be said to have first made visible, as the first flash of lightning does the coming storm, the commotion and revolution which the meeting of concurrent forces that had been long at work produced in the Protestant Reformation.

Though not associating himself with the Reformers, Erasmus continued to be helpful to them through carrying on the very same kind of work by which he had done so much to prepare the way for them. Before the memorable day on which the Pope's Bull was burned by Luther, Erasmus had sought to popularize the Bible by issuing a paraphrase of some of Paul's Epistles, and a few years afterwards he did the same for the whole of the New Testament—the Apocalypse excepted. The fame of the author helped the book to sell, and ere long it found a place in every parish church in England.

Previous to the publication of this there appeared a second edition of the "Familiar Colloquies"—the book which, of all Erasmus wrote, became the most popular, and contains so much that is opposed to the Roman Catholic system that it was condemned some years after it was issued by the Theological Faculty of the University of Paris, and placed by the Inquisition among "the first-class" of prohibited books.

But Erasmus, though he continued to help the Reformation movement in this indirect way, believing that he saw in it an influence that was adverse to the cause of learning, in which he had so deep an interest, regarded its progress with a feeling akin to dismay. And though the Reformation was ultimately favourable to literature—though it quickened intellectual activity and stimulated research; though it spread information among the people and awakened them to a sense of their interests; though it circulated the Bible and sowed principles the development of which helped to usher in the brightness of that day that burst upon the world in "Great Eliza's golden time," yet its immediate effects were different. So much so, in the opinion of Goethe, that he was led to say, as quoted by Froude, that "Luther threw back the intellectual progress of mankind for centuries by calling in the passions of the multitude to decide on subjects which ought to have been left to the learned." And as Erasmus saw this—saw religious zeal and the questions of the day absorb the attention of the ablest minds—saw the movement which Luther was heading carry away in its sweep such men as Von Hutten, and Melancthon, and Reuchlin—Saint Reuchlin as after his death he called him—and who had been doing for Hebrew what Erasmus had been doing for Greek, he regarded it as nothing short of a calamity.

But another reason Erasmus had for deprecating the new movement was the disturbances both in Church and State to which it gave rise. The unsettling of the old-established order led, as it could hardly otherwise do, to violent controversy and political rebellion. But to Erasmus, in his way of looking at things, it was better to tolerate error and injustice than seek their removal if that could be effected only through the application of means that were violent. He declared "he hated discord so much that he would dislike the truth itself if it were seditious." "By a natural instinct," he wrote, " I so abhor all kinds of quarrels that if I had a large estate to defend at law I would sooner lose it than litigate."

Feeling in this way, and seeing the commotion that was likely to arise from a man of Luther's strength and temperament opposing himself to the head of the Church, shortly before the burning of the Pope's Bull he sent him a letter, in reply to one he had received, in which he addressed him as "My dearest brother in Christ," and exhorted him to moderation. But he might as well have tried to curb the wind, or alter the stars in their course, for Luther believed that, in what he was doing in relation to the Pope's authority, he was possessed by a divine impulse, and as much called upon freely to fulfil the divine purpose as the wind, or the stars, or other objects of God's creative power, that have no will of their own to refuse compliance with the divine behests, but are and do as God commands.

These two men were different, entirely different, and it was only in an indirect way they could co-operate. Great as Erasmus was in his power of acquisition, and in the measure of his knowledge, he was not like Luther —a spiritual force that could shape the history of all coming time through moulding by its inherent strength opposing circumstances so far to its own nature as to make them subserve its purpose, but was pliable enough, through his sensitiveness and dread of conflict, to have even his conceptions of truth and duty affected in his seeking to fall in comfortably with his surroundings. What was in itself right, did not always seem to him, specially perhaps in later years, the first consideration in determining the course of conduct he would pursue, but what was safe or prudent. " There was a certain pious craft and innocent time-serving," he thought, " could be used without doing injury to the interests of true religion." As for the truth, " he had," he said, " no inclination to die for it. Every man has not the courage to be a martyr, and I am afraid if I were put to the trial I should imitate St. Peter."

And yet there was a limit to the measure in which his conception of duty could be affected, and in so far as he heard the voice of conscience he seemed willing to obey it. And though, in his frankness, he speaks of himself as he has done, there is no saying how much he would have been willing to suffer had he thought that through his suffering the interests of humanity or of true religion would have been promoted. It is not those who have boasted of their fearlessness and devotion to truth that have shewn in a righteous cause the greatest powers of endurance, or the greatest readiness to suffer; and had Erasmus believed there was good occasion for it, he might have proved himself—as many a woman has done in the hour of extremity—possessed of a courage that was invincible. It was probably a very genuine feeling, and more than a mere passing one to which he gave expression when he said that though he had " no wish to be martyr for Luther, he was ready to be a martyr for Christ, if He gave him strength to be one."

Religion on its practical side—religion viewed as "morality touched by emotion" that had its exciting cause in a belief of the Holy One—had the greatest interest for him, and he "could honour piety," he said, "wherever it was found, provided only it was genuine." But for mere theological truth, or religion viewed as a system of dogmas, he cared very little, regarding it as valuable, like rites and ceremonies, only as it tended to promote "a pious disposition of the heart."

Had he been asked to formulate a creed, in complying with the request he would have drawn out a very short one. "Formerly," he wrote in his introduction to his edition of St. Hilary's works, "faith consisted in the life rather than in the profession of a multitude of articles. By-and-by it became necessary to impose articles of faith, but these were at first few in number, and of apostolic simplicity. Then the perverseness and malice of heretics caused the Holy Scriptures to be more diligently discussed, and points of doctrine to be determined by the authority of synods. At length faith ceased to be a matter of the heart, and was wholly transferred to written documents; and there were almost as many confessions of faith as there were persons capable of drawing them up. Articles increased, but sincerity decreased. Contention waxed warm, charity waxed cold. The doctrine of Christ, which at first repudiated all strife of words, began to look to the schools of the philosophers for protection; this was the first step in the decline of the Church. Wealth increased, and power too. The interference of the authority of the Emperors, moreover, was not very conducive to sincerity of faith." And elsewhere he says: "It would be better for the Church not to decide so dogmatically upon so many speculative points and make them articles of faith, but only require assent to those doctrines which are manifestly laid down in the Holy Scriptures as necessary for salvation. These are few." What these are, however, he does not seem inclined to inquire. Theological truth had too little interest for him to tempt him often, or far, it would appear, in its investigation, and when he enters upon it he manifests a sceptical tendency in the indulgence of which he is restrained through fear of differing from the Church and giving ground for a charge of heresy. Possessed of a mind that was keen and quick in its movement, but broad rather than deep, receiving many impressions rather than any one with intenseness, he saw difficulties and felt doubts in connection with theological truth of which men with less true piety than himself had no experience: and finding he was apt to get unsettled on points that the Church had settled, and regarding the form which these assumed as a matter of comparatively little moment, he satisfied himself, as so many have done, with that spurious rest that is found in bowing to the authority of the Church. So much did that authority weigh with him, he said, that he "could be of the opinion of the Arians and Pelagians if the Church had approved their doctrine." To leave the Church and join the Reformers he regarded as a mere change of masters, and as he honestly differed from their leaders in some of their views, he was content to remain where he was.

His opposition to Luther showed itself specially in

his controversy with him on the subject of Free Will. Though Luther's view that the will of man was in bondage by reason of sin, and that he could will freely only in so far as divine grace enabled him to do so, was to him, as he said: "a matter serious, necessary and eternal, of such momentous interest that it must be defended at the risk of life itself," the whole question to Erasmus had an interest of a merely speculative kind, and he was only led to deal with it to gratify his friends in the Church, and to satisfy them that he was not, as he was so much blamed for being, either with the Reformers or one of them.

Though he did not join them, and protested often, and strongly, against his name being associated with theirs, he had, as he could not but have, after all he had done that tended to prepare the way for them, much true sympathy with them in the work in which they where engaged. Luther, Erasmus regarded as a remedy "bitter and drastic," which the unhealthy condition of the Church required; and while he deprecated his violent temper and thorough-going ways, he had a true admiration for his character; and it was only after frequently excusing himself, and much delay, that he took up his pen to write against him. No good came of the controversy. Erasmus charged Luther with unworthy motives, and Luther, in bad temper, called his opponent, "that enraged viper, Erasmus of Rotterdam, the vainest creature in all the world."

Luther was not the only one of the Reformers who got angry with Erasmus. With some of them, indeed, specially with Melancthon, whom Luther loved, he remained on terms of friendly intercourse. But the majority of them could not understand how one who had done so much to promote the cause into which they had thrown their strength, should have refused to join them when they broke away from the Romish Church and put themselves in opposition to it; and the more violent of them attacked him with violent language and applied to him opprobrious epithets.

But Erasmus had to suffer attacks from another side. The priests and monks were enraged at him, and could not but be after having written about them in the way he had, and done so much that tended not only to weaken their influence and blast their reputation, but undermine the system the interests of which they regarded as bound up with their own. With more truth than he was willing to acknowledge they declared: "Erasmus had laid the egg and Luther had hatched it." And the monk of whom Erasmus tells us who took his picture and hung it up in his chamber "that he might get spitting upon it," is an indication of the bitterness of feeling with which many of them regarded him. "And thus," he says, "I am well rewarded for all my labours by being pelted on both sides. Among ourselves I am universally accused of being a Lutheran, while among the Germans I am evil-spoken of as an adversary to the Lutheran faction. I would, however, give not only my good name, but life itself, to calm this most disastrous storm."

Despite these troubles, Erasmus did not lose his merry-heartedness, nor did his vigour grow dull. During these years, while the Reformation controversy was raging, and he was defending himself for the middle course he seemed to be pursuing of sympathizing with much in the spirit of the Reformation, and yet keeping friendly with Rome, he continued to pursue in his own peaceful way, and with as much earnestness as ever, the kind of work in which he had been so long engaged. For eight years, beginning in 1521, he worked at " Froben's mill," as he termed the printing press of his friend, issuing now a new edition of one of his own books, or writing an introduction to one by somebody else; publishing a commentary on part of the Bible, or editing one of the classics or fathers; No longer entreating his friends for money or presents, but receiving many, and as acknowledged to be the brightest luminary of his age, making the greatest of those who sent them feel honoured if they received a letter in return.

The troubles in Basle arising from the Reformation movement, and the suspicion in which he was there held by those who were favourable to it, induced him to seek refuge for a time in Friburg. But he returned; and here in 1536, beside the swift-flowing Rhine, and near the printing press from which had issued the first published New Testament in Greek, Erasmus died, " sine lux, sine crux "—without candle, without crucifix— so years before an ignorant monk had reported to his friends he had died, thinking apparently it would be an agreeable piece of news to know that one who had spoken about them as Erasmus had done, had departed without the consolations of the Church, or the hope which the Church could give. And it was better that this man who had sought to direct human faith to a higher source of help than that which the ceremonies of the Church could afford, should have died without any priest or priestly rite intervening between his spirit and Him to whom he prayed with his departing breath the prayer, "O Jesus, have mercy"; "Lord, have mercy"; "Lord, make an end."

Thus passed away Desiderius Erasmus—the amiable, so his name means, and in the signification we have an index to one of the special features of his character, for whatever else he was, he was amiable. And if we could wish that with his gentleness and kindness he had had more firmness and force of will; that with his keen intellect he had had a clearer perception of the value of truth even in its formal expression; that with his hatred of discord he had hated more all manner of unrighteousness; that with his humanistic breadth he had had greater evangelistic zeal, we can still esteem him for what he was and admire him for what he did. Possessed of the greatest abilities, he devoted them to the best of ends. Though he delighted in peace, his life was one of continual conflict, and the foes he did battle with were ignorance and superstition. If the truth and freedom which have come down to us as the fruit of the Reformation movement are valued by us, then we have reason to be grateful to him; for without him the Reformers of his time would not have been what they were, or have accomplished what they did. It was he, more than any anyone else, who

> "Stemm'd the wild torrent of a barbarous age,
> And drove those holy vandals off the stage."

And now, in leaving him, though we may differ in opinion as to the excellence of his character or the value of his work, as those have done who were best able to estimate both, we may all at least join in the prayer with which he closed his most popular book: "May that Spirit which is the pacifier of all, who uses His instruments various ways, make us all agree and consent in sound doctrine and holy manners, that we may all come to the fellowship of the New Jerusalem that knows no discords. Amen."

Luther.

DURING a midsummer afternoon of the year 1415, on the bank of the beautiful lake of Constance, a memorable scene was witnessed. In pursuance of the sentence of condemnation passed by the Church Council assembled in the town, and in defiance of the imperial safe-conduct, John Hus was burnt at the stake. For many years he had laboured and written in his native Bohemia, for the reformation of the Church. But, although he had gathered round him a large party of his countrymen like-minded with himself, the authority of Pope and Council was against him, and he died the heretic's death. There is a tradition to the effect that in the hour of death's approach—that hour when sometimes the soul has seemed to be gifted with a prophetic power, and the dying eyes have seen into the future with more than mortal vision—the martyr, playing with the meaning of his own name, declared to his judges that now they burnt a goose, but that in an hundred years a white swan would come whom no one would be able to destroy.

Never had prophetic word seemed less likely of fulfilment: and as the years wore on there was little indication that the hope which it breathed would be realized. The ashes of the faithful confessor were cast into the river Rhine, which here issues from the lake. His martyrdom became the watchword of a long and dreadful war between the people of Bohemia and the German Empire. In this war the Hussites were repeatedly and decisively victorious. But success proved more dangerous than might have been defeat; for through internal discords, the indulgence of carnal passions, and the imperfect apprehension of Christian doctrine, the reforming movement, which had been so full of promise in the hands of Hus, lost its strong impulse, and fell into a languishing condition.

The worst effect, however, of this great religious feud was the alienation of the German mind from all doctrines akin to those which were inscribed on the banners of the men who had put to disgraceful rout the imperial armies. The national honour had already been touched by a dispute in the University of Prague in which Hus's party remained masters of the situation; and the feeling of soreness was intensely aggravated by the bitter and bloody war which proved so humbling to the military reputation of the Germans. The Hussite victories had shut and sealed the mind of Europe against the Hussite doctrine; and there was nothing from which a German, whether ecclesiastic or lay, shrank with greater horror than any suspicion of being tainted with the Bohemian poison. Even Luther himself was at first cautious in admitting kinship or sympathy with the Reformer of Prague.

No doubt there were voices in the night which gave unmistakeable, though fragmentary, utterance to some parts of the truth which became full-voiced in Luther and the later Reformers. Thus, for instance, John

Wessel, who taught in Paris during the latter part of the century, attached such importance to faith as the turning-point between the natural and the spiritual life, that Luther calls him a rare and lofty spirit, and says, " If I had read Wessel first, my adversaries might have imagined that Luther had taken everything from him." So, too, such men as John of Goch, in Germany, Savonarola in Italy, and others, amid much that was defective, emphasized the great central truth that religion consists in a direct and immediate relation between the soul and the work of Christ. These teachings, however, never became rallying centres of fresh thought and life. And although, along with many of the secular influences of the century—such as the revival of classical learning, the decay of Scholasticism, which fell in great part by its own weight, leaving a want which the culture of Humanism could not satisfy, the invention of printing, which was to the Reformation what the universal diffusion of the Greek language was to primitive Christianity, the widening of the horizon of common life by geographical discovery and commercial enterprise—they combined to predispose men's minds for the reception of new truth, yet their visible effect was very limited.

On the other hand, the Church of Rome appeared to renew and consolidate her power. Councils met which, by their mild and utterly insufficient attempts at outward reform, gave a further sanction and fixity to the abuses of the Papal system. Towards the close of the century the Inquisition seems to have been established with renewed vigour in Germany. The Roman Court, becoming supremely confident in its apparently impregnable security, set no bounds to its excesses, and the

Papal chair was repeatedly occupied by men whose lives were stained with the foulest worldliness and immorality. When, on the 16th day of March, 1517, Leo X. brought the fifth Lateran Council to a triumphant conclusion, not a whisper of revolt was to be heard through the wide realm of his spiritual sovereignty. There was scarcely an indication that Europe was on the eve of the mightiest change in her history which has taken place since the day when an apostle landed on her shores.

Yet even then, almost in the same hour, an unknown hand came forth and wrote strange words of destiny within sight of all. Little more than seven months had elapsed since the close of the Lateran Council, when, on the last day of October, an Augustinian monk, without informing anyone of what he was about to do, appeared at the Castle Church of Wittenberg among a crowd of relic-worshippers, and, standing under the arched doorway, posted on the door of the church a paper containing ninety-five short Latin theses concerning indulgences, which in a prefaratory note he offered as subjects of a public disputation to be held under his own presidency. While Leo was devoting himself to those autumn pleasures of which he was passionately fond—hawking and fishing and hunting, being splendidly entertained by the princes of the Church in their country palaces—a writing was written, although he did not at once see it; and the interpretation of it was, that the vast system of religious worship and life of which he was the head, had been weighed in the balances and was found wanting. These theses, which remain to this day, graven in brass, on the spot where they were first set up, formed the beginning of the

Reformation, and were the edge of the axe laid to the huge and monstrous growth of mediaeval superstition.

Even before this, just the one hundred years from the very day on which the martyr's spirit ascended in its chariot of fire at Constance, this monk, who was also a doctor and professor, was finding in the Bible, and in his university lectures was declaring to others, the truth which had been hidden for long ages, and which Hus had but dimly descried. The white swan was indeed come, and a new and glorious doctrine—the true message of the everlasting Gospel itself—was being unfolded, out of the heart of a deep experience and Scriptural knowledge, to the roused intelligence and spiritual consciousness of the hearers.

It was by no rapid process that Martin Luther had become capable of such teaching, and of such an act. The vehemence of his language has somtimes led people to think of him as reckless and revolutionary, self-confidently assuming the *rôle* of Reformer. Nothing could be further from the fact. He was a man whose convictions ripened slowly; and it is remarkable that almost all the great crises of his life had their occasion, though doubtless not their deepest cause, in outward compelling circumstances. At this time he was 34 years of age, and the publication of his theses was the outcome and climax of a distinct experience of 14 years' duration—from the day on which he found a Latin Bible in the University Library at Erfurt, till the time when his penitents came to him seeking absolution on the authority of Tetzel's letter of indulgence. Let us mark the steps of this progress.

Born almost under the shadow of the Harz mountains at the town of Eisleben, to the copper mines near which his father had come in search of work, he early learnt the meaning of poverty. Blessed with excellent and kind parents, he seems, however, to have been subjected to a somewhat stern discipline. In his schools he was unfortunate, till he went to Eisenach, where his young heart expanded under the sweet motherly influence of Ursula Cotta, and the instruction of the wise, far-seeing Trebonius; so that he ever afterwards looked back to his "dear" Eisenach as a green spot in the journey of his life. At the age of 18 he is a student at the University of Erfurt, remaining there for four years, and in the middle of that period making his momentous discovery of a copy of the Vulgate—the first complete Bible he had seen. And although his readings in this book were, as yet, but like the driftwood which Columbus saw, revealing the existence of a new world yet undiscovered, they quickened in him those spiritual fears and longings which had already begun to make themselves felt.

By what looks an accident, and in consequence of a vow uttered in a moment of terror, and which he himself said that he for a time regretted after it was made, he enters the convent at Erfurt. Not seldom God deepens the darkness ere he leads to the light; and it was needful that Luther should know to the uttermost the hard yoke from which he was to be God's instrument for liberating the bodies and souls of men. The student, whose work had been full of promise. and for whom his father and his friends were anticipating a brilliant career in the profession of the law, at first tells no one of his new resolve. A fortnight afterwards, on a July evening, he invites a number of his college friends to supper; after a few pleasant hours have been spent, before the merry party breaks up, informs them that this is his farewell to the world; and, notwithstanding their entreaties, that very night knocks for admittance at the door of the Augustinian Convent.

For the young graduate there was at first total and bitter disappointment. He entered with devotion into the life which he had chosen. He made full proof of the monastic discipline. But the thought of sin, which had become a reality to him even while he was at the University, deepened, and overspread his whole consciousness; while, on the other hand, the character of God seemed equally terrible. He brooded over the word "righteousness," but in the Divine "righteousness," or "justice," he could find no comfort. He felt the intense need which the Mystics before him had felt, of communion with God; but in his case there was interposed a tremendous conviction of sin, which had been almost wanting to them. An immense gulf yawned between God's holiness and himself as a sinner—a gulf which seemed only to widen as he strove, by all the prescribed methods, to narrow it. He sought carefully in fastings, and vigils, and prayers, and all kinds of penances and mortifications, for the secret of peace; but he could not find it. "I was a pious monk," he said; "if ever a monk came to heaven though a monkish life, I would have come thither."

Gradually, however, a change takes place. He pores over the Word of God—first the red-leather convent Bible, chained to the wall, and then a copy which he obtains as a present. He reads the pages of Occam and Augustine. And, above all, he is brought into contact with Staupitz, the Vicar-General of his Order, who at this time paid a visit to the convent, and through whose means it was largely that the blindness was at last taken from his eyes, and he saw, as he tells us, the light of the Gospel dawning out of the darkness in his heart. The young monk, who had at once attracted the eye of his superior, unbosoms to him all his difficulties—his experience of the mastery of sin, his fear of the Divine justice. "Why torment thyself with these things?" says this spiritual father. "Look to the wounds of Jesus Christ: then shalt thou see the grace of God. Instead of making a martyr of thyself for thy faults, throw thyself into the arms of the Redeemer." "But," objects Luther, "I must be changed before God can receive me." "No repentance is true," replies Staupitz, "save that which begins with the love of God and of righteousness. If thou wouldst be converted, dwell not upon all these macerations and tortures: love Him who first loved thee." He finds, to his intense surprise, that the word "penitentia," which had seemed so bitter to him as he read it in his Vulgate, does not mean the penance which he has deemed so necessary, but repentance. He comes to see that the righteousness of God is not to be deserved, but to be received as a gift by faith. Accordingly he is able to write, in one of his letters, that all the passages of Scripture which "used to frighten him, now seemed to rise up from all sides, smiling and leaping, and sporting with him." "As I had previously," he says, "hated the words 'righteousness of God,' so from that time I began to esteem and love them, as words most sweet and most consoling. Indeed they were to me the true gate of Paradise." The Vicar-General was deeply impressed by his conversations with Luther, and he predicted for him a great future. "It is not without cause that God exercises you by so many combats: be assured He will employ you in great things as His minister."

The enlightening process goes on. During the second year of his stay at the convent, while he is prostrate under a severe illness, and is again shaken with spiritual terrors, an old monk repeats to him the article of the Apostles' Creed, "I believe in the forgiveness of sins," impressing upon him the fact that we must believe not only that David's or Peter's sins, but that our own sins, are forgiven; and the words become a rock in the surging sea of his troubled thoughts. While he is pursuing his studies in the University of Wittenberg, to a chair in which he had been appointed by the Elector, he is struck with the sentence in the Epistle to the Romans, "The just shall live by faith," which became the heart of his religion and his theology, and which has proved to be one of those fontal texts from which truth, for a time condensed and sealed, has flowed forth in a mighty stream, showing itself to possess an infinite significance and power of expansion. Again and again during his life these words sounded in his ears—at Bologna, where he lay dangerously sick; at Rome, while climbing up Pilate's staircase on his knees, and elsewhere. Forming first one of the practical means of his personal salvation, they became the basis and starting-point of the great doctrine of Justification by Faith, which he framed into a scientific expression in after years.

One event happened during those years which exerted

an important influence upon him as a reformer of the Church—his visit to Rome. He approached the city in a spirit of deep devotion, falling upon his knees, and exclaiming, "Hail to thee, holy Rome!" but he left it with the dream of its sanctity rudely broken. In the Holy City fifteen centuries of Christianity had brought men round again to the condition of pagan Rome, in which, according to a celebrated testimony, two augurs could scarcely meet without laughing. At ecclesiastical dinner-tables, and elsewhere, he heard the holiest mysteries of his religion made a jest of, and he was utterly shocked by the wickedness and unbelief which abounded on every side. And although he was careful to distinguish between the religion and its unworthy ministers, the facts of which he had been an eye-witness sank deeply into his mind. "I would not have missed seeing Rome for a hundred thousand florins," he afterwards declared; "for I might then have felt that I had done some injustice to the Pope."

The years which followed his return from Rome show him to us still quietly engaged at his studies and lectures. During all this time he seems to have had no presentiment of the great work which was awaiting him. Far from counting it a prize to be eagerly grasped, that he should change the thoughts of men about religion which had served them in the past, the strong language which he used in the midst of later labours gives evidence of the intellectual modesty and spiritual reserve with which he yielded to the fulfilment of his mission. "Had I known what I now know," he said afterwards, "not ten horses would ever have dragged me into it." "God hurries, drives me. I am not master of myself. I wish to be quiet, and am hurried into the midst of tumults." Staupitz had the utmost difficulty in persuading him to preach. "In asking me to do this," he exclaimed to his chief, "you wish to kill me. I shall not live for three months, if you make me go on." "Very well," was the reply, "so be it, in God's name; it would be a noble offering to make. And up yonder, too, our Lord has need of able and devoted men." And so, first, in a small wooden chapel, thirty feet long, temporarily used as the convent church, and then in the town church, that voice began to speak which was afterwards to be heard in tones of thunder by the world. The touching reluctance, thus repeatedly struggled with and overcome, is the highest modern rendering of the apostolic "Necessity is laid upon me."

At length a flagrant abuse confronts him in his ordinary work. Among his duties was that of confessor. In the year 1517 Tetzel, Chief Commissioner of Indulgences for Germany, under the Cardinal-Archbishop of Mayence, set up his establishment at Jüterbok, a few miles from Wittenberg; and Luther, who had already begun to feel an aversion to the system of indulgences, became fully alive to its enormity when some persons, coming to the confessional, claiming from him, as priest, unconditional absolution for their sins, and being refused the Church's forgiveness except after promise of amendment, at once produced Tetzel's paper bearing the authority of the Pope. According to the terms of this document they had received the remission of all penalties for sin, including the pains of purgatory, and had been re-established in the purity of the first hour of their baptism.

The chief means by which this writing had been obtained was the payment of a sum of money. It was the custom of the Commissioner to enter the town, which from time to time he fixed as his head-quarters, in a grand procession, with the Papal brief carried in front on cloth of gold. Before the altar a large red cross, on which hung a silk banner bearing the Papal arms, was set up; and before this cross was placed a great iron chest, to hold the money. Before the money could be received, confession had to be made, and contrition felt. But it was frequently arranged that confession should be made wholesale, while the contrition deemed satisfactory was of the vaguest kind. The chief stress was laid on the giving of the money; all else was practically lost sight of in regard to the living, while the tinkling of the coin in the box was declared to achieve the instantaneous deliverance of the dead from purgatory. All the bad features of this system were rendered doubly bad through its management by a man like Tetzel, a vulgar and shameless braggart, distinguished by incredible effrontery and license of speech. With stentorian voice and brazen audacity he recommended his wares, in the style of an auctioneer or a quack, urging the people not to lose such a splendid opportunity of buying their salvation. In Tetzel's appeals we have the loudest and most unblushing contradiction to the language of the New Testament and the ancient prophets, which offers the gifts of God without money and without price.

These indulgences were no new thing in the Church; and it is important to get a clear understanding of what they mean, for in them Luther's whole controversy with the Church is illustrated, and brought to a focus. As the subject was discussed in all its bearings, and when he found that his theses, instead of being approved by the Pope, as calling attention to the gross mismanagement in the administration of indulgences, were condemned, he was led to re-consider the whole question of Christian doctrine and authority. Little more than three years had elapsed when the same hand which fixed the theses on the church door committed the Pope's bull to the flames.

We must remember, then, that the effect of an indulgence was supposed to extend to the temporal punishment of sin, whether in this world or the next, that is, all punishment till the day of judgment, which had still to be borne after its eternal punishment was remitted. This temporal punishment was twofold, consisting, on the one hand, of penances imposed by the Church, and, on the other hand, of the chastisements laid, especially in the future life, on the sinner by God, notwithstanding the forgiveness of the guilt of his sin. Now it was these penances and chastisements which in early centuries the Church, and in later times especially the Pope, had claimed the power of remitting. There is no doubt that the existence of such a claim finds its explanation in the overwhelming sense of sin which dominated the mind of the early Church, together with a partial obscuration of the meaning and value of Christ's atonement. The effect of that atonement was practically more and more confined to the eternal aspect of sin—the removal of its guilt and of its remote penalty in the eternal future; while as to its temporal aspect there was, under the management of the Church, what can be called nothing less than a copy or imitation, on the scale of human merit, of the supreme work of the Saviour. It was granted that

Christ's sacrifice was an absolute and complete atonement for the guilt and eternal punishment of sin; but these severe penances, which were imposed originally on those who had committed great offences, were regarded as having an expiatory effect for the temporal penalty.

The burden was too great to be borne. Accordingly, relaxations were gradually introduced. At first these were bestowed at the request of the martyrs and confessors, whose superabundant merit was held to have a vicarious value, and who were in the habit of granting letters of commendation on behalf of those who were undergoing penance, whose penalty was on this ground remitted to them. Certain good works, however, were still imposed on the penitent before he was restored to the communion of the Church, partly as a test of sincerity, and partly for the reason that the merits of the martyrs were not regarded as an absolute equivalent for the whole temporal penalty. In subsequent times these good works were commuted for contributions of money towards some religious object, such as the building of a church. The danger of such a system is unmistakeable; and it had reached its grossest development in the time of Luther. The full-blown theory then was, that the Pope had authority over an inexhaustible treasure consisting of the merits of Christ and the supererogatory works of the saints, and that he could dispense this treasure for the benefit of those who were willing to give money for so good a purpose as the building of St. Peter's Church. In the case of the living this contribution was to be made by each individual; while in regard to the souls in purgatory, it could be made by others on their behalf.

No doubt it may be said that in the original conception of indulgences, as thus historically traced, there is nothing inherently ignoble, or necessarily of a corrupting tendency; and the practice may be idealized by sophistical reasoning. But it rested upon an absolute fiction. There is no such treasure of martyrs and saints; and such a conception of Christ's work as the theory involved is entirely without foundation. Cardinal Cajetan, before whom Luther appeared at Augsburg, maintained that "one drop of the blood of Christ being sufficient to redeem the whole human race, the remaining part was left as a legacy to the Church, and might be distributed by indulgences from the Roman pontiff." It is obvious that on such a fantastic principle of the interpretation of Christian facts as this, any doctrine whatever might be framed. Moreover, it was practically inevitable that a system which made the remission of sins and the assurance of peace with God obtainable, in however refined and indirect a way, by means of money, should become an encouragement, rather than a preventive, of sin. The refinements of subtle thought, especially when founded on an ecclesiastical figment, were lost sight of, and the bare result, stripped of all disguise, amounted to this, that a tax, according to a graduated scale, was levied on sins, which thus became luxuries which all might enjoy who could afford to pay for them.

With Tetzel's proceedings there was a widespread dissatisfaction, and the matter had become a public scandal. No one, however, dared to raise a voice in opposition to what was going on, for excommunication had been threatened against all who obstructed the indulgences. But Luther's conscience was set on flame. And when the matter is brought home to his own responsibility as a pastor of souls, he feels that he must do what he can to drive these vile and profane traffickers in sin out of the temple of God; he will beat a hole in Tetzel's drum. And so he appears with his remarkable theses, which were the trumpet-blast to waken Europe to a new life.

Yet it is remarkable how cautious and conservative Luther is in this celebrated protest. He does not even commit himself to maintain any of the propositions; but according to a custom of the age, which allowed the utmost latitude in public discussion, he simply offers them as matters to be inquired into, in order that the truth on each point may be reached. Moreover, if we regard each of the theses as expressing Luther's own opinion, what he retains is almost as remarkable as what he rejects. He upholds the validity of the Papal pardon, although at the same time he says that the Pope has no power to remit sin except in declaring it to have been remitted by God. What he protests against is the abuse of the Pope's commission by those who sold the indulgences. All through he appeals from the Pope's agents to the Pope himself. He denies that there is any such thing as purgatorial penance imposed by the Church, although he believes in the existence of purgatory; so that, since the Pope can remit no penalties except those which he has himself imposed, indulgences have no value for the dead. He declares further that every Christian who feels true repentance has a full absolution from punishment and guilt, even without letters of pardon (Thesis 36). And, although the remission imparted by the Pope is not to be despised (Thesis 38), although he even goes the length of saying that God never remits any man's guilt without at the same time subjecting him to the authority of His representative, the priest (Thesis 7); yet he affirms that works of mercy, and even necessary household expenses, are far more acceptable to God than the buying of pardons (Thesis 45, 46). The indulgence, therefore, being not commanded (Thesis 47), seems to become a spiritual luxury which it is allowable to possess only after the more important duties of life and religion have been performed. He protests against the "errors" and "dreams" of those who preached the pardons, and declares that if the Pope were acquainted with what they did, he would prefer that the basilica of St. Peter should be burnt to ashes rather than that it should be built up with the skin, flesh, and bones of his sheep (Thesis 50). The practical and distinct result of the whole document is, that the true treasure of the Church is the gospel of the glory and grace of God (Thesis 62); that true repentance, which is life-long and is not to be confounded with outward penance, obtains a plenary remission; and that it is better to give to the poor, or to provide for common necessities, than to purchase an indulgence.

Although some of the propositions seem, and perhaps were meant, to be contradictory, although much of the old error is bound up with the new truth, yet such statements as those last quoted, when received by the popular mind, could not but have the effect of paralyzing the whole system; and no long time elapsed before Luther himself saw that the stroke which he had aimed against the abuses of the indulgence went much further than he had thought of, gathering momentum as it travelled. The impulse which enabled him to write the ninety-five theses carried him onward to the denial of many things which are enshrined in them as undoubted truth, and the affirmation of many other things which left the controversy concerning them far in the distance. But the study of their phraseology and meaning will always possess a living interest. In their contents we behold together, the darkness and the light, phantoms and facts. The ghosts that were vanishing at day-dawn strangely mingle with the shapes of the great world of truth and reality. These theses form the rubicon between the mediæval and the modern world; and the master-spirit who takes us across them, became the hero, mightier than Cæsar, who, by the grace of God, conquered for us the wide and glorious realm of Christian freedom and faith.

The effect produced in Germany was instantaneous and profound. The public conscience, which had been juggled, was satisfied by this utterance of truth and soberness. The matter was at first treated lightly by the Pope; but at the Roman court there never seems to have been the slightest idea of giving a favourable reply to the obscure monk's appeal. When at last Leo roused himself to see the true state of the case, one effort after another was made to dislodge him from the position he had taken up, but with the result only of convincing him more entirely that he was right. At Augsburg, where, in Cardinal Cajetan, he encountered the calm impassiveness of authority which would accept nothing short of a simple retraction, he appeals from the Pope ill-informed to the Pope better-informed. And when a bull sanctioning the whole doctrine and practice of indulgences was published in December,

1518, he had already appealed to a Council. At Altenburg, in the interview with Miltitz, he parries the kindly but keen diplomacy which sought to win him to submission. At Leipzig he engages in a public Latin disputation of nine days' duration with Dr. Eck, who seems to have been, what Tetzel was in a lower rank, a clever but shallow and blatant quibbler. While, at Augsburg, he had set the Scriptures above the Pope, he now strenuously denied that the primacy of the Pope was of divine appointment; and in declaring that four of Hus's propositions, condemned at Constance, were perfectly orthodox, he virtually asserted that Councils might err. At each stage the scales dropped from his eyes, one error after another was put aside: and although for a time he saw men as trees, walking, yet his position became more and more clear to himself, and he rapidly attained to a complete understanding of the truths, both negative and positive, which were henceforth written deep on the heart of the new movement.

At length the rent in the unity of past ages became an outward fact. But it was the doing, not of Luther, but of the Pope and his Roman advisers, who would allow no place to the work of purification within the limits of the unbroken Church. A bull published on the 16th of June, 1520, rejected forty-one of Luther's propositions, sentenced his books to be burnt, and declared him excommunicated if he did not recant within sixty days. And the Reformer, having been thus cast out from the Church, at length himself took the final step, after which no return was possible. At nine o'clock on a winter morning, at a spot outside the east gate of Wittenberg, still marked by an oak tree, he, with his own hands, cast the Papal bull into a blazing pile, kindled by one of the Masters of Arts, in sight of a great crowd from the University and the town. It was the boldest act of his life—one of the boldest acts ever done by man; and he who was capable of it was fitted to be the leader of his country and of Europe into a new era.

These years, till the close of his stay at the Wartburg in 1522, were the most fruitful period of Luther's life. During their course he produced his three great Reformation treatises, his first Commentary on the Epistle to the Galatians, and his translation of the New Testament. Yet, although he thus steadily advanced, it is interesting and touching to notice with what hesitation the great mind turns away from the institutions and thoughts of the past. There are moments when he seems almost willing to stop. He promises to Miltitz that he will be silent, and let the affair, as he says, "bleed itself to death." He writes letters to the Pope in which, though declaring his inability to retract, he uses expressions of profound humility and respect. And, in his subsequent opposition to the iconoclastic proceedings of Carlstadt, he shows himself fearful of laying a rude hand on any of the old usages of worship. While Carlstadt and the more thorough-going party held that everything should be abolished which was not commanded in Scripture, Luther laid down the principle that everything might be retained which was not directly contrary to Scripture. With regard, indeed, to these earlier pauses and indications of a spirit of submission to the Church and the Pope, he has been accused of dissimulation; his inconsistencies of language have even been interpreted as part of a deep scheme for outwitting Italian policy, and proving that a rude German could meet Roman *finesse* with its own weapons. And it has been too much the fashion for Luther's biographers to represent him as possessing from the first an unwavering consciousness and full-orbed conception of the work he had to do. We believe such a view to be the very opposite of a correct interpretation of the facts; for it is in entire contradiction to the essentially and manifestly progressive character of Luther's mind. His new creed was as far as possible from emerging, like Minerva from the brain of Jupiter, perfect and complete. For a long period it was continually growing and expanding, and receiving new elements. His expressions of attachment to the old system of belief and practice are not irony, but the marks of a sincere mind in a state of transition. And, as the poet tells how the winding Tweed turns and turns again, as loath to leave the lands through which its waters have flowed: so, as we watch the course of the great Reformer's thought, while we behold it broadening and deepening, now flowing majestically, and now hurrying forward, and now letting itself break into a foaming cataract, we see also the yearning regret, the turnings of a noble reluctance, which are precious to us as indications that we have here the procedure and career not of a reckless enthusiast, blinded to the excellence of what he was leaving, but of a reasonable man, slow to change, willing to yield to the ancient authority, if that be possible, and only moving onward by the irresistible power of the truth of God.

It was during this period that he brought into full and definite statement the doctrine of Justification by Faith. What is the meaning of this great principle which in modern times has been identified with the Reformation? and how far was the expression given to it by Luther satisfactory?

It may be said that religion lies in a connection between the seen and the unseen, between that which is material, temporal, bodily, and that which is moral, eternal, spiritual, between the human and the divine. And the truest realization of religion consists in the complete subordination of the lower element to the higher. When God is supreme, and man is the obedient creature, the holy child, of God, when the material is made the perfect instrument of the spiritual, when the human is the image of the divine, there is an attainment of the ideal condition, which was the purpose of creation. Now in religion, as in all lesser departments of human interest, one of the most widely-spread tendencies has been to make the material, in some of its manifold forms, encroach upon the spiritual: so that the lower becomes first the principal organ of, and then a substitute for, the higher. A memorable and beautiful expression of this tendency has been preserved for us in Greek mythology, in which the divine and spiritual world is a copy and reflection of the natural. And for all worship and religious life there is a right relation between the two, a relation which is recognized in the Christian Sacraments and means of grace. But the history of Christianity proves how great a danger there is that the spiritual shall not be allowed its due and supreme place. In the system of the mediaeval Church—that system whose greatest representative is Gregory VII.— we see the fullest endeavour which has ever been made to realize man's highest life by the direct means and instrumentality of what is outward, sensuous, material. By the theory of ordination which brought into existence a distinct class of men gifted with mysterious supernatural power, together with the theory of the *opus operatum* in the administration of the rites of the Church, grace and holiness became unspiritual and external. The sacrifice of the mass attached an extraordinary importance to an outward act of man, through which both the living and the dead were supposed to be benefited. A like fictitious value was given to innumerable ceremonies and penances. Good works, even in the barest form, and almost apart from the motive, were held to possess an absolute merit. The character of God was obscured, the significance of Christ's salvation defaced, by the worship of saints and the introduction of a thousand mediating influences, which largely undid in men's practical experience what had been accomplished by the incarnation and the atonement. Images and relics were holy things. The worship of the congregation was conducted by the priest in a dead language.

The climax and culmination of this system was reached in the extreme development of indulgences. Further than this it was impossible for the materializing process to go. One of its highest expressions was the episode of the Crusades, in which the whole enthusiasm of the Church was concentrated upon an outward object—an object of interest to Christian feeling, but never, during the pure ages, itself a centre of pilgrimage and devotion. But, whether in its higher or its lower forms, the development of this tendency led to a distinct, and often gross, materializing of the spiritual. Practically, in all but the best minds, the higher element was almost altogether superseded by the lower, in regard to every aspect of religious life.

Now, from all this the Saxon Reformer delivered the minds of men. He restored the spiritual, which had been obstructed and oppressed, to its true place in the estimation of the Church. He made inward faith once more the regal, all-controlling principle of the Christian life. When the body crushes the soul, we have, in natural life, the animal nature; in religious life, superstition. This superstition Luther swept away; and the spiritual life, which had been all but smothered, breathed freely again. He made faith, what the New Testament makes it, the beginning and centre of all else, the heart and pulse of the whole body of religion. Nothing need come between the soul and the divine object of its worship. No human nor creaturely mediator—neither priest, nor pope, nor council, nor saint, nor angel, nor weary round of penance, nor long list of meritorious works—shall stand in the way, when man seeks his God. Faith alone is needed—the believing of the heart, the clinging of the soul.

This was in itself a far-reaching reformation. The true value of faith, however, depends on what its object is. In those ceremonies and rites, those continual masses and penances, there was the distorted perception and the stammering utterance of a grand truth—a truth which was sometimes dimly prefigured in heathen religions, but has been in a complete and unique way revealed through the gospel—the truth, namely, that God must *do something on behalf of sinful man*, if the purpose of man's being is to be reached. The idea latent in all the sacramental and ceremonial acts, unspiritual as they were, was that God produced some effect, for the benefit of the worshippers, which was independent of all qualifications on their part, except the external act of submission or reverence; and further, that this effect depended on an historical act done by God long before, for all the sacrifices of the mass, fictitious as they really were, would have been valueless apart from the first sacrifice offered on Calvary. And the Roman doctrine may be described as a compromise between the human, sensuous, materializing tendency and the truth that a work of absolute grace and atonement has been accomplished by God on our behalf. It is the element of sin which so frightfully complicates the problem of the relation between the spiritual and the natural. Both instinct and experience teach that the only effectual way of dealing with sin is, that God shall forgive it—that he shall put it away and implant within us a new nature, a holy character. The utmost which the popular system, prevailing at the commencement of the sixteenth century, attained, was a mere fragment or caricature of this truth. But it is this which, according to Luther, is the object of faith—the word of God declaring that this has been done in Christ. The sole object of faith is the merit and righteousness and mediation of Christ, and this so accepted as to be distinguishable in thought, yet really inseparable from a holy life, as its consequence. The sinner is justified by the act of God for Christ's sake; and the faith which receives this justifying act is not a barren thing, it produces right action. Thus the doctrine, as stated by Luther, is twofold. In virtue of the faith which is commanded we draw near to God, free from all interposing obstacles whatsoever—whether our sins themselves, or supposed means of our own for putting them away; while, on the other hand, there is the still more important truth, that God has already drawn near to us in Christ, for whose sake He is willing at once to absolve us from guilt, and give us power to be good and to do good.

Luther's doctrine has been charged with Antinomianism, and his faith has been accused of being indistinguishable from a mere abstract confidence. It cannot be denied that he occasionally uses exaggerated and paradoxical language. He sometimes speaks contemptuously of the law; and, in many passages, he seems to exalt trust in Christ's merits and the divine forgiveness to a solitary and giddy pinnacle of elevation. The very fact of his well-known depreciation of the Epistle of James,—a depreciation which is, however, less than it is often supposed to be,—is an indication of a shrinking consciousness that his conception did not absolutely square with the whole language of the New Testament. But there is overwhelming evidence, in the rest of his writings, that such language is to be explained as due to the reaction from Roman materialism, and to the enthusiastic desire to hold up in undimmed splendour of illumination the truth which had been so long concealed. The momentary, incidental exaggeration was amply corrected by the whole mass of the reformer's teaching. Faith, he calls "a living, busy, active, mighty thing," and declares that " it is as impossible to separate works from faith as heat from fire." The great sentence which he places in the fore-front of his treatise " Concerning Christian

Liberty"—" a Christian man is the most free lord of all, and subject to none: a Christian man is the most dutiful servant of all, and subject to everyone ;" as well as that inscribed on the bronze pedestal of his statue at Worms—" Faith is but the right and true life in God," indicates that his real doctrine did not halt in a one-sided failure to give their due place to good works as the necessary fruits, and unfailing evidences, of a true faith. And just as the amusing practical errors respecting quantity and magnitude which are recorded of the author of the " Principia," do not disprove his mathematical genius or discredit the law of gravitation, but indeed were rather due to the very perfectness of his mathematical conceptions ; so these expressions of Luther, when fairly interpreted and when due allowance is made for the exigencies of the immense controversy in which he was engaged, do not invalidate the moral perfection of his doctrine ; nor do they carry in them the least design to loosen the indissoluble link which in all true religious teaching must ever bind together belief and practice, the inward and the outward, the faith which justifies and the works which are the body and right hand of the justified life.

Another objection made to Luther's statement is the too subjective character he gives to faith. At times he fails to distinguish it from assurance. Moreover, his relation to the Word of God seems to be made too dependent on his own interpretation of that Word, as is shown in his language about several books of the Canon, and in the unreasoning tenacity with which he clung to his own rendering of the Eucharistic words. We must acknowledge that there is some truth in this charge. It is interesting to notice how Luther's original grasp of justification by faith was a thing individual and personal—so much so that for years the idea never occurred to him that it involved a reconstruction of the whole of Christian doctrine. And even when he was able to give it an independent dogmatic form, there was a tendency to make the subjective phase predominate.

In Luther's character the contemplative, self-introspective side was always very strong. This is observable in his intensely realistic conception of sin. Probably few men have apprehended with such extraordinary vividness the idea of temptation. The tempter was a continual presence to him. Yet it is unquestionable that many of his statements on this subject, though having in them an element of reality, as giving expression to his belief in a personal power of evil, were in great measure simply the reflections of his own state of mind. The same subjective bias is observable, though not to the same extent, in his language with regard to justification. "Be in any way sure that you are saved, and you are saved; only feel yourself safe, and you are certainly safe." Nothing short of this absolute assurance, this exercise of simple confidence, is, he implies, of any real avail. The emphasis was practically laid on the inward feeling rather than on the absolute and divine object, on the subjective, and not the objective, element in justification. This is the weak side of much of Luther's language. And under such a representation the spiritual life was too apt, as was proved by some of the social phenomena of the new movement, to "sink, like a sea-weed, into whence it rose." However, it is in Luther but an occasional and passing phase of exaggeration. It was perhaps unavoidable in one who had just escaped from the abyss of unreality, in which assurance was attached to what was little more than an external bodily act; while the antidote was contained in the Reformer's own complete and sober doctrine.

One other remark may be made on this subject. Luther, taking the ceremonial observances, with which he had been so familiar, as the type of all works, frequently appears oblivious of the fact that there may be in some works a spiritual element, a something which is pleasing to God and is akin to faith, even apart from or previous to the great act of confidence, in which the whole word and work of Christ is accepted. Just as, in a subsequent controversy, to those who asserted that there is nothing in the knowledge of the intellect which is not already contained in the knowledge of the senses, Leibnitz added by way of reply—" Except the intellect itself." So, when it is said that there is no spiritual justifying element or instrument in works, this is quite true in regard to the works as such, and in regard to human merit; it is quite true, except in so far as it can be shown that some works are complex things, and contain in them faith itself. It is a fact of spiritual experience that a single act of obedience to Christ, one good work done as the commandment of God, may be the very occasion and birthplace of faith in the soul, or at least may be attended by the faint stirring of the great principle. Within the outer shell of the actual good work there may be that which makes the whole acceptable to God for Christ's sake. The earnest performance of a new duty is often a channel in which begins to run the thin, thread-like stream of a higher trust and devotion. Good habits may be, in the order of Providence and of Grace, practically the provocatives and suggesters of faith, themselves already possessing something of its secret essence. There are acts which are anticipatory or prophetic of faith, and have in them a latent virtue and a light reflected from its coming glory. It is quite true that, as Luther says, "Good works never make a good man; but a pious, good man does good works." Yet good works may have a provisional, educative value, and may contain the minute germ implanted by the Divine Spirit, which, if unchecked, subsequently becomes a fully-developed trust in the whole person and work of Christ. There is a Light that lighteth every man, and a Spirit who worketh in all.

It is this aspect of the subject which is not sufficiently allowed for in many of Luther's statements, and especially in his frequently extreme language against the law. A perception of this fact would have prevented Augustine from going far beyond the language of St. Paul in his description of the good works of the heathen as *splendida peccata*, and would have saved Luther from making his polemic against works occasionally short-sighted. Too absolutely he made faith a thing of explicit consciousness, and complete acquaintance with the whole doctrine, depriving of spiritual value every good act which did not come up to this standard, and putting it beyond the pale of acceptance with God. He makes what is the best condition of religious life to be the only true one. No work, however, which is anything more than a mere external observance, is to be despised, for it may contain within itself, though in a dim and crude way, the root of a living faith. Faith alone justifies, on the ground of the perfect merit and righteousness of Christ; but a "work," besides being the distinct result of faith, may be, consciously or unconsciously, a means and organ for its manifestation.

Luther, however, was called not only to words, but to deeds. In the spring of 1521, when he is in the thirty-eighth year of his age, he is cited to appear before the Diet at Worms. Although he lay under the ban of the Papal excommunication, a safe-conduct was sent from the Emperor, and an Imperial herald, in coat-of-arms, rode in front of him on the long and memorable journey. Hus's fate is before his eyes; but, notwithstanding the dissuasion of friend and of foe, he goes calmly on, speaking here and there grand utterances of courage, which have ever since been household words, and trumpet-calls to self-sacrificing duty. Leaving his home on the 2nd of April, in a carriage provided by the magistrates, at ten o'clock on the morning of the 16th of April he enters Worms. It is probable that as he came within sight of the towers and tiled roofs of the ancient city, he formed the idea of his great hymn, the "Marseillaise," as it has been called, of the Reformation, though the whole hymn was not published till nine years afterwards. We see him surrounded by the eager crowds, who throng to meet him when his appearance has been signalled by the sentinel stationed in the Cathedral tower. We see the poor miner's son, the excommunicated monk, thin and pale, with the marks still upon him of an illness with which he had been seized during his journey, appear on the evening of the next day, amid the glory of a bright sunset, before the august assembly, which represented the highest spiritual and temporal power on earth—Emperor, and princes, and nobles, nuncio, and cardinals, and bishops, knowing that among them he had a few who were friendly, but well aware that most were coldly indifferent, or bitterly hostile. We see him agitated and nervous, seeming to hesitate, asking a day's respite to consider his answer. We overhear the wonderful words of prayer, fragments of which have been preserved for us, which broke from his lips when, left alone in the silent night, he wrestled with God and was bowed down in a great agony, in listening to which we seem to enter the holy place of a human soul, where it has immediate access to the Most High. On the next evening he made a noble speech, first in Latin and then in German, worthy of the great occasion, to the delight and admiration of his friends, in which he modestly but firmly refused to retract, unless he were refuted from Holy Scripture. When further pressed, his reply was—"Here I stand: I can do no otherwise: God help me. Amen"— words which have been ever since one of the grand texts of religious liberty, and a very fountain-head of quickening influence for devotion to truth and for all the noblest life of man. They were spoken amid the lights and shadows that flickered in the great hall of the bishop's palace, for the April evening was now well-advanced, and torches had been lighted. The noble speaker is conducted to his lodging amid the congratulations of his friends and the scornful hisses of the Emperor's Spanish attendants. He feels all the gladness of victory, stretching out his hands when he arrives at the house, and joyfully exclaiming—"I am through, I am through." Had Luther yielded then, the new movement would have been incalculably weakened. The period was one of crisis; and his highest praise is that in this Thermopylæ of the Reformation, himself more than the Leonidas of the momentous struggle, he stood steadfast, defending the new-won realm of a purified Christianity, and bidding humble but sublime defiance to the gathered might of Church and Empire.

If the Reformer's life rises at Worms into epical grandeur, his concealment at the Wartburg, amid its scenes of sylvan beauty, is one of the romances of religious history. Indeed, if the record were to stop here, we do not know where a grander or more perfect life could be found. It was, of course, marked by human infirmity; but, after this allowance has been made, there is almost nothing to dim the moral admiration we feel regarding it. Most of the things that we would wish away come afterwards. They are of comparatively slight importance, and only one of them can be referred to in this lecture with any fulness.

Though the ban of the empire was pronounced against him after his departure from Worms, so powerful was now the influence in his favour, that it remained a dead letter; and after his return to Wittenberg, he continued to work unmolested. His task was laboriously to build up a new system of Church life and doctrine, and to this his whole strength was devoted amid the countless difficulties and hindrances created by the very principle of private judgment which he had so successfully asserted. He was grieved beyond measure to see the new cause compromised by what seemed to him the too sudden and radical changes advocated by Carlstadt (towards whom he acted somewhat overbearingly), and especially by the excesses of the Anabaptists and of the Peasants' War. With regard to the latter, he at first took up the attitude of peacemaker, rebuking the lords and urging the peasants to desist from violence. But when the insurrection had become a terrible fact, and the subversion of all authority was threatened, he pressed the nobles to adopt the severest measures, though, as he afterwards explained, he had spoken not against the conquered, but only against those engaged in actual rebellion. It was in many respects an iron time in which Luther lived; and something of its hardness, perhaps, entered on this occasion into his feelings.

In 1525 he was married to Catherine von Bora, a young lady of noble family, who, having escaped from the convent in which she was placed at nine years of age, had taken refuge at Wittenberg. One of the motives of this marriage undoubtedly was to break, by so decisive an act as the union of a monk and a nun, the hard and evil yoke which the Church had so long laid on her ministers; and the result of it was to set again the happy home close to the very heart of the highest religious life.

The burning question referred to in his controversy with Erasmus has now become, to a large extent, an extinct volcano, at least in the form in which it presented itself to Luther and Erasmus alike. In the dispute, each combatant aims formidable blows which strike the air; and probably Luther's bondage of the will is as little contradicted by Erasmus's freedom, as St. Paul's faith is contradicted by St. James's works. Throughout this passage of his history, Luther shows in several ways to disadvantage, although the strong moral motive by which he was animated raises him far above his gifted opponent.

That which in the Reformer's conduct we would most desire to see blotted out, is the advice he gave in regard to the matter of the Landgrave of Hesse. The most that can be said is, that it was an honest error of judgment, and that Luther, by the way in which he subjected the whole matter to the test of Scripture, supplied the corrective of the mistake he made.

In his doctrine concerning the Lord's Supper, the excellences, peculiarities, and defects of Luther's type of Christian thought are strikingly concentrated. We see here the new element of the Reformation truth brought into union with other parts of his theological experience—his Scholasticism, his Mysticism, his surviving Roman doctrine—and formed into a strange amalgam; while as to his personal advocacy of his own view, his warmest admirers can but deplore with amazement the narrow and uncharitable disposition he showed.

His procedure in regard to the whole mediæval doctrine of the Eucharist was, in the first place, destructive. That tendency to substitute the material and the human for the spiritual and the divine, to which reference has already been made, may be expressed by saying, that in ecclesiastical history it is a tendency to substitute the Church for Christ, to put tradition, to a greater or less extent, in the place of Revelation. Perhaps the most stupendous example of this is to be found in the almost total inversion of thought which gradually took place in regard to the Lord's Supper. Its purely sacramental function was largely obscured by the new sacrificial character given to it. Instead of being looked on as something coming from God to man, as a means of grace in which Christ's blessings and presence were brought to His people, it came to be actually regarded as something brought to God by man, as nothing less than a propitiatory offering from man to God. The Sacrament became the Mass, and every mass was supposed to be a veritable renewal of the sacrifice on the Cross. Although, doubtless, it was held that Christ offered Himself anew by the hands of His minister, the priest, yet practically it was the Church, in the priest, which had the power, at will, of repeating the one supreme act of atonement which had been accomplished in the death of the Saviour, the object of this repetition being the direct application of its efficacy to the whole body of the people, as well as to individual souls, whether living or dead. Thus, in the most directly gross and material way, the value of Christ's sacrifice was supposed to be appropriated. The deepest cause of this distortion of Christian doctrine was the strong conviction of sin, which was compelled to seek in this strange way the satisfaction for which it craved, because it was prevented by other causes from understanding adequately the absolute worth, and eternal spiritual significance, of Christ's atonement; but it was all the more firmly upheld, since payment for masses, especially masses said for the benefit of the souls in purgatory, was the source of an immense revenue to the Church.

This utter mistake and abuse Luther swept away. To the place occupied by the mass he restored the truth which it had so largely concealed. He set the one supreme sacrifice in its true position of solitary grandeur and sufficiency; so that every other propitiatory offering was felt to be worse than useless.

The Lord's Supper was thus seen to be a means of grace provided by Christ for the Church. Its sacrificial character being demolished, it became the memorial of the infinite sacrifice; and, thus disencumbered and simplified, it assumed its full value as a true sacrament. Here emerges Luther's second divergence from the Roman doctrine. According to that doctrine the elements of the Eucharist conveyed grace to the communicant in consequence of their consecration by the priest. The chief condition of this sacramental efficacy was intention on the part of the priest; while the actual administration of the sacrament was held to confer grace through an inherent virtue belonging to it. But it was distinctly held that faith was not a necessary qualification on the part of the recipient. Now, it was this qualification which Luther asserted as absolutely necessary. Without a living faith the sacrament was inoperative, no grace was conveyed. He did indeed so far keep to the position of the Roman doctrine as to assert strongly that there was in the Eucharistic elements themselves an inherent power, a virtue which exists independently of faith, a virtue which is conveyed to them by the power of the Word of Christ, and which, he says, belongs to them as truly as the healing virtue resided in Christ before the woman touched the hem of His garment. Indeed, Luther attributes not only to the Sacrament, but to the whole Word of God, a peculiar supernatural virtue, a power which it possesses absolutely in itself, as truly as fire possesses heat. But whether for receiving the power which is in the Word, or the power which is in the Lord's Supper, the only true and beneficial medium of communication on man's part is Faith. The feeling of the communicant, not the consecration by the priest, is the vital human element of the sacramental act. Faith, then, here, as everywhere else in the relation between Christian doctrine and Christian life, delivers men from a hard, unspiritual, material relation to divine truth, and is the open secret whereby possession is obtained of all the riches of God's grace. And thus was removed at a stroke, by the one mighty principle, all that world of superstitious feeling which in the great majority of cases, and in the average popular mind, made spiritual safety and holiness dependent on the due performance of an external rite.

The question remains, How is the grace of the Lord's Supper conveyed? in what manner does Christ through the Sacrament bring blessing to His people? what distinguishes it as a means of grace from every other means? wherein lies its unique character? The teaching of the Roman Church was that the whole substance of the bread, as well as of the wine, is changed into the body and blood of Christ, nothing of the elements remaining except the "accidents," or appearances. Luther, on the other hand, holds that the body of Christ is present "in, with, and under" the elements. While, however, according to the Roman theory, the change is effected by a direct and ever-repeated miracle, Luther explains the supposed corporeal presence of Christ by means of a peculiar dogma, which he held before making this application of it, and which, though up to that time it had been a mere speculation entertained by some of the Fathers and of the Schoolmen, and not sanctioned by any creed, seemed to him to furnish a philosophical or theological basis for the doctrine of the Real Presence: he said this Presence was due to the ubiquity, or omnipresence, of Christ's body. According to the view embodied in this word the human and divine natures were so united in Christ, that the qualities of the divine nature, and among those qualities ubiquity, were communicated to His body. If, then, Christ was present in the Sacrament, he was so, not only spiritually, but corporeally. In virtue of its ubiquity, the body of Christ was everywhere; and in virtue of the Word of Christ pronounced by a minister of the Church it came into manifestation in the sacramental act, in connection with the bread and the wine, though outwardly indistinguishable from them. And Luther did not shrink from expressing in the strongest possible language the physical reception and oral manducation by all the communicants, believers and unbelievers alike—the partaking with the very mouth of the body of the Saviour. It is precisely at this point that he introduces Faith. The body was present to all. Only, however, to the communicant who had faith did it convey any grace; while, in the case of a communicant who was without faith, its effect was that of spiritual injury and condemnation. Thus in so complete, extraordinary, and memorable a way, in contradiction to ordinary reason and the evidence of the senses, did Faith, according to Luther, prove its unique power.

It seems strange, unless we take into account the varied intellectual and spiritual influences to which he was subjected, that the Reformer, who had so thoroughly emancipated himself in most ways from the materializing tendency of Roman doctrine and worship, should in this particular have adhered so closely and uncompromisingly to the old view. He himself admits that there was a time when he had a leaning to a far simpler view, and would gladly have had it proved to him that there was " nothing but bread and wine in the Supper."

No doubt his doctrine represented powerfully one side of the truth in regard to the Sacrament, a side which it cannot be denied was too much overlooked by Zwingli and his friends; and it was, moreover, quite in accordance with the deep mystical character of Luther's feeling. In the form, however, which it assumes under his treatment, it rests on a hollow basis of assumptions and contradictions. Perhaps it was a recrudescence of Roman dogma in his mind. It may have been a reaction from the too subjective character he was sometimes inclined to give to faith—a reaction from the spirit which was ready to put aside books of Scripture, to a condition of absolute bondage to the letter of Scripture. Or perhaps the strange and unalterable attraction it possessed for him lay in the secret intellectual and spiritual delight which he had in subjecting everything to the great spiritual principle he had asserted, and in being conscious of this most signal triumph of Faith over, as he said to Zwingli, "reason, common sense, carnal arguments, and mathematics." Faith which justifies the soul, which makes the Word of God itself operative, which is the impulse and guarantee of all works, finally accomplishes even this,—that the believer receives into himself the real body and presence of the Saviour. However, whatever be the psychological explanation, the marked and specific importance he assigns to believing goes far to rob such a doctrine of its power for injury. Conceived unspiritually, as in the Roman system, its inevitable tendency is to deaden the inward life; but depending for its practical value and operation altogether on Faith, it escapes the heaviest part of the condemnation under which any development of superstitious thought and feeling must lie.

The matter was the subject of a famous discussion held at the castle of Marburg in the autumn of 1529, on the urgent invitation of the Landgrave of Hesse. Luther and Zwingli, with their friends, met face to face under the sumptuous hospitality of the Landgrave, who was anxious to see the schism which was dividing the Reformation healed. Zwingli had on this point gone to the furthest extreme from the German Reformer, holding the Lord's Supper to be no more, or little more, than a simply commemorative rite; although, at the same time, he was exceedingly desirous to approximate, as far as possible, to the other view, and to aid in framing a harmonious statement which might form a meeting ground for both parties. Luther consented to come very unwillingly, having no hope of any good result.

The scene of the conference was a large apartment in the castle, and it was held in presence of the Landgrave and a considerable assemblage of nobles and theologians. The four theologians who conducted the debate sat together at a table. Before the speaking commenced, Luther took a piece of chalk and wrote in large letters on the velvet cloth which covered the table, the words of institution, "This is my body:" and during the whole conference he always returned to the absolutely literal interpretation of these words. Œcolampadius and Zwingli urged the figurative meaning of the verb in other passages, and the significance of such a text as, "The flesh profiteth nothing;" but the German Reformer exclaimed, "'This is my body.' To seek to understand it is to fall away from the faith. God speaks: men, worms, listen. Let us fall down, and humbly kiss the Word:" and kept laying his finger on the chalked text before him. Zwingli, appealing to the article of the creed, "He ascended into heaven," urged that, since it is against the nature of a body to be in several places at once, Christ's body, which is in heaven, cannot be in the bread. To this Luther's reply was that Christ's body was not in the bread *as in a place*. When, however, Œcolampadius wished to take advantage of this admission, and to look for a link of agreement in an inquiry as to the nature of Christ's *non-local* bodily presence in the Sacrament, Luther, seeing the design, exclaimed, "You shall not take me a step further;" and seizing the velvet table-cover, he held it up, with the chalked words, in the face of his opponents. "I abandon you to God's judgment," he said, "and pray that He will enlighten you." Zwingli, deeply affected, burst into tears.

At this point, on the evening of the second day, the news was brought that the fearful epidemic called the sweating sickness, which was desolating Germany, had broken out in the town; and this hastened the breaking-up of the conference, though it was practically terminated already. On the following day Zwingli held out the hand of brotherhood to Luther, who rejected it, saying repeatedly, "You have a different spirit from ours:" and his friends concurred with him in declaring that they could not receive the Swiss as brethren in Christ, or as belonging to the communion of the Christian Church. At last, Luther was induced to offer "the hand of peace and charity," which did not, however, imply a recognition of Christian brotherhood: and all the members of the opposing parties shook hands. Before they separated fifteen Articles were drawn up by Luther and signed by the theologians, which affirmed agreement in doctrine to exist in all points except the corporeal Presence. This point of difference is confined to the second part of the fifteenth Article, which also contains a recommendation that the two parties should show Christian charity to each other "as far as conscience permits." This, however, was but a momentary relenting on Luther's part, and he soon afterwards gave evidence, in different ways, that he recoiled from the mild statement of the doctrine in the Marburg Articles, as well as from the kindly spirit they inculcated.

In regard to the doctrine itself of which he was the champion at this conference, the imperious dogmatism with which he defended it, and, especially, the cold and unbrotherly spirit he showed towards his antagonists, Luther appears in a very unfavourable light. However, although we are compelled deeply to regret the position he took up, nevertheless—remembering that there was a sharp contention even between apostles—remembering that a greater man than Luther, the leader out of an earlier bondage, was provoked at the waters of strife and spake unadvisedly with his lips—remembering that God gives not all His gifts, either of fortune or of grace, to any one of His servants—remembering that there is some ground for believing a report that he said to Melancthon long afterwards, "Dear Philip, I confess to have gone too far in the affair of the Sacrament"—remembering that the highest charity is that which thinks charitably of the uncharitable—we can surely be generous to forgive, for his intolerance on this occasion, the representative of a system which treats its adversaries with, at worst, hard words and cold looks, and which, historically, has delivered Europe from the terrible sway of that other system whose unfailing arguments were the prison, the rack, and the stake.

Thus in mingled light and shadow, amid polemical warfare, and with the care upon him of all the Churches, amid private joys and sorrows, amid frequent journeyings and the severe attacks of disease, Luther's life passed on till, "spent, worn, weary," as he describes himself, with his hair white and having lost the sight of one of his eyes, he reached his sixty-third year. The end came while he was on a visit, at the close of an inclement winter, to his native town of Eisleben; and he was buried in the Castle Church of Wittenberg, on the doors of which he had nailed his theses twenty-eight years before.

As we look back over his wonderful life, we catch sight of him, almost at every turn, in some scene which touches our imagination or our heart. We see him lying on the floor of the cell at Erfurt, and restored from his death-like swoon by the sweet voices of the choristers; facing the venomous Eck, in the great hall of the Pleissenburg, with a bouquet of flowers in his hand; to Serra Longa's sneering question, "Where, then, do you mean to take refuge?" replying with untroubled serenity, "Under heaven;" at his "Patmos," the Wartburg, laboriously translating the New Testament; at Coburg, writing gaily about the diet of the rooks, who flapped their wings, and sent their mandates through the air, in front of his windows. We see him kneeling beside his little daughter Lena, as, at fourteen years of age, she lay on her death-bed, and writing afterwards in a letter, "Although my wife and I ought only to thank God for her happy departure, yet so strong is natural love that we cannot bear it without a bitter sense of death in ourselves. So deeply printed on our hearts are her ways, her words, her gestures, when she was with us and when she was leaving us, that even Christ's death cannot drive away this agony." We see him rise from his dinner-table, which was usually well-furnished with guests, and touch, with skilful hand, his favourite lute, or take part with the others in song or hymn. We see him watching the games of his children, and walking with Catherine under the starlight in his garden. We see him in the full flow of conversation, grave or humorous—for he was the Doctor Johnson of his time, and was attended by a whole army of Boswells. We see him now bursting into merriment, now weighed down with melancholy—a deep vein of which lay in his character; now enjoying to the full the innocent pleasures of life, and now engaged in stern, quaintly-expressed conflict with Satan. We see him with his portly presence—though in his earlier years, and even when he was at Leipzig and at Worms, his body was thin and wasted; with his face slightly upturned, according to his habit, and bearing in its expression a mingled pathos and kindliness and calm; with his deep, dark eyes, which "sparkled like stars." According to the testimony of his contemporaries, his voice was clear and melodious, his conversation was agreeable and witty, he was never at a loss, and had the art of pleasantly adapting himself to every-one in whose company he happened to be.

He had his failings, and does not belong to that prim, self-conscious type of character which is "faultily faultless." In his greatest violence, and seeming coarseness, of language, there are no doubt pure flashes of that righteous indignation which has found its highest expression in the denunciations of the book of Psalms and our Saviour's rebukes, yet the smoke often mingles thickly with the flame. When we hear him say that "he wrote best when he was angry," we regret the want of a more judicial tone in the great Reformer's writings, even when we make allowance for such a saying as the mere hasty half-truth of conversation. His perceptions of truth were intuitive and penetrating, but often lacking in breadth; while he saw one principle with extraordinary vividness, and though his character was broad and many-sided, he not seldom failed to discern some aspect which was necessary to a complete view. Yet these and other defects are nothing more than the small dust of the balance, when we estimate the influence of his character and his work.

Under Luther, as quickened and guided by the Divine Spirit, there took place a regeneration of religious thought and life, a new beginning of Christianity, the liberation of the human mind from the shackles of man's authority. He breathed into the awakened intellect of Europe a spirit of religion, and did more than anyone else to prevent the revival of letters from becoming, as it seemed only too ready to become, a new paganism. He, largely without assistance, translated the Bible, being thus in himself a Tyndale and company of Translators, united. He brought forth again into fullest light and life the great doctrine which had so long lain crushed under mountains of untruth, though, like the buried giant Enceladus, it had at intervals made the incumbent mass shake above it. He stood at Worms, in the face of Europe, the very embodiment and impersonation of the Christian conscience. In his marriage and home he broke down that middle wall of partition which had been built up in the name of the holiest religion between man and woman.

In his principle of the universal priesthood of Christians—a priesthood conferred, as he held, in baptism—he closed that wide and unnatural gulf which made an absolute separation of the clergy from the laity. In his famous hymn he sang the battle-song of his Church and of his country. Adorning with a grace all his own the least thing he touched, he wrote to his little boy, Hans, what an eminent historian has called " perhaps the prettiest letter ever addressed by a father to a child." In addition to these varied achievements, he formed the German language; he was a voluminous letter-writer; he was almost ceaselessly engaged in composing books, which, as he says, "rained, hailed, and snowed" from his pen. He was a professor, a pastor, a great orator. He was thus not one man, but many men; his life-work resembling his own river Elbe, close to whose waters at Wittenberg he lived during so many years, which, in its long progress from the mountains to the sea, pays toll to near a score of different governments, through whose territories its vessels pass.

The Reformer was a patriot, and, in a sense as full as would be true concerning any similar assertion of the influence of an individual upon a nation, it may be said that Luther is Germany, his influence an enduring impulse in the German Church, as it has been a powerful prompting towards a united empire. Yet he was a true patriot, because he was much more, a religious leader, being at once the Wallace and the Knox of his country. While, further, notwithstanding his intensely national character, more than any other of the Reformers of the sixteenth century, he has commanded the sympathies of other peoples, and given his name to be the common inheritance of all the Churches. That name, not Graecized, like those of many of his contemporaries, but remaining the simple German, has become for everyone a very synonym for freedom and for faith.

Through all, and in addition to all, he has shown us a noble type of character, which, as it is distinguished by the possession, in fullest measure, of spiritual genius, so it was thoroughly honest—honest with itself, honest with every question of moral and theological truth, honest with opponents; which, as it was deeply religious, was also simple and natural; as it was learned in Scripture, so could find delight in nature, and recreation, and amusement; as it was heroic, was at the same time gentle, and pitiful, and playful; as it was capable of great self-assertion, was so because it was still more deeply capable of great self-surrender, and therefore could be no less modest and humble than it was decided and confident, and was no less characterized by sobriety of judgment and practical discernment than by courage and devotion. There was in him no hard, granite stoicism; his nature, while it was strong, was deeply sympathetic, and, in the full round and sweep of his experience, resembled rather the oak-tree, with its play of varied movement, now standing serene and grand, and now bending to the earth, in seeming weakness almost rent asunder, yet rooted more firmly by the storms which shake it. From the night on which he fixed his destiny by knocking at the door of the Erfurt convent, his life was "a battle and a march." He came onward "like a spectre-ship, sailing right against the wind," yet no spectre, but a divine life, and mighty, spiritual movement. He had a great, in many respects an awful work to do, a work which was largely against the natural bent of his moderate and deeply reverent character, a work which seems easy since it has been successful, yet was essentially the struggle of a minority; this work was given him to do, and he did it. If, as has been said, the three highest titles which can be given to man are those of martyr, hero, saint, there is not one of them which does not of right belong to the great Reformer of the sixteenth century.

It has been remarked that, amid all his journeyings, we never meet with Luther by the sea-side. Yet there is no place, in nature, in which we could more fitly imagine that we see him, than on the border of the great deep, where we think that he might have watched "the children sport upon the shore," and heard "the mighty waters rolling evermore." The ocean, with its unfathomable depths and its sunny ripples, in its loud tempests and the gentle lapse of its wavelets, is a type of Luther's whole spirit and varied disposition. He himself was not only many-sided, but belonged to that class of characters which suggest to us the infinite and the eternal.

We do not call him Master; we do not give to his thoughts the seal of infallibility, or the reverence due only to inspiration: we do not allow even him to stereotype, and fix finally for all ages, the expression of Christian truth. But we feel the almost unexampled greatness of his service to the Church and to the world. He destroyed, but he also built up. He was emphatically a son of thunder, but he was no less really an apostle of love. He looked wistfully on the past, with its thousand years of Roman authority and teaching, but he resolutely put his hand to the plough of the task which belonged to the present and the future. He spoke of an inward invisible faith, yet his life was a giant's labour. He was finely and most loveably human; yet, more than anyone, since the last of the Twelve fell asleep, he has brought God's truth and God's presence near to men.

John Calvin.

THE place deservedly assigned to the commanding personality of Luther in connection with the sixteenth century Reformation should not blind us to the fact that the spiritual movement which bears this name had not one, but several distinct origins. Zwingli in Switzerland, and Lefevre and Farel in France, were already preaching a pure Gospel, ere yet Luther's name had been heard of. It was natural that, once Luther had spoken, his name should overshadow those of pioneers in other countries. The inherent greatness of the man, his open rupture with the Papacy, the conspicuous stage on which he figured—in conflict with Pope, Emperor, and princes—above all, the bold, fresh, original character of his utterances—shaking Europe as with thunder-claps, and rousing men's hearts as by the sound of a trumpet—gave him, in the eyes of Christendom, a representative position in relation to the whole movement. But both in Switzerland and France, notwithstanding Luther's influence, the Reformations retained very much of their indigenous character. Distinct in origin, the streams were kept still further distinct in their after flow by the disputes which early arose between the German and Swiss Reformers on the subject of the Sacraments. Luther had, properly speaking, no successor. At a later period, the Swiss and French Reformations found a point of meeting in John Calvin, who, a Frenchman by birth, and a Swiss in virtue of his world-famous connection with Geneva, fitly represented both.

From another point of view, in France, Switzerland, and Germany alike, the Reformation movement was one. It took its origin in all three countries from the same general causes; it was characterized by the same return to Scripture, as the living fountainhead of truth, in distinction from Papal dogma and the philosophy of the schools; it expressed the same revolt of the human conscience against hierarchical domination, and the superstitions and abuses by which that domination was maintained; it gave the same prominence to the cardinal truths of justification by faith, and the sole mediatorship of Christ. On closer inspection, no doubt, different standpoints reveal themselves. In Germany the personal, in Switzerland the Biblical, element predominates. With Luther, the central point is the certainty of salvation; with Zwingli, the chief place is given to the outward Word. Luther moves among dignitaries and princes; in Switzerland the Reformation is on democratic ground, and Zwingli, with his ardent patriotism and love of freedom, is its appropriate apostle. But in essence, spirit, aim, the movements are one. The unanimity of the Reformers is the more remarkable that, in most cases, their views were reached by independent study of the Scriptures. Even in regard to Predestination, it may be noted that Zwingli and Luther were as strenuous upholders of this doctrine as Calvin himself.

When Calvin entered on his work as Reformer, the first wave of the Reformation movement had already spent itself. Luther's views had taken root not only in large parts of Germany, but in Sweden, Denmark, and the Netherlands, and were rapidly leavening Europe. Most of the Swiss Cantons had embraced the Reformation, but Zwingli had fallen on the fatal field of Cappel. The fervid Farel was evangelizing with singular success in the neighbourhood of Lausanne, Morat, Neuchatel, and Geneva. On the other hand, Francis I. had decided for Catholicism, and Paris was blazing with martyr fires. Politically, Europe was rent with divisions, and distracted with the intrigues of Pope, King, and Emperor. The Reformation itself had let loose fanatical and anarchic tendencies which, at different points, threatened its destruction. The time had clearly come for a new order of man to arise, an equal to Luther in genius, but differently endowed—not an originator, but a consolidator, a thinker and organizer, rather than a man of action—one who, to those gifts of soul which must appear in every great Reformer, and with full devotion to the objects of Reformation, would unite the highest power of intellect, and a rare faculty of construction and systematization—in short, a man capable of being a spiritual leader and adviser of his age, and of recasting in forms that would endure alike the theology and the polity of the Church. Such a man was Calvin—the subject of our present lecture—and this, as we shall see, was the nature of the service he rendered to the Reformation.

John Chauvin or Calvin was born at Noyon, in Picardy, on the 10th of July, 1509. He was the second of a family of six—four sons and two daughters. His father, Gerard Chauvin, was Procurator-Fiscal for the county and Secretary to the Bishop of the Diocese. He is described as a man of excellent business capacity, but withal of somewhat severe character. Calvin's mother, on the other hand, is spoken of as a lady not less distinguished for her beauty than her piety. From the former parent the Reformer may have inherited, besides his methodical habits, that gravity of disposition, tinctured with censoriousness, which led even his schoolmates to fasten on him the nick-name of the "Accusative." From the latter he probably derived his fine nervous organization, his delicately chiselled features, his native courtesy of manner, and perhaps, also, that constitutional shyness and timidity which to the end of his life he never wholly overcame. Calvin's boyhood can only be briefly sketched. Thoughtful and grave, the light of a penetrative intellect already shone in those burning eyes of which all his biographers speak, and his gifts could not long be hid. Soon we find him taken under the patronage of the great, and pursuing his studies in company with the children of the noble house of Mommor, the most honourable in the neighbourhood. This intimacy had important results for Calvin, both as imparting to him that air of good-breeding and refinement which never afterwards left him, and as securing for him the advantages of a thoroughly liberal education. How different with Luther, coming from the miner's hut, and fighting his hard battle with poverty by singing on the streets for bread! Meanwhile, Calvin's father was exerting himself to lay the foundation of preferment for a son of so much promise. A chaplaincy had become vacant in Noyon Cathedral. This, through

Gerard's influence, was given to Calvin, then a boy of twelve years of age, a step which necessitated his receiving the tonsure, or shaving of the crown. The transaction startles us, but it was no uncommon one in these times of secularization of sacred things. It may be added that this and other preferments which he received were voluntarily surrendered by Calvin in 1534.

From Noyon, in 1523, Calvin proceeded, still in company with the Mommors, to study in the University of Paris. Here he remained for four years, perfecting himself in Latin under Corderius, and familiarising himself with logic and philosophy. Then his studies took a different turn. Of this change he himself gives the following account in that wonderful piece of autobiography which forms the Preface to his Commentary on the Psalms—" When I was yet a very little boy, my father had destined me for the study of theology. But afterwards, when he considered that the legal profession commonly raised those who followed it to wealth, this prospect induced him suddenly to change his purpose. Thus it came to pass that I was withdrawn from the study of philosophy, and was put to the study of law." Calvin himself does not seem to have been consulted in this step, but, governed in all things by a sense of duty rather than by inclination, he lost no time in giving effect to his father's will. Leaving Paris, he repaired first to Orleans, then to Bourges, where distinguished teachers of jurisprudence were lecturing, and applied himself with incredible industry to his new study. His success may be estimated by the fact that, when yet a youth of nineteen, he was frequently called to conduct the class in the absence or illness of the Professor; and, when leaving Orleans, had bestowed upon him, unsought, the highest honours which the University had to give. At Bourges, in addition to his legal studies, he availed himself of the presence of Wolmar, a German Protestant, to acquire a knowledge of Greek, and thus had opened to him, for the first time, the Scriptures of the New Testament in the tongue in which they were written.

Looking back on this period of training, extending to the death of Calvin's father in 1531,[1] it is not difficult to discern in the direction given to events the secretly guiding hand of Providence, preparing the Reformer for his future work. At Paris, Calvin's mind was brought into contact with the best knowledge of his time. He beheld there the old and the new in conflict. The Sorbonne, watchful of its orthodoxy, might thunder forth its anathemas, but there could be no question with any thoughtful onlooker that the times were big with change. From the throne downwards, a new taste for letters was diffusing itself; the fountains of classic learning were unsealed; the Scriptures were circulating in the vernacular; new opinions were freely discussed; persecution had begun, and martyrs for the truth of Christ were marching grandly to the stake. Calvin profited in this new learning above many his equals. His attenuated frame bore witness to the diligence of his studies. The old Roman literature he devoured with avidity. It formed his taste and style, and he never afterwards lost his love for it. His first work, published in 1532, was a commentary on Seneca's treatise,

[1] The date is fixed by registers in Noyon.

"De Clementia." Cicero's writings he is said to have read through every year till a late period of his life. Calvin's Latinity has often been extolled, but it is not so well known that, through the strength, grace, flexibility, precision, and fire of his compositions, he rendered a service to his native tongue not unlike that which Luther, by his translation of the Bible, rendered to German—in short, became one of the creators of modern French. This power over language, consecrated by him to give weighty and eloquent expression to Christian truth, is doubtless attributable in part to his ripe acquaintance with the Roman classics. Not less valuable as a discipline was Calvin's laborious study of the principles of jurisprudence. The knowledge acquired from his teachers in this department proved of incalculable service to him in his later attempts at devising a satisfactory constitution for Church and State at Geneva.

We come now to the great crisis in our Reformer's life—that which changed him from a devoted adherent of the Romish faith into a not less uncompromising defender of the Reformed doctrines. The steps in this change can only be hurriedly indicated. Calvin's life, from his boyhood, had been marked by a sincere moral aim. His youth was irreproachably pure—so pure as to be a sort of marvel to his gayer and less earnest companions. But his mind at this time was tenaciously wedded to the beliefs in which he had been brought up. "I was obstinately addicted," he tells us," to Papal superstitions." It goes without saying that whatever system of beliefs Calvin adopted, he would adopt it with his whole soul, and would not be readily moved away from it. At Paris, he must have been perfectly aware of the new doctrines that were being taught, but, absorbed in other studies, he probably gave them little attention. Yet the young student was not at peace. His experience during these years resembled that of Saul the Pharisee. His correctness of moral conduct did not satisfy him, and his assiduity in the practices of piety failed to assure him of Divine forgiveness. The law which he strove so faithfully to obey entered into his conscience, and convinced him ever more deeply of sin. Absolutions, penances, intercessions, proved ineffectual for relief. "I tried all these methods," he says,[1] "but without obtaining relief or peace of mind. As often as I looked into myself, or attempted to lift my eyes to Thee, O God, I was filled with a dread which no penances or satisfactions of mine could mitigate. The more narrowly I inspected myself, the deeper did the sting enter into my conscience, so that at last I could find no ease but by steeping my mind in forgetfulness." Considerable influence seems to have been exerted on his mind by his kinsman Olivetan, a disciple of Lefevre's, and future translator of the Bible into French, who directed him to the study of the Scriptures. But it was not till a later period that the light broke, and he was brought, as he expresses it, by "a sudden conversion"[2] to a subdued and teachable frame of mind. This was the decisive turning-point. The idea of the Church occasioned him some difficulty, but only till he was able to distinguish between the Church as a visible society, and the true, invisible Church of Christ, consisting of all

---

[1] In his answer to Cardinal Sadolet.
[2] Preface to Psalms.

faithful souls, whether in communion with the visible society or not.

The precise date of Calvin's conversion is uncertain. Some place it as early as 1529, while Calvin was yet a student of law at Orleans or Bourges; others as late as 1532, after the publication of his first work. It favours the earlier date that we have distinct accounts of his teaching and evangelizing in Bourges and its neighbourhood about this period. But whenever or however the change was brought about, its effects were immediate on the young scholar's plans of life. Earthly distinctions stood awaiting him, but these he was willing to renounce for Christ's sake and the Gospel's. His place henceforward was with the friends of the Reformation, and his powers were to be devoted to the service of the God who had been graciously pleased to reveal His Son in him. Not yet, however, had Calvin any thought of mixing with public affairs, or even of coming forward as a regular preacher. On the contrary, he shrank from such work, and desired only to have opportunity of pursuing his studies in retirement, hoping, perhaps, as Providence might guide, to be able to serve the Reformation with his pen. Man proposes, but God disposes. The retirement which Calvin sought seemed to flee from him. Now we get glimpses of him at Paris, now at Noyon, now at Orleans, now at Angoulême, at the chateau of his friend Du Tillet, now at Poitiers, now again at Paris, but wherever he went, friends sought him out, so that, he says, "All my retreats were like public schools." At Paris he taught, preached, and evangelized, encouraging many who were soon to glorify God by martyrdom. Here, in 1533, an incident occurred which shows that Calvin's name was becoming known. Nicholas Cop, rector of the University, took occasion of an inaugural address to deliver an oration on "Christian Philosophy," which, it turned out afterwards, had been composed for him by Calvin. The boldness of the ideas, and the evangelical character of the sentiments, excited a storm of disapprobation. Cop had to flee, and suspicion falling at once on Calvin, his house was searched, and papers were discovered implicating himself and several of his friends. The Reformer had barely time to make his escape, disguised, it is said, as a vine-dresser. At Orleans, in 1534, he published his first theological work, a treatise entitled "Psychopannychia," directed against the Anabaptist tenet of the sleep of the soul after death. At Poitiers he formed a small congregation, and the Lord's Supper was administered in a cave near the city, known to this day as "Calvin's Grotto." Calvin revisited Paris in 1534, then, still seeking seclusion, betook himself first to Strassburg, afterwards to Basle. Here an event took place which raised him at one stroke to the position of foremost influence among the Reformers. We refer to the publication of the "Institutes of the Christian Religion."

The "Institutes" of Calvin is one of those epoch-making books, like Bacon's "Novum Organum" or Newton's "Principia" in science, or Kant's "Kritik of Pure Reason" in philosophy, the interest of which is enduring. Hitherto no book had appeared which took commanding rank as an exhibition of the doctrines of the Reformed Churches in their systematic unity and connection. Melancthon's "Commonplaces" appeared in 1521, but hardly served the purpose. Yet this was a work necessary to be done, both as a satisfaction to the mind of the Church, and that the Reformation might have something to oppose to the imposing and compact systems of the Middle Ages. Calvin undertook the task, and accomplished it with decisive success.

The motive which led to the composition of the book was, however, anything but a dogmatic one. The "Institutes" have been compared to various works—to Aquinas's "Summa Theologia," to Augustine's "City of God," to those noble "Apologies" presented by the early Christians to the heathen emperors, asking justice for their cause, and vindicating it from the calumnies of their enemies. The last comparison is as true as any. A fresh outbreak of persecution had taken place in France. Calvin's soul was stirred by tidings brought him of holy persons—many of them members of his former flock—burned and tortured for their adherence to the Reformed views. Still more was it stirred to hear them denounced as enemies of civil order. Hitherto he had contemplated nothing higher than the preparation of an elementary manual of doctrine for the instruction of his countrymen. Now his work was to take the grander shape of a vindication of his wronged brethren. He would plead their cause in the ears of Christendom; he would state and defend the doctrines for which they suffered; he would vindicate their principles from the aspersions cast upon them. This being the purpose of the book, we can imagine the spirit that reigns in it. It is anything but a dry compendium of doctrine. Its motive raises it almost to the dignity of a prose poem.

On some points in the theology of the "Institutes" we may remark hereafter; meanwhile it will suffice to give a general idea of its method and contents. The book, as published at Basle in 1536, was a small volume, which subsequent editions enlarged to many times its original size. It was written in Latin, and afterwards translated into French. Prefixed to it is a Preface, addressed to Francis I., which is justly regarded as one of the *chefs d'œuvres* of literature. It is composed in a strain of noble eloquence; reminds the Sovereign of his responsibilities as minister of God; asks him to undertake the investigation of a cause unjustly condemned; and replies to the objections urged against the Reformed doctrines as being new, unsupported by miracles, opposed to the teaching of the Fathers, destructive of the idea of the Church, and provocative of sedition. The additions subsequently made to the body of the work gave it architectural completeness, but wrought no change in its essential contents. The plan is simple, following the order of the Creed. Treating first of the knowledge of God as Creator, Calvin shows that the mind is naturally imbued with this knowledge, yet needs Scripture as a guide and teacher in coming to God as a Creator. Here he investigates the grounds of our confidence in Scripture, passing from this to the consideration of the Triune nature of God, the creation and original condition of man, and the doctrine of Divine Providence. His doctrine of Providence gives equal prominence to the will of God, as the last ground of explanation of all that is, and to human volition as the means by which the purposes of God are carried out. The second book treats of the knowledge of God as Redeemer. This portion of the work discusses the doctrine of the Fall, man's corrupt and enslaved condition through sin, the gradual steps in the revelation of the purpose of salvation, and, finally, the person, offices, and work of

Christ. In the third Book, we proceed to the work of the Holy Spirit. Here Calvin treats of faith and repentence, of gratuitous justification, and the sanctification of the believer, combating Romish errors on each of these subjects. He sketches in beautiful language the life of the Christian man, and towards the close of the Book unfolds his doctrine of eternal election to salvation, with its logical counterpart, the reprobation of the wicked. It ought to be noticed that, however fundamental this doctrine is in Calvin, it is brought in, not at the head of his system—not, *e.g.*, in the place it holds in the Westminster Confession— but rather as a corollary from what has been shown of the dependence on Divine grace of all that is good in man. The last Book treats of the Church, of Church government, of the Sacraments, and of the province of the Civil ruler. It is well known that in his views on the Sacraments, Calvin steers a middle course between the High Church Lutheran view, which affirms baptismal regeneration and a corporeal presence of Christ in the Supper, and the lower view, which would degrade the Sacraments into mere signs. The Sacraments, with Calvin, are connected with a real presence of Christ and a real work of the Spirit, but the presence is spiritual, and the reception of blessing is conditioned by the faith of the recipient. All this may seem familiar enough and trite enough to us, but it was different with the Reformers, to whom the Scriptures had newly been opened, and on whose minds these doctrines had burst with the power of a grand discovery. Now they saw them set in their relation to each other, and expounded and defended with constant appeal to Scripture, by a mind that perhaps had no equal in Europe. They saw this done, moreover, not in the stiff, repellent phraseology of the schools, but in language of surprising force and freshness, largely free from technicalities, and glowing with the fervour of personal conviction. The greatness of the "Institutes" lies in its combination of these two sets of qualities. It is great in constructive power. It took the matter of the Reformed doctrine, and reduced it once for all to coherence—gave it compactness, unity, system. Its grasp is wonderful, especially in those parts where Calvin puts forth his full original strength. Men cavil at Calvin, but it is easier to cavil than to meet the Reformer on his own ground, and solidly refute him. Not less great is the book in the fire, force, and freshness with which its ideas are expressed. Considering that Calvin was at this time but twenty-six years of age, his work must be regarded as one of the most surprising examples in literature of early intellectual maturity.

The toil of these months of seclusion in Basle was not to remain unrewarded. The sensation produced by the publication of the "Institutes" was immense. The book was speedily translated into the languages of Europe, and passed through innumerable editions. As if a meteor had appeared in the sky, men's attention was everywhere arrested by it. Calvin published his work anonymously, but his was a name not easily concealed. Friends felt that a new David had risen to do battle for them with the Philistine, and were correspondingly overjoyed. Enemies wreaked their rage on the book by burning it. As evidence of its popularity we may mention that versions of it exist in modern French, Italian, Spanish,

Dutch, German, English, and even in the language of Hungary, in Greek, and in Arabic. But the effects of the "Institutes" were not confined to Calvin's contemporaries. Its influence on posterity was yet more remarkable. It passed through the creeds into the thoughts of men, moulded the life of nations, became the soul of Puritanism in England, of Republicanism in Holland, of Democratic institutions in America, identifying itself in every land to which it went with the undying principles of civil freedom.

Calvin has published his great work—what shall he do next? Far from him as ever is the thought of entering upon public life. Rather, with the bookish man's love of retirement growing upon him, he is increasingly captivated with the idea of some quiet retreat, where he may pursue his studies uninterruptedly, and use his pen in the interest of the cause for which he had taken it up. Besides, has he not proved his strength in this department of service, and may he not reasonably infer that it is in this way, rather than by a life of action, that the Master, who giveth "to every man his work," intends him to take his part in the battle of the time. Whither shall he go? We find him for a space in Italy, at the Court of the little deformed daughter of Louis XII., Renée, Duchess of Ferrara, whose love of the Gospel forms a bright spot in the dark ambition-stained records of the houses with which she was related. We get a trace of him at Piedmont; we see him recalled to Noyon by the death of his elder brother Charles, an ecclesiastic, but also, alas, a sceptic and a libertine; we find him, ultimately, resolving on return to Basle, that fair city on the Rhine, whose reformed government, flourishing University, busy printing-presses, and learned society, made it so tempting an abode for a man of letters. But again the hand of Destiny seems on our Reformer. Other work is to be found for him than that which he contemplates. Yonder, under the shadow of the Alps, on the banks of Lake Leman, at the junction of its waters with the Rhone, stands a brave, liberty-loving little Republic, whose citizens, having fought and won the battle of their independence, have just opened their gates to the Reformation. This was the place Providence had chosen as a new centre and nursery of the truth, and to it, by circumstances apparently fortuitous, the Reformer's steps were guided. War had broken out between Charles V. and Francis I., and the direct route to Basle through Lorraine was blocked. The agitated condition of the country compelled Calvin to make a long detour, and thus, late in August, 1536, we find him at Geneva. He entered the city, intending to remain only a single night; with the exception of a short interval of banishment, he never afterwards quitted it. Before, however, describing Calvin's connection with Geneva, it will be proper to bestow a glance or two on recent events in the history of the city itself.

From an early period the Genevese people had been distinguished for their love of liberty. Their Bishop was also their ruler, but the constitution was popular. There were ancient franchises and customs, which the Bishop on his accession took an oath to respect. The management of affairs was in the hands of a Council of Twenty-Five, consisting of four Syndics or Magistrates, elected by the people, twenty councillors, and a treasurer. Over this was a Council of Sixty; over this again a Council of Two Hundred; and above all was a General Assembly of the whole body of the citizens. These liberties of the Genevese had not been maintained without a struggle. The neighbouring lords of Savoy, jealous of the independence and covetous of the territories of the little Republic, had long sought to reduce it under their power. They received aid from Pope Martin V., who, in 1513, having deprived the people of the right of electing their own Bishops, nominated to the vacant see a creature of the House of Savoy. The new Bishop made over the temporal sovereignty to the Duke, and a struggle commenced, lasting over twenty years, in which much patriotic blood was spilt. The citizens themselves were divided into two parties—one, the patriotic party, known as the Eidgenossen, and the other, adhering to the Duke, known as the Mamelukes. The fact that in this conflict Pope and Bishop were on the side of the enemies of their liberties, naturally tended to inflame the minds of the Genevese against their ecclesiastical superiors; and the hostility with which they regarded them was increased by the scandalously dissolute lives of all orders of the clergy, and by the refusal of the latter to bear any part of the expenses of the patriotic contest.

This was the state of matters when, in 1532, William Farel, who had been labouring in the neighbourhood, first entered Geneva, preaching the Reformed doctrines. He did not meet with immediate success, but the word took root, and, furthered by the teaching of Anthony Froment, whom Farel, when compelled to withdraw, sent to fill his place, the new ideas made rapid progress. From this point the struggle between liberty and despotism becomes inextricably intertwined with the deeper struggles between Evangelical truth and Popish error and superstition, the Reformers drawing their chief strength from the patriotic party, while the Mamelukes lent their utmost support to the priesthood. The Magistrates, meanwhile, fearful of offending powerful allies, temporized, but the movement was growing with a volume they could not resist. A church was conceded to the Protestant preachers; a disputation, after the usual fashion of the times, was held before the Council, in which the defenders of Rome were worsted; in 1534 the Bishop, having left the city, was deposed by the Council as an enemy of the public peace; finally, in 1536, the worst danger being over, a General Assembly of the people was convened, and the citizens, "lifting up their hands, promised and sware to God that by His help they would live according to the holy Evangelical religion and Word of God lately preached to them, renouncing the mass, idols, images, and every other Papal abuse, and that they would live in union and obedience to justice."[1] Immediate steps were taken to apply the ecclesiastical revenues to purposes consonant with the reformed faith—to the support of an hospital and public school, and to the payment of the preachers.

Thus far had the Reformation advanced in Geneva on that memorable evening when Calvin might have been descried entering its gates. The city was impoverished and disorganized by its long struggle; men's blood was still hot with the spirit of faction; morals, owing to the absence of all effective restraints, the bad example of the great, and the long unsettled

[1] M'Crie's "Early Years of John Calvin," p. 168.

condition of public affairs, were exceedingly corrupt. Not a few had accepted the Gospel from the heart, but the masses had embraced the Reformation more from detestation of the priests and love of change, than from any intelligent understanding of Christian doctrines, or desire for the kind of life to which the Gospel constrains men. There were immense congregations, but there was no proper organization of churches, or provision for exercising church discipline. Laws had been re-enacted against vice and profaneness, but there was no power adequately to enforce these laws. Affairs in the city, in short, were largely in a condition of chaos; a revolution had taken place, but the actors in it had not as yet had time to comprehend what it involved, or what new forms of life it would impose.

Calvin, as we have seen, had not intended to remain in Geneva longer than a single night. Providence, however, had ordained otherwise. His presence, which he had thought to keep secret, was discovered, and reported to Farel, who, feeling deeply his own inability to cope with the elements of disturbance around him, lost no time in waiting on the Reformer, and implored him to come to his assistance. The scene that follows is dramatic in its interest. Calvin, shrinking with his whole soul from the task sought to be forced upon him, made every excuse he could think of. He was a studious man; he did not wish to bind himself to one Church, but would endeavour to serve all; he was timid and loved retirement. But Farel was not to be daunted. With something of the energy of an old Hebrew prophet, he suddenly placed himself before Calvin, and proceeded to pronounce a curse on the studies he held so dear, if they kept him from coming to the help of the Lord against the mighty. "I declare unto thee," he said, "on the part of God, that if thou refuse to labour with us here in God's work, He will curse thee; for in pleading thy studies as an excuse for abandoning us, thou seekest thyself more than God." This "fearful obtestation," Calvin tells us, filled him with such terror that he felt powerless to resist any longer. He recognized that the call of God had come to him, and, laying aside his own preferences, prepared at once to obey. He commenced by permission of the Magistrates to give lectures in theology, and soon afterwards was formally appointed pastor.

Calvin's entrance into Geneva falls exactly midway in his life, and it marks also a natural division in his history. Henceforward we are to see the Reformer in a different light from any in which we have hitherto considered him. He remains as before the man of thought and learning, but it is now to be discovered that the timid, retiring student, anxious only to be left alone with his books, is no less extraordinarily endowed with the faculty of rule, that the genius of organization and control exists in him in as powerful a degree as the genius of dogmatic construction. His labours to attain his ends involved him, as we shall see, in long protracted conflicts, but the principles he fought for ultimately triumphed, and made Geneva the astonishment of Christendom for civil order, administration of justice, pure morals, liberal learning, generous hospitality, and the flourishing state of its arts and industries. We shall best review this period of Calvin's life, interrupted, after about two years, by a temporary banishment from the city, by considering first, in connection with a sketch of his polity, his conflicts with the Libertine party in Geneva; second, his much misunderstood share in the trial and condemnation of Servetus; and, lastly, the period of the triumph of his principles.

The stormy events of Calvin's earlier residence in Geneva—that which ended in his expulsion from the city—can be briefly narrated. Hardly had he commenced his labours before his reforming activity began to show itself. It went out in the three directions of the Church, education, and the reform of public morals. One of his first tasks was to draw up, in conjunction with Farel, a short Confession of twenty-one articles, to which, after it had been ratified by the Council of Two Hundred, the citizens, in parties of ten each, solemnly gave in their adhesion. This laid the basis of that theocratic constitution which Calvin afterwards toiled so zealously to perfect. At the same time he prepared a short form of discipline. He next directed attention to the schools, and sought to establish throughout the Canton a system of compulsory education. Calvin rightly felt, however, that if the Republic was to be Christian at heart as well as in name, a reform was needed more urgent than any of these—to which these, indeed, were but means—a reform of the manners and morals of the State, and to this, also, he earnestly addressed himself. The agencies which presented themselves for the accomplishment of such reform were three-fold—preaching, exhortation, and reproof in the pulpit; a rigorous enforcement of the laws of the State by the Magistrates; but, above all, the right inherent in the Church of excluding moral offenders from the Lord's table.

Laws were already in force in Geneva when Calvin

entered it, not only forbidding vice, but laying down regulations in regard to dress, food, and ornament, and requiring attendance at the services of public worship; to which, therefore, no objection could be taken on the score of want of strictness. As respects these, Calvin could only use his influence with the Magistrates to put them in execution; but the power of excommunication was with himself, and he did not hesitate to employ it against notorious evil-livers. The Magistrates, however, warmly seconded his efforts. These measures could not be carried out without encountering strong opposition, and a party soon developed itself bitterly hostile to the new regimen. This party received the name of "Libertine," and not unjustly, for obviously the best portion of the community was with Calvin, and the soul of the opposition consisted of men of profligate and abandoned character. Joined with it, however, may have been members of the old patriot party, naturally jealous of Calvin's influence, and resentful of what they regarded as a new attempt to deprive them of their liberties. In course of time, the party of opposition gained an ascendancy in the Council, and then the contest began in earnest. A point of even greater soreness with the malcontents than the rigour of the laws, was the power claimed by Calvin to debar the unworthy persons among them from the Sacrament; but on this point, a vital one for the purity of the Church, the Reformer stood firm, notwithstanding that his conduct exposed him and his associates to the coarsest public insults. The dispute was still proceeding, when a message came from Berne urging the Genevese to restore certain holidays, and to keep the Sacrament with unleavened bread. The Reformers opposed these changes, and immediately the Libertines were inflamed with an eager desire to see the Holy Supper observed without leaven. Matters reached a crisis on Easter Day, 1538. During the previous week, the city had been torn with dissensions, and when the Lord's Day came, the churches were filled with armed and riotous men. Under these circumstances, Farel and Calvin announced that the Lord's Supper would not be dispensed that day. Furious tumults ensued, and the lives of the Reformers were threatened. Next day the Council met, and pronounced sentence of banishment on the two preachers. Calvin received the decision with calmness, remarking, "Had we been the servants of men, we would now be ill repaid; but we serve a great Master, who never lets those who serve Him go unrewarded, and who even pays them what He does not owe them." Then, in company with Farel, he left the city.

His disputes with the Libertines were not his only troubles during this residence in Geneva. He had early to oppose the Anabaptists, whose extravagant opinions tended to subvert Church and State alike. Specially was he annoyed by the attacks made on him by one Caroli, who impeached his orthodoxy, and even had him brought before a synod to clear himself of the charge of Arianism. It is curious to see Calvin—hard dogmatist as we are apt to think him—called to account for not using the terms "Trinity" and "Person" in his teachings on the Godhead, and having to defend himself for his preference for simple Scriptural expressions. When blamed by Caroli for not accepting the ancient creeds, he "rejoined," say[1] the Genevese preach-

---
[1] In a letter to Berne.

ers, "that we had sworn to the belief in one God, and not to the creed of Athanasius, whose symbol a true Church would never have admitted."

The next three years of the Reformer's life were spent tranquilly at Strassburg in ministering to a congregation of French refugees. Save for interruptions of bodily sickness—the effects of toil and anxiety upon a frame not naturally strong—these quiet years of exile were perhaps the happiest Calvin ever knew. He did not indeed permit himself repose. He preached, lectured, wrote incessantly. But the labour was congenial. Here, in 1539, he revised and recast his "Institutes," giving the book substantially its present form. Here also, in the same year, he issued from the press his Commentary on the Epistle to the Romans—the first of that noble series of Commentaries which, in their sober regard for the historical and grammatical sense of Scripture, in their skill in detecting and aptness in expressing the meaning of the sacred writers, and, generally, in their depth and penetration—bear so remarkably modern a character, and are to the present day aids in the interpretation of Scripture which no exegete can afford to despise. The Emperor Charles V. was at this time engaged in schemes of mediation between Protestants and Romanists, and Calvin went as delegate to several conferences in Germany, where he made the acquaintance of Melancthon, and of other leaders of the German Reformation. A yet more tender interest attaches to this sojourn in Strassburg. It was here that Calvin married. The lady who won his affections was Idelette de Bure, a widow, distinguished for discretion, virtue, piety, and a cultivation and elevation of mind which made her a fit helpmate for the Reformer.

The union lasted for but nine years. Idelette seems to have been devoted to her husband's interests. "She was," says Calvin, "the best of companions, who, if anything harder could have happened to me, would willingly have been my companion, not only in exile and in want, but in death itself."[1] Calvin, on his part, cherished for his wife not only high esteem, but tender love. His letters show that her death in 1549 left him well-nigh inconsolable. The fruit of the union was one son, who died in infancy.

What, meanwhile, of Geneva? Bitterly by this time had it repented of its treatment of the preachers. Only disorder had reigned since their departure. The citizens had had a taste of Libertine rule, and did not relish it. Laws were set at nought. The grossest licentiousness prevailed. Of the four Syndics who expelled Calvin, one "was found guilty of promoting an insurrection, and endeavouring to escape through a window, fell and broke his neck. Another was accused of murder, and beheaded. Two others, guilty of treason, were obliged to flee."[2] No power existed in the city itself capable of restoring order, and soon the cry arose to bring Calvin back.

The Reformer, however, had too vivid a recollection of his Genevan experiences to be easily persuaded to return. "Why not rather submit to be crucified?" he says in one of his letters, "It would be better to perish at once than to be tormented to death in that chamber of torture." At length he consented, and re-entered Geneva on the 13th September, 1541, amidst general popular enthusiasm. The magistrates provided him with a house and garden, gave

---

[1] Letter to Viret, 1549. [2] Beza.

him cloth for a coat, and settled on him a salary of 500 florins, twelve measures of wheat, and two tuns of wine. His conflicts were not over—the worst, indeed, lay before him—but for the moment he was in honour. The next five years of his life might be described as peaceful, but for a dispute with Castellio, tutor of his school, whom Calvin, for some acrimonious attacks made on him in public, had removed from his office.

The time had now come for a complete remodelling of the constitution of Church and State in Geneva, and before proceeding further, some account must be given of the new polity thus introduced. It may seem a bold thing to say, but we think it true, that the logical consequence of Calvin's principles would be the entire separation of Church and State. Civil and spiritual government he holds to be distinct. However friendly may be the relations of the two powers, however freely they may co-operate in matters of common interest, they yet represent distinct jurisdictions, each has its own responsibility, and neither is subject to the control of the other. The spiritual is not at liberty to control the civil, and as little is the civil entitled to control the spiritual. This perfect independence of the two jurisdictions can only be secured by keeping them apart. Even granting to Calvin that the Magistrate should profess the Christian religion, and that his care extends to both tables of the law, the conclusion based on the distinctness of the jurisdictions is not affected. The more numerous the points which the jurisdictions touch in common, the greater the need that each should be left free to act on its own responsibility. Calvin, however, did not thus conceive of his principles in practice. Starting from the duty of the Magistrate to put himself at the head of a work of Reformation, and from the consent of the citizens to the articles of the Christian faith, he thinks he finds a basis for a Christian Republic—a theocracy. The model constitution figures itself to his mind as one in which the two powers do not remain apart, but are united for mutual support, and for the attainment of common ends.

Constructing the Genevan Republic under this idea, Calvin began with the Church. The city was divided into parishes, and a minister was alloted to each; elders were appointed; rules of Church government were drawn up; order was introduced into the services, including a liturgy, and congregational singing. In the civil department, Calvin undertook the revision of the laws. Under his superintendence, the laws and edicts of the State were collected, such changes were made on them as was necessary, and the whole was reduced to a well-digested code.

But in a theocracy, Church and State are so far identified that the whole body of the people are by profession Christians—the two jurisdictions apply to the same body of people. Accordingly, the third part of Calvin's work, and that by which he is best known, was the drawing up of a code for the joint use of the civil and ecclesiastical authorities in those matters which, on the theocratic principle, came under the cognizance of both. This code—the famous "Ecclesiastical Ordinances"—was properly a code of morals. It laid down rules for the regulation of the life of the citizens of Geneva, entering minutely into social, and even domestic details, but specially aiming at the suppression of the darker vices—profanity, drinking, gaming, lewdness, and the like. On the ecclesiastical side, it was a code of discipline. As such, it was administered by the Consistory, a court composed of ministers and elders, which sat weekly to hear and to dispose of cases. If ecclesiastical discipline did not produce amendment, the case was reported to the Council, which dealt with the offence as against civil order, and punished it accordingly. The laymen—twelve in number—who sat in the Consistory, were chosen from the Councils, and formed the link between the two jurisdictions.

This polity of Calvin's has been the subject of much animadversion. It is no easy matter to do it justice. Viewing it theoretically, it is obviously not without grave faults. Its fundamental idea—that of making Christian profession the basis of civil privilege—modern society justly rejects as incompatible with the full recognition of the rights of conscience. On the other hand, the idea of *theocracy*—of a fair Divine order in society, of an earthly state organized in all respects in obedience to, and in perfect harmony with, the Divine will, of a kingdom of God among men, is surely in itself a noble one, a conception which human society cannot forego, but must ever keep before it as its goal. Yet Calvin errs in the shape he gives to his conception. Two jurisdictions are recognized, but their spheres are not kept distinct. The civil ruler is invested with functions which do not properly belong to him. The Church invites his aid in matters with which he has no right to interfere.

Viewing it as a practically working system, the Genevan polity is not less open to criticism. It undeniably went too far in interference with individual liberty, and tended to confound the follies of society with its vices. When, however, we find fault with its details, it is important to remember that the *laissez-faire* doctrine of government is essentially a modern one, and that sumptuary laws were not peculiar to Geneva.[1] It is to be pointed out, further, that most of the provisions of the "Ordinances" were based on existing enactments. "It can be shown," says Dr. Hagenbach, "that strict prohibitions against cursing and blaspheming, against games of chance, masquerades, dances, magnificence in dress, &c., had been issued by the Geneva Government as early as the fifteenth and the beginning of the sixteenth century, and that Calvin, consequently, cannot be regarded as the originator of such laws."[2] Calvin drafted the code, but the Councils revised and amended it, and, says the above-quoted writer, "It has been proved that not only in political affairs, but even in ecclesiastical matters, the civil authorities of Geneva insisted jealously upon their rights, and reserved to themselves the prerogative of final decision; and that there were not lacking instances when their opinions conflicted

---

[1] "Sumptuary laws were in great favour in the legislation of England from the time of Edward III. down to the Reformation. Statute 10, Edward III. . . . . enacts that no man, of whatever condition or estate, shall be allowed more than two courses at dinner or supper, or more than two kinds of food in each course, except on the principal festivals of the year, when three courses at the utmost are to be allowed. All who did not enjoy a free estate of £100 per annum were prohibited from wearing fur, skins, or silk, and the use of foreign cloth was allowed to the Royal Family alone."—Chambers's Encyclopædia, Art. "Sumptuary Laws." See also Hallam's "History of Europe during the Middle Ages," chap. ix.

[2] "Hist. of the Reformation," vol ii. p. 313 (Eng. trans).

with those of the Consistory."[1] Calvin, therefore, cannot fairly be held responsible for everything the code contains. Valuing it mainly as an instrument in repressing vice, there is no evidence that he attached much importance to its pettier details.

The code, once enacted, was administered with wholesale rigour. The highest families in the Republic were required to yield obedience to it, or if they did not, were summoned before the Consistory. This rigour had its reprehensible, but it had also its salutary side. A system is best judged of by its moral fruits, and Calvin's need not shrink the application of this test. The moral state of Geneva was such that drastic treatment was necessary. The Consistory had a sufficiently high idea of its functions; both Consistory and Council occasionally erred in the severity of punishments meted out to small offences;[2] but the effect of their work was to recover Geneva out of the hands of a lawless and flagitious faction, whose vices were destroying it, and to raise it to the first rank in Europe as a city of pure morals, of enlightenment, peace, and order.

Libertinism reared its head again in Geneva in 1546, this time in darker colours than before. It now appeared in connection with Pantheistic and Atheistic doctrines, breathing a fierce hatred of Christ, and openly justifying the most shameless immorality.

---

[1] "Hist. of the Reformation," p. 323.

[2] It is worth observing that the instances commonly quoted of excessive severity in the punishment of minor offences mostly belong to a period subsequent to Calvin's death. A boy, for example, was beheaded for striking his parents in 1568. Yet the Genevan code fairly enough reflects Calvin's severely judicial spirit.

"The Libertines or 'Spirituals,'" says Dr. Philip Schaff, "combined a Pantheistic creed with licentiousness and free-lovism, and anticipated the worst forms of modern infidelity to the extent of declaring the Gospel a tissue of lies of less value than Æsop's Fables."[1] This party, with which the ribaldry of the city speedily associated itself, found a leader in Amy Perrin, the Captain-General, a former friend of Calvin's, but now, on account of some proceedings taken against his wife's relations, the Reformer's bitterest enemy. Perrin demanded that the Council should deprive the Consistory of its power of excommunication, and assume the power into its own hands. He was not at first successful, but in 1549, his party having gained in numbers and influence, he was elected First Syndic, and the old conflict was renewed. Calvin behaved with great courage. He presented himself in 1547 before the Council of the Two Hundred, and facing the drawn swords of his enemies, said, "If it is my life you desire, I am ready to die. If it is my banishment you wish, I shall exile myself. If you desire once more to save Geneva without the Gospel, you can try." This ended the matter for the time.

A second crisis in the struggle was in 1553. Calvin's influence in this year was at its lowest ebb. Popular feeling ran strongly against him. His enemies, insolent in their triumph, "resorted to personal indignities and every device of intimidation; they named the very dogs of the street after him; they one night fired fifty shots before his bed-chamber; they threatened him in the pulpit."[2] At this juncture,

---

[1] "History of the Creeds of Christendom," p. 471.
[2] Ibid., p. 471.

one Berthelier appeared before the Council, asking it to rescind a sentence of excommunication passed upon him by the Consistory. Calvin withstood him, but Perrin's influence prevailed, and the Council reversed the sentence as desired. It went further, and transferred the power of excommunicating from the Consistory to itself. This decision was ratified in the popular assembly. The next Sabbath was the day of Communion in St. Peter's. Curiosity was strung to its highest pitch, for Berthelier was expected to present himself, bearing the warrant he had received from the Council. Calvin, however, was resolute. When the moment arrived to dispense the sacred elements, and the Libertines made a move forward as if to seize the bread and cup, he covered the symbols with his hands and cried, "You may break these limbs and shed my blood; I would rather die than dishonour the table of my God." His opponents were awed, and retreated in silence. The service was then quietly proceeded with.

The final conflict was in 1555. The spiritual supremacy had by this time been restored to the Consistory. But the enemies were untiring in their opposition. So far at length did their rage carry them, that a tavern-house plot was formed for the massacre of refugees resident in the city. The plot failed, and its authors were brought to justice. Four persons were beheaded, Perrin had to flee, others were banished. From this period Geneva had rest.

Thus ended the conflict with the Libertines. In justice to Calvin's enemies, it should be remembered how unbearably galling it must have been to freer spirits in the Republic—many of them belonging to old native families, and accustomed to hold their heads high among the citizens—to find themselves suddenly stopped in a career of pleasure, and put under Calvin's hard moral yoke—forbidden the wine-shop, the card-table, the revel, rigorously limited in dress and manner of living, compelled to attend sermons in which their vices were unsparingly castigated, and required, on pain of humiliation, to yield unquestioning obedience to the dictates of a Consistory. They saw, as they thought, a new Popedom established in their midst; they found themselves put under a yoke more rigorous than that from which they had escaped; they rebelled that they, the children of the soil, should be subjected to this hateful tyranny by an alien; they beheld the city filling up with refugees, and they clamoured that the native influence was being illegitimately swamped. Flesh and blood would not be what it is if such rule had been endured in quietness. Nor is it wonderful that the Magistrates were jealous of a power which they saw growing up in the State rivalling their own, which they thought bore hardly on the life of the people, and which kept them embroiled with leading citizens. We will not dispute that the influence of the Council on the Consistory was on the whole a moderating one. Yet it must be repeated that Calvin's discipline proved wholesome for Geneva.[1] It was no Popedom, but rule in accordance with a Constitution which had been established by the free votes of the citizens, and which, it must be said for them, amidst all the heat of their disputes, they never seem to have desired to alter.

[1] Hooker somewhere says, "This device I see not how the best then living could have bettered, if we consider duly what the existent state of the Genevese did then require."

Passing by other controversies of this period, as those with Pighius and Bolsec, both on the subject of Predestination, and other labours, as those for the union of the Swiss Churches, we come without further delay to that episode in Calvin's life which more than any other has left a stain of reproach upon his memory; we refer to the episode of the trial and burning of Servetus. Of this mournful transaction—so impossible to justify at the bar of the modern conscience—we shall endeavour to speak impartially, not screening Calvin from the share he actually took in it, but at the same time endeavouring to show that this share has popularly been very much exaggerated.

To his own age Servetus was a monster and blasphemer; we may be permitted to give a calmer account of him. He was a Spanish physician, who, in 1531, had published a work against the Trinity, and, again, in 1553, had printed clandestinely a book entitled "Christianismi Restitutio," in which he further developed his views of a perfectly reformed Christianity.[1] He was a man of undoubted talent and accomplishment. His genius, however, was erratic, his mind restless and speculative, and his manner of dealing with Divine things daring and irreverent.

It is not easy in short compass to give a coherent account of his doctrines. They were of a very crude order. With a denial of the distinction of persons in the Godhead, and consequently of the eternity of Christ's Sonship, he seems to have combined Pan-

---

[1] He was born in the same year as Calvin (1509), and, like Calvin, had studied both theology and law.

theistic notions of the relation of God to the universe. One passage-at-arms between him and Calvin in the trial at Geneva will serve to illustrate the character of his views, as well as give an example of the levity of his manner of treating sacred subjects. "When he asserted," says Calvin, " that all creatures were produced from the proper essence of God, and that therefore all were filled with gods, I was so hurt by this wretched absurdity that I assailed him with these words— 'What, unhappy man! if anyone treading on this floor should say to you that he was treading your God under his feet, would you not be scandalized at such an assertion?' He answered, 'I, on the contrary, do not doubt but that this footstool, or anything else which you may point out, is the substance of God.' When it was again objected to him, 'Then will the devil actually be God?' he answered, with a peal of laughter, 'And can you doubt it? This, however, is my general principle, that out of the substance of God all things have arisen, and that the nature of things is actually the Spirit of God.'"[1]

Sentiments like these, in Calvin's day, were not only regarded with abhorrence, but by both Protestants and Catholics were held to be justly punishable by the sword of the Magistrate. In separating from the Church of Rome, the Reformers had no idea of challenging the principle of that Church, that heresies ought to be restrained and suppressed by the civil power. They upheld that principle. Their own defence, when the secular sword was unsheathed against them, was not that the Magistrate ought not to punish error, but this, that what they taught was

[1] Henry's "Life and Times of Calvin," vol. ii. p. 196.

not error, but manifest truth. They appeared before their judges ready to support their doctrine by appeal to the Scriptures. If what they taught was error, by all means let the civil ruler correct them for their error, but if it could be shown to be truth according to God's Word, they ought not, they held, to be made to suffer for it. In two ways only this principle of Rome was modified. First, mere opinion was not to be punished, but only the active diffusion and dissemination of errors; and second, forbearance was to be shown to minor aberrations. But attacks on œcumenical doctrines, such as those of Servetus, were supposed to be beyond all bounds of toleration. "The more we reflect on it," said the Church of Berne, speaking of the errors of Bolsec, "the more we are convinced that it is not necessary to proceed with too much severity against those who are in error, lest in seeking at all hazards to maintain purity of doctrine, we come short of the measure of the Spirit of Christ." Yet this same Church, when consulted two years later about the heresy of Servetus, replied, "In effect he has reckoned himself free to call in question all the essential points of our religion, wholly to overthrow it by new explanations, and utterly to corrupt it by reviving the poison of the ancient heretics. We pray the Lord that he may give you a spirit of prudence and counsel and strength, that you may put your own and other Churches beyond reach of this pest; and that in the meantime you may do nothing which might appear unseemly in a Christian Magistrate."[1] The one charge that can be brought against Calvin is, that, sharing this all but universal opinion of his age, he

[1] Quoted by Rilliet, Henry, &c.

did not hesitate, with the consistency of a logical mind, to give effect to it.[1]

The connection of Servetus with Calvin began as early as 1534. Calvin was then at Paris. A meeting was arranged for, but Servetus did not keep his appointment. In 1546, he sent to Calvin the manuscript of his "Christianismi Restitutio." The Reformer gave him his opinion of the writing, and in reply to an expressed wish of Servetus to come to Geneva, very plainly hinted to him that if he did, he would not be responsible for his safety.[2] In 1553, he was apprehended at Vienne, and would have suffered death at the hands of the Roman Catholic authorities of that place, but for a timely escape from prison. Servetus always regarded Calvin as the cause of this arrest. The accusation, however, has no further truth in it than that the real accuser, one De Trie, a French refugee, residing at Geneva, succeeded, after much pressure, in obtaining from Calvin certain documents incriminating Servetus, and establishing his identity with the author of the "Restitutio."[3]

This leads to the remark that, deeply as we deplore

[1] Calvin was not in spirit a persecutor. This is shown by his friendly relations with Lælius Socinus, and others of free-thinking tendencies, in whom he thought he discerned an earnest disposition for the truth.

[2] He wrote to Farel at this time, "If he come, I shall not suffer him to depart alive, as far as my influence can avail." To Servetus himself he wrote, "I neither hate you nor despise you, nor do I wish to persecute you; but I would be hard as iron when I behold you insulting sound doctrine with such audacity."

[3] "I must, however, plainly confess to you that I have had great trouble in obtaining from Mr. Calvin what I now send you. . . . But I so wore him with my importunities, showing that the charge of levity would be cast upon me if I had not his help, that at last he yielded, and gave me what you see."—De Trie's letter in forwarding the documents.

the fate of Servetus, unjustly as we think him to have been treated, he is not a man for whose character it is possible to feel much respect. At Vienne his career was one of long-continued dissimulation. In his trial in that city, he did not hesitate to avail himself of the weapons of falsehood—palming off upon his judges false statements in regard to almost every particular in his history. At Geneva, the same arts of deception were resorted to. He was plausible or defiant, humble or insulting in turns, according as he thought it would best serve his purpose. A man of this stamp, whatever other qualities there may be about him to interest us, is without genuine moral backbone; he may win our sympathy, but cannot command our esteem.

Servetus escaped from Vienne in April, and came to Geneva in August. Why, of all places on earth, he should have come to this one, it is difficult to conjecture, unless he had the hope of finding friends among the enemies of Calvin. It was the year 1553, when the conflict with the Libertines was at its height, and Calvin's influence was at its lowest point. The Council was hostile to him. It was during the trial of Servetus that those events occurred which we have already described—the reversal of the sentence of excommunication on Berthelier, the stripping of the Consistory of its power of debarring from the Lord's Supper, the memorable scene in St. Peter's. Calvin's spirits were so depressed at this time that he sometimes felt as if he could wish to die. On the evening of that day when he made his stand in St. Peter's, he had an affectionate farewell meeting with his flock, expecting fully to be banished on the morrow.

On the other hand, it was the Libertines who stood by Servetus. Their temporary triumphs in the Council nearly turned his head, and led him, confident of victory, to indulge in unmeasured invective against the Reformer, who, warmly aroused, did not spare injurious epithets in reply.

Calvin, hearing of Servetus' arrival, and dreading his influence in the city, had him at once arrested, and, through his secretary, La Fontaine, instituted proceedings against him. The Magistrates, whatever their private sentiments, had no alternative but to investigate the charge. Some days were occupied with preliminary examinations, then La Fontaine and his fellow-pursuers were discharged from their connection with the case, and the trial passed into the hands of the Council, and was conducted by the public prosecutor. We need not recount its different stages. The services of the ministers were sometimes required to cast light on points of doctrine; in particular, Calvin was ordered to extract, and give in, without note or comment, a list of the passages in Servetus' book which he thought objectionable, and to this Servetus replied. But the Council jealously kept the trial in its own hands, and gave attention less to the abstract theological error of Servetus' opinions than to their supposed bearings on the peace and good order of society.[1] Servetus, on his part, showed exceptional adroitness in turning the tables on his accusers, and though he often quibbled and evaded, many of his answers to the charges brought against him were solid and well reasoned. He was specially keen in his attacks on Calvin, against whom he brought counter articles of charge, and whom he

[1] The writings of Servetus were at this time widely circulated.

wished to pursue "till," as he said, "the cause be terminated by the death of him or me."

We hasten to the end. Before finally deciding, the Council resolved to take the opinion of the Swiss Churches on the case, and accordingly sent copies of the documents to the Churches of Berne, Zurich, Schaffhausen, and Basle, requesting their advice. The replies they received were unanimous as to the guilt of Servetus. Nothing remained but to pronounce sentence, and on the 26th October it was decreed that the unhappy man should expiate his errors in the the flames.

Was the verdict challenged ? Yes, one man challenged it—one whose name does not readily occur to us in such a connection—this man was Calvin. Calvin agreed with the Council that the errors of Servetus were such as deserved death, but he shrank with horror from the infliction of a death by burning, and, with his colleagues, did his best to induce the Council to substitute a milder form of execution. The Magistrates would not enter into his views. "It is to him, notwithstanding," as one has said, "that men have always imputed the guilt of that funeral pile which he wished had never been reared."[1]

Servetus was publicly burned on 27th October, 1553. The first announcement of his doom utterly unmanned him, but he afterwards recovered some composure, and died in protracted agony, calling on "Jesus, Son of the Eternal God." It is a mournful spectacle, yet perhaps the pile of Servetus was needed fully to awaken the conscience of Protestantism to the perception of the error of the principle which, in

[1] Rilliet.

inconsistency with its own grand truth that "God alone is Lord of the conscience," it had unthinkingly adopted. Servetus was right in maintaining that a man ought not to be punished for error in his opinions, and his avowal of this principle, however little we may respect himself otherwise, makes him a martyr for liberty of conscience. The shock which men received at seeing this burning pile raised by Protestant hands was itself an indication that there was something wrong, and only a little reflection was needed to discover what it was. To condemn Servetus for opinions arrived at in the exercise of his undoubted right to search the Word of God for himself,—or, generally, his right of thought and inquiry, —was, for Protestants, to go in the teeth of their own claim—to outrage in his person the very principles for which, in their own case, they were nobly contending. The defence, of course, was, "Ours are true views; his are pernicious errors." But this is to overlook that the concession of the right of inquiry involves the right to form an independent judgment on the truth of the matters submitted. It is clearly illogical first to grant a man the right of judging of what is true, then to punish him for the use he makes of it. Nor, pondering the nature of the tribunal before which grave theological questions of the Trinity and Sonship of Christ were debated—a secular tribunal, presided over by Perrin the Libertine, and composed of men all unversed in such subtleties— could thoughtful minds fail to be struck by the absurdity of entrusting to such tribunals the final decision of what was to be held true and false in doctrine. In fine, the stake of Servetus brought better home to men's minds than a hundred arguments could do, the untenableness of the fundamental assumption that it belongs to the civil Magistrate to restrain and punish heresy—showed it to be alien to the Gospel, a confounding of civil and spiritual jurisdictions, inimical to free inquiry, and destructive of rights of conscience.

Calvin's share in this painful transaction can now be fairly appraised. With the later stages of the trial of Servetus he had really little to do. His influence on the final decision was all but *nil*. The Magistrates had taken the matter into their own hands, and Calvin at the time was the object of their distrust. "Their folly and rage have increased to such a degree," we hear him saying, "that all which we state is received with distrust. Were we to say it is light at noon-time, they would immediately begin to doubt it."[1] It was against Calvin's wishes that the Swiss Churches were consulted. It was against his will that Servetus died by fire.

On the other hand, there can be no question that Calvin, in common with most of his age, held that blasphemies such as those of Servetus were punishable by death; that he instituted proceedings against Servetus in Geneva; that he anticipated and desired a capital sentence; and that he held the decision of the Council to be just, though he could not approve of the manner in which death was inflicted. And this, be it owned, is a heavy enough indictment.

Nine years yet remained to Calvin after the expulsion of the Libertines, and this was the period of the triumph of his principles. More than ever, acting on

[1] Letter to Bullinger, 1553.

his conviction that the State has one sphere and the Church another, he withdrew from political business, and devoted himself to spiritual labours. The distrust of him by the Council seems soon to have cleared away, and people and Senate cordially supported him in his efforts. Many tokens exist of the high respect in which Calvin was held in his later years. The work he got through during this period, considering his weak physical constitution, and the numerous maladies which incessantly preyed on him, was enormous. He preached two or three times a week, lectured every third day, presided in the Consistory on Thursdays, and fulfilled the other duties of his pastoral office. His pen was unceasingly busy, writing new books, revising old ones, conducting an extensive correspondence, taking part in the controversies of the time.[1] His abode was in Geneva, but his heart was in the Church of God everywhere. His reputation in Europe was yearly rising. His commentaries and theological writings gained for him renown as an author; among his correspondents were kings, nobles, and persons of highest position in all countries; his advice was sought on matters small and great. His name was a familiar one in courts and conclaves. His letters were prized as literary treasures, as well as for the worth of their contents. Not a Church was in difficulty, hardly a martyr went to the stake, but received from him some message of guidance or consolation.

Under his influence, Geneva became an asylum for the persecuted, and numbers of persons of rank, learn-

[1] Of these the chief were the Sacramentarian controversies with the Lutherans.

ing, and piety, found refuge within its walls, many of whom were admitted to the rights of citizens. One such refugee was John Knox, who resided in Geneva at intervals between 1554 and 1559. He became intimate with Calvin, and throughout life revered him as a father. As the city opened its gates to the distressed, so out of it again, in bands of Evangelical labourers, trained by Calvin, and despatched to spread the Gospel in neighbouring kingdoms, went forth a renewing power on other countries. Specially did he interest himself in the progress of the Church of France, which, from a single congregation in 1556, had, notwithstanding furious persecutions, increased by 1561 to 2150. Calvin had the satisfaction of seeing this Church consolidated, and his polity set up in it in an even purer form than at Geneva. He strongly deprecated the religious wars, telling the leaders that "if they wished to establish their rights by the sword, they would prevent God from helping them." "One single drop of blood," he said, "shed by you will overflow all France."[1]

One work on which Calvin had long set his heart was the founding of an Academy in Geneva, which, uniting the interest of letters with that of religion, would make the city still further a centre of enlightenment. This work, in 1559, he saw accomplished. A building was reared dedicated to learning; Theodore Beza was appointed Rector; and provision was made for instruction in Greek, Latin, Hebrew, philosophy, and even law, in addition to divinity. This institute gave new glory to Geneva. In the train of culture, and pure moral living, came the arts. The city had

[1] Quoted by Henry, vol. ii. p. 409.

trials, but frugality and industry enabled it to surmount these, and it steadily rose to influence. The citizens, too, had learned to trust and honour the man through whom this greatness had come to them—who, to apply the boast of Augustus about Rome, had found their city brick, and left it marble. In the midst of all, Calvin was sometimes very poor. His expenses were great, exercising hospitality, assisting refugees, aiding churches abroad, relieving the necessitous at home, and he had often little left for himself. "That which made the strength of that heretic," said Pius IV., after his death, "was that money was nothing to him."

The time now approached that Calvin should lay down the weapons of his earthly warfare. His body, the seat of many disorders, some of them inflicting on him excruciating agony, was rapidly breaking up. For years, Beza says, he took only one meal a day, and that a very sparing one. Only his indomitable will carried him through the multitudinous labours, from which, in spite of exhausting physical weakness, he could not be persuaded to desist. In 1558, he was prostrated by the quartan-ague, and never afterwards was free from pain. In his sorest anguish he was often heard to murmur, "O Lord, how long!" His last sermon was preached on 6th February, 1564. The delivery of it was interrupted by violent coughing and spitting of blood. After this, he caused himself to be carried on several occasions to Church, and on Easter Day partook for the last time of the Sacrament, joining with trembling voice in the concluding hymn, "Lord, let thy servant depart in peace." On 27th March, he was borne to the Council Chamber, and took an affectionate farewell of the members; and a month later, on 30th April, he received a deputation from the Council in his own chamber, and, solemnly addressing them on their duties, bade them a yet more formal adieu. Two days previously, he had summoned and taken farewell of the ministers of the city. On 19th May, when the ministers met in his house at a common meal, he had himself carried into the chamber where they were, and ate a little food with them, but he had to leave before the meal was concluded. The few days that remained to him were spent almost wholly in prayer. His form was so wasted that it seemed as if only the spirit were left; but his eyes, witnesses tell us, burned with their old lustre till the close. He had made his will in due form, and on 27th May, peacefully breathed his last. Great was the mourning at Geneva, and intense the excitement which the news of his death thrilled through the Christian world. Professors, clergy, citizens, all classes of the population, many of them in tears, followed his dust to its quiet resting-place in the city church-yard. It was Calvin's own wish that he should be buried without pomp, and that no stone should be raised to his memory. The exact spot where he sleeps is accordingly unknown.[1]

The intellectual and moral qualities of the distinguished man who, in the fifty-fifth year of his age, was thus called to his repose, will be sufficiently apparent from the review we have given of the events of his chequered career. Calvin's intellectual and moral build is entirely different from Luther's. The contrast of the two men is seen in their portraits—the one,

[1] A small stone, marked with the simple letters " J.C.," has for about twenty years marked the supposed place of his interment, but the identification is conjectural.

spare, fleshless, thin and refined in feature; the other, sturdy, strong, masculine, almost coarse in face and form. Calvin wants Luther's geniality, his rich, overflowing humour, his human many-sidedness. But he is Luther's equal in unbending loyalty to conscience, and in grandeur of intellect is incontestably his superior. The three powers that appear in him in almost naked severity are intellect, conscience, and will. To a mind calm, lofty, and comprehensive in its views of truth; clear and logical in its processes of thought; endowed with singular penetration into men's characters and motives; and statesmanlike in its grasp of the complex features of an involved situation, he united a strength of moral conviction, a straightforwardness of aim, and an inflexibility of purpose, which, whatever the sphere of his action, made him a force in that sphere. Calvin has been compared with the Apostle Paul in his early struggles of conscience, his experiences of sin and grace, and his soaring habit of contemplating all things in the light of the Divine counsel. They may be compared also in the purity of their motives and the singleness of their aims. But, above all, Reformer and Apostle are alike in the union they present of logical, argumentative powers of mind, with intense fervour of practical piety. Perhaps, after Paul, Calvin is the greatest example of this union.

Calvin was not without faults. His disposition tended to severity. He specially blames himself for impetuosity of temper, and begs forgiveness of those whom he may have wounded by harsh and uncharitable expressions. Like every man of strong convictions and decided will, he was apt to have little sympathy with those who set themselves in opposition to his views and wishes. Upright in motive himself, he felt only scorn for duplicity or meanness in others. When roused, he could express himself with great vehemence. His writings contain passages of keen sarcasm, of biting, caustic wit. His character, as has been said, had in it more of the Old Testament than of the New, reflected more the holiness than the love of God.

Yet Calvin was not cold. Those who speak of him in this way have not gone far down into his inner life. His letters show that beneath the reserved exterior, there beat a warm, true, loving heart. His intimate friends loved him as few men are loved. On the death of his infant son he writes:—"The Lord has indeed inflicted a grievous wound on us by the death of our little son, and we feel it bitterly. But He is a Father, and knows what is necessary for His children." When his wife was removed from his side, he tells—"If I had not exercised the whole force of my spirit to soften my agony, I could not have borne it." "I do what I can not to sink under the weight of this misfortune." His spirit went on mellowing as years advanced. How touching his sigh for rest on hearing of the death of Melancthon—"O Philip Melancthon, for I appeal to thee who art now living in the bosom of God, where thou waitest for us till we be gathered together with thee to a holy rest! A hundred times hast thou said, when, wearied with labour and oppressed with sadness, thou didst lay thyself familiarly on my breast, 'Would that I could die on this breast!' Since then I have a thousand times wished that it had been our lot to be together." [1]

---

[1] Henry, vols. i. pp. 265-7; ii. p. 296. Tulloch, "Leaders of the Reformation," p. 188.

In truth, these letters of the Reformer, admitting us to the inmost recesses of his soul, reveal to the reader a very different man from the Calvin of traditional opinion. Accused of pride, we find in these letters a man of very humble heart; accused of arrogance, we find that the terms Calvin most constantly applies to himself are shy, timid, bashful, pusillanimous; accused of tyranny, he was able to write—" How groundless the slander is that I am a tyrannical ruler, I leave my colleagues to judge, for they certainly have never complained that they felt themselves oppressed by my power; on the contrary, they frequently object to me that I am too shy, and do not act freely enough when there is need of the exercise of my authority, which all regard as beneficial."[1] Stern where the honour of God was involved, he was quick to forgive where the injury was personal; prone to anger, he was ready to confess his fault, and ask pardon for it. Still, he had not the genial, popular qualities of Luther; his manners were those of the well-bred gentleman, grave and courtly, rather than those of the man of the people; his interests and work naturally withdrew his affections from the ordinary channels, and absorbed them in the good of the Church at large; so that it is not wonderful that those outside his immediate circle admired him at a respectful distance rather than regarded him with warm love. This is not, however, the want of sympathy, but a cosmopolitan sympathy swallowing up the personal and local.

Calvin has been blamed for want of love of nature. Nature's fairest scenes were stretched around him, yet

[1] Henry, vol. i. p. 347.

his letters take no more notice of them than if he had lived in a desert. The same objection has been taken to the letters of the Apostle Paul. Of both men it may be said that with their hands full of the work they had to do, they were not likely to get much time to æstheticise. Yet passages might be quoted to show that Calvin was far from insensible to the grandeur of God's works in the natural world. "Whither could men turn," he wrote, "without hearing vocal testimonies to the existence and glory of the Great Architect in the admirable mechanism of the universe, proclaiming all around with loud and swelling voice the majesty of the One Supreme. There were as many heralds of His boundless glory as there were beings He had made, and even those creatures which were dumb had in this respect a tongue for man. The birds in their warblings sang of God, and the lowing steers more loudly told of Him, while the heavenly bodies moved on in silent adoration; the mountain resounded His praise, and fountain and flood pointed to Him with their glance, and every herb and flower seemed to woo man to His maker."[1] Whatever may be said of the feeling for natural beauty—which is a modern taste—Calvin does not fall under the reproach of the man "that hath not music in himself," and "is not moved with concord of sweet sounds," for he had a genuine appreciation of both poetry and music. He promoted a metrical version of the Psalms, had appropriate tunes composed for them, introduced congregational singing at Geneva, and himself wrote a few pieces, including a hymn of praise to Christ, which, says Schaff, "are worthy of Clement

[1] Preface to Olivetan's New Testament, 1535. See also "Institutes," Book I., sect. 5.

Marot, and reveal an unexpected vein of poetic fervour and tenderness."[1]

The Reformer has been called narrow. But Calvin's mind, whatever its defects, was not a narrow one. While not free from the inevitable limitations of his age, it was vast, capacious, comprehensive. It was not narrow as despising culture. What could breathe a juster spirit than the following remarks on heathen wisdom—" It is granted by all that truth, of what kind soever it is, is precious. But as the Deity is the fountain of all that is good, you should think with yourself that you incur the charge of deep ingratitude if you do not welcome every portion of truth, in whatever channel it may come to you, as proceeding from God, and receive it as if it were spoken to you by a voice from heaven. For if it is criminal to despise the gifts of God, to ascribe to men what properly belongs to God is flagrant impiety. Wherefore philosophy is to be viewed as a rare gift from heaven, and those wise men who have appeared in every age were raised up by God to point the world to the knowledge of truth."[2] It was not narrow as overridden by dogma. This is shown by the Commentaries, which anticipate the best modern works of their class in their freedom from dogmatic prejudice, and honest desire to discover the exact sense of Scripture. It was not narrow as unable to stretch across wide gulphs and embrace men of very different opinions. The Reformer had a friendship with Lælius Socinus, and wrote of Luther that though the latter should call him a devil, he would

[1] Creeds of Christendom, p. 440, and Guizot's St. Louis and Calvin, p. 264.

[2] Quoted by M'Crie, p. 23.

still regard him as a chosen minister of God. Luther, however, had a high respect for Calvin. Finally, it was not narrow as stickling for trifles and accessories. Himself favouring a particular form of government, he freely recognized the advantages of other forms; a Presbyterian in Church polity, he was not hostile to Episcopacy; he withheld the Sacrament from the Libertines, but he defended charity in judging of men's characters, as against the narrowness of the Anabaptists; he had his own opinion of holidays and ceremonies, but he constantly held such things to be indifferent; the Lord's Day was strictly observed at Geneva, but Calvin's views on the Sunday question are what would be called broad. His austerity was not such, that of an evening he could not unbend to a quiet game with the Magistrates at the pastime of "the Key," or permit himself the gentle exhilaration of the bowling green.

Calvin's system is the reflection of his mind—severe, grand, logical, daring in the heights to which it ascends, yet humble in its constant reversion to Scripture as its basis. Mounting to the throne of God, Calvin reads everything in the light of the eternal Divine decree. Man in his state of sin has lost his spiritual freedom, and the power to do anything truly good, though Calvin freely admits the existence of natural virtue, and attributes it to a working of Divine grace, even in the unregenerate. God's providence is all-governing and all-embracing, taking up into itself every act of man, and every event, natural and spiritual. Everything that happens is thus the bringing to light of part of an eternal counsel. Whoever is brought into the kingdom of salvation is brought there by a free act of grace, and even the passing by of the unsaved, however mysterious, must be traced back to an origin in the eternal Divine will. The will of God thus contains in itself the ultimate reasons of all that is. It is not an arbitrary, but a holy and good will, though the reasons for what actually takes place in the government of the world are to us inscrutable. We will not ask how much in this grand scheme belongs to Paul, how much to Augustine, how much to Calvin himself. It contains great truths, but it may be questioned whether, in carrying his theology to such heights, following

"Knowledge like a sinking star
Beyond the utmost bound of human thought,"[1]

Calvin has not placed these truths in a light which seriously imperils the plain Scripture doctrine of the love of God to humanity at large. A system, however, to be criticised, must be understood, and many popular objections apply, not to the theology of Calvin, but to unintelligent caricatures of it, and have their origin in failure to rise to Calvin's own point of view. The difficulty in every doctrine of predestination is, how to reconcile it with free-will and responsibility; but the problem is as much a philosophical as a theological one. Much depends on how we define freedom on the one hand, and on how we connect predestination with the free act on the other. The real knot of the difficulty lies farther back—how a free act can even be foreknown. A free act, in the sense of the objector, is one which springs solely from the will of the creature; it has no causes beyond that will; it rests with the agent alone to say what it shall be. This raises the difficulty of supposing it to be foreknown what an action shall be

[1] Tennyson's Ulysses.

before even the creature who is to determine what it shall be has so much as been brought into existence. On the other hand, granted unerring foreknowledge of how the individual will act in any position in which he may be placed, and it is not difficult to see that a plan may be formed consistently with freedom, yet shaping the course of the world's history down even to its minutest details; taking up free action into itself as the means of realizing its purposes; and so giving actuality to the free actions of men, otherwise regarded as bare possibilities. One thing is certain, that neither the materialist nor the idealist of our day can logically take up the stone against Calvin. Not the school of Huxley, Tyndall, Maudsley, or Galton, who deny free agency from the physical side; not the school of Mr. Spencer or Mr. Bain, who are necessitarian on the metaphysical side; not even the Hegelian school, which, with a higher aim, yet sees in all things the working out of an eternal necessity.

We have not left ourselves space to speak as we would have wished of the influence of Calvin. His Church polity extended itself to may countries. His system, passing like iron into the blood of the nations which received it, raised up in the French Huguenots, the English Puritans, the Scotch, the Dutch, the New Englanders, brave, free, God-fearing peoples. Abasing man before God, but exalting him again in the consciousness of a new-born liberty in Christ, teaching him his slavery through sin, yet restoring to him his freedom through grace, leading him to regard all things in the light of eternity, it contributed to form a grave, but very noble and elevated type of character, reared a race not afraid to lift up the head before kings. Mr. Froude may well ask "how it came to pass that if Calvinism is indeed the hard and unreasonable creed which modern enlightenment declares it to be, it has possessed such singular attractions in past times for some of the greatest men that ever lived; how—being, as we are told, fatal to morality, because it denies free-will— the first symptom of its operation, wherever it established itself, was to obliterate the distinction between sins and crimes, and to make the moral law the rule of life for States as well as persons; why, if it be a creed of intellectual servitude, it was able to inspire and sustain the bravest efforts ever made by man to break the yoke of unjust authority."[1] Since Calvin's day, the world has not stood still. Men's thoughts have widened. Other forms of society have taken the place of those with which he was familiar; new questions are agitating the Church; infidelity has extended its line, and is showing a different front. Scripture itself is cast into the crucible, and is being tried by processes the Reformer would have shrunk from. Yet was his battle essentially the same as ours—the battle with moral disorder, the battle with Antichristian error, the battle with Atheistic unbelief. His work will stand the scrutiny of the ages. To the end it will be testified of him—"He served his generation by the will of God."

[1] "Calvinism" in Short Studies, 2nd Series, p. 6. Mr. Froude, however, is wrong in saying that Calvinism denies free-will. See "Calvinism and the Doctrine of Philosophical Necessity" in Cunningham's Reformers and the Theology of the Reformation, p. 471.

Lollards of Kyle and other Precursors of the Scottish Reformation.

No picture of the Scottish Reformation can be complete in which the three great figures—Hamilton, Wishart, and Knox—are represented only as standing out against the common background of the conventional portrait-painter. History demands more. They must be set in the midst of their times. The distance and the middle-distance must be rubbed in with breadth and boldness, so as to bring out the historical perspective of events. The salient features of the past must be restored upon the canvas, so as to intensify the interest which must necessarily be focused on the three principal figures of the foreground.

Our duty is simply to sketch the background of the historical picture, and to introduce into the middle distance the few, though by no means unimportant, Reformers who assisted in preparing the times for the Reformation. Others will paint in the three great figures who lived in "the fulness of the time" and stamped it with their personality.

The Reformers of whom we treat appeared for the most part in the fifteenth century. That century, however, was the resultant of forces long in operation, and can only be understood by tracing these forces to their origin. The history of the Scottish Church dates back at least a thousand years from the Reformation, and is divided almost equally into two epochs—the Columban and the Roman. From the sixth till the sixteenth century, from Columba to Knox, there is a historical development which necessitates at least a brief reference to the remoter and nearer past.

Let us look for a moment to the sixth century. In 563, when Columba set his foot on the shore of Iona, the dawn broke over Scotland, and the Scottish Church may be said to have been born. Against the horizon only a few figures are discernible other than by name; and even these few seem for the most part only like "men as trees, walking." They are majestic and real, however, in spite of the mist of tradition in which they move. We see Columba austere and energetic, as visionary as a crusader, but as practical as a politician—a preacher and organizer, busy, ubiquitous, full of that contagious enthusiasm which made his numerous monasteries brilliant light-centres that smote the darkness of the age; St. Mungo, Columba's contemporary, sweetening the rude life of Pict and Briton with the amiability of his own character; St. Aidan, of Lindisfarne, redeeming the fortunes of Northumbria; and St. Cuthbert, the gentle-hearted Prior of Melrose, the Chrysostom of the early Scottish Church, preaching to the rude chieftains and the cheerless peasantry of the Cheviots. The lives of these early saints cover a memorable century, the golden age of the Church. As yet the Church was poor and pious, fired with the unselfish zeal of youth. The Bible was venerated and put to use. The monks were missionaries, whose spirituality was not yet crushed out by machinery nor emasculated by luxury. The influence of that age never wholly died out. Columba reappeared in John Knox.

"Every beginning is cheerful; the threshold is the place of expectation." The golden age of the early saints soon degenerated into brass. The expectation perished almost at the threshold of the new era. The next four hundred years, during which the Culdee Church feebly existed, are almost a historical blank. The monasteries became religious only in name. The ashes of young enthusiasm lay cold upon the altars. The offices of the Church became hereditary, and the wives and children of the priests claimed a share in the offerings made to God, whilst the abbots not infrequently were laymen who plundered the endowments of the monasteries.[1] Reform soon became imperative.

In the middle of the eleventh century a brilliant though superficial reformation was inaugurated. But in the very effort to reform, the seeds of a worse deformation were sown. It is here we find the nearer beginning of the evils that called for the thorough, radical, evangelical Reformation of the sixteenth century.

If Ireland gave us Columba, England gave us Margaret. In 1066 she sailed up the Forth an exile, but remained a queen and a conqueror. The influence of Margaret can scarcely be overestimated. Like Columba, she introduced a century of brilliant reform, which may be said to have culminated in the reign of her son, the "Sair Sanct," David I. During that century Teutonic and Norman influences did much to civilize the wild

[1] Laing's Lindores Abbey, p. 30.

Celt and to develop both his individuality and his patriotism. With the south wind there appeared signs of returning spring. The old Culdee Church was peaceably supplanted by the Roman. That of England was taken as the model for the Scottish reconstruction. The Culdee monasteries were restored and gradually filled with monks, native and foreign. The various orders were imported according to the fashion of the day. The rudimentary parochial system of the Culdees was perfected, and parochial clergy were stationed over the country. New bishoprics were founded. Cathedrals, abbeys, and monastic houses beautified the wild landscape. It was an age of crusades, of beautiful fanaticism and visionary romance, effectual in this at least, that men's purses opened wide as their hearts, and untold treasures were poured, not without great and increasing injury, into the monasteries and other ecclesiastical foundations.

Although Margaret's Reformation was not the best, it was the best possible. The times were not ready for radical remedies and internal upheavals. The revival of learning, printing, maritime discovery, and democracy had to appear before a radical doctrinal reformation could be attempted with the hope of success. Meanwhile the reconstruction offered a temporary remedy to many of the national grievances. Vast tracts of soil were brought under monastic government. The peasants, who had been alternately plunderers and plundered, could till the ecclesiastical lands with security and in peace. Agriculture was encouraged, and the fields around the monasteries were browned by the plough rather than reddened by battle. " Repose was the one thing most wanted, and the people found it under the protection of the crosier."[1] Learning, too, was fostered, and men who, many of them, loved the pagan classic lore more than their Bibles, were content to tolerate the grossest superstitions in order to secure an asylum for study not elsewhere to be found.[2] Yet the Reformation of Margaret and her sons was superficial, spite of all its regal splendour. It was only a reorganization of the effete Culdee Church. "The Church had risen from its Culdee tomb with more than Columban vigour."[3] There was "more than Columban vigour," but it lacked Columban spirituality. The Columban movement was essentially dynamical, as Carlyle would term it. In the sixth century religion "was spread abroad by the 'preaching of the Word,' by simple, altogether natural and individual efforts; and flew, like hallowed fire, from heart to heart."[4] In the eleventh and twelfth centuries the Reformation was mechanical, external, superficially splendid. The Church got a new suit of costly armour, but she eventually fell beneath its resplendent weight.

When James Resby, the protomartyr of Scotland, ventured across the Border into our country at the beginning of the fifteenth century, he found the people labouring under political and ecclesiastical oppression. Scotland was just recovering, under the House of Stuart, from the effects of its long struggle for independence. Wallace and Bruce had bought our nationality at an immense price. It took a long

---

[1] Cosmo Innes, quoted in Laing's Lindores Abbey, p. 32.
[2] Pinkerton's History, vol. i. bk. v.
[3] Ross's Scottish History and Literature, p. 39.
[4] Carlyle's Signs of the Times.

time to liquidate the account. But even after our nationality was won against the English it had to be preserved against the barons, whose power soon increased to a dangerous enormity. The people felt

"The anger, na the wretched doom
That is coupled to foul thraldom." [1]

Froissart,[2] who visited Scotland about ten years before Resby, shudders at the penury and barbarity of the country. The handicrafts were so little known that the Scots could not make a horse-shoe nor a saddle. Nor did the Church do much to alleviate the people's thraldom. Europe was scandalized by the exasperating intrigues and shameless vices of a long series of Popes. When the fifteenth century opened two rival successors of Peter—a Roman and a French—were entertaining the Christian world with their conflicting claims and their reciprocal anathemas. A locust-plague of monks infested Europe. Scotland, too, was visited and eaten up. Indulgences for sins committed, and for sins contemplated, were hawked about by the friars and sold to the highest bidder. Repentance was not requisite. The Pope was needy, his emissaries were willing, and the consciences of the people demanded the only relief which money could buy. Nor is it surprising that in such an age the grossest superstition should prevail. Even the sober, voluminous Bower of Inchcolm devotes a chapter to a miracle wrought by the mass. Through having previously celebrated the mass, three of his brother monks were saved from shipwreck in a storm which overtook them in Aberdour Bay when returning from the shore with a

[1] Barbour's Bruce.
[2] Pinkerton's History, vol. i. p. 148.

comfortable cargo of barrels of beer.[1] Relics were vended at the market-places. Bands of pilgrims set out to Whithorn marching to the bagpipes, the wild music of which was varied by the most wanton songs.[2] Salvation was bought and sold. But the price was works—money, pilgrimages, adoration of relics, and almost every form of self-redemption. Faith and grace were unknown terms. Christ—the Christ of the Bible—had become stranger to priest and people "and he could there do no more mighty work."

James Resby was only the local exponent of a movement which soon became European. The Councils at Pisa, Constance, and Basle had failed in their attempts at mechanical reform. The correction of abuses would no longer suffice. What was wanted was not new machinery but new motive power. The appearance of Wyclif on the scene was epoch-making. He was not the first, but the first great, Reformer. Two things characterized his efforts. He attacked doctrinal error and appealed to the common people.[3] This he did by emphasizing the need of faith and by translating the Bible into the people's language. Wyclif died in 1384. "Inspiration," says Alexander Smith, "not unfrequently has travelled, like summer, from south northward." The breath of reform blew gently over Scotland and gave it the first quickening of hopeful spring

It was probably about six years after Wyclif's death when James Resby came to Scotland. In the year 1400, Henry IV., son of that Duke of Lancaster

---

[1] Scotichronicon à Goodall, lib. xv. cap. xxxviii.
[2] Pict. Hist. Scot., vol. i. p. 275.
[3] Kurtz, Church Hist., vol. i. p. 476.

who had so often befriended Wyclif, bought the favour of the Church by renouncing his father's policy and polluting the English statute-book for the first time with an Act "De Haeretico Comburendo." Resby, who was probably one of Wyclif's "Poor Priests," may have come north to escape persecution; but he remained to preach the Gospel and suffer for it. Little is known of this protomartyr save what is found in Walter Bower's continuation of Fordoun's Scotichronicon. "Tradition tells us that Resby was extremely tall, spare, of commanding aspect, and with an eye which burned with earnestness and enthusiasm."[1] But Bower is so overcome with the horror of heresy that he does not even give us a side-glimpse of the noble heretic's personality. That he was not an unlettered man is, however, evident. His writings were long cherished during these dark times in many a Scottish home, "at the instigation of the devil," says the orthodox Bower, who adds with pathetic naïveté, that to these Lollards "stolen waters are sweet and bread eaten in secret is pleasant."

But Resby's power was in his preaching. At last a dynamic force was at work. The Word of God was brought out of the dull, damp monasteries, and carried over the breezy Scottish heather to speak in the rude vernacular in the turf-huts of the people. Resby made his appearance at a favourable time. England and Scotland were at peace. The Border was quiet. The peasant had laid down his well-used sword and battle-axe, and was ready to listen. When we picture in our imagination the tall, spare priest

[2] Laing's Lindores Abbey, p. 104. The source of the tradition is not indicated.

in russet gown and with bare feet, gathering the crowds around him in the fields of Kyle or in the little burghs of Perth or Fife, exposing the festering sores of the Church, the wounded Body of Christ, and pouring into them the forgotten balm of the Gospel, we can understand how Resby merited the sneering commendation of the chronicler, "for his preaching he enjoyed a very high repute among the simple." It was a new thing in Scotland to appeal to the people as the Church of Christ. Hitherto the clergy were the Church. The people were only the source whence the priesthood derived its wealth. The shepherds pastured the sheep for the sake of the wool. When reform was attempted, the voice of the people was not heard. Deputations to Rome, a change of order of monks, an episcopal remonstrance, were the extremest measures adopted. But Resby, like Wyclif, appealed to the people and preached the radical doctrine of salvation by grace, and thus became the first precursor of the Reformation of John Knox.

Had James Resby only thundered against the clergy the minor charges of simony, laziness, and uncleanness, he might have passed through Scotland unnoticed. These were small matters. But when he ventured upon doctrinal reform, he had touched the Ark of the Covenant, and must die. Resby was heard by the common people gladly. "Enough for the disciple to be as his Master." The old history was repeated in miniature. The chief priests and Pharisees held a council and said among themselves, "Perceive ye how ye prevail nothing? Behold, the world is gone after him!" Lawrence of Lindores, "a most solid and famous ecclesiastic, especially blessed for the sanctity of his life,"¹ played the rôle of Caiaphas and counselled death. "The Inquisitor of Hæretical depravity," as Lawrence was called, found a willing coadjutor in the Duke of Albany, who acted then as Regent during the exile of young King James I. Much less could a Regent than a hereditary king dispense with the favour of the Church when he found himself surrounded by a host of "Butcher-Barons." Arundel's coronation-whisper to Henry IV. seems to have reached Albany's ear—" To consolidate your throne, conciliate the clergy and sacrifice the Lollards." Perhaps instinct taught Albany what Arundel learned by experience. Albany, at least, was not unwilling to make the purchase at any price—even the life of an English "Poor Priest." Lindores, whose sympathies went with France rather than with England,² and who feared the new dangerous light of Wyclif that had sent this stray flash piercing through the Scottish darkness, was willing to negotiate. James Resby escaped the fires of Smithfield, which Archbishop Arundel fed so assiduously with English Lollards, but he met a like fate in the land of his exile. Being consigned, along with his writings, to the flames at Perth in the year 1407,³ he attained the proud distinction of dying as Scotland's first martyr for the cause of Christ.

Lawrence's refutation of Resby affords an interesting glimpse into the theology and logic of the age. Resby

---

¹ Scotichronicon, lib. xv. cap. xx.

² Tytler's History of Scotland, vol. iii. p. 282.

³ The date is uncertain. The Scotichronicon reads—"Eodem anno——die——combustus est Jacobus Resby," etc. The *same year* may refer to 1406 or 1407, cited at the close of the preceding chapter. Spotiswood gives 1407.

was accused of forty heretical conclusions, against which Lawrence of Lindores tried his dialectic skill. If the patient, prosy monk of Inchcolm has faithfully reported Lawrence's refutations in the two folio pages devoted to that purpose, they reveal a wonderful zeal without knowledge. The only two heretical tenets cited are these—" That the Pope is not *de facto* the Vicar of Christ," and " that no one can be Pope or Vicar of Christ unless he be holy,"—two theses which gained pungency from the Papal scandals of Resby's times. The refutation begins with a pathetic remark upon the hopelessness of the heretic. " They who are imbued with and rooted in the teaching of this most pernicious doctrine seldom or never reach the unity of the faith. Rarely also, or never, do I remember to have seen such fall asleep in the Lord in a Christian manner." The Lollards are then described in a series of curious pictorial epithets, which Lawrence or Bower seems to have mistaken for arguments. We can only give a few. They are, "Gog and Magog," "worshippers of Antichrist," " dragons," " the seed of Canaan," " wicked, lying, inveterate children, wavering from the paths of the law." The epithets being exhausted, the artillery of Scripture and of the saints is made to do duty. Lawrence, however, was more telling in epithet than in quotation. One almost fancies he sees a smile pass over the face of the tall, pale heretic as he hears such fatal verses as these made to do service in Resby's condemnation—" So I sware in my wrath they shall not enter into my rest." " I know thy works, that thou art neither cold nor hot; I would thou wert cold or hot. So, then, because thou art lukewarm, and neither cold nor hot, I will spue thee out of my mouth." "In the latter times, some shall depart from the faith, giving heed to seducing spirits and doctrines of devils." The Inquisitor then, by describing a series of logical circles, in which we cannot hope to follow him, proves to his own satisfaction, and evidently to that of the Council, that the Pope *is* the Vicar of Christ; and closes triumphantly with a quotation from the Revelations of St. Bridget, the Royal Swedish Nun, which are warranted to confute the Lollards and all such. We should like to have heard something of James Resby's reply. But the chronicler is silent. Who was Resby in comparison with the mighty Lawrence that his words should be chronicled? We suspect that the only argument which told effectually was that to which the others offered only an ingenious pretext—the argument of the fire at Perth.

The cause of evangelical truth suffered little by this first martyrdom. The Scottish peasantry had tasted the new wine, and, spite of all the specious attempts to demonstrate that the old was better, an indestructible remnant of the people held to their conviction. The enemies of the new heresy themselves did much to prepare the soil for the detested seed. Henry Wardlaw, Bishop of St. Andrews, upon whose memory, otherwise blameless, the death of Resby, says Spotiswood, "lieth heavily," has the undying honour of founding the first university in Scotland. He had studied at Oxford, where Baliol College had been founded about a hundred and fifty years before this time. Three years after Resby's martyrdom, he provided lectures at St. Andrews on various subjects for the Scottish youth—a venture which received the

Papal confirmation in 1413 amidst great rejoicings.[1] Nor is Lawrence of Lindores without a merited meed of praise. He helped the Reformation in other ways than by martyr-making. He encouraged that genuine love of learning which is the iconoclast of all priestly superstition. That "great theologian and man of venerable life,"[2] being the first to assist Wardlaw in his memorable undertaking, like a faithful "inquisitor of heretical depravity," lectured upon Peter Lombard's "Sentences," which formed, during the close of the middle ages, the supreme standard of orthodoxy. Lawrence's zeal for orthodoxy seems, however, not to have entirely accomplished its end. Lollardism had evidently become a popular phase of belief. In 1416, rumours of the great Bohemian movement being abroad in the land, his hand is seen at work in the records of the new university enacting that all Masters of Arts should swear the following:—"You shall defend the Church against the assaults of the Lollards, and, according to your ability, shall resist all those who adhere to that sect."[3]

But the movement indicated by this oath was not confined to the East. Outside the university and in the West of Scotland, where Lawrence's influence could scarcely be felt, Lollardism was agitating the mind of the people. It seems to have become necessary in these quarters to make another public example of the detested sect. A heretic, whose name even is unrecorded in the martyr-roll of our country, and of whom absolutely nothing but his death is known, was com-

[1] Scotichronicon, lib. xv. cap. xxii.
[2] Idem.
[3] Knox's Hist. of the Reformation, Ed. Laing, append. vol. ii.

mitted to the flames at Glasgow in 1422.[1] Two years after this event, which is the only indication of the progress of the new opinions in the West, James I. returned from his long exile, and a new era began in the history of Scotland.

It has been well said by one of the old historians[2] that "James was one of the worthiest of all the Kings of Scotland till his Times. Of the former Kings it might have been said the Nation made them Kings, but this King made that People a Nation." The thirteen years of his active reign fill one of the brightest pages in Scottish history. He was a man of Protean accomplishments—statesman, philosopher, musician, linguist, poet—"much obliged to the gifts of nature." He left an impression upon Scotland which neither the minorities of future sovereigns nor the baronial feuds ever wholly extinguished. James had a great work before him, and he set about it with more than royal earnestness. Whether to begin with Church or State must have been the question that presented itself to such a king. There was little to choose between them. The one was as corrupt as the other. The barons, however, were politically the more troublesome. During his exile they had risen into dangerous power; but during his exile he had by his character and education accumulated a force that would hold them in check at least during his lifetime. To reform the State became the object of James, and for that purpose he had to become the patron of the Church. But he did more good by elevating the material condition of the people than he would have done by reform-

---

[1] Laing's Edition of Knox, vol. i. p. 5.
[2] Drummond of Hawthornden.

ing the corruption of the clergy. He did for democracy what Wardlaw and Lawrence had done for learning. The state of civilization which he found on his arrival in Scotland was deplorable. Scotland was far behind the land of his fortunate exile. Enea Silvio, who became afterwards Pious II., gives an interesting glimpse into the domestic history of the land. "The towns are unwalled," he writes, "the houses commonly built without lime, and in villages roofed with turf, while a cow's hide supplies the place of a door. The commonalty are poor and uneducated, have abundance of flesh and fish, but eat bread as a dainty."[1] Sorners, beggars, fools, and jesters vied with the friars in amusing and plundering the people. "Everywhere we behold a barbarous scorn of law, savage insolence, sanguinary feuds, and cruel tragedies."[2] James ventured to crush these evils. He encouraged honest labour by laying a strong hand upon the beggar. He attempted to make property more secure. The statute-books were rapidly filled with laws, which, had it been possible to enforce them, would have prevented a hundred years of fruitless national struggle.

But James was more than an iron-handed legislator. He loved and encouraged good society; and his queen, so romantically wooed and won, "turned new-fangle the Court" with English fashions and the foibles of the day. Even the Church began to rebuke the king. The good Henry Wardlaw and "the severer sort of the clergy began to carp," and forbade furs and ermine, gold and silver lace, pearls, jesters and buffoons.[3] But we may still follow the King in his lighter moods, and enjoy his

---

[1] Quoted in Pinkerton's Hist. Scot., vol. i. book v.
[2] Ross's History and Literature of Scotland, p. 110.
[3] Drummond of Hawthornden, Hist. of James I.

homely, humane interest in the common people of his day. We can accompany him in his journeys amongst the simple folk, and can see him laugh at their follies, and take notes of their rollicking amusements. We can go with the royal poet to "Peblis to the play," and admire "the wenches of the West," with their curches and hoods and tippets; and the men of Tweeddale, with "birken hats" on their heads, dancing to the shrill music of the bagpipe. We meet on the road the typical fish-cadger and his wife, with their creels and their "great grey mare"; or we can go with them to "Christ's Kirk on the Green," the antitype of Burns' Holy Fair, and learn more of the flesh and blood of the history of his reign than we will find in all the learned chronicles. There we see the priest-ridden, baron-ridden peasantry enjoying themselves in their own rude fashion. We meet Tam Lutar the minstrel, and Robin Roy, and the "hasty hensure"[1] Harry, and Lowry the arrowmaker, and the town soutar with "full gowden" hair, and the miller "of manly mak'," and the sturdy herdsmen of the Cheviots.[2] We cannot but rejoice in their wild horse-play. The indomitable spirit of the Scotchman was not to be crushed out by adversity. Here are the men who made history, or helped to make it—if history be more than a game at backgammon between kings and nobility.

But James had no favour, or at least showed none, for the new light. He had seen the rosy dawn of letters in England, but he was blind to the parallel

---

[1] Giddy fellow.

[2] In the text we have accepted the tradition which ascribes to the author of the King's Quhair the minor poems referred to, though their authorship is disputed.

awakening in religion. He introduced Chaucer to his countrymen, but not Wyclif. His training under Henry IV. and Henry V., whose statecraft he made the model of his own, was fatal to the Lollard cause. The English kings had adopted a policy of extermination, and James found it easy and politic to do likewise. Accordingly in his first Parliament, in 1424, seventeen years after Resby's martyrdom, a law was passed "Anentis Heretikis and Lollardis," to the effect that every bishop, wherever any heretics be found, should cause inquiry to be made by the inquisition of heresy, and that the heretics be punished as the law of the Holy Kirk requires; and, if necessary, that the secular power be called in for the support and help of the Holy Kirk.[1]

It is not to be supposed, however, that James was wholly blind to the evils of the Church, which policy, if not inclination, induced him to conciliate. He was too keen-sighted to imagine that the State could be healthy when the Church was corrupt. Bower[2] has preserved a characteristic letter of the King to the Benedictine and Augustinian monks, in which the King uses "great plainness of speech." He complains of the "rapid decay and threatening ruin of holy religion," which, he says, is daily degenerating from its ancient foundation, and feels constrained to arouse somewhat sharply their "torpid minds," and to awaken them out of the "sloth of their drowsiness," that they might live more consistently with their profession. In order to set before the other Orders in Scotland an example

[1] Acta Parl. Scotiæ, vol. ii. p. 7 Quoted in Laing's Appendix to Knox. Cf. Tytler, vol. iii. p. 231.
[2] Scotichronicon à Goodall, lib. xvi. cap. xxxii.

in preciseness of living, he introduced the Carthusian monks, for whom he built and endowed a beautiful monastery at Perth.[1]

But a fresh impulse was given to evangelical reform by the appearance in Scotland of another martyr— Paul Crawar. Little is known of the personal history of this adventurous Reformer, save that he was a Bohemian and a physician. Our imagination, however, can without historical anachronism picture him as a boy listening in the Bethlehem Chapel in Prague to John Hus, of "pale and meagre countenance,"[2] whilst the pious orator preached the old Gospel which was new to Prague, both to its priests and its people, or as a youth catching a holy zeal for Christ from the martyr-pile of the same dauntless Reformer. At any rate he had drunk the new wine of Bohemia, and, driven thence by persecution or by the impulse to head a new movement in Scotland, he had set himself to evangelize our country.

It is not known when Paul Crawar came to Scotland. In 1433, however, a new zeal for orthodoxy had sprung up in the Church. Columba Dunbar, Bishop of Moray, and John Cameron,[3] Bishop of Glasgow, had been sent to Basle as delegates from the Scottish Church to the Council held there that year. One of the exciting questions of the Council was that of the Hussite doctrine. The four Calixtine Articles—the Eucharist under both forms, the free preaching of the Gospel in the vernacular, strict discipline among the

---

[1] Spotiswood's Hist., p. 57 (ed. 1655).

[2] Mosheim.

[3] Vid. Dr. Gordon's Scotichronicon, vol. ii. p. 499, and Tytler Hist. Scot., vol. iii. p. 286.

clergy, and that the clergy should not possess secular property—were discussed for fifty days, and at last nominally conceded to be afterwards ignored.[1] The Taborites, another sect of the Hussites, stood out against this temporizing policy of the Calixtines and argued for a thorough and Scriptural reform. Feeling ran high, and we may justly suppose that the Scottish bishops caught the contagion of the persecuting policy and brought it home. It was not difficult for them to induce the doughty Lawrence of Lindores, "inquisitor of heretical depravity," to buckle on his armour once again for the fray, and all the less difficult when it was known that the Scottish movement was being headed by one of these turbulent Hussite Bohemians,[2] Paul Crawar, the heretical physician.

We may tell the story of the only day of the martyr's life of which anything is known in the quaint vernacular of Bellenden's translation of Hector Boece. "Nocht lang efter was tane in Sanct Androis ane man of Beum namit Paule Craw, precheand new and vane superstitionis to the pepyl, specially aganis the sacrament of the alter, veneration of sanctis, and confession to be maid to Priestis. At last he was brocht afore the Theologis, and al his opinionis condampnit. And because he perseuerit obstinatly to the end of his pley, he was condampnit and brint. He confessit afore his death that he was send out of Beum to preiche to Scottis the heresyis of Hus and Wiccleif. The King

---

[1] Kurtz, vol. i. p. 488. Cf. Scotichronicon à Goodall, lib. xvi. cap. xx.

[2] "Qui nunc in maleficiis nimium praevalebant." Scotichr., lib. xvi. cap. xx.

commendit mekyl this punition."[1] A few suggestive touches may be added to this narrative of the scholarly Principal of Aberdeen from the earliest record of the event—that of Bower. The very title of the chapter in the *Scotichronicon* which records the martyr's death is indicative in itself of the prominent part which Crawar has played in Scottish religious history. Resby was entitled a heretic, Crawar an "arch-heretic."[2] Resby was said to be held in high repute for his preaching by the simple. Crawar is recognized as a man of learning worthy of Lawrence's steel, "prompt and practised in sacred letters and in adducing the Scriptures." He had come, it is added, with commendatory letters from Prague to practise the art of medicine, in which he excelled. But Lindores, "who," says the admiring Bower, "never gave rest to the heretics or Lollards within the kingdom," discovered him and brought him to bay, and confuted him by much invective and a bonfire in St. Andrews on the 23rd July, 1433.

To which of the Hussite sects Crawar belonged is not certainly known. From the minute description which Bower gives of the Taborites, we may imagine that Crawar was a follower of that party which was led by Procopius the Great. The Taborites were democratic. They had adopted the policy of no surrender, and despised the Calixtines for their compromise with the Church, which they considered rotten, root and branch. At once the strength and weakness of the sect was its severe spirituality which rejected forms

[1] Laing's Knox, Append. ii.

[2] "De Combustione Pauli Crawar arch-haeretici, et de Lolardis," lib. xvi. cap. xx.

and human aids of every kind. They threw off all the fetters of rule and ordinance, cleared away images, indulgences, relics, saint worship, pilgrimages; advocated the abolition of ecclesiastical possession of secular property, and gave the people the sacrament in both kinds. Bower,[1] whose vivid description argues that he had his information from the records of an eye-witness—probably of one of the delegates to Basle—tells with horror how Procopius, dressed in a long tunic with sleeves, marched with his followers to celebrate the mass without being furnished with the holy vestments, the Epistles, or Gospels, or any of the usual adjuncts of that occasion; and how, after a stirring Dominican oration, he served the company of common people with wine out of a common bowl and with common bread *cum magna quantitate*. But the strength of the Taborites was their weakness. They became visionary, and forgot that the Church was still militant. They cleared the deck and the hold of the ship not only of the ecclesiastical rubbish, but of the needed ballast and steering gear and other necessary appliances; and so in the end out-puritaned the Puritans and "virtually condemned all the literature, education, offices, and law as then existing."[2] To this democratic and radical sect it is very probable that Paul Crawar belonged. Bower's description of Procopius becomes significant only when we apply it to the Bohemian Taborite in Scotland.

In what manner Paul Crawar was tried and condemned is not known. Knox, indeed (upon what authority we do not know), gives one interesting and graphic detail of the scene. It is said that the martyr

[1] Scotichronicon, lib. xvi. cap. xx.
[2] Kurtz, vol. i. p. 498.

was delivered over to the secular judge by the Bishops, who followed Pilate, "who both did condemn and also wash his hands." "To declare themselves to be the generation of Satan, who, from the beginning, hath been enemy to the truth and he that desireth the same to be hid from the knowledge of men, they put a ball of brass in his mouth, to the end that he should not give confession of his faith to the people, neither yet that they should understand the defence which he had against their unjust accusation and condemnation."[1] In the *Scotichronicon* there are two folio pages of allegorical abuse in which heaven and earth are almost exhausted of all evil imagery by way of refutation. We need only cull a few of the choice phrases. These Lollards are "wolves in sheep's clothing," "foxes of Samson," "a brood of vipers," "horned serpents," "pigmies," "erratic stars moving against the motion of the firmament," "hypocritical Pharisees," "Sadducees," "Stoics and Epicureans," "clouds without water," "walkers in the way of Cain and the errors of Balaam," "horned owls," "sowers of the devil's seed," "apostates from the faith," "shameless dog flies and locusts with long spikes and winged locusts whose end is the destruction of the fruit of the Church,"[2] etc. But enough. The chronicler might have enriched the martyrology of our country had he condescended to write ten lines of plain history in lieu of these folio pages of harmless vituperation. Yet there is historical value even in all this invective. The chronicler immortalizes the intellectual condition of his time. He takes us into the monastery and lets us hear the

[1] Laing's Knox, vol. i. p. 6.
[2] Scotichronicon, lib. xvi. cap. xxi. xxii.

monks speaking of the new light that was breaking so slowly and so intermittently over the land. We hear their exclamations of horror, their hopeless attempts at refutation by inappropriate texts and garbled Scripture and uncharitable jargon, and we understand somewhat whence the fire came that kindled the martyr-pile at St. Andrews for the adventurous Bohemian.

The murder of James I. in 1437 was the greatest national calamity of the century. The hopes of political and social reform were suddenly crushed under the feet of the assassins; and, although the King's influence was never effaced from the annals of our country, the evils of the minorities and the unpatriotic ambition of the nobles did much to hinder the progress of civilization so happily begun. James II. was only six years old at the death of his father. One needs only glance over the mournful pages of Lindsay of Pitscottie's Chronicles to learn what a tragic calamity a minority was to Scotland in these days. The wild hunt for power began. Murder became the chief pastime of the nobles. Laws were haughtily despised. The arm of State authority was paralysed. No regent had sufficient power to enforce a law against a Douglas or a Livingston. The brutality of the times is witnessed, for instance, in the bloody encounter between the Ogilvies and the Crawfords at Arbroath in 1445, narrated in such tragic matter-of-fact detail by Pitscottie, who thereafter makes the *naïve* remark, which he more than justifies in the course of his history— " Efter this thair followed nothing but slauchter in this realme. In everie pairt ilk ane laid wait for otheris, as they had been settand themselffis for slauchter of wyld beastis."[1] The House of Douglas especially became the scourge of Scotland, and we see how hopeless the struggle for progress must have been when it could be said of the most powerful noble of the realm, " to theife and traytour he was ane sicker targe, and be the contrair, ane plaine enemy to good men."[2] Nor was this lawlessness confined to the minority of James II. The battle of the kites and crows revived during the minorities of the next three kings, and during the majority of each was only varied, more or less, by the monarch himself becoming a new party in the struggle. Respect for property had almost died out. Burning became the fashionable revenge of the nobility. Within a few years Stirling, Strathbogie, Forres, and Inverness were laid waste by fire in the rude settlement of private feuds. The voice of justice was smothered; her arm, which was partially released by James I., was again bound by the lawless nobility. " Even so late as Mary's reign," says Pinkerton, " the balance of justice was commonly used in weighing which bribe was heaviest." How grievously these calamities oppressed the commonalty and exhausted the resources of the country may be seen from the old chronicle at the end of Wyntoun. Against the year 1482 we find the following suggestive entry, which gives the other side of the picture—how it fared with the commons whilst the nobles were playing at knightly murder:—" Thar was ane gret hungyr and deid in Scotland, for the boll of meill was for four pounds; for thar was blak cunye (coinage) in the realm, strikkin and ordinyt be King James the Thred. . . . . And

[1] Pitscottie's Chronicles, vol. i. p. 55 (Ed. Edinburgh, 1814).
[2] Idem, p. 68.

als was gret wer (war) betwix Scotland and Ingland, and gret distructioun throw the weris (wars) was of corne and catell. And thai twa thyngs causyt bayth hungar and derth, and mony pur folk deit of hungar."[1]

Under such political and social conditions it is not to be expected that the cause of religion could thrive. The commonalty had not leisure to lead or be led in any new religious movement. The priests had the leisure but not the desire to advance the claims of truth and righteousness in times which demanded them both. So lazy became the habits, so base the lives, so shameless the extortion of the rank and file of the clergy, that the censure and excommunication of the Church were despised by the common people, and had to be enforced by the secular power. But its enormous wealth was the Church's curse. The world was too much with it. So vastly had its endowments increased that its property was equal to that in the hands of the whole laity.[2] But this princely affluence exposed the Church to the intrigues of avarice, sacred and secular. Its prizes were vehemently competed for by the Pope and the King. Bishoprics had long been sold to the highest bidder by the Pope, who would not give his coveted bull for nothing. But in 1471 James III. enacted that it was treasonable to purchase a benefice or other office at Rome, and gradually assumed to himself the right of nomination to all vacant offices in the Church.

The effect of this unwise legislation, which simply transferred the evils of simony from the Pope to the King, was to fill the parishes and the monasteries

---

[1] *Vide* Pinkerton, vol. i. Append. xxi.
[2] Pinkerton's Hist., vol. i. p. 414.

with royal hirelings, who loved leisure and the larder more than the cure of souls. When the recruits among the clergy were enlisted from a nobility which was as infamous in its crimes as notorious for its ignorance, we must grant that the Church, when it escaped the plunder of the Pope, suffered much at the hands of the avaricious King. Many of the rich livings were held by mere boys, some even by infants, and not a few by men imbecile in mind.[1] The evils of simony were felt even by the clergy themselves, who, however, would rather have been fleeced by the Pope than by the King, and find expression in the lines of a poem of the times, The Three Priests of Peebles, in which the royal simony is blamed for the loss of the Church's spirituality—

> For now on days, is neither rich nor poor
> Shall get ane kirk, all through his literature.
> For science, for virtue or for blood,
> Gets nane the Kirk, but baith for gold and good.
> Thus, great excellent King! the holy Ghaist
> Out of your men of good away is chast. . . .
> Sic wickedness there is this world within,
> That simony is counted now nae sin.

Between the martyrdom of Paul Crawar and the trial of the Lollards of Kyle there elapsed a period of sixty years. During that long period of baronial feuds, ecclesiastical lethargy, and national adversity, the evangelical reforming spirit was quiescent, if not quenched. If there was a noble remnant left it was hidden. The times were too insecure to admit of agitation in favour of evangelical reform. Yet it must not be understood that nothing was done to remedy the abuses of the clergy. If the Church as a whole was corrupt, there

[1] *Vide* Laing's Lindores Abbey, p. 111.

were within its pale a few conspicuous exceptions, whose probity, purity, and patriotism redeem it from sweeping obloquy.

Lawrence of Lindores, even, " the inquisitor of heretical depravity," was in his own way a reformer, and stands out from the common priesthood with unstained character, and disinterested, though misdirected zeal for the welfare of the Church and the glory of God. One would rather remember him gratefully as one of the founders of the first university than for his martyr-making. Bishop Henry Wardlaw, too, the first of three successive Bishops of St. Andrews who attempted to allay the worst symptoms, if not to cure the disease of the Church, must not be forgotten in speaking of the Church's internal reformers. Though so unhappily associated with the death of Resby and Crawar, he is to be patriotically remembered as the founder of our first university, who, by his learning, unselfish generosity, and faithfulness to the duties of his distinguished office, adorned for thirty-five years the ancient see of St. Andrews, and did much to banish ignorance and evil from the Church.

But Bishop James Kennedy stands without an equal in Church or State during his times, and has left an indelible impression upon both. During the reign of James II., and part of the reign of James III., he stood at the helm in the height of the storm—almost the only man of his day for whom history has a word of enthusiastic praise. As a Churchman he did not attempt to destroy the germs of the Church's disease, but he closed, at least for the time, her putrid sores. Historians have only good to say of Kennedy. He repaired with some success the broken-down ecclesiastical machinery, and set the Church somewhat in order. Spotiswood says that "upon his translation to S. Andrews he did put all things in such order as no man then living did remember to have seen the Church in so good an estate."[1] But we have to turn to the pages of Pitscottie to know the nature of the good Bishop's work. The historian's magnificent eulogy is invaluable not only as a portrait of a noble historical figure, but, by implication, as a suggestive picture of the average clerical life of the times, to which Kennedy was at once an exception and an example. "This bischop Kennedie was vondrous godlie and wyse, and was weill learned in divine sciences, and practised the same to the glorie of God, and weill of his Church; for he caused all persones and vicares to remaine at thair paroche kirkis, for the instructions and edificing of thair flock, and caused thame preach the Word of God to the people, and visit thame that war seik; and also the said bischope visited every kirk within the diocie, four tymes in the yeir, and preached to the said parochin him selfe the word of God, and inquyred of thame if they war dewlie instructed be thair persone and viccar, and if the poore war susteaned, and the youth brought vp, and learned according to the ordour that was taine in the kirk of God; and quhair he found not this ordour keipit, he maid great punischment, to the effect that Godis glorie might shyne in his diocie; leiving guid example to all archbischopis and kirk men to caus the patrimonie of God's word to be vsed to his awin glorie, and to the commounweill of the poore."[2]

Bishop Kennedy died in 1466, having been Bishop

---

[1] Spotiswood, p. 57.
[2] Pitscottie's Chronicles, vol. i. p. 170.

of St. Andrews for twenty-two years. He was succeeded by his half-brother, Patrick Graham, who inherited many of the qualities which distinguished Kennedy. Patrick Graham may rank also among the Reformers and, in certain respects, as a heretic and a martyr. He suffered much by Kennedy's greatness. Such a man as Kennedy, on account of his probity, made many enemies among the nobles, and they, in the fashion of the times, determined to avenge themselves upon his kinsman Graham. Graham's appointment as first Archbishop of St. Andrews was received with much disfavour. It excited the spite of the bishops, who refused to tolerate a superior whom they were not prepared to imitate. "He came among them with the odious commission of an Apostolic Nuncio, to extort a tithe of their benefices for a war against the Turks. In their indignation they taxed themselves in 12,000 marks, and, making common cause with the King and the Court, precipitated a conflict which proved fatal to Archbishop Patrick Graham."[1] Nor was the Papal appointment acceptable to the common clergy, who became alarmed at the well-known reforming propensities of the new Archbishop. His commission from Rome authorized him to reform the abuses in the Church and to correct the dissoluteness of the clergy. It was not difficult for the clerical party to enlist the sympathies of the nobles, who themselves had a large interest in the ecclesiastical maladministration. Graham's spirit was foreign to the Church and the nobility. Few, if any, desired reform. The abuses were too splendid and profitable to be so lightly remedied. Graham was accused of heresy, schism, and, among other things, of

[1] Gordon's Scotichronicon, vol. i. p. 224.

saying three masses in the day, "whereas in those times it was difficile to find a Bishop that in three months did say one mass."[1] The noble and pious Graham became the subject of a tedious persecution. He was stripped of his honours, imprisoned in various places, and at last, his reason having given way, he died in St. Serf's and was buried there, and with him passed away a brilliant but abortive attempt at reform from within the Church itself. Although these bishops cannot be classed among the Evangelical Reformers of our country, no account of pre-Reformation Reformers could be complete which ignored their noble services on behalf of Church and State.

On the death of Patrick Graham the Church went "daily from ill to worse." The few internal Reformers whom he represented retired hopelessly into private life. But the leaven of reform began to work in another sphere, outside the universities and the ecclesiastical circles—among the common people of the West, who became known as the Lollards of Kyle. The fire of Lollardism had never been quite quenched; but how it suddenly burst into flame in 1494 remains still a mystery. There was at this time no outstanding movement in England nor on the Continent. In the Low Countries John Ruchrath and John Wessel, the "lux mundi" so much admired by Luther, had been advocating a reform which was mainly theological, quiet and local. Savonarola had begun to illuminate Florence with his bold enthusiastic oratory. But his appearance was meteoric, strange, brilliant, evanescent. None of the contemporaneous movements spread beyond the localities in which they originated. The

[1] Spotiswood, p. 59.

Kyle movement seems to have been indebted to no foreign influence. One little incident, indeed, may be supposed to throw a thin ray of light upon the subject. About this time the study of the Bible in the vernacular in manuscript seems to have been not uncommon in the Ayrshire district. This is evident from a letter which was written sometime afterwards to James V. by Alexander Alesius.[1] In that letter, in which it is argued that the Scriptures should be read in families at home, the pious example of John Campbell of Cessnock is cited. He, it is said, had a priest in his own house who read to the family, to their great edification, the New Testament in the vernacular. Being a hospitable and tolerant gentleman he entertained the monks to dinner and to after-dinner dissertations on theology. But the monks, "passing by the eating-table and the salt," reported to the bishop, and Campbell and his lady were accused of heresy. Campbell being a very modest man, and, like Moses, of "uncircumcised lips," found a vigorous advocate in his wife, who by appropriate Scripture and sound mother-wit so successfully disposed of the monkish vagaries that King James IV., before whose tribunal they were summoned, "rising up, caressed the woman, and extolled her diligence in Christian doctrine." To this custom of reading the Scriptures, probably introduced long before this time by followers of Wyclif, may be traced the effort at reform made by the Lollards of Kyle. The Kyle movement was not confined to any one family. It seems to have been popular over the greater part of Ayrshire. The leaders in the movement were drawn neither from the nobles nor from the common people,

[1] Annals of the English Bible, vol. ii. quoted Pict. His. of Scot.

whose wars and feudal relations gave them little leisure, but from the intermediate class, the comparatively independent gentry of the shire. That the movement was carried on with some success and determination is seen from the fact that no less than thirty of the leaders were summoned by the Archbishop of Glasgow to appear before the Great Council of the King. The names of six of these are given by Knox and are worthy of remembrance—George Campbell of Cessnock, Adam Reid of Barskimming, John Campbell of Newmilns, Andrew Shaw of Polkemmet, Helen Chalmours lady Polkellie, and Marion Chalmours lady Stair.[1]

The trial was conducted in the presence of King James IV., who was then in the sixth year of his reign. James was a gifted monarch, beloved of nobles and commons, not hated by priests. He had much of the brilliant talent of James I., but little of his earnestness and love of learning. By turns he was a sensualist and an ascetic, a humble pilgrim and a reckless freeliver. His curiously mixed character may be summed up in the couplet of a poet and the epigram of a historian—

"For he was myrrour of humilitie,
Lode sterne and lamp of liberalitie;"[2]

"A monarch whose faults were few but fatal, whose virtues were many but useless."[3] But James was not by any means priest-ridden. Notwithstanding all his own spasmodic penances and eccentric pilgrimages he knew the hollowness of the priestly life and the insincerity of much of their doctrine. To him the trial of these

[1] *Vide* Knox's Ref. by Laing, vol. i. pp. 6-12.
[2] Sir David Lindsay.
[3] Pinkerton.

Lollards had little gravity. He treated it in the Gallio fashion. Robert Blacader, who acted as inquisitor, had only lately won for Glasgow the honour of an archbishopric.[1] He is said to have been noble and wise, a good diplomatist in State affairs, superstitious, however, and morose, known during his fatal pilgrimage to the Holy Land as the "rich Scottish bishop." But in his attempt to signalize his archiepiscopal zeal by persecution, he incurred alike the ridicule of the witty heretics and the laughter of the good-natured king.

The articles of which the Lollards were accused by Blacader are interesting as an indictment against the life of the clergy and the policy of the Church. Knox, who copied them from the Glasgow records, which are not known to be now extant, enumerates thirty-four, of which the following are the most important:—That images are not to be had nor yet to be worshipped; that the relics of saints are not to be worshipped; that Christ gave power to Peter only, and not to his successors, to bind and loose within the kirk; that after the consecration in the mass there remains bread, and that there is not the natural body of Christ; that tithes might not be given to ecclesiastical men; that every faithful man or woman is a priest; that the Pope is not the successor of Peter, but where He said, "Go behind me, Satan"; that the Pope deceives the people by his bulls and indulgences; that the Pope cannot remit the pains of purgatory; that the priests might have wives according to the constitution of the law; that the Pope forgives not sins, but only God.

In these sweeping accusations it is not difficult to perceive the influence of Wyclif and his followers, the

[1] In 1491, *vide* Scotichronicon by Dr. Gordon, vol. ii. p. 515.

English Lollards. Almost every one of these charges could have been quoted against the Reformers across the Border. But they were not aimed by the Lollards of Kyle against imaginary evils. Scotland knew more of priestly pride, imposition, and scandal than even England. As regards the evil of the worship of images and of relics, the extent to which it had developed may be seen by glancing over an inventory, made in the middle of the fifteenth century, of the ornaments, relics, and jewels in the church of Glasgow.[1] Among other things we notice—" Four Precious Clasps for Copes, bearing the embroidered Image of the Annunciation of the Blessed Virgin; another, more precious, representing her coronation; a third with the image of the crucifix; a fourth with the image of our Lord seated on a Throne with the Four Evangelists, one or either in the four corners: all of silver richly gilt. A cross, or the image of the crucifix, with two collateral Figures of good size, of Silver." The vestments of the bishop and his ministers are of brown velvet, white silk or red silk ornamented with flowers of gold and images of silk. There are several altar cloths with golden images. In fact images are represented as appearing on almost everything under the care of the sacristan. But the list of relics in the inventory reveals a still grosser credulity and superstition. There is, of course, " a small piece of the true cross of our Lord"; a phial with the hair of the blessed Virgin; portions of the hair shirts of Saints Kentigern and Thomas of Canterbury; a particle of the skin of St. Bartholomew the Apostle; a bone of St. Ninian; "a small portion of the girdle of the blessed Virgin Mary"; a small por-

[1] Scotichronicon, by Dr. Gordon, vol. ii. pp. 451-457.

tion of the crib of our Lord; and four bags of bones of various saints. There is little wonder that the enlightened people of Kyle revolted against the image and relic worship which had grown to such dimensions in the diocese of the very bishop who was now their accuser.

Nor were the other Articles framed against vices and superstitions that would shock only fanatics. The monks and priests winked at the vows of their order.[1] Their richly dowered daughters competed more than favourably with the daughters of the nobles in securing the prizes of matrimony. Indulgences were sold like common merchandise at markets and fares. Goods and lands were bequeathed by almost every one who had property for founding altars, in order to "assuage and terminate the pains of purgatory" for the donor.[2] The Pope had made himself so hateful by the practices to which he resorted in order to extract money from the people, that his pardon and blessing and excommunication were despised. But the Lollards of Kyle, with their Bible in their heart, met the arrogance and pomp of the priests by advocating the priesthood of the faithful people, and cut themselves adrift from work-righteousness and fictitious remedies by proclaiming with Lutheran boldness "that the Pope forgives not sins, but only God."

But turn for a moment to the scene in the Great Council. The heretics were more than a match for their accusers. There is an enjoyable Scotch pawkiness in the manner in which Adam Reid of Barskim-

---

[1] Cf. Register of the Collegiate Church of Crail, by Dr. Rogers, p. 23. Ross's Hist. and Lit., pp. 401, 402.
[2] Register of the Coll. Ch. of Crail, p. 31.

ming defended the cause of himself and his comrades. Knox's narrative of the trial is too happy to be improved upon. " Albeit that the accusation of the bishop, and his accomplices, was very grievous, yet God so assisted His servants, partly by inclining the King's heart to gentleness (for divers of them were his great familiars), and partly by giving bold and godly answers to their accusators, that the enemies in the end were frustrate of their purpose. For, while the bishop, in mockage, said to Adam Reid of Barskyming, ' Reid, believe ye that God is in heaven ? ' He answered, ' Not as I do the sacraments seven.' Whereat the bishop, thinking to have triumphed, said, ' Sir, lo, he denies that God is in heaven.' Whereat the King, wondering, said, ' Adam Reid, what say ye ? ' The other answered, ' Pleaseth your Majesty to hear the end betwixt the churl and me.' And therewith he turned to the bishop, and said, ' I neither think nor believe as thou thinkest that God is in heaven ; but I am most assured that He is not only in heaven but also in the earth. But thou and thy faction declare by your works, that either ye think that there is no God at all, or else that He is so set up in heaven that He regards not what is done upon the earth ; for, if thou firmly believedest that God were in heaven, thou shouldest not make thyself checkmate to the King, and altogether forget the charge that Jesus Christ the Son of God gave to His Apostles, which was to preach His Gospel, and not to play the proud prelates, as all the rabble of you do this day. And now, Sir,' said he to the King, ' judge ye whether the bishop or I believe best that God is in heaven.' While the bishop and his band could not well revenge themselves, and while many taunts were given them in their teeth, the King, willing to put an end to further reasoning, said to the said Adam Reid, 'Wilt thou burn thy bill?' He answered, 'Sir, and the bishop, an ye will.' With these and the like scoffs the bishop and his band were so dashed out of countenance that the greatest part of the accusation was turned to laughter."[1]

The trial, which under a more fanatic or less independent king might have ended in martyrdom, was hushed up in mockery. The Lollards returned home, but we hear no more of the progress of their agitation. Knox says that "after that diet, we find almost no question for matters of religion, the space of nearly thirty years." The reason may be found in the fact that the attempts at reform were yet, to a great extent, only negative. They were made against abuses rather than in favour of the great truths of the Christian religion. What was needed to give vitality to the movement was a few cardinal truths to fight for. But the doctrines of justification by faith alone, and of redemption by the merits of Christ, not having been fully discovered, were not fully and freely insisted upon. Till the radical Reformation inaugurated by Luther gave a new direction and a fresh force to the movement in Scotland, Christ did not receive His position as chief corner-stone in the doctrinal edifice. There is a great advance even from the thirty-four articles of the Lollards of Kyle to the Brief Treatise of Mr. Patrike Hamelton, called Patrike's Places. In the latter "Christ is all and in all," and the Gospel receives at last a distinct evangelical utterance. Yet, till Hamilton and Knox came, there was work to be done—

[1] Knox's History, vol. i. (Paisley: David Gardner. 1791.)

the work of still further demolition preparatory to reform.

The work of demolition was to a great extent effected by two men, William Dunbar and Sir David Lyndsay, the former of whom, at least, manifested no sympathy with the evangelical movements of the past nor of his own day. If they cannot be called Reformers, they certainly were forerunners of reform. They did much to make the rough places smooth for the more positive work of John Knox by rendering the priests ridiculous and the Church suspected by the common people. Dunbar and Lyndsay were, however, assisted in their work of demolition by the circumstances of their times. Education was at last being looked upon as something more than a monkish accomplishment. On the very year in which the Lollards of Kyle were tried, a third university was founded in Scotland. Two years after that, the first compulsory education Act was passed, to the effect that the eldest sons of barons be sent to school when they were nine years of age. The reign of James IV., spite of its licentiousness, was one of prosperity. Scotland began now to feel the impulse of the so-called revival of learning, which in Western Europe was maturing vast changes, in which Scotland also was destined to participate. Quite a galaxy of poets had suddenly appeared. Dunbar's Lament of the Makaris makes the patriotic Scotchman both proud and sorrowful. Only one of the number for whom the bard laments is well known—the gentle-hearted, sententious schoolmaster of Dunfermline, "good Maister Robert Henrisoun." The others have disappeared, or have left behind them only fragments which are indicative of the great works we have lost.

But the beginning of the century witnessed a revival of letters unprecedented in Scotland. The classic Bishop of Dunkeld, Gavin Douglas, who forfeited a larger fame as a poet by his notoriety as a political prelate, had introduced Virgil to his countrymen in a translation in which the Renaissance first finds distinct expression in the Scottish tongue. Hector Boece, the studious Principal of Aberdeen, whom Pinkerton so unceremoniously dismissed as "one of the most egregious impostors that ever appeared in any country," was busy with his Lives of the Bishops of Aberdeen, in which we have a pleasing proof of his own quiet industry, and a noble tribute to the otherwise scarcely known virtues and excellencies of the godly remnant of the clergy. Joannes Major, the far-seeing radical professor of theology, teacher of Hamilton and Knox, was unconsciously leavening the youth of the country with new ideas about democracy, divine right of kings, and excommunication,[1] which could not but bear fruit in the hour of action when the hour and the man had come. He did for the Scottish religion what Socrates did for the Greek mythology, superseded it without open opposition. In this, like Socrates, he became a corrupter of the youth. "Although not a heretic himself," says Dr. Ross, "he was singularly successful in breeding heretics."[2]

But in commerce as in letters there were vast changes at work prophetic of some still vaster. The passion for maritime discovery, which between 1492 and 1497 led to the discovery of America by Columbus, the doubling of the Cape by De Gama, and the

---

[1] Cf. Ross's History and Literature, 233, etc.
[2] Id., p. 237.

discovery of Newfoundland by Cabot, was felt in Scotland, and led to the building of the " Great Michael " and the " Flower " and the " Yellow Carvel." In Sir Andrew Wood of Largo, and Sir Andrew Barton, the spirit of maritime adventure found a chivalrous expression, which made Scotland a formidable rival to all others on the sea. Commerce now began to flourish. Seaports rose into importance, and towns gradually attained an independence which helped to check the presumptuous selfishness of the nobles. The spirit of democracy was being nourished by healthy remunerative labour. Intercourse with other nations broadened men's sympathies. The old feudal relations were being rudely questioned, and men began to look with bewilderment and disgust upon the childish fables and the shamefaced imposture of the Church which they had so long tolerated.

It was in the midst of these times that Dunbar appeared to assist Lyndsay in exposing the spiritual corruption which overshadowed this material prosperity. Having been clerk to some of the numerous embassies employed by James IV., he knew the world, and he did not hate it. He was a keen-sighted man, with a warm love for nature and a penetrative insight into humanity, but not moral enough to detest the pleasures of the clergy which providence did not permit him to enjoy. When we read the Golden Targe, or The Thistle and the Rose, we feel at once that we are walking through well-known Scottish scenes with a companion who intensely loves the landscape which his genius has painted with an artist's colouring and a poet's insight. Had he written no more than these two healthy allegories we might have called him the pure, the gentle-hearted, the refined. But Dunbar had been a Dominican monk. He knew the insincerity and indelicacy of his order. He was versed in the spiritual anatomy of the priests, whom he dissected unmercifully but without disgust. He was a courtier but also a place-hunter, hungering hopelessly for a good fat benefice that would take the satiric sting out of his mouth and make him comfortable like others. Disappointment made him a satirist and kept him so; but his love of natural scenery, combined with his misanthropic indifference to the foibles and vices of humanity, saved him from becoming a pessimist. He certainly deserved a benefice, if not for his own virtues, for his exposure of the vices of others. In him, as in Lyndsay, we get the history of the times presented to us in flesh and blood. We are introduced to veritable priests and people by a humorist who, with dismal realism and fierce wit, smote the vices of both without mercy or without indignation.

But the priests are the special object of ridicule to this unintentional reformer of abuses. We need only turn for proof to one of his poems. The Dance of the Seven Deadly Sins is a weird, grotesque, and somewhat ghastly satire upon the priestly vices of the age. The poet has a dream in which he sees "baith heaven and hell." In the latter region "Mahoun gart cry ane dance" of the wretches "that were never shriven." We see the "holy harlots" trooping in haughtily "with mony sundry guise," yet there is never a smile upon the face of the fiendish master of ceremonies as they prepare for the dance. But immediately "the priests come in with bare shaven necks" to be spectators of the infernal scene, there is a wild chorus of laughter and mockery that fills the nameless place with impious joy. The fact that a poet, who was himself a priest, could venture to offer to his countrymen a satire in which their religious instructors were brought into such irreverent juxtaposition with harlots and in such a place, argues that the priests were doubly-dyed in guilt, the Church blind to her vices, the people prepared either to laugh or weep over the tragic farce of religion.

Sir David Lyndsay of the Mount, though not so great a poet, was a more popular and more humane satirist than Dunbar. He was a lover of righteousness and of men, and hated cant and vice with a fierce hatred that burst through all the canons of delicacy and æstheticism in its irresistible expression. The blunt but kindly squire was the poet of the people. He created and expressed their opinions in popular language and memorable form with a plainness which the people could enjoy, and for which we marvel that he escaped the bonfire or the axe. But Lyndsay was in earnest: so earnest that he did not shrink from exposing the obscenities of his times with a coarse vehemence which itself is only redeemed from the charge of obscenity by its healthy scorn. Dryden says he "lashed vice into reformation." We certainly could not expect such work to be done by a kid-gloved philosopher. It needed one who was not afraid of the dirt he would encounter in his ungenial task. Such was Lyndsay, who did so much for the cause of reform, but withal pure-souled, righteous, "a man of unsuspected probity and veracity," says Buchanan, not to be judged by any modern standard of taste but by that of his own age.

No man, till Knox and his coadjutors appeared on the scene, did more for the Reformation than this honest country squire, the Lyon King of Arms. "If we do not reckon him as one of the Protestant Reformers," says Laing, "it would be a greater mistake should we hesitate for one moment in asserting that his satirical writings had a powerful effect in preparing the minds of his countrymen, by his exposure of the manifold corruption and errors of Popery, for the final triumph of the Reformation, accomplished mainly by the dauntless energy of our great Reformer, John Knox."[1] Lyndsay's picture of his times is sadder because more serious than that of Dunbar. The times of James V. seem to have waxed worse than those of his chivalrous father who fell at the fatal Flodden. Although the Act passed in 1525 against the Lutheran heresy boasted that the country had ever been "clene of all sic filth and vice," there were "filth and vice" as of an Augean stable to be cleaned out of the Church so soon as a Hercules was found. Before the Hercules came Lyndsay created the needed popular disgust which made the cleansing imperative. This he did by his satires, which were the popular literature of his times.

We may examine briefly the chief of these historical pictures of Scotland in the beginning of the sixteenth century. In The Dreme which he addressed with such pathos to James V., whom, as a child, he had carried in his arms and amused with the lute and fairy-like dances and ghost-stories and improvised farces, he gives a vision of the infernal regions as hideous if not so extensive as that of Dante:—

[1] Poetical Works of Sir David Lyndsay, by Laing, vol. i. p. 50. Cf. the exquisite chapter on Lyndsay in Ross's History and Literature.

> " The men of kirk lay bounden into bings ;
> There saw we many careful cardinal,
> And archbishops, in their pontifical;
> Proud and perversed prelates out of number,
> Priors, abbots, and false flatter and friers."[1]

The " lady of portraiture perfite," who acts as Beatrice to this Scottish Dante, reveals the cause of their "punition" generally as " covetice, lust, and ambition." But more specific charges are brought against them. His gentle guide informs him that they are in "this painful poisoned pit"

> " Als they did not instruct the ignorant,
> Provocaut them to penitence by preaching."

But still worse sins than those of neglect were laid to their charge. They had abused and squandered the "Holy Kirkis patrimony" on "cards and dice, on harlotry," content to see

> "Their kirkis riven, their ladies cleanly cled."

In The Complaynt, so tender and fearless, the King is exhorted to reform the spirituality, which is the only thing in the land " without good order." Lyndsay had a deep concern in the education of the poor, and looked to the Church for that help which in later times it did not withhold. The terms of his appeal are as radical and even more evangelical than any used by the Lollards, whose work he was indirectly carrying on. There is a ring of Lutheran doctrine in the lines in which he urges the duty of the priests—

> " To preach with unfeigned intents,
> And truly use the Sacraments,
> After Christ's institutions,
> Leaving their vain traditions,
> Which do the silly sheep illude,

---

[1] The quotations are given in somewhat modernized spelling.

> For whom Christ Jesus shed His blood:
> As superstitious pilgrimages,
> Praying to graven images,
> Express against the Lord's command."

But another phase of shame-faced priestcraft is exposed with a delicate humour that casts a lurid light upon many a death-bed scene of the times, in The Testament and Complaynt of our Soverane Lordis Papyngo. The Papyngo, the king's favourite parrot, is dying and holds a communing with her "holy executors," the Pye, the Raven, and the Gled—a canon regular, a black monk, and a holy friar. They are deeply anxious about her "goodis natural," that she may dispone her gear to them who have the power to bring her "quite to heaven." The poor parrot listens to the counsels and promises of the pious plunderers to this effect:—

> "And we shall sing about your sepulture
> Sanct Mungo's matins, and the meikle creed;
> And syne devoutly say, I you assure,
> The auld Placebo backwards and the beid;
> And we shall wear, for you, the mourning weed.
> And, though your sp'rit with Pluto was professed,
> Devoutly shall your Diregie be addressed."

But the pawky parrot, though dying, is quite a match for them. Not without humour does she remind them, in the midst of their priestly offices for her eternal welfare, that she saw them one day

> "pyke
> Ane chicken from ane hen under ane dyke,"

but she receives the unabashed reply, which confirms her suspicion that their conscience "be nocht gude":—

> "I grant, said he, that hen was my gude friend,
> And I the chicken took but for my teind."

The whole picture is painted from life under the thin guise of allegory. One almost sees the figures in flesh and blood becking and whispering around the bedside of their wealthy victim. At last the Papyngo tells into their ears the history of the decline and fall of the priesthood, and dies, and the clerical harpies pounce upon her and part her body among them while the poor parrot is still hot.

But if The Papyngo introduces us to the death-bed, The Monarchy takes us to church, where

> "Unlearned people on the holy day
> Solemnedly they hear the Evangel sung,
> Not knowing what the priest doth sing or say,
> But as a bell when that they hear it rung."

The sight of the simple folks listening to the Gospel in a foreign language made Lyndsay a brave advocate for the use of his mother-tongue in church. He loved his own language and knew its power. People knew more of Lyndsay than of any of the Apostles. He wonders why the "heavenly wark" should be unknown to common men, and he argues well that it had been a "savourless jest" had God given the law to the Jews in Greek or Latin; and adds with homely pathos—

> "He gave the law on tables hard of stone
> In their own vulgar tongue, Hebrew,
> That all the bairns of Israel, every one,
> Might know the law and so the same pursue."

It is, however, in the Pleasant Satyre of the Thrie Estaitis that the vices of nobles, clergy, and commons are most severely impugned. It was acted for the

---

[1] *Vide* Laing's Memoir of Lyndsay.

first time in Linlithgow[1] in 1539-40 before the King, Queen, ladies of the Court, and nobility, between nine in the morning and six in the evening. It is here that the state of the Church is revealed at its worst. It is, indeed, a sickly revelation, almost unbelievable. The Church has scarcely a rag of virtue left to cover its nakedness. We cannot quote. Nuns, monks, friars, priors, and prelates monopolize the cardinal vices and relate their shameless practices with a matter-of-fact indifference that shocks every finer feeling and makes us stand aghast at the corruption. It seems as if a thousand voices became, at the bidding of Lyndsay, clamant for reformation.

But let us leave his works and look at the man. He is not a Reformer in the common acceptation of the term; but we may question if John Knox's work would have been so successful if Sir David Lyndsay had not lived before him. He did much by his negative work of demolition to make Knox's work of construction possible. The people knew from Lyndsay the disease and were ready to accept the remedy from Knox. He did not live to see the full day of the Reformation. He saw only the first glimmerings of the dawn. His work was that of the iconoclast. He was a redresser of wrongs. Spite of all his honest coarseness, Scotland shall never liquidate her debt to the fearless righteous Sir David Lyndsay, from whose godly heart shot

> "The flash of that satiric rage,
> Which, bursting on the early stage,
> Branded the vices of the age
> And broke the keys of Rome."[1]

[1] Scott's Marmion.

But our work is done. We have filled in roughly the historical background of the picture of the Scottish Reformation. We leave the unfinished canvas for others to complete it by painting in the three great figures of the foreground—Hamilton, Wishart, and Knox.

Patrick Hamilton and George Wishart.

WHAT Lollardism attempted in the fifteenth century John Knox achieved in the latter part of the sixteenth. Between the attempt and the achievement, linking them together as parts of one great movement, stand Patrick Hamilton and George Wishart. There were others, indeed not a few, who during the intervening period laboured strenuously and suffered nobly for the truth, but these, so far as history is concerned, must take a subordinate place. The prominent parts in that act of the drama were played by Hamilton and Wishart. On them the historian necessarily fixes his thoughts, for round them the figures and incidents of the time naturally group themselves. Like the loftiest peaks of a mountain range, they arrest the eye and cast the shadow of their commanding altitude on the lower heights. In them the Reformation succession was continued; through them the Reformation force moved onward, deepening and expanding as it moved; by them the Reformation impulse, weak and wavering at first, but becoming ever stronger and more intense, was transmitted to that shrewd, vigorous, brave man who, by the strength of God, was to complete the overthrow of the kingdom of error, and to secure the establishment of the kingdom of truth in our country.

Unfortunately, we know little of the history of either Hamilton or Wishart. Much we should have been glad to know has been lost, apparently beyond recovery; while not a little has come down to us in a form so vague and fragmentary as to leave room for opinions the most diverse regarding its value and bearing. This is disappointing and oftentimes perplexing. We can only endeavour by careful investigation to arrive at the actual facts and to gain a just estimate of their importance.

Patrick Hamilton was born about the year 1504. More definitely than this we cannot fix the date. For this approximation to it we are indebted to Francis Lambert, who tells us that in 1527, when attending the University of Marburg, his young friend was twenty-three years of age. The place of his birth is as uncertain as the date. In the records of the University of Paris he is designated "Glasguensis," which seems to imply that he was born within the diocese of Glasgow; and as Stonehouse, near Hamilton, was the only property belonging to his father in that diocese, it has been fixed upon by some writers as the scene of the event. But in the album of the University of Marburg he entered himself "Litgoviensis," and this points to the parish of Linlithgow as his native district, and gives support to the view that at Kincavel, which was near the town of Linlithgow, and was also owned by his father, the future martyr first saw the light. With the information which we at present possess it is impossible to decide between those two places.

Happily we are in no doubt as to his descent; it was

noble, even royal. His father was Sir Patrick Hamilton of Stonehouse and Kincavel, who was the eldest of three illegitimate sons borne by Miss Witherspoon of Brighouse, to James, first Lord Hamilton, before he married Princess Mary, sister of James III. and Countess of Arran, by whom he had one son, James, afterwards second Lord Hamilton and first Earl of Arran. His mother was Catherine Stewart, daughter of Alexander Duke of Albany, second son of James II., and Catherine Sinclair, daughter of William Earl of Orkney. Though of high parentage, Catherine was, like her husband, illegitimate; this was the result of a divorce obtained by Alexander on the ground of propinquity, though only of the fourth degree. Her maternal grandmother was Lady Margaret Douglas, daughter of Archibald, fourth Earl of Angus, and Margaret Stewart, eldest daughter of Robert III., and therefore aunt of the famous Gavin Douglas, Bishop of Dunkeld. Thus in the veins of the first Scottish martyr there flowed royal blood, and round him there fell a faint reflection of the light that "beats upon the throne"; he was the great-great-grandson of Robert III., the great-grandson of James II., and by his grandfather's marriage he was virtually related to James IV., who was King at the time of his birth.

Regarding his early education no information has come down to us, but that it would be carefully attended to admits of no doubt. From his infancy, indeed, he would breathe a cultured atmosphere. Among his relatives, both paternal and maternal, there were many who were remarkable for their refinement and courtesy, for their polish and accomplishments, for their love and pursuit of learning. Whether he was sent to one of the grammar schools that were then making their appearance in Scotland or committed to the care of his friends, we cannot say, but that everything was done that could be done to secure for him the best possible instruction we may be sure : nay, that this was the case we have proof in the ability and attainments by which he was distinguished in after years.

The school is not, however, the only educating influence under which a youth comes. He has other teachers than those that guide him in his studies. The events of the time, his social and political surroundings, these do their part, often a very important part, in moulding his character and fitting him for the work that lies before him; and the general character of the events witnessed by Hamilton and of the surroundings amidst which he grew up we can easily discover. The times were troublous ; the political sky was often overcast; violent storms frequently swept across the country, and to these the Hamilton family could not remain indifferent : in the issue they had not seldom the deepest interest. In 1513, when Patrick was a boy of ten years of age, the battle of Flodden, with its crushing defeat, filled the land with woe and lamentation; in that fell disaster many of the wisest and bravest and best of Scotland's sons were smitten and slain by the side of their King. The minority that followed gave ample opportunity for intrigue and treachery on one hand, and for honour and patriotism on the other. The French and English parties in Scottish politics were then taking shape. The houses of Hamilton and of Douglas, too, were settling down into mutual jealousy and hate. Stirring times they were ;

and to all that was being said and done the young Patrick must have been fully alive; in every incident he must have taken a keen interest. It was indeed impossible for him to act otherwise. The fortunes, the very existence of the family, often depended on the result of struggle and negotiation. Sir Patrick was more than once in imminent danger, and did eventually lose his life in the well-known encounter in the High Street of Edinburgh with Angus and his followers, called "Cleanse the Causeway." Thus, inheriting his father's brave and chivalrous spirit, he was reared in circumstances the most congenial for its development, and, by the experiences of his boyhood and youth he was prepared for exhibiting a bravery and a chivalry that would win for him fame and glory greater far than had been won by his father in the tournament and in the battlefield.

Of the domestic circle and the spirit that reigned there we are ignorant. Concerning his mother only one item of information has reached us, but it is most valuable, supplying, as it does, strong and touching testimony to the purity of her character and the beneficial influence exercised by her on her children. When bound to the stake, and face to face with death, her son spoke of her with tenderness and affection, recalling, doubtless, not only the care with which she had nursed and tended him in early years, but also, and most of all, the high principles she had inculcated, the spiritual truths with which she had familiarized and impressed his young mind, and the noble, holy life she had led, confirming and illustrating by her example the lessons she taught.

He was early directed by his parents to the Church as the sphere within which he must seek place and promotion. At that time there were many rich and enviable ecclesiastical appointments, and these were eagerly sought after and easily gained by the sons of the nobility. Such appointments, while in themselves honourable and lucrative, did not demand the exclusive attention and effort of those who held them; they in no way interfered with activity, either in politics or in war. The ecclesiastic might take his full share—often took more than his share—in the government of the country; he also might, and often did, exchange the mitre and the crosier for the helmet and the sword, and not a few Church dignitaries signalized themselves more by their martial skill and valour than by their evangelical fervour and activity, by their exploits in the field of battle than by their proclamation of the Gospel of Peace. At the very time when young Hamilton's mind was directed to it, the Church was betraying marked signs of weakness and corruption. Worldliness was blighting its spirituality, vice was stifling its morality, hypocrisy was discrediting the truth, of which it proclaimed itself the repository and the teacher. The most shameful devices were resorted to to gain rich benefices, and the revenues thus gained were diverted to the most shameful uses. Bishops stooped to any artifice in order to secure an archbishopric. The qualifications demanded or appealed to were not those of the New Testament—they were power to bribe a superior, skill to outwit or force to crush an opponent. With carnal weapons men fought for spiritual positions, and, having secured them, they employed them for carnal ends.

Of the precise state of affairs Patrick cannot have been ignorant. The disgraceful scramble and struggle for the Archbishopric of St. Andrews, rendered vacant by the death of Alexander Stewart at Flodden, he must have watched closely. Like most such transactions, it was as much political as ecclesiastical in its bearings. On the one side or the other the nobles ranged themselves, according as the leanings of the candidate were towards them or their opponents in the State. One of the candidates was Gavin Douglas, his mother's cousin; but with their relative the members of the Kincavel household could show little sympathy, for he belonged to the Angus party, with which, at this time, the Arran party, to which the Hamiltons belonged, were at variance. Of the feelings with which the future martyr watched the contest we have no record, but, if the boy was father to the man, he must have been deeply wounded and greatly scandalized. In harmony, though it unhappily was, with the ideas of the age, the glaring inconsistency it presented must have struck—and struck forcibly and painfully—the youth who in a few years was to display an acute intellect touched by a pure morality and a high spirituality.

Shortly after the settlement of this dispute he himself received an appointment in connection with the Church: he was named titular Abbot of Ferne, in Rossshire. This appointment was received in 1517—probably the summer of 1517, as his predecessor died on 17th June of that year. It appears as if this office was sought in order that the emoluments attached to it might enable him to prosecute his study in a manner that would qualify him for the highest offices and honours in the ecclesiastical sphere. Nor did his duties as abbot interfere with his study; it was not needful that he should at once attend at the abbey, and we do not know that he ever even saw the religious house whence he took his title and gained his income. Indeed there is good ground for believing that at this period the abbey was in a dilapidated state, so that the appointment was in the fullest sense a sinecure.

In this same year he went to Paris, attracted by the fame of its university. In all probability he attached himself to the Scots' College, which had been founded there in the time of Robert the Bruce for the benefit of those going from this country to France to complete their education. But whatever college he entered, the transition from Scotland to Paris would be, in an intellectual respect, great and important. The university of the French capital was then the most illustrious school of philosophy and theology in Europe. More valuable, however, than the lectures delivered by its professors was the spirit of inquiry and investigation that was abroad in this centre of learning and culture. At once the student, who took up his residence there, experienced the quickening influence of the new life that was pulsing in every member of the body intellectual of the civilized world. The dreary night of Scholasticism had begun to yield slowly and reluctantly to the dawn of free and vigorous thought that was heralded by the Renaissance, and on Paris the first beams of the coming day had fallen with a brightness that gladdened some, while it startled and terrified others. The voice of Erasmus had been heard, and had awakened a sympathetic response. The result of his appeal was distinctly seen in a deepening dissatisfaction with the barren subtleties of the old systems, and a deepening desire for the living and life-giving fruits of past civilization. Peter the Lombard and Thomas Aquinas were being forsaken for Plato and Aristotle. The "Sentences" ceased to prove attractive when the "Dialogues" were exposed to view and offered to all.

But another voice besides that of Erasmus had been heard in Paris; another appeal, more vigorous and thrilling even than that of the gentle, timid humanist had been addressed to the thoughtful and the devout in that city as elsewhere. That same year in which Hamilton went abroad, Luther nailed his theses to the door of the church at Wittenberg, and the strokes of his hammer were echoed in the French capital. Much consternation, too, did those echoes cause; much disputation did they occasion. For a whole year the Sorbonne was occupied considering the writings of the Saxon monk; and in their work the liveliest interest was manifested. Luther's reply, hurled at the learned doctors of this famous school, quickened this interest, and impelled those in whom it had been excited to investigation—investigation for which they had been prepared by Erasmus, but of which Erasmus was not always ready to approve. Under such influences as these the young Scotchman came—he could not escape them, nor did he desire to do so. His open, candid mind, thirsting for truth, received communications from every quarter, and accepted whatever was valuable, by whomsoever offered. The ordinary course of study pursued by him was such as he would have followed had he gone to Glasgow or St. Andrews, but this was a less fruitful element in his education at the French capital than his contact with the spirit of the age. Indeed, the prescribed curriculum yielded him

negative rather than positive gain. It revealed to him
the poverty of the systems and the teaching that were
offered in the name of philosophy and theology, and
convinced him that, if satisfaction were to be enjoyed,
he must turn to the new treasures that were being discovered and unsealed.

In 1520 he took his degree. On 30th April of
that year his father was killed, but this event did not
hasten his return home. After his graduation he went
to Louvain. There Erasmus was living, and there the
Trilingual College had been founded. His object in
going thither was doubtless to see and hear Erasmus,
and to reap the fruit of the new learning as that was
presented in the college. While there, therefore, his
Erasmian tendencies must have been confirmed; his
thirst for truth would be intensified, and his determination to reach the fountain at which alone it could
be quenched would be strengthened.

We next meet with him at St. Andrews. When he
returned home we cannot tell; we only know that
on the 9th June, 1523, he was incorporated in the
University of that ancient city. This act made him a
member without admitting him to any of the Faculties;
but on 3rd October, 1524, he gained admission to the
Faculty of Arts. We need not be surprised that he
should have resolved to settle for a time in St.
Andrews. For a youth of his tastes and attainments
no spot in the country could present stronger attractions. It was the ecclesiastical capital of the kingdom,
the seat of the oldest university, and the centre of learning. Connected with its cathedral, its colleges, and its
monasteries, there were many men of elevated tastes
and wide culture. There more than anywhere else in

z

his native land was the graduate of Paris, "*ingenio summo et eruditione singulari*," likely to find congenial society and to experience quickening impulses.

With which of its three colleges he connected himself we have no certain knowledge. His leanings, however, were most in accord with the spirit that animated the heads of St. Leonard's. Not that in it the new systems had been adopted and the new learning gladly received. Though founded in 1512, only twelve years before Hamilton's admission, it had in its arrangements more affinity with the old than with the new methods and pursuits. But in St. Andrews, as in Paris, there was a movement outside the recognized course which was stirred and sustained by the intellectual revival that was now affecting even the "Ultima Thule"; and that movement found ampler scope amongst the members of this institution than amongst the members of the Pedagogy or of St. Salvator's. To it, then, rather than to either of the other two he would go. And this conclusion, drawn from a general view of the circumstances, is confirmed by some facts that are known to us. While at St. Andrews he composed a mass, arranged in parts for nine voices, which was sung in the cathedral under his leadership. This is a proof of his refinement and accomplishment; it also indicates the high respect in which he was held by those in authority. But most important of all in the present reference, it points to connection with St. Leonard's, for the Canons of the Priory with which St. Leonard's was associated were the Canons of the Cathedral, and singing was one of the regular prescribed exercises in that college for those who displayed an aptitude for music. On those connected with the Priory, indeed, seems to have devolved the care of the choral part of the service in the cathedral; only, therefore, in all probability, to a member of the Priory College would permission have been granted to superintend the execution of his own composition. Amongst those, too, who were Canons of the Priory and members of St. Leonard's, Hamilton found in after years his warmest friends, and more than one became conspicuous by their profession of and adherence amidst difficulties to Reformation principles.

Hamilton doubtless sought admission to this university in order that he might study theology. As an aspirant to ecclesiastical honours this subject would demand attention, and his residence at Paris, tending, as it evidently did, to give him a high idea of the work of a priest, would urge him to seek the best guidance in his study that was available. At St. Andrews there was at this period one who had already acquired fame as a teacher in this department—viz., John Major, who was a Doctor of the Sorbonne. He was lecturing in Paris during the first year at least of Hamilton's stay there, so that in all likelihood the two had met in France. It is interesting, also, to note that both were incorporated in the University of St. Andrews on the same day; and it is at least permissible to suppose that the incorporation of the student was due so far to the incorporation of the professor. After leaving the French capital, Major had gone to Glasgow, and thither his name had drawn students from all quarters. Among those who sat at his feet in the West was John Knox; and now in the East Patrick Hamilton was to listen to his prelections. Soon both were to outstrip their leader in the search for truth—

the one to die in its defence, and the other to suffer and at length to conquer in its name.

John Frith, in his preface to "Patrick's Places," tells us that Hamilton became a priest when at St. Andrews: his statement is, "To testifie the truth, he sought all meanes and tooke upon him priesthode (even as Paule circumcised Timothy to wynne the weake Jews) that he might be admitted to preache the pure Word of God." Could this statement be accepted by us as true, it would be most valuable and instructive; it would indicate the point which the future martyr had reached, and would illustrate the gradual nature of his advance to Reformation ground. But there are several weighty objections to its acceptance. In the first place, at the time referred to Hamilton was too young to be admitted in ordinary course to the priesthood, and there was no reason why, in his case, the ecclesiastics should take advantage of the permission granted them to set aside the rules, when by so doing the interests of the Church would be served; there was indeed very good reason why they should refuse so to act, considering the foreign and pernicious influences under which the applicant had come. In the second place, there is no reference whatever to his ordination in the documents relating to his trial. He is called *magister*, but not *presbyter*, in the summons issued and in the sentence pronounced; and he was not, as were the law and practice of the Church, divested of his sacerdotal authority and dignity before he was handed over to the secular power to be punished. Laxity and haste might, as has been urged, account for the latter omission, but not for the former. In the third place, Alexander Alesius, to whom we are indebted for nearly all the trustworthy information we possess regarding him at this period, does not mention his taking upon himself the priesthood. This silence is all the more significant since he is careful to tell us that "such was his hatred to monkish hypocrisy that he never assumed the monkish habit." Reference to his attitude toward the abbacy would naturally, we may even say certainly, have led to a reference to his attitude toward the priesthood, had he taken orders. And of the step Alesius could not possibly have been ignorant, as he was in St. Andrews throughout Hamilton's residence at St. Leonard's, and was evidently on terms of the closest intimacy with him. For these among other reasons the assertion made by Frith must be looked upon as at least doubtful—in all probability a mistaken inference on the writer's part from the Reformer's general position. Could we be certain that Frith, as is alleged, met Hamilton at Marburg and enjoyed his fellowship for some months, his testimony would gain in value, but evidence on this point is wanting; authorities, indeed, seem to point in the opposite direction.

Whether ordained or not, he did not conceal his views on religious matters. Before the beginning of 1527 he had made his theological position quite clear to those with whom he came into contact. That it was a position that exposed him to danger he knew full well. In 1525 an Act was passed by Parliament condemning Lutheranism, and forbidding strangers to "bring with them any books or works of Luther or his disciples," or "to rehearse his opinions unless it be to the confusion thereof." This Act was due to the exertions of the bishops, due especially to David Beaton, who had lately come from France to Arbroath, and who from the date of his arrival till his death controlled in a large measure the action of the Church. But despite the condemnation and the warning, which it published, the new opinions and the heretical books found their way into the country, and with them came, in large quantities, Tyndale's New Testament. And the way was prepared for these by the state of the Church. Those who filled its offices and wore its titles did not preserve its purity or commend its truths; they were often ignorant of the Scriptures, stained by profligacy, more deeply concerned with politics than with religion. So rapidly did the proscribed volumes and pernicious doctrines spread that in 1527 it was found needful to extend the provisions of the Act of 1525 so as to embrace the King's lieges; they were to be punished in the same way as strangers, should they be proved to be "assisters to such opinions," and only "clerks in schools" were granted permission to dispute. Before this, however, the Archbishop had dealt with Hamilton. While in residence at St. Leonard's he did not attempt to hide his liking for the truths proclaimed by Luther: in discussion and in conversation he declared his approval of them with all the energy and fervour of one who had experienced their power. This was more than the Church dignitaries could permit; whatever else they did or failed to do, they must show themselves zealous for the truth as that had been defined by the Fathers and the Councils. For some time, indeed, Hamilton was left free to set forth his opinions and to argue in their defence. This liberty of speech was due to the civil complications in which Beaton was involved. These diverted his attention from the events that were taking place in his diocese;

they even brought him into disgrace and exposed him to danger, so that he deemed it needful to seek safety in disguise. In the garb of a shepherd he tended sheep on the hills of Fife until his money and the efforts of his friends secured his return to power. During that period no action could be taken against heresy or heretic; and thus, notwithstanding the condemnation and the penalty proclaimed by authority of Parliament, the heresy spread and the heretic laboured. But the restoration of the Archbishop to place and favour was the signal for vigorous effort. During Lent, 1527, that effort was directed against Hamilton. Beaton, having made inquiry, found him "infamed with the heresy of Luther," and summoned him to appear and answer the charges that were to be brought against him. Hearing of the danger that threatened him, Patrick left St. Andrews and betook himself to Germany. He was not yet fully qualified for the martyr's work and the martyr's crown. He must have a firmer grasp, a clearer view, a richer experience of Divine truth than he yet had before he could suffer for its sake. And he went where he was likely to gain these—to the land of Luther.

Apparently his destination was Wittenberg. Thither he was attracted by the fame of the great Reformer and of those who had gathered round him in the university; from their lips he was desirous of hearing the words of Life. But his desire was not to be gratified. At that time the plague was raging violently in the town, and he either, on hearing this, turned aside before reaching it, or else, because of the danger, left it earlier than he had intended. Certainly he did not enrol himself as a student.

At Marburg he settled. The University there had just been founded by the Landgrave of Hesse. Among the distinguished teachers who had joined it was Francis Lambert, the famous theologian. For the young Scotchman he would have special attraction, and to him he would afford much help. Listening to his lectures, Hamilton's convictions would be deepened and his zeal would be quickened. The whole surroundings, indeed, would contribute to this result; the air was charged with Reformation principles and Reformation fervour. That he reaped much benefit, and made considerable progress, we have conclusive proof in the only work from his pen that has come down to us. It was written during his stay in Marburg, and contains theses put forth and defended by him at the university. It was published at the request of Lambert, and thus testifies to the high esteem in which the student was held by the professor.

At this university he remained only one session. That short period sufficed so to expand his views of Divine truth, and to strengthen his devotion to his "good and gentle Lord," that he felt himself prepared to meet the difficulties and dangers from which he had fled. He was persuaded that it was his duty to do what lay within his power to enlighten his countrymen, and he resolved, at whatever cost, to discharge that duty. Leaving the two companions who had travelled with him to Marburg, he returned to Scotland. On his arrival he went to Kincavel, now the property and residence of his brother, James, Sheriff of Linlithgow. There he remained for some time. At once he began to preach "alse weal in publict as in secret," and he continued to do so until prevented by the action of the

Archbishop. His preaching was much appreciated and highly beneficial not only to the members of his brother's household, but also to the inhabitants of the adjoining districts. He had "a great following," and those who listened to his fervent presentation of evangelical truth, experienced quickening, enlightenment and comfort.

Shortly after his return he married. Who the lady was who became his bride we do not know: indeed the fact of his marriage was only lately discovered. It was known that he had left a daughter, but it was supposed that she was illegitimate, and the supposition cast a shadow on his otherwise pure and noble character. That the supposition was incorrect we learn from Alesius, who states distinctly that Hamilton "shortly before his death married a young lady of noble rank."

Not long did the pair enjoy the happiness and the comforts of married life; not long was Hamilton permitted to proclaim the Gospel of Jesus Christ. His return and his activity in disseminating heresy were duly reported to Beaton. Of these the Archbishop must take account; even if he were willing to treat them lightly, there were those by his side, notably his nephew David, who were determined to proceed to the extremest measures in order to stamp out the evil. And by his conduct the Reformer had thrown down a challenge which the ecclesiastics must take up if they wished to retain their hold on the people. When summoned to appear before the Court of the Primate and meet grave accusations of doctrinal error, he had made his escape, and, after a few months' absence in that country the very atmosphere of which was tainted with heresy, he had come back to set himself even more openly and more distinctly than before in opposition to the authorities. In his utterances he did not after his return confine himself to the statement of evangelical principles; he did more than preach salvation by faith; he attacked the institutions, denied the authority, and defied the power of the Church. Once more, then, he is cited to appear at St. Andrews. The terms of the citation are important, shedding light, as they do, on the position taken up by the Reformer. He is charged with teaching that neither the laws, the canons, the ordinances and decrees of the Fathers, nor human institutions are to be obeyed; that the keys and censures of the Church are to be despised; that no reliance is to be placed on the Sacraments of the same; that churches are not to be attended; that images are not to be worshipped; that prayers are not to be offered for the souls of the dead; that tithes are not to be paid to God and the Church; that good works do not of merit secure salvation, and that evil deeds do not of desert entail punishment; that our ancestors, trusting in the Church of God and in the Sacraments of the same, died in a corrupt and false faith and were buried in hell.[1]

It was easy for Beaton to issue his summons; it was not so easy for him to carry it into effect; he must act with the utmost caution. The heretic had many powerful relatives who were ready to defend him. The Hamiltons and the Douglases, too, were then on

[1] Citatio Patricii Hamilton e Formulari Vetere Andreano. This document was recently discovered in the library of St. Andrews University by Prof. Mitchell, to whom I am indebted for a copy. On its issue I base my arrangement of the events connected with his apprehension.

friendly terms, so that if the Archbishop acted hastily and carelessly he might array against himself their combined opposition. Most important of all, the young King was interested in the young preacher, and might exercise his authority on his behalf. The two must have met frequently. In the palace of Linlithgow, "the Versailles of the period," James often lived, and at Kincavel, in its vicinity, Hamilton resided with his brother when not attending the university; the two families were also closely connected. It is therefore impossible to suppose that they were not acquainted with each other, even though no definite statement to this effect remains. In any case James might be approached either by the Reformer or by his friends; and he was. When the citation was issued, an appeal was made to him. And anxious to shelter one for whom he had a high regard, but unwilling to offend the clergy by taking a decided stand, he recommended Patrick to endeavour to come to terms with the Archbishop, and with the view of helping on this result he suggested a conference. To this suggestion Beaton readily agreed; in all probability it was his own. At any rate, since the conference was to be held at St. Andrews, it would further his plan, for it would bring his victim within his power, so that should he refuse to recant he could be easily seized; it would also afford him and those associated with him longer time to negotiate with Angus, and in this way to secure not only his favour, but also that of the King, who was practically under his control. Knox says that the Archbishop "so travailled with Maister Patrick that he gat him to Sanctandrosse." And this would be true if, as is likely, he strove to give to the conference a plausible look, and to hold out hope that by means of it a reconciliation might be effected. In harmony with this view was the conduct of the Primate. For the suspected preacher he provided lodgings; after his arrival he met with him more than once, discussed the need for certain changes, and even professed agreement with many of the points urged by him. Indeed, his whole bearing toward him had at first the appearance at least of friendship. He allowed him to enjoy perfect freedom; he permitted him to receive at his lodgings all who visited him, and to move about amongst his former acquaintances without let or hindrance.

But Hamilton was not deceived by the conduct of Beaton. He yielded to the King's wish, and expressed himself willing to confer with the Primate. But he entertained not the faintest hope of either securing his own release, or bringing about reform. He saw precisely how matters stood in the civil sphere. The recommendation of James, to seek peace with the Archbishop, taught him that neither he nor Angus could or would shield him from harm. This they could only do at the risk of breaking with the clergy, and that was a step neither was prepared to take. Each was anxious to retain the favour of the Church, and so to ensure its aid when that might prove helpful; hence the King's reluctance to interfere, and Angus's readiness to acquiesce. Fully aware of the state of the case, Hamilton left Kincavel convinced that he was going to his doom. While still at liberty in St. Andrews he was urged both by his friends and opponents to flee; he was even assured on the best authority that the Archbishop would be pleased if he accepted the advice offered. But he steadily refused to do so; he as steadily sought to dissuade his friends from having recourse to physical force on his behalf. He had fled before, but he would not do so again; he would remain at his post, and, if need be, by his death prove the sincerity of his profession and the power of Divine truth to strengthen for duty and sustain under trial.

For a month he was allowed to enjoy perfect freedom. That interval he employed in presenting Reformation doctrines to all whom he met. The conviction that had taken possession of him that his time was short influenced his teaching. It not only rendered him more ardent in his endeavours to impress his hearers, but it led him to confine himself more particularly to the exhibition of saving truth. While at Kincavel he had dealt with the externals of the Catholic system, as well as with the great essential doctrines of Christianity; at St. Andrews he followed a different course; he was anxious to teach men and bring them within the benign and vivifying influence of the Gospel, feeling assured that if he succeeded in thus affecting them he would prepare efficient instruments for accomplishing the work which he had been compelled to abandon. And his efforts were not altogether fruitless; some who came to converse with him in the hope that they might bring him back to the orthodox faith were, by his cogent reasoning, themselves drawn away and led to accept the new system. This was strikingly the case with Alexander Alane, afterwards called Alesius, who conceived a strong affection for Hamilton, an affection that led him, a few years after his death, to embody in his Commentary on the 37th Psalm a brief narrative of the martyr, which contains much information not to be found in any other volume. And the depth of his affection for the Reformer was an indication of the depth of the impression made on his heart by the Reformer's utterances; though he escaped death, he passed through much suffering because of his attachment to the Lutheran doctrines taught him by Hamilton, and he only preserved his life by flight.

Not a few, however, sought an audience with him from another and entirely different motive. They came as emissaries from the "chief priests" to catch him in his words, or rather, to extract from him his opinions, and report them to those that sent them, in order that material for weighty accusations might be gathered and witnesses might be secured to prove the charges made.

At length all was ready. It was notified to Hamilton that, in terms of the citation served upon him, he must attend on the day named therein to explain his position with regard to certain statements contrary to the orthodox faith, said to have been made by him. He did attend; he even anticipated the hour of meeting, so eager was he to face his accusers and declare in their presence his convictions. Thirteen articles of heresy were read over, and these he was charged with having taught and defended. Six of the thirteen he admitted to be disputable, but he refused to condemn them until stronger reasons against them than he had yet heard had been adduced. The remaining seven he confessed having taught and defended; and he declared himself prepared to defend them still further, absolutely refusing to recant or modify his utterances. These charges, with the arguments advanced by him in support of them, were referred to a body of theologians for examination. The result was, as might have been expected, that they were condemned; all the points submitted were declared to be at variance with the teaching of the Church. It was arranged that this condemnation should be presented to an ecclesiastical court, to be held in the cathedral on the last day of February, and by it ratified.

After his examination, Hamilton was permitted to return to his lodgings, and, pending the report of the theologians, he was to be allowed to enjoy the freedom hitherto accorded. Such at least was the intention of the Archbishop, but he saw cause to alter his plans. Hamilton's friends had determined to accomplish his release, and for this purpose they decided to call out and arm all the men at their command. Patrick's brother, the Sheriff of Linlithgow, did gather his forces together, and was only prevented marching on St. Andrews by a violent storm that rendered the passage of the Firth of Forth impossible until too late. Duncan, of Airdrie, also collected his few retainers, and was on the way to attack the Primate when he was met and overpowered by the Primate's soldiers.

Learning that such attempts at a rescue were being contemplated, Beaton deemed it desirable to secure his victim, and gave orders for his apprehension. His orders were at once carried out. At night the captain of the Castle drew a body of armed men round the house in which Hamilton was living. He at once surrendered himself, beseeching the friends who were with him to offer no resistance. He was conveyed to the Castle, and kept there till the day fixed for the trial. On the day appointed a vast concourse of

Church dignitaries assembled in the cathedral. To Friar Campbell was assigned the task of conducting the case. This task he greatly disliked; secretly, as Hamilton reminded him, he sympathized with the heretical opinions which he had to denounce. In private he had often acquiesced in the views expressed by the Reformer, and it required not a little effrontery to accuse in public the man with whom he had agreed in private. Campbell first read over the written charges which Hamilton had already admitted, and which had been adjudged heretical. These the accused met so firmly and defended so ably that it was thought needful to add others in order that those present might be convinced that he was indeed worthy of heavy punishment. Campbell being instructed to do so, took up points which, though of minor importance, were more serviceable than the others, because they were within the comprehension of the audience. These concerned the lawfulness of reading the Word of God, of worshiping images, of praying to saints, and in particular to the Virgin Mary, and the existence of purgatory. With regard to these matters the accused stated his opinions clearly and courageously; and those opinions were distinctly at variance alike with the views of the judges and the beliefs of the people. Knowing this, Campbell turned triumphantly to the tribunal and said, "My Lord Archbishop, you hear he denies the institutions of the holy Kirk and the authority of our holy Father the Pope. I need not to accuse him any more." Unanimously he was condemned, and sentenced to be delivered to the secular power for punishment. His condemnation seemed to rest on "trifles," but it really rested on the weightiest matters of the law, though for the sake of gaining popular approval the former were emphasized.

The sentence was carried out that very day. The only civil warrant obtained was one signed by the Archbishop's own bailiff. No time was allowed for an appeal to the King; indeed such an appeal would have been useless. The King, as we have already seen, had been approached when the citation was issued, but without success; and, lest any subsequent application might be successful, the Church authorities had arranged with Angus that James, who was under his control, should visit the shrine of St. Duthac in Ross-shire. When the sentence was pronounced, then, he was far beyond the reach of Hamilton or of his friends; and that no opportunity of reaching him might be afforded them, the sentence was executed with most unseemly haste.

At noon the stake was prepared in the area in front of St. Salvator's College. Hamilton calmly awaited the fatal hour in one of the rooms of the Castle, and when the captain intimated that the pile was ready he walked forth with a quick, firm step. To a friend he gave his copy of the Evangelists, and to his servant his cap and gown, and other upper garments. He was urged to recant, but refused to do so. Having been bound by a chain to the stake, he sought in prayer strength for himself and enlightenment for his country. His sufferings were severe and prolonged. The fire when first applied only exploded the gunpowder, but did not ignite the faggots; partly burned, he asked them to fetch more gunpowder and wood. While waiting for these his agony was intense, but he showed no sign of impatience; on the contrary, he spoke comforting words to those who were present. At length the flames kindled round him, but so slowly did they do their work that it was six o'clock before his body was consumed. Thus for six hours the execution lasted, but during all this time, says Alesius, who was an eyewitness of the scene, "the martyr never gave one sign of impatience or anger, nor ever called to heaven for vengeance upon his persecutors, so great was his faith, so strong his confidence in God."

Of Hamilton's theological position we have a clear indication in "Patrick's Places." This work is interesting as the first statement of doctrine that was called forth in connection with the Scottish Reformation. It is distinctly evangelical in tone and scope. It has been called Lutheran, but that term, suggestive as it is of the later peculiarities of German theology, is somewhat misleading when applied to Hamilton's theses. They present a lucid and pointed summary of the vital truths that the Wittenberg monk had, by his own experience, been led to set before his fellow-countrymen. They deal with such fundamental questions as the difference between the law and the gospel, faith and works, justification and holiness. And the ease and maturity with which he discusses these matters is truly remarkable when his circumstances are fairly considered. With a steady hand he traces the dividing line between truth and error; with singular precision he marks off the respective spheres of law and gospel; with striking accuracy and rare felicity he expounds and illustrates the relation between faith and works. The key-note of the whole is faith; faith as the ground of justification and sanctification; faith as the root whence spring hope and charity; faith as the bond linking us to Christ, and so enabling us to keep the

Commandments. These were the doctrines he proclaimed in his preaching and upheld in his discussions: doctrines that were vastly different from those to which the people had been so long accustomed; that were instinct with life, aglow with love, and bright with hope; that struck a death-blow at the system of empty rites and dead ceremonies with which the country had hitherto had to be satisfied; that, by setting forth the possibility of salvation apart from sacerdotal instrumentality, undermined the pretensions of priest and of Pope; that, by proving the necessary connection between a Christian profession and purity of life, brought out into striking prominence the inconsistencies that marked the lives of the clergy. When we appreciate aright the nature of Hamilton's teaching, and remember the condition of the country and the Church, we shall not wonder that when he spoke men listened and responded to his appeal, and the Cardinal trembled and felt compelled to silence his voice.

When we read "Patrick's Places" we perceive the distinction between Hamilton and the Lollards. The latter dealt with the fruits, the former went down to the root. John Resby and those who followed him pointed out and attacked many evils and errors, setting forth at the same time the truth as it bore upon the matters referred to; but they failed to reach, or at least to see distinctly, the ground and source of all these evils and errors. This, Hamilton, following Luther, did. Seizing firmly the spiritual aspect of religion, discerning clearly that the act by which we become Christian is a movement of the heart, he understood fully the fallacy on which the Church of Rome had reared its system. If justification was by faith, and by faith alone, then it was folly, worse than folly, to identify salvation with external processes, to permit any man to intervene between the individual soul and God, to believe that one who was vicious in life was, or could be, the channel of Divine grace. When this doctrine was distinctly apprehended and emphatically declared, the pretensions of Rome were proved to be unfounded, arrogant, aye blasphemous.

"The reik of Maister Patrick Hamilton has infected as many as it blew upon:" so said Johnnie Lyndsay to James Beaton, and there was more truth in the saying than the Archbishop was ready to admit. The extreme measures resorted to, so far from arresting the spread of the new doctrines, as was intended, gave them a wider currency. Men of all classes felt constrained to ask why one so pure and gentle, so noble and good, should have suffered martyrdom, and the inquiry wrought in them the belief that the martyr was right and that his persecutors were wrong. Thus he exercised a more powerful influence by his death than by his life: many were affected by the pains he endured who would have paid little heed to the words he uttered. Indeed, until Wishart began his work, the teaching of Hamilton continued the moving spring of the Reformation in Scotland; so far as we can gather, those who, in the intervening period stood forth to bear witness to the truth, and, if called upon to seal their testimony with their blood, assumed substantially his doctrinal position.

Naturally the first and most decided effects of Hamilton's influence appeared in St. Andrews—the scene of his earlier and later teaching and the place of his martyrdom. Those living in that ancient city ad seen the man, had listened to his words, had felt the charm of his sweet and beautiful character, had been impressed by the calm heroism with which he met his fate. This was specially true of the canons of the priory, many of whom, both when he was in residence at St. Leonard's and when he moved amongst them under suspicion, had recognized and admitted the force of his appeals and arguments. Of these, several now ranged themselves on the side of Lutheranism.

But the leaven was not confined in its working to St. Andrews; it spread throughout the land, making its presence and operation manifest in many directions and in many forms. In the circumstances it could not well be otherwise. On St. Andrews no fewer than twenty-eight religious houses were dependent; between these institutions and their head there was frequent communication; a movement at the centre could not fail to make itself felt at every point in the circumference. These religious houses again had their dependencies—their members doing parochial work in connection with the churches of the surrounding districts. In this way the light that had been kindled by Hamilton and fanned into bright glow by the fury of his adversaries shed its guiding and cheering radiance far and wide.

Nor was its diffusion limited to the monasteries; it touched also the laity, and especially those occupying high positions in the social and intellectual spheres. Many of the sons of the nobility were studying at the University of St. Andrews when the Church pronounced and carried out its cruel sentence, and, like the others who were in the city, they turned their attention to the matters in dispute, with the result that some accepted the heresy of Luther as the truth of God. When they visited their homes they carried with them the doctrines they had received and commended them to their friends. Apart from this, however, the death of Patrick Hamilton would have excited interest amongst the titled classes. He was related to those who bore honourable names; he could claim kinship with some of the noblest in the land, even with the King himself. It was therefore impossible that his death could be passed by without notice or comment. The prelates did not desire that it should; it was designed to act as a warning to those who were tempted to stray from the path of orthodoxy. In many cases, even amongst the nobility, it had the very opposite effect. Men thought, and thought rightly, that if one so devout and holy as Patrick Hamilton had been, had not walked in the path of orthodoxy that path could not be the way of righteousness.

Thus, despite the death of the Reformer, the Reformation went on, taking an ever-wider sweep and an ever-stronger hold on the nation. It is, however, no easy task to mark accurately the course it took or the extent of its operation during the period that elapsed between the martyrdom of Hamilton and the preaching of Wishart. That it was advancing there is abundant evidence—evidence frequently of a sad and painful kind, but the advance itself we cannot trace or estimate with certainty. This is due in great measure to the political troubles and complications of that epoch, and to the relations, oftentimes subtle and intricate, between the two parties in the civil and the two parties in the religious sphere. The maintenance of the Church became associated with one faction in the State, its reformation with another; and it is well-nigh impossible to unravel the web and set forth accurately what was due to zeal for the truth and what to baser and less worthy motives.

The main features of the period may, however, without difficulty be briefly sketched. It runs practically parallel with the reign of James V., from his escape from the power of Angus till his death. His flight from Falkland to Stirling took place a few months after Hamilton was burned, and he died in December, 1542.

As a result of the restraints imposed on him during his minority the King entertained feelings of keen enmity toward the barons and of bitter hatred toward the Douglases. He thought that the nobility had been growing in importance, and had been invading the possessions and the prerogatives of the Crown, and he determined to humble them and to regain what he had lost. But if he separated himself from the aristocracy, to whom could he look for support? There was but one party—the clergy, and into their arms he threw himself. James had no special love for the Church or her ministers. He was fully aware that there was need for reform in the manners of the clergy, and he often urged them to mend their ways; but he required their aid in order to oppose the nobility, whom he reckoned his enemies, and consequently he could not deal hardly with them, or compel them to make the changes which he saw clearly were necessary. Thus the two parties in the State became more sharply defined than they had been before. Behind each stood a foreign power; behind the Church, France, and sometimes the Emperor; behind the nobility, England. France was ready to support the Church, always because of its devotion to the Pope, and sometimes because of its opposition to England. England, on the other hand, anxious for political reasons to gain a share in the management of Scottish affairs, and perceiving that the clergy were its most determined opponents, offered support to those who were willing, for whatever reason, to crush the ecclesiastics, at the same time pressing upon James the desirability of carrying forward without delay the work of reform. It is easy to understand how difficulties and complications arose; easy to understand, too, the vacillations of the King—at one moment showing himself determined to suppress the heresy, at another appearing altogether indifferent on the subject. He was being wooed by two different suitors, and he was dazzled in turn by the charms and possessions of each. But on the whole the Church was able to offer the strongest attractions; not only could she confer high titles and bestow rich gifts, she could also promise military aid from France in cases of emergency. To the Scottish Court there came a Papal legate; with him he brought a cap and a sword that had been consecrated by the Pope on the anniversary of the Nativity, and as he laid them at the feet of the King he addressed him as "Defender of the Faith"— a title that had been conferred upon Henry VIII., but of which he had proved himself altogether unworthy. His illegitimate sons also, infants though they were, received from His Holiness permission to hold offices in the Church, and the revenues drawn from these sources were to be augmented by a year's revenue, which he was authorized to demand from all vacant benefices. Considering the efforts and sacrifices which the Church was ready to make, we need not wonder that the power of the clergy increased, and that James felt himself drawn to them in ever closer union. His French marriages also added new links to the chains that bound him to the ecclesiastical faction. He had sold himself to the Church that he might gain independence. For a time he apparently deluded himself with the idea that he had gained what he sought. Now and again he stood apart and thought and acted for himself, and he mistook this for liberty: his delusion was soon to be rudely dispelled.

Turning from the political to the religious aspect of events, we discover that notwithstanding the general confusion and strife of parties it is possible to note a definite advance in the dissemination of Reformation principles. Of this we have proof in the Acts that were passed for the purpose of suppressing the heresy and in the martyrdoms that took place at different times during this period. In 1532 the sale, possession, or use of the Scriptures was prohibited by the bishops; in 1535 the enactment of 1525 was made more stringent, all who had heretical books being required to deliver them up within forty days; and in 1541 all religious discussion was forbidden. In 1534 and 1539 there were numerous instances of persecutions, and in each of these years men and women suffered for their attachment to "the truth as it is in Jesus." This last date is important, as it marks the accession to full power of David Beaton, who had been acting for a few months as colleague to his uncle. Previous to this, as we have seen, his hand may be detected in the government of the country, but for the next seven years he becomes the chief actor in Scottish affairs. A deadly foe to Henry, because of his apostacy, the Archbishop exerted his extraordinary powers to frustrate all endeavours to bring Scotland under English rule, to outwit the supporters and agents of the King, and to crush those who, because of their desire for Church reform, might lend him their countenance.

James had long found it difficult to maintain his position between the two parties in the State, and at length he fell a victim to the division. The defeat of Solway filled him with despair, under which he sank and to which he speedily succumbed. After his death there was found in his pocket a list of one hundred noblemen, all friendly to the Reformation, whom the Cardinal had advised him to put to death. The roll had been offered to him once before by Beaton; he had rejected it then with scorn and anger, but the necessities of the case had later become too strong for him, and he had yielded. This diabolical plan, had the King lived to execute it, would at once have been a death-blow to the English influence in Scotland, and have rendered the Church safe from spoliation. More than once Henry, through his ambassadors, had advised James to follow his example in the destruction of the monasteries and the appropriation of their wealth, and more than once when his treasury was empty James had been tempted to follow his advice. The design of the Archbishop was intended to deprive such a suggestion of all force by supplying the King with riches sufficient to gratify even his extravagant tastes.

Immediately after the King's death, Beaton claimed the regency in virtue of a testament which he produced bearing the King's signature. The claim was refused, the testament being declared a forgery, and Arran was appointed. His appointment gave much satisfaction to the Reformers, for he was understood to be favourable to the new doctrines. Indeed, he had attached to his household Rough and Williams, two preachers of Lutheran views. The satisfaction was, however, of short duration. Influenced by his half-brother, the Abbot of Paisley, Arran recanted at Stirling on 3rd Sept., 1543, and became reconciled to Beaton, whom a few months before he had cast into prison. This act carried with it the most serious consequences for the country; it was a violation of the treaty concluded with Henry regarding the marriage of Edward and Mary, and Henry was not slow to take revenge, ravaging the land with fire and sword.

The Acts passed from time to time, the martyrdoms that took place, the roll of condemned reforming nobles drawn up by Beaton, and the temporary favour shown by Arran to the movement, all furnish evidence that the Reformation was gaining ground in the country, and that the number of its adherents was increasing. The most signal proof, however, of its advance is offered by an Act passed in March, 1543, which provided that "all men and women should be free to read the Holy Scriptures in their own tongue or in the English tongue, and that all Acts passed to the contrary should be abolished." Well might the Archbishop of Glasgow protest against this enactment, for by it the way was paved for the overthrow of Papal authority and the downfall of the Catholic Church.

But this brings us almost to the time when Wishart began his labours; we must therefore pause, that we may trace his early career.

George Wishart was the only son of James Wishart of Pitarrow, and Elizabeth Learmont, his second wife. Of the place and date of his birth no record remains. It seems, however, fair to conclude that he was born at Pitarrow, the family seat, which is situated fifteen miles from Montrose, and an inscription on what is said to be a painting of the Reformer fixes 1513 as the year in which the event occurred. The testimony of the inscription harmonizes with what we gather from two legal documents connected with the family: the one is dated 28th Oct., 1510, and is in favour of James Wishart and Janet Lindsay, his spouse: the other is dated 30th April, 1512, and is in favour of James Wishart and Elizabeth Learmont, his spouse. As it follows from these dates that James Wishart must have married Elizabeth Learmont shortly before 30th April, 1512, we may, without hesitation, accept 1513 as the year in which their only son was born.

The Wisharts were an ancient and distinguished family. In the affairs of their country they had always taken a deep interest, and more than one of their number had filled places of honour and importance in the State. George's father was no exception to the rule; he was appointed, by James IV., Justice Clerk and King's Advocate, and was a member of the Council that assembled at Perth in November, 1513, to meet the ambassadors from Louis XII.

Elizabeth Learmont was the daughter of Learmont of Balcomie, in Fifeshire, who was descended from the Learmonts of Ercildoune or Earlston, of which house Thomas the Rhymer was the most illustrious member. Her brother was James Learmont, who played a somewhat prominent part in civil affairs about the time when Wishart came to the front; he was Master of the Household in the reign of James V., and was one of the Commissioners who went to England to treat with Henry about the marriage of Mary and Edward; he was also Provost of St. Andrews when Beaton was murdered.

Regarding George Wishart's childhood and youth, no information has reached us. Not until he is twenty-three years of age do we meet with any authentic references to him. These tell us that he taught Greek in a school that had been founded in Montrose by John Erskine of Dun when Provost of that burgh; they also tell us that not only did he teach Greek, he also supplied his pupils with a text-book—the best of all text-books, the New Testament. Of his doings, John Hepburn, Bishop of Brechin, heard, but did not in the least approve. So far from being pleased with the attempt being made to spread culture in his diocese, he was angry, and resolved to put a stop to it at once. He summoned Wishart to appear before his court. But Wishart did not obey the summons; he fled. He was not yet ready to take his stand and suffer for the truth; he was only groping his way out into the light, guided by his study of the sacred volume.

We next catch a glimpse of him at Bristol, where he has been preaching. How he came to be there, and there in the capacity of a preacher, is involved in mystery. It would seem as if in some way he had been introduced to Latimer, who was then Bishop of Worcester, and by him had been sent to that part of his diocese to labour; but in what way that introduction was brought about we cannot say. The suggestion has been made that he went to Cambridge and there came under the notice of the Bishop, but of his residence in Cambridge at this period of his history we have no notice.

In letters written in connection with his visit to Bristol he is called "the reader," and by Bishop Lesley, who was a contemporary, he is referred to as "a clerk." These statements appear to imply that he had been admitted, by Latimer probably, to one of the inferior orders, and thus furnished with authority to preach. In any case he did preach, and in the course of his preaching he gave expression to erroneous views. While officiating in the Church of St. Nicolas he declared that "Christ nother hathe nor coulde merite for him nor yett for" his hearers. It has been contended that in this sentence we should read "mother" for "nother," and understand that Wishart was attacking Mariolatry, but this cannot be allowed; the statement is plain and definite, and all the circumstances of the case go to prove that he had accepted and was teaching mistaken opinions regarding the Atonement. His heretical utterances were made the subject of complaint by the clergy. In consequence of this he was arrested by the Mayor, and subsequently sent to London to be tried by a court over which Cranmer presided. He was condemned, and was sentenced to burn his faggot. This he did in St. Nicholas' Church on Sunday, 13th July, and in Christ's Church on Sunday, 20th July, 1539. His conduct in this matter was in every way creditable to him, and foreshadowed the noble course he was to pursue later. His love of truth compelled him at once to recant, when convinced of his error, despite the humiliation entailed by doing so; that same love of truth was in after years to preserve him from recanting, when no such conviction was produced, although by his refusal to do so he had to face not only humiliation but also suffering—even death itself.

After burning his faggot he went to Germany and Switzerland. On the Continent he remained two or three years, but no account of his journey or his residence abroad has been preserved. Returning to England, he entered Bennet's or Christ's College, Cambridge, intending both to study and to teach. Emery Tylney, one of his pupils, who knew him well and loved him intensely, has supplied us with a simple but graphic description of his appearance and character. By him he is represented as earnest, sober, at times even stern, yet tender, amiable, charitable; a man of simple habits and elevated tastes; longing to grow in knowledge and willing to impart to others what he had himself acquired; devout in tone, pure and gentle and good.

From Cambridge he came to Scotland. The statements regarding the date of his return which we possess are, unfortunately, indefinite, and capable of more than one interpretation. As the point is of prime importance, because of its bearing on other questions regarding the conduct and character of the Reformer, it demands close attention and careful treatment.

Our two authorities on the subject are John Knox and Emery Tylney. The former says: "In the myddest of all the calamities that came upoun the realme after the defectioun of the Governour from Christ Jesus came in Scotland that blissed martyre of God, Maister George Wisharte, in company of the Commissionaris before mentionat, in the year of God 1544." In this statement there are three notes of time: (1)

the calamities, (2) the return of the Commissioners, (3) the year of God 1544. Of these, the first and third agree with each other, but from both the second appears to differ. Let us look at each, that we may understand both the agreement and the apparent difference.

Knox speaks first of all of certain "calamities." What these calamities were there can be no doubt. He has just given a long account of them. Their beginning and cause, indeed, he marks very distinctly in the passage quoted: "They came," he says, "after the defectioun of the Governour from Christ Jesus." That defection took place, as we have already seen, in September, 1543. Knox, having written fully regarding it, proceeds to narrate the invasion of Scotland by Henry in May, 1544, adding, "This was a parte of the punishment which God took upoun the realme for infidelitie of the Governour and for the violatioun of his solempned oath." He then relates the arrival of the French troops in June, 1545, and only after having done so does he speak of Wishart's return. From this it is clear that in the sentence under review he points to a period not earlier than May, 1544. In conformity with this reference is the third note, "The year of God 1544." And in dealing with this, as with other dates, we have to remember that the year began then on 25th March, and not as now on 1st January.

From these we turn to the second clause, "in company with the Commissionaris before mentionat." The only "Commissionaris before mentionat" are those that were appointed to negotiate with Henry about the marriage of Edward and Mary, and these left Scotland in March and returned in July, 1543. This statement, then, seems to contradict the other two, and that there is a difficulty occasioned by it cannot be denied. The question naturally suggests itself, Were there any Commissioners sent to England at a later date with whom Wishart might return, and with whom Knox might confound those "mentionat" by him? The answer is, that there were none of precisely the same kind, but that there were others who went on a different footing and for a different purpose. By the English faction in Scotland, at the head of which were Lennox and Glencairn, representatives were sent across the Border in 1544, and in connection with their visit a treaty was concluded with Henry on 17th May of that year. It is quite possible that Knox might be thinking of these Commissioners, and might through ignorance or inadvertency identify them with those to whom he had previously referred. And there are two considerations that favour this view. First, those who went up in March, 1543, representing the Governor and Parliament are called in the State papers "Ambassadors," while those who went up from the English party are called "Commissioners." Second, the former were sent on a purely political errand; the points in the treaty concluded bore solely on civil affairs, but the latter demanded and secured as one of the heads of the arrangement entered into that the people should be left free to read the Bible in their own tongue: they had thus a religious side to their negotiations. And the presumption is surely in favour of Wishart's returning with those who dealt with the ecclesiastical as well as with the political affairs of the country, rather than with those who dealt solely with the political.

It is true that in support of the earlier date it may

be urged that when the Commissioners from Parliament set out for England Arran was professedly favourable to the Reformation, so that circumstances seemed to invite the exiled Reformer to come north and render help to the cause he had so much at heart; also, that Wishart's uncle, Sir James Learmont, was one of the Commissioners, and that he, as a supporter of the Reformation, would doubtless emphasize the invitation presented by the circumstances and endeavour to persuade his nephew to accompany him to Scotland. But these contentions imply that Wishart would only return to his native country when there were no dangers to be faced, and this is not in accord with his conduct at other times.

Knox has certainly run into error; and in deciding where the error lies we must consider in what direction he was most likely to err. Taking his statement as it stands, the balance is in favour of a late date, since two clauses point to 1544, while only one points to 1543. And looking at the matter generally we reach the same conclusion. We may present the matter thus—If Wishart returned with "the Commissionaris before mentionat," then he neither came in the "myddest of the calamities" nor in 1544; but if he came in "the myddest of the calamities" then he might come in 1544. Putting it thus, we perceive that the question which we have to answer is: Regarding which point was Knox most likely to make a mistake, regarding the Commissioners with whom Wishart returned, the condition of the country at the time of his return, or the year in which he returned. In discussing the question we must remember that Knox was brought into close contact with Wishart in the end of 1545, and that he had therefore ample opportunity of gaining information regarding his earlier movements. He wrote, too, only twenty years after the event he was recording took place, and wrote with a distinctly religious aim, dealing with political matters, as he constantly tells us, only in so far as these touched closely the history of the Church. In such circumstances he was surely much more likely to err regarding the people with whom the Reformer returned than regarding the date of his return or the state of the country at the moment. What would fix itself in his memory would be the defection of the Governor, with the evils following, all of which had for him a religious significance, and the sudden illumination of the darkness that had settled on the land by the appearance of a bright and shining light. He might readily forget in whose company Wishart travelled north, especially as there were then frequent deputations passing between England and Scotland; he might even forget the year, though this is not likely, seeing that it was a year that was eventful in the history of the nation; but he would not readily forget the circumstances of the time—circumstances so sad and painful that they must have indelibly impressed themselves on the mind of one who was alike an ardent patriot and a fervent Reformer.

In so far as the statement of Tylney bears on the subject, it confirms the conclusion reached. He says, "About the year of our Lord a thousand five hundredth fortie and three there was in the Universitie of Cambridge one Maister George Wishart." He speaks of "the whole year of my being with him"; and he states "that he went into Scotland with diuers of the nobilitie that came for a treaty to King Henry the Eight." The phrase " about the year a thousand five hundredth fortie and three," taken in connection with the expression, "the whole year of my being with him," suggests that 1543 was the year in which the pupil enjoyed the benefit of this tutor's friendship and instruction—the year, therefore, with which he most naturally associated his stay at Cambridge. Had he left in July, 1543, he would have lived in Cambridge only one quarter of that year, according to the reckoning then in use, and, had this been so, Tylney would scarcely have written as he has done.

Once more, the terms in which he refers to those with whom he went away suggest rather the representatives of the English faction than the ambassadors from the Governor and Parliament: " He went into Scotland with diuers of the nobilitie that came for a treaty with Henry the Eight."

Despite, then, the difficulty occasioned by Knox's statement as to the " Commissionaris," we seem forced to accept the later date, and to understand that Wishart returned either in May, 1544, or subsequent thereto.

This is not the general opinion. Tytler says, "All are agreed that Wishart arrived with the Commissioners, and they certainly arrived in the interval between 16th and 31st July, 1543;" he says, further, that the date " has been mistaken by Knox and all our ecclesiastical historians." That Knox has made a mistake is clear; but that the ecclesiastical historians, who accept a later date than July, 1543, have not made such a serious mistake as Tytler's statement implies, is as clear. He himself is at fault in the matter. He takes one part of a statement and rejects two, although, as has been shown, the two are more reliable than the one, and must be allowed to a certain extent to interpret it.

After his return from England Wishart taught for a time in Montrose in a house hired by him for the purpose. Thence he went to Dundee, where he expounded the "Epistle to the Romans" to large audiences, drawn together by his fame as a preacher. There he continued to labour till forbidden to do so by the municipal authorities. Prior to their interference, two attempts had been made to intimidate him and bring his expositions to a close. The Governor, instigated doubtless by the Primate, had charged him to cease holding public meetings, but this charge he had refused to obey. In order to compel obedience, the Church lent the force of its censures to the menaces of the civil power. Because of his refusal the Bishop of Brechin cursed[1] him and delivered him into the Devil's hands, and gave him commandment that he should preach no more. But the ecclesiastical malediction proved as powerless to arrest him as the civil injunction had done; notwithstanding, he did "continew obstinatlye." Frustrated in their attempts to terrify into silence the preacher of righteousness and grace, the clergy sought to work on the fears of the magistrates, who had hitherto afforded him protection and enabled him to defy all the threats hurled at him. At length they succeeded. And, at the close of one of his services, Wishart was inhibited from addressing congregations in the burgh. This inhibition was delivered to him by Robert Myln, a magistrate, who had formerly professed attachment to Lutheranism, and had even suffered because of his profession. Wishart

---

[1] *i.e.*, excommunicated.

was much affected when he heard the proclamation, but it would have been folly for him to disregard it. He had not hesitated, as he reminded them, to remain amongst them, even at the hazard of his life, so long as they had been willing to listen to his words, but now that they were forsaking him and withdrawing from him their countenance he must leave them and seek opportunities of usefulness elsewhere. He, however, warned them that since they were rejecting God's message, afraid of the trouble its proclamation might bring upon them, God would send upon them other troubles that would be unaffected by "horning and cursing."

Driven out of Dundee by priestly machinations, he betook himself to Kyle, "that ancient receptacle of God's people." The efforts of Lollardism in that district had not been altogether fruitless; there were still some who had come under its quickening influence, and who were yearning for fuller and clearer views of Divine truth. Aware of this, Wishart felt sure that in the West he would find many willing to listen to him. He also knew that in Ayrshire there were several gentlemen of position who sympathized heartily with his views, and would be ready to defend him if he were attacked.

In Ayr he preached at the Cross; this he did because he was prevented entering the church by Dunbar, Archbishop of Glasgow, who was alarmed by this evangelical invasion of his diocese. At Mauchline, where the church was also closed against him, lest the crowds that assembled to hear him should destroy a valuable shrine which it contained, he preached from a dyke, and preached with great power and effect. Galston, however, was the chief scene of his labours. There he remained for some weeks, under the protection of John Lockhart, of Barr, and during his stay he preached regularly in the surrounding districts. Wherever he went crowds gathered to hear him, and of those who came not a few by their profession and conduct testified to his success in presenting the truth so as to touch the heart and influence the life.

But, inviting though this sphere was, the time came, and came soon, when he must leave it. In Dundee the plague was raging; it had begun four days after his departure, and its ravages were so terrible that "it almost passed credibilitie to hear what number departed everie foure-and-twenty houris." The information which he received regarding the condition of the people, in whom, despite their harsh treatment of him, he had still a deep interest, seemed a call to return and resume amongst them the work that had been so suddenly brought to a close; and this call he obeyed without hesitation or delay, "to the regreate of many." His appearance in the plague-stricken city was hailed with joy by the "faythful." At once he addressed himself to the work that lay to his hand, ministering in many ways to the comfort of the diseased. Shortly after his arrival he preached from the East Gate. This place was resorted to on account of the pestilence, enabling as it did the preacher to address two congregations at the same time; "the whole sat or stood within, the seik and suspected without the porte." His text on the occasion was, "He sent His word and healed them," from which he discoursed in a manner fitted to comfort and guide the inhabitants in their peculiar circumstances. And the place selected as a pulpit gave point to the words chosen as a text, for in its immediate vicinity was the monastery of St. Roque, the saint who was invoked in times of sickness. Thus by implication, if not by actual statement, the preacher turned the thoughts of his hearers from the false to the true source of health and healing.

Wishart remained in Dundee till the pestilence had almost passed away, and was unwearied in his endeavours to aid, both in things temporal and in things spiritual, those who were in affliction. But he was not permitted to continue undisturbed his labour of love. The Cardinal had heard of his return, and had determined to silence him. He however knew well that, in the circumstances, it would be folly to attack him directly, since the people would defend him from any force sent to take him, and would be estranged from the Church by any attempt made to arrest him. But what he feared to do openly he sought to do secretly. He employed a priest, John Wightone by name, to carry out his design. Stationed at the foot of the stair, with "his whinger drawin into his hand under his gown," he intended to stab Wishart as he came down from the pulpit, but Wishart, who was "most scharpe of eie and judgment," suspecting him of some foul purpose, seized him by the hand that held the dagger. When he saw that he was discovered and overpowered he made full confession. The crowd were so enraged that they would fain have taken summary vengeance on him, but Wishart embracing him, cried out, "Who troubles him troubles me," and so saved him from the danger to which he had exposed himself.

When the plague had well nigh ceased, Wishart went for a short time to Montrose. His aim in going thither was to secure rest and leisure for meditation. He had been invited to Edinburgh by the Earls Glencairn and Cassilis, who had promised him that at a meeting of the Provincial Synod to be held in January he should have an opportunity of discussing publicly with the bishops various matters requiring reformation; and for this he was anxious to prepare himself fully.

But the malice of the Cardinal followed him into his retirement. Sending him a message that his friend Kinneir, of Kinneir in Fifeshire, was ill, he sought, by inducing him to travel thither, to bring him within the reach of a body of soldiers which he had placed in ambush. His plan almost succeeded. The Reformer set out in haste to visit his sick friend, but suddenly he stopped and refused to proceed, declaring that evil was intended by his enemies; thus he was saved by his "scharpeness and wisdom."

Thus far I have sketched the career of Wishart after his return from England, without reference to dates. This omission has not been accidental. I have purposely abstained from marking off definitely the several periods embraced in this section of his life because of the acknowledged difficulty that has to be faced in the attempt to do so. To the subject we must, however, now devote our attention. And it may be well to begin by considering the views of those who accept July, 1543, as the date of his arrival in Scotland; these are varied and diverse, and demand examination, because of their bearing on the character of the Reformer.

One view is that he remained in obscurity at Pitarrow till the spring of 1545; and that consequently his activity on behalf of the Reformation lasted for only nine months. His retirement is accounted for by the change that took place in the Regent's religious convictions, or rather profession. But apart from the fact that nine months is much too brief a period for all that was accomplished, the shrinking from service and danger which such a retirement would imply is altogether antagonistic to the character of the Reformer. He was ever eager to teach, and when prevented from doing so he looked upon himself as "nothing better than a dead man, except that he ate and drank"; he was also brave, willing to risk his life in the attempt to instruct those who would listen to him. Surely a man animated by such a spirit could not remain quietly in concealment for almost two years, no matter how serious the difficulties to be overcome, and how terrible the dangers to be faced in the discharge of duty.

Another view is as follows: Immediately on his arrival in Scotland he began to preach in Montrose, and shortly thereafter he went to Dundee. Evidence of his early appearance and efforts in the latter town is furnished by the popular demonstrations which took place there in September, 1543, in connection with which most of the monasteries were destroyed. After these demonstrations he continued his labours till the Governor and the Cardinal came thither in January, 1544, to make inquisition and to punish those found guilty of heresy. At their approach he and his congregation fled and remained in hiding till the danger was past; thereafter he returned and continued some months till, in consequence of the interference of the magistrates, he was obliged to cease teaching, and to leave the town. He then set out for the West, where he lived and taught till, on hearing that the plague had broken out in Dundee, he felt called upon to return to the East; and the plague visited Dundee in the summer of 1544. From the date of his return till the autumn of 1545, he continued in that town preaching and comforting the afflicted, ceasing to do so only when his arrangement with Glencairn and Cassilis called him to Edinburgh.

Now this view is not only at variance with the facts, it does the Reformer serious injustice; it makes him responsible for disorderly riots and wanton destruction of property; and it implies that he was cowardly enough to flee from the Governor and Cardinal when they came to Dundee to hold inquisition. That it is a mistaken view may, however, be easily proved. It can be satisfactorily shown that Wishart had and could have no connection with the disturbances that led to the demolition of the monasteries, even admitting that he reached Scotland in July, 1543; that he was not in Dundee in January, 1544, and therefore did not flee when the Governor and Cardinal visited the town; and that after his return from Kyle he did not remain so long in Dundee as is required by this theory.

As to the riots, these took place before 3rd September, 1543; a more exact date cannot be given, but this is sufficient for our present purpose. What, then, does this view imply when fully stated? It implies that within a month Wishart visited his friends, hired a house in Montrose and preached in it, left Montrose and went to Dundee, where he expounded the Epistle to the Romans, and by his exposition so excited the populace that they attacked the sacred buildings. We may truly say that if, in such a brief period, and, it may be added, with such an unpromising theme, Wishart could so influence his audience, he must have been a much greater man than the most enthusiastic martyrologist has ever ventured to suggest. But he did not; his name is not even hinted at by the writers of the period who refer to the disturbances; and it would undoubtedly have been mentioned had he been the instigator and moving spirit.

If further proof be required on this point it will be furnished by what we learn regarding his supposed presence in Dundee in the beginning of 1544. One, if not the chief object which Arran and Beaton had in visiting Dundee in January of that year, was to punish those who were responsible for the demonstrations that had proved so disastrous to the monasteries. Where then was Wishart? We are told that he had fled. We at once reply that this is not the conduct we should have expected from one who was so conscientious and courageous. But, apart from this, we are constrained to ask, even if he had fled would not the civil power, impelled by the ecclesiastical, have sought him out and brought him to trial? Would it not, at any rate, on his resumption of work in the town, have apprehended and punished him? In the course of the following month some were cited to answer for their share in the riots, but amongst these we do not find the Reformer, prime mover though he is said to have been. At this very time, too, others were seized because they continued to teach the new doctrines. Of these the most notable was John Rogers, who was taken, imprisoned, thrown from the Castle wall and drowned in the sea at St. Andrews; and his offence was that he persisted in preaching in Angus and Mearns. And yet we are to believe that, while all this was taking place, Wishart was left undisturbed, and permitted to complete his exposition of the " Epistle to the Romans." When all the facts are considered by us, we are forced to the conclusion that wherever he was in the beginning of 1544 he was not in Dundee, and his absence from Dundee at this period confirms the result already reached that he was in no sense responsible for the destruction of the religious houses in that town.

The next point requiring consideration is the assertion that, as the plague began in Dundee in the summer of 1544, and as Wishart returned from Kyle immediately after its outbreak and continued till the autumn of 1545, he must have been there at this time fully a year. This assertion is not borne out by the terms in which Knox speaks of the subject. He says, "When the plague was ceased that almost thare was none seak, he tooke his leave of them." These words imply that, when he left, the effects of the pestilence had not quite passed away; there were still some "seak." And this tells against such a lengthened residence as is necessitated by the theory which we are discussing. The promise, too, that Glencairn and Cassilis gave Wishart before he left Ayrshire, that they would arrange a public discussion when the Provincial Synod met in January, points in the same direction. It is not distinctly stated that this Synod was to be held in the January following the date of the promise, but that is the natural inference: it would be strange if the promise had been given in reference to a Synod that was not to meet for eighteen months. Once more, though the exact date is doubtful, there is good authority for saying that the plague visited Dundee in the summer of 1545 and not of 1544.

And this brings us to the arrangement that suggests

itself on the supposition that he did not return from England before May, 1544. Going to Montrose, he hired a house and taught for a few months, living the while at Pitarrow. Leaving Montrose about the close of the year, he came to Dundee, where he laboured till the following summer. On being prohibited by the magistrates of that burgh, he betook himself to the West. A month or so later, he returned to preach and tend the "seak." When all were nearly recovered—probably in the month of October—he went to Montrose to meditate, so that in November he might be ready to set out for Edinburgh. According to this disposition he would labour in Dundee six or nine months before the inhibition was served upon him by Robert Myln; and this would leave ample time for the injunction of the Governor, the cursing of the Bishop of Brechin, and the negotiations of the clergy with the municipal authorities, which resulted in his expulsion. He would also spend two months, or thereby, ministering to the diseased after his return from Kyle; and some such period is in harmony with the statement of Knox.

In whatever way we deal with the interval between his arrival in Scotland and his journey from Montrose to Edinburgh, it is quite certain that the latter was undertaken in November, 1545. It was undertaken, too, in opposition to the wishes of his friends, especially of his early friend, John Erskine of Dun. Despite their earnest entreaties he was determined to go, and determined to go notwithstanding his firm conviction that troubles awaited him. Duty called him, and the call of duty he dared not disobey. But though his response was willing and immediate, he did not comply without a struggle. His frequent references to the shortness of his time, his sleeplessness and midnight walks, his request for the prayers of his friends that he might remain firm to the end, all imply that he experienced the full intensity of his trial, and that only after severe inner conflict and victory through grace was he enabled to pursue his course with joy.

On his way to Edinburgh he used due precaution; he did not take the direct route through Fife, since that would have brought him within the power of the Cardinal, but went by Perth, Kinross, and Kinghorn. He reached the Capital before his friends Glencairn and Cassilis, and was advised by those who received him to remain silent till they arrived. For a time he yielded to their wish, but becoming sorrowful in spirit, he was allowed to preach. He did so in Leith on the second Sabbath of December, and afterwards at Inveresk, Tranent, and Haddington. At Haddington his audiences were small, owing to the influence exercised in the district by the Earl of Bothwell. Before entering the pulpit the second time, he received intimation that Glencairn and Cassilis were not coming to Edinburgh to meet him. By this he was much troubled, saying to Knox, whom he had met at Longniddry, and who was constantly with him bearing a sword before him, that he "weryed of the world," for "men begane to weary of God." In his discourse he bewailed the lack of interest on the part of the people in Gospel truth, and prophesied that evil times would come on them because of their indifference. That night he was apprehended in Ormiston House, the residence of Cockburn, who, along with Crichtone and Douglas, had taken him under their protection, by the Earl of

Bothwell, who gave his word that he would preserve him from harm, and in particular that he would hinder the Governor and the Cardinal from having "thare will of him." He was taken to Elphinstone Tower and shortly after, despite the promise given by the Earl, he was delivered over to the Cardinal, who sent him to St. Andrews and confined him in the sea-tower or bottle dungeon of the castle, a dismal cell cut down into the solid rock. Here he was kept for a month. This period was requisite for the needful arrangements. The Cardinal first sought the assistance of the civil power; he asked "a commissioun and ane judge criminall to give doom on Maister George if the clergy fand him guiltie." This request the Governor refused, in the hope that he might be able to prevent Beaton doing Wishart serious injury; but Beaton was at the moment too powerful to be hindered by the Governor's refusal; he resolved to act on his own responsibility. But, before he could proceed, he must surmount another obstacle; he was not on friendly terms with Dunbar, Archbishop of Glasgow. Shortly before this an unseemly quarrel had taken place between them at the door of the Cathedral in Glasgow, because each claimed the chief place, and the "enemitie" that resulted "was judged mortall and without all hope of reconsiliation." But much as the Archbishop of Glasgow disliked the Archbishop of St. Andrews, he disliked heretics still more—disliked this heretic in particular, because he had invaded his diocese. Heartily, therefore, he responded to the invitation sent him, and on the day appointed, 28th February, he took his place by the side of the Cardinal and gave his voice against the troubler of the Church.

Wishart, when brought before the tribunal which had been assembled in the Cathedral, asked that he should be judged by the Governor whose prisoner he was; this request was treated with contempt, and he was bidden answer the charges that were brought against him by Lauder, who acted the part of accuser. These were eighteen in number, and for the most part bore on the Sacraments. Wishart having prayed for guidance, answered sweetly, but his answers only increased the wrath of his judges. He would neither recant nor modify his utterances, unless convinced of their error from the Word of God; to the Scriptures he made his appeal, and on them he grounded all his statements. But those ecclesiastics had not come together to discuss with a heretic the Scriptural character of the Church's faith; they had come to condemn, not to convince. When the trial, if trial it could be called, was over, the people were excluded and sentence was pronounced. The prisoner was ordered to be burned on the following day, and the order was carried out in front of the Castle. From a window in the eastern tower, Beaton and Dunbar watched the execution of the sentence they had been in such haste to pronounce; and lest there should be any attempt at a rescue the ordnance of the Castle was directed to the spot and "the gunnaris ready and standing by thare gunnis." Wishart was first strangled and then burned. His death was in harmony with his life. He willingly forgave his executioner, on being asked to do so; he spoke kindly and cheerfully to those who were standing by; he submitted bravely and calmly to his fate. Having with childlike trust committed his spirit into his Father's hands, he assured his friends that he would "sup with Christ" that night, and went home to the "rest that remaineth for the people of God," and to the reward that awaits those that are "faithful unto death."

Three months after Wishart was burned, Beaton was murdered. Into the details of the bloody deed we are not called upon to enter, but to the deed itself we must refer, because it has been asserted that the act had been long meditated, and that Wishart was privy to the plot, nay, was largely responsible for it. In order that we may investigate the matter carefully and satisfactorily, we must discover on what ground this assertion is based; and in order that we may understand the ground of the assertion, we must recall the position of affairs in the sphere of politics. At the time with which we are concerned, Henry VIII. was anxious to conclude a marriage between his son Edward and Mary, the infant daughter of James V.; but all his attempts to do so proved futile, and he was fully aware that the chief opponent to his scheme was the Cardinal. Naturally he was desirous that he should be removed—either apprehended or slain. Sadler, the English ambassador, through whom Henry was negotiating with the Scottish authorities, was compelled in November, 1543, to leave Edinburgh. It was of course necessary that he should have full information of all that was being done if he were to carry out his master's wishes, and, with the view of gaining this, he employed, as his secret agent and spy, Crichtone of Brunstone. In a letter dated 17th April, 1544, from the Earl of Hertford to Henry, that nobleman says, "This daye arryved here with me the Erll of Hertford, a Scottishman called Wyshert, and brought me a letter from the Larde of Brunstone;" and then he proceeds to state that the "said Wyshert" has two proposals to lay before His Majesty, one of which is "that the Larde of Grainge, late thresaurer of Scotlande, the mr. of Rothes, the Erl of Rothes' eldest son, and John Charter's eldest son wolde attempt eyther to apprehend or slee the cardynall at some tyme when he shall passe thorouhge the Fyf lande, as he doth sundry times, to Sanct Andrewes," if they knew His Highness' pleasure. At intervals between this date and the death of the Cardinal letters appear in the State papers which clearly prove that the conspiracy, though delayed, was not forgotten: now these letters are from Crichtone, now from Glencairn and Cassilis, but all deal more or less distinctly with the same subject. As in none of them, however, does the name "Wyshert" occur, we have no special concern with them. The point, the one point, requiring consideration is, was the "Scottishman called Wyshert" in the Earl of Hertford's letter George Wishart the martyr. This is the question on the answer to which all turns, for, had this name not appeared in this communication, the martyr would never have been charged with having a share in the plot. Now this question has practically been answered in the negative; it has been shown that Wishart did not return to Scotland before May, 1544, and the letter referred to is dated 17th April, 1544; it is therefore impossible that he could be the person spoken of. Not being in Scotland, he could not be the bearer of a letter from the "Larde of Brunstone" to the Earl of Hertford.

But it may be maintained that the date of Wishart's

return has not been conclusively settled; it may be well, therefore, to deal with the matter generally. And our discussion of the question will be most satisfactory if we begin by asking what those who charge him with complicity have to say in support of their view.

Hill Burton says, "To the observer from without, Wishart the martyr is part of the group occupied in the affair; removing him from that group breaks it up almost more than the removal of any other." A more unwarrantable statement it would scarcely be possible to conceive; though it must be admitted that it is in perfect harmony with Burton's general account of the Reformer. What are the facts of the case? For two years, at intervals, longer or shorter according to circumstances, letters were passing between a party in Scotland and Henry VIII. as to the disposal of the Cardinal; in only one of these, and that the very first, does the name "Wyshert" occur. He who bore the name, whoever he was, was a trusted agent employed to carry the letter in which the proposal to remove the Cardinal was contained, and to discover the King's mind on the subject; and that is all. Never again throughout the correspondence is that name even referred to. Now, admitting for the moment that the "Wyshert" mentioned was the Reformer, what have we? We have the fact that he was employed to carry a communication from one who had been retained as an English spy—the earliest, too, of many communications that were forwarded on the subject—and we have nothing more; and yet, because, eighteen months after the date of that communication,* this spy is named, along with Glencairn and Cassilis, as friendly and as affording protection to the martyr, it is declared that the martyr was the central figure of the group, and that on him it depended for existence and cohesion. But it may be replied that all concerned in the plot were professed Reformers, and that Wishart, as the leader for the time being of the Reformation, formed the connecting link. To speak in this way is to overlook the character of the plot. The Cardinal was to be removed, not because he held fast the old doctrine and ritual, but because he opposed the advance of the English power. The conspiracy was distinctly political in its basis and aim. The death of Wishart undoubtedly gave to the murder something of a religious aspect, but that was by no means the main, certainly not the original reference of the scheme. It is true that while preaching in Ayrshire Wishart met both Glencairn and Cassilis, and enjoyed their protection. What the extent of their intimacy was it is difficult to say. Knox's statement seems to imply that the Reformer went to Kyle of his own free will, and apart altogether from their knowledge. But, if our supposition as to the circumstances in which he came from England be correct, it would follow that he had made their acquaintance at the time of his return. Even if this were the case it would not prove that he was informed of their design. A man may be associated with other men and yet not be privy to all their schemes. In any case, putting Wishart's stay in the West at the earliest possible date, it was two or three months subsequent to the despatch of the letter in question, and supplies no evidence whatever that he was involved in, still less that he was the moving spirit of the plot. We may safely say that whatever Wishart the martyr was, he was not the centre of the group occupied in the affair. Intimate with some of the members of the group he unquestionably was, but it is altogether unwarrantable to infer from this that he was the "Scottishman" referred to in Hertford's letter.

Yet Burton is not alone in thus arguing—Tytler had taken the same line. He asserts that from the date of Wishart's return, Brunstone was his great friend. This assertion is totally unsupported by evidence. We do not know that Wishart ever even saw Brunstone till within a few weeks of his death. Tytler's statement, like that of Burton, is a vicious *petitio principii*. From the occurrence of the name "Wyshert" in the letter from Brunstone, the early intimacy of the Reformer with Brunstone is inferred, and then by this the identity of George Wishart with the "Scottishman" is proved. But Brunstone's interest in Wishart can be sufficiently accounted for without assuming a long and intimate friendship. He was anxious to ingratiate himself with the party who were opposed to the Cardinal, so that, even if we suppose him to have been nothing more than a "dark intriguer," as Tytler calls him, we can easily understand why he should be eager to do a favour to the man whom many were ready to receive with acclamation and to obey with alacrity.

It thus appears that, even admitting that he returned in July, 1543, there is no ground for holding that the Reformer was specially intimate with Crichtone and his associates; that, on the contrary, the facts support the opposite conclusion. This being so, the only basis that remains for the accusation is the name; the Scottishman was called "Wyshert" and the martyr was called "Wishart," a slender and insufficient basis surely! Despite Burton's sneer it may with force be urged that there were other "Wisharts," even other "George Wisharts," in Scotland at that period; and it may be added that the designation of the Reformer was "Maister" George Wishart, a designation that would scarcely have been omitted in a letter from the "Larde of Brunstone" to the King of England.

There are, however, other considerations of a positive kind that may be adduced in support of the contention that the Scottishman Wyshert was not the future martyr.

A man's character may with justice be appealed to in deciding such a point as that under discussion; and Wishart's character is known to us. It is presented in detail by Tylney, and his portraiture suggests a temperament far enough removed from deeds of violence. But we are not dependent on the warm eulogy of a devoted pupil; we have many indications of his disposition in his conduct. On all occasions he opposed strenuously the use of force either on his own behalf or on behalf of the cause he had at heart. During his stay in Ayrshire, he more than once prevented a riot by dissuading his friends from breaking into the churches that were closed against him. And when the assassin was caught by him in Dundee, and would have been visited with swift and severe punishment by the enraged congregation, he pleaded on his behalf, nay, positively forbade them, to lay hands on him; and he did so fully aware that this same man might, in a few days, be employed and be willing to act in the same capacity. Indeed, all that we learn of Wishart testifies to a spirit the very opposite of that which would be implied in active participation in a conspiracy to commit murder, even according to the ethical code of the sixteenth century; his whole action and bearing spoke of a tender and peaceable disposition; alike in word and in deed he breathed the spirit of Him who said, " Put up again thy sword."

But there is another argument that may to some minds carry greater weight than that just urged. It is, that Wishart was not the kind of man to be used as a confidential messenger in connection with a conspiracy, not even the kind of man likely to be admitted to the knowledge of a plot by those concerned in it. This is the view that is supported by the record of his career which we possess. What does Hill Burton say of him? He says, " He had little or none of the political activity and worldly sagacity of John Knox." In this he is right, and yet he does not hesitate to declare that this man, devoid of " political activity and worldly sagacity," was entrusted with a secret and important proposal, nay, was the centre, the binding thread, the heart and soul of the group whence the communication emanated! To my mind it would be much more in harmony with the circumstances to say that, recognizing the simplicity and purity of Wishart's character, the conspirators were careful to hide from him the design they had formed and were seeking encouragement to carry out.

Another argument on the same side may be drawn from the silence of John Knox on the whole subject. Had Wishart been in East Lothian in April, 1544, as he must have been if he were the Scottishman called " Wyshert," Knox must have been aware of it, for he was then tutor at Longniddry and Ormiston; or, had he later had anything to do with the plot, Knox could not have been ignorant of it. But he says nothing about it in his History; and there was no reason at all why he should not have stated everything he knew concerning it. He does not think or speak with horror or regret of the murder; he writes of it with a savage glee that somewhat offends us as we read his recital of the details. Tytler says, and says truly, that "he considered the deed justifiable and praiseworthy." Had he, then, been aware of the plot and of Wishart's alleged connection with it, he would most undoubtedly have mentioned them. His silence proves that he was not, and this ignorance can mean only one or other of two things; either that Wishart had nothing to do with it, or that he had to do with it but that his connection with it was kept secret from Knox. And the latter supposition seems to me to be a simple impossibility. If Brunstone and his associates felt it needful to conceal the matter from Knox, who, though he had yet taken no part in political matters, was thoroughly capable of understanding these, how much more needful must they have felt it to be to conceal it from Wishart, who was without guile. Without hesitation I accept the former alternative, and regard the Reformer's innocence as fully and conclusively established.

Wishart left no original work, and the parts of his sermons that have come down to us are too fragmentary to enable us to discover his standing ground. Fortunately, however, when on the Continent, he executed a translation of the Helvetic Confession, and from his having done so we may infer with certainty that in it we have an accurate expression of his doctrinal position. A study of it proves him to have been in substantial agreement with Hamilton, in advance of him only in fulness and accuracy of statement. He has considered " the Sacraments," " the Constitution and Power of the Church," " the Chosynge and Duties of Ministers and Officers," and other such matters not dealt with in " Patrick's Places," not raised, indeed, when that work was published. Wishart has only kept pace with the Protestant Churches abroad in their efforts to develop and apply Scriptural principles, and of the two main lines along which this effort moved he chose the Reformed rather than the Lutheran. In making this choice he prepared the way for his great successor, who was to carry forward the work of reform, and to present to Scotland a complete and carefully arranged system of Divine truth.

At Dundee he expounded the " Epistle to the Romans," and the selection of this part of the New Testament as the subject of exposition confirms the belief that in the " Confession " we have a true reflection of his creed. This being so, we need not be surprised that large congregations flocked to hear him, and that his preaching was with power. For his work the country had been undergoing preparation. Since Hamilton taught, the Scriptures had been widely circulated ; men's minds had been directed to the truth; dissatisfaction with the existing arrangements had been deepening; the people were ready to listen with joy to the Evangel when it was proclaimed, and proclaimed it was by George Wishart.

God took the workmen, but He continued the work. Patrick Hamilton and George Wishart were snatched away in the beginning of their days, before, to human view, they had fully entered on their labours; but the good cause did not suffer by their removal, it rather benefited. The fires in which they perished kindled enthusiasm for the Gospel in hearts that previously had been cold or lukewarm; and this enthusiasm proved contagious, touching with its fervour an ever expanding circle, and deepening in intensity as it spread, till it burst forth into fierce flame, and with its glowing heat consumed the falsehood that had been permitted to usurp the place of truth. The results of this refining process we enjoy. Recognizing their value, we should honour highly those who, when there were few to applaud or sympathize with their act of self-sacrifice, heroically surrendered themselves, that the spark which was to ignite the mass might be struck, or when well nigh extinguished, be fanned into bright blaze. When we review the past we should not permit ourselves to be so dazzled by the glare of the great conflagration by which the Church was purified, as to forget the feeble flickerings from which it grew. And while we recall and revere those who struggled and suffered, we should emulate them in their determination to hold fast only "the faith once delivered to the saints." Animated by this spirit we shall prove ourselves worthy of such noble ancestors as Patrick Hamilton and George Wishart.

John Knox.

To the east of the White Cart, and about a mile to the north of Paisley, the level plain which skirts the Clyde is broken by a rising ground near the summit of which stands a farmhouse called to this day the Knock. Here in former times was a lairdship, and the owners, as the custom was, took the name of their lairdship, and were the Knocks of that ilk.[1] This, we believe, is the origin of the surname Knox, so illustrious in our Scottish annals; for it is a long-received tradition that the Reformer's "father was a brother's son of the house of Ranfurlie"[2] —a neighbouring estate in possession of the proprietors of the Knock. There is nothing inconsistent with the tradition in the Reformer's statement to the Earl of Bothwell that his "grandfather, goodsher, and father" had served under his lordship's predecessors, and some of them had died under their standards;[3] nay, the statement rather confirms the tradition, for it seems to

[1] A History of the Shire of Renfrew, by George Crawford (1710), pp. 41 and 68.

[2] Life, by David Buchanan, prefixed to his edition of Knox's History (1644).

[3] Knox's History of the Reformation, vol. ii. p. 323. This and all subsequent references to the History and to Knox's other works are to Laing's edition.

indicate that it was only in the time of the Reformer's grandfather that his family had settled in the Lothians.

The district of which the Knock is the centre is thus of singular interest. At Elderslie, about two miles to the south-west, William Wallace was born; and King's Inch, about two miles to the north-east, was the home of the Stewards of Scotland, who became the Royal Family. The three great rivers of southern Scotland, the Clyde, the Annan, and the Tweed, all rise on the same hill; and we have a parallel to this in the fact that three of the greatest forces in our history had their springs within a circuit of a few miles. It is specially striking that the ancestors of John Knox and of Mary Stuart should have been so near neighbours. Doubtless there were old contendings between the sturdy lairds of the Knock and the powerful founders of Paisley Abbey, to foreshadow the conflicts of a later day between their respective descendants, the preacher and the Queen, at Holyrood.

Though Knox came of a western stock, he was born in East Lothian—not indeed at the village of Gifford —though Beza styles him *Giffordiensis*—for that village did not exist till the latter half of the seventeenth century;[1] but at Giffordgate, a suburb of Haddington, connected with the county-town by the old stone bridge across the Tyne. There, in a house opposite the eastern end of the Abbey Church, Knox first saw the light in 1505—the year in which Luther entered the Augustinian convent at Erfurt. His mother's name was Sinclair, and often in troublous times he used that name in signing his letters.

He received a liberal education in the ancient

[1] Laing. Knox's Works, vol. vi., Preface, p. xviii.

grammar school of Haddington; and we may probably recognize his sense of indebtedness to that foundation, in the provision of the First Book of Discipline, that the schoolmaster be "suche a one as is able, at least, to teache grammar and the Latine toung, yf the toun be of any reputatioun."[1]

At the age of seventeen Knox entered the University of Glasgow, in the "Annales" of which his name appears among the "Incorporati" for the year 1522.[2] It is possible that his choice of this University, instead of that of St. Andrews, to which a native of Haddington would naturally have gone (Edinburgh not having been founded till sixty years later), is due to his family connection with the West; but it is more probable that he was attracted by the fame of John Major, who was then Principal and Professor of Philosophy and Theology at Glasgow. If, as some have supposed, he followed Major to St. Andrews, when the Professor was transferred to the older seat of learning in 1523, there is no direct evidence of the fact. But whether he was a longer or shorter time under him, it hardly admits of doubt that he was powerfully influenced by his teaching. Major was a disciple of Gerson, of the University of Paris, the able defender of the liberties of the Gallican Church against the absolute authority of the Popes; and in his Commentaries on Petrus Lombardus, his Exposition of St. Matthew, and his History of the Scottish Nation, Major comes to the same conclusion with regard to the Bishop of Rome's claim to supremacy and the validity of Papal excommunications as those of which Knox was the vehement

[1] History, vol. ii. p. 209.
[2] M'Crie's Life of Knox, Note B.

assertor; he speaks of the rapacity, ambition, and
worldliness of popes, cardinals, and bishops in terms
that might have been used by the Reformer himself;
and he asserts the right of a people to "depose a king
for his offences and exclude his family from the throne"
with a boldness which his pupil hardly sur-passed.[1]

No evidence can be found that Knox took his
degree at the University. Indeed, there is evidence to
the contrary in the fact that when he was a priest he
was designated "Schir" John Knox—a title given to
the priesthood as knights of the Pope, but given only
to those of them who had not the right to the then
exclusively academic title of "Mr."[2] Since he had
no degree it is certain that he could not have taught
philosophy at St. Andrews and improved on the dialectic of his master, as Beza and Melchior Adam
say he did.' The fact is that, after we see him as an
entrant at Glasgow in 1522, he disappears from view
till we have glimpses of him in the garb of the priesthood at the market-cross of Haddington, acting on
behalf of James Ker in Samuelston, December 13th,
1540; again two years later as one of two umpires in

[1] See M'Crie's Life, Period I. and Note D; and Ross's Scottish
History and Literature to the period of the Reformation, pp.
227-239.

[2] We have his own testimony in 1550 to the fact that he was
ignorant of Hebrew—"Vindication," Works, vol. iii.p. 47—though
he then avows "a fervent thrist to have sum entrance thairin."
Whether he acquired this language in middle-life, when it is
believed he learned Greek, we cannot tell. From the many
references to, and long quotations from, the Hebrew prophets in
his writings during his exile at Dieppe and Geneva, when he
had abundant leisure, we are disposed to conclude that he did.
A reference to the original in his Sermon on Isaiah xxvi. 13
(Works, vol. vi. p. 221), preached in 1565, seems to point to this
conclusion.

a dispute regarding a chalder of victual; and yet again on 27th March, 1543, when he signed as notary an assignation by Elizabeth Home, Lady Hammilton of Samuelston.[1] In the peculiar attestation which he affixed to his signature on this deed—"Testis per Christum fidelis, cui gloria, Amen"—we have an indication that, though still doing duty as a priest, he had already embraced the Reformed faith; and we have other evidence that it must have been before that date, that he came under the influence of one of the preachers to the governor, the Earl of Arran, who was then professing the Reformed doctrine.

This preacher was a Black Friar, named Thomas Gulliamme. Calderwood tells us that "He was the first man from whom Mr. Knox received any taste of the truth."[2] Knox himself testifies that "the man was of solid judgment, reasonable letters (as for that age), and of a prompt and good utterance; his doctrine was holsome, without great vehemency against superstition." It would be interesting if we knew more of Knox's spiritual father, and of the nature of the teaching which gave the Reformer a "taste of the truth." We learn from his dying words that it was in the 17th chapter of St. John's Gospel that he "first cast anchor"; and we can believe that the preacher who guided his earliest experiences, being "without great vehemency against superstition," would often choose his themes from those chapters of the fourth Evangelist in which vehemency has given place to gentleness, as of one who lay in Jesus' bosom. Since it was in the

[1] Laing. Knox's Works, vol. vi. Preface, pp. xxi. and xxii., with fac-simile of deed.
[2] History of the Kirk of Scotland, vol i. p. 156.

gentleness which pervades the upper room that Knox cast anchor, we must attribute it to the storms he had to ride that he manifested in his life so much of the earlier vehemency of St. John, and resembled the Son of Thunder more than the reclining disciple. The first time we see him openly enlisted on the side of Protestantism, the vehemency which characterized him to the end had already appeared. In 1545, when Wishart came to East Lothian, Knox attached himself to the fervid preacher, whose life was known to be in peril, and carried a two-handed sword before him. By this time he had become tutor to two sons of the Laird of Longniddry, and to a son of the Laird of Ormiston ; and when he proposed to go with Wishart on the night on which he was taken, Wishart said to him, "Nay, return to your bairns, and God bless you. One is sufficient for one sacrifice."[1]

It will be observed that at this period Knox had reached his fortieth year. We have a noteworthy coincidence in the fact that the destined leader in the exodus of his nation from bondage, had attained that age before he in any public way identified himself with their struggle. These years of obscurity were the best preparation for his peculiar work. It is not without regret that we have been constrained to give up as unhistorical the pictures, drawn by the hands of fond biographers, of the brilliant young teacher of philosophy at St. Andrews, surrounded by admiring students and eclipsing the reputation of his master; but the less romantic labours of a " Rood Priest," with no university distinction and belonging to none of the monastic establishments, quietly doing his work according to his

[1] Knox's History, vol. i. p. 139.

light—settling disputes about chalders of victual, signing deeds in behalf of high-born ladies to whom the art of writing was unknown, and then, when the new light had dawned upon him, instructing his "bairns," "nourishing them in godliness," he called it, in the chapel of Longniddry, in presence of eager rustics who came to listen to unaccustomed truth—were after all the best training for the part he had to play, as the stern resister of courtly influences arrayed against the gospel and the liberties of the nation, and as the legislator for a Church which had to set itself to the task of civilizing a rude and barbarous people. He was of the people, and by long intercourse with them he learned their needs.

His open adherence to Wishart at last brought Knox under the surveillance of those in authority. He tells us that he was "wearied of removing from place to place by reason of the persecution that came upon him," and had made up his mind to leave Scotland and visit "the schools of Germany"; but he yielded to the solicitation of the fathers of his pupils that he would not desert his charge; and so he and the young men, at Easter, 1547, took refuge in the Castle of St. Andrews, which was held by the conspirators who had avenged the martyrdom of Wishart by the slaughter of Cardinal Beaton. He sought this refuge in common with a large number of the more earnest adherents of the Reformation; because, since the defection of the Regent, it was the only place in Scotland where they could safely maintain the profession of their faith. Their going there did not necessarily involve approval of the deed which had been done by those who held the stronghold though it is evident, from the terms in which Knox writes of that deed, that he did not reckon it an assassination, but a vindication of outraged law against a notorious offender, who would in ordinary course of justice have been put to death, if he had not himself had control of the executive authority. While fully recognizing the peril of approving such vindications, we are unable to share the "extreme pain and disgust" with which a recent historian of the Scottish Church reads Knox's graphic record of this event.[1] Knox could not reasonably be expected to pity Beaton, whose hands were red with innocent blood, and if, as was his wont, he saw the comedy that mingled with the tragedy of the persecutor's death, we cannot greatly blame him.

Knox's residence in the Castle was very short—less than four months; yet during that time he made his influence powerfully felt in the ecclesiastical capital and beyond it. The prominence he obtained was not of his seeking. He resumed in the chapel of the Castle the instruction of his pupils in the Gospel of St. John at the point he had reached when he left Longniddry, and the garrison and refugees gathered in to listen to his teaching. Among the listeners were John Rough, who with Gulliaume had been one of the Regent's chaplains, and was now preacher in the Castle; Henry Balnaves, a Lord of Session, whose treatise on Justification was so highly commended by Knox; and Sir David Lyndsay of the Mount, whose satires had done so much to prepare the Reformer's way. The two first named "perceaving the maner of his doctrin, begane earnestlie to travaill with him, that he wold tack the preaching

[1] Church History of Scotland, by Dr. Cunningham, of Crieff. vol. i. note to page 252.

place upoun him. But he utterlie refuissed, alledgeing 'that he wold nott ryne whare God had nott called him,' meanyng that he wold do nothing without a lauchfull vocatioun."[1] In this ground of refusal we recognize the first germ of that principle which has proved so fruitful during all the after history of our Scottish Church—the principle that no one is entitled to assume the preacher's office without the "lawful call" of those to whom he is to minister.

Rough and Balnaves took steps to provide the necessary call. They consulted with Lyndsay, and in the plan they devised we see the hand of the Lyon King of Arms, accustomed to study dramatic effects. The scene they arranged can be best described by quoting the words of Knox himself, whose dramatic power was hardly inferior to that of his forerunner. "Thei concluded that they wold geve a charge to the said Johnne, and that publictlie by the mouth of thare preachear. And so upoun a certane day, a sermone had of the electioun of ministeris, What power the congregatioun (how small that ever it was, passing the nomber of two or three) had above any man, in whome thei supposed and espyed the giftes of God to be, and how dangerous it was to refuise, and not to hear the voce of such as desyre to be instructed. These and other headis (we say) declaired, the said Johnne Rowght, preachear, directed his words to the said Johnne Knox, saying, 'Brother, ye shall nott be offended, albeit that I speak unto yow that which I have in charge, evin from all those that ar hear present, which is this: In the name of God, and of his Sone Jesus Christ, and in the name of these that presentlie calles yow by my mouth, I charge

[1] History, vol. i. p 186.

yow, that ye refuise not this holy vocatioun, but that as ye tender the glorie of God, the encrease of Christ his kingdome, the edificatioun of your brethrene, and the conforte of me, whome ye understand weill yneuch to be oppressed by the multitude of labouris, that ye tak upoun yow the publict office and charge of preaching, evin as ye looke to avoid Goddis heavye displeasur, and disyre that he shall multiplye his graces with yow.' And in the end he said to those that war present, 'Was not this your charge to me? And do ye not approve this vocatioun?' Thei answered, 'It was; and we approve it.' Whairat the said Johnne, abashed, byrst furth in moist abundand tearis, and withdrew himself to his chalmer. His conteannance and behaveour, fra that day till the day that he was compelled to present himself to the publict place of preaching, did sufficiently declair the greaf and truble of his hearte; for no man saw any sign of myrth of him, neyther yitt had he pleasur to accumpany any man, many dayis togetther."[1]

The scene is memorable and instructive. It is the way of prophets thus to shrink from the speaking of God's Word, and from the baptism with which they are baptized who speak it faithfully. "Who am I that I should go? I am not eloquent, but I am slow of speech." "I am a man of unclean lips." "Ah, Lord God! behold I cannot speak, for I am a child."[2] By and by the Word, from speaking which they at first shrink, is in their hearts as a burning fire shut up in their bones, and they are weary with forbearing and they cannot stay. Very soon it was so with John

---

[1] History, vol. i. pp. 186-8.
[2] Moses, Isaiah, Jeremiah.

Knox. "The necessitie that caused him to enter in the publict place, besydis the vocatioun foirsaid," was the position taken up by "Deane Johne Annan (a rottin Papist)." To a man of apostolic spirit, not only a great door and effectual, but many adversaries, are needed to constitute an irresistible call. Annan, Knox tells us, having long troubled Rough in his preaching, and being beaten in argument at last in the parish kirk of St. Andrews, fell back on the authority of the Church, "which authoritie (said he), damned all Lutherianes and heretikes; and tharefoir he nedith no farther disputatioun." This was more than Knox could bear, and so on the following Sunday he mounted the pulpit and chose his text from the prophecy of Daniel, concerning the other king who should arise, and "speak great words against the Most High and should wear out the saints of the Most High." Having "sufficientlie declared" three heads of positive truth, "he entered to the contrar," and hurled argument and invective against the Papacy—showing that its doctrine and its laws alike are "contrare to Christ," and that therefore it is Antichrist; and he closed by addressing a challenge to his audience, in which were his old master John Major, the University, the sub-prior and many canons, with some friars black and grey, to controvert his argument if they could.

The delivery of this, John Knox's first sermon, marks an epoch in the history of Scottish Reformation. His hearers recognized that it did so, for some of them said, "Otheris sned the branches of the Papistrie, but he strykis at the roote to destroy the hole." It was true. Other leaders of the Reformation came slowly and sorrowfully to the conclusion that the system of

Popery, the errors and defects of which they would fain have corrected, was itself essentially evil, and that no reform short of uprootal would avail. The assertion of this was the very first public utterance of our clear-eyed, practical Scottish Reformer.

The excitement produced by the sermon culminated in a public disputation, in which Knox held his own against Wynrame, the sub-prior, and Arbuckle, a Franciscan, whom in the end Wynrame found rather an inconvenient ally, for when they were driven from Scripture to Scripture by the remorseless logician, the friar "whill he wanderis about in the myst, he falles in a fowll myre; for alledgeing that we may nott be so bound to the woord, he affirmed that the Apostles had not receaved the Holy Ghost, when thei did write thare epistles; but after thei receaved him, and then thei did ordeyn the Ceremonies." The sub-prior deemed it necessary to wash his hands of that argument; the friar was fain to flee to the authority of the Church; and when Knox, summarizing in a sentence the fundamental position of the Reformation, replied, "That the spouse of Christ had neither power nor authority against the word of God," his opponent exclaimed, "If so ye will leave us no kirk;" and Knox, with the humour with which this healthful soul never failed to lighten grave debate, answered, "Indead in David I read that thare is a Church of the malignantis, for he sayis, *Odi ecclesiam malignantium*. That church ye may have without the word."

Though the authorities took care that Knox should not preach again on a Sunday, but confine his ministrations to week-days, the effect of the Reformer's teaching was such that not only all the refugees in the Castle but many of the inhabitants of the town openly professed the Reformed faith. Towards the end of July a French fleet cast anchor in the bay, the siege by land was made more stringent, the plague broke out in the garrison, and by the last day of the month the Castle had capitulated, and Knox, in flagrant violation of the terms of capitulation, found himself chained to the oar as a galley-slave. For nineteen weary months, through winter cold and summer heat, now on French rivers and now on the open sea, did he toil on; but nothing could break his spirit. He and his companions, though "threatened with tormentis yf thei wold not give reverence to the Messe," stood firm. When the *Salve Regina* was sung "the hole Scotishmen putt on thare cappes, thare hoodis, or such thing as thei had to cover thare headis"; and on one memorable occasion "a paynted brod (which thei called 'Nostre Dame') was brought in to be kissed, and, amongis otheris, was presented to one of the Scotishmen then cheyned. He gentillye said, 'Truble me nott; such ane idole is accursed; and tharefoir I will not tuich it.' The Patron and the Arguesyn, with two officeris, having the cheaf charge of all such materis, said, 'Thow salt handill it;' and so they violentlie thrust it to his face, and putt it betwix his handis; who, seeing the extremitie, took the idole, and advisitlie looking about, he caist it in the rivare, and said, 'Lett our Lady now saif hirself: sche is lycht aneuch; let hir learne to swyme.' After that was no Scotish man urged with that idolatrie."[1] Though Knox modestly conceals his name, no one can doubt that it was he who wrought this happy deliverance for his fellow-captives. By wasting fever he was brought

---

[1] History, vol. i. p. 227.

to the very gates of death; yet he never lost heart or hope. Once when the galleys were lying between Dundee and St. Andrews he, though he was "so extreamlye sick that few hoped his lyeff," said cheerily, " I see the stepill of that place, whare God first in publict opened my mouth to his glorie, and I am fullie persuaded, how weak that ever I now appear, that I shall nott departe this lyif till that my toung shall glorifie his godlie name in the same place." He never during the dark days of his servitude forgot his " best beloved brethren of the congregation of the Castle of St. Andrews." His first literary effort, like his first sermon, was for their behoof. It was an essay introductory to a treatise written by Henry Balnaves in his prison at Rouen, on the Reformation doctrine of Justification, which Knox deemed so valuable that he sent it home to Scotland, accompanied with a summary of it which he made in the form of a Confession of Faith.

During these months matters were going ill in Scotland for the cause of reformation. The English Protector, Somerset, who had weakly abandoned the garrison of St. Andrews to their fate, and thus let the firmest upholders of the English alliance be made exiles and prisoners, resolved on an invasion to enforce the fulfilment of the engagement, into which the Scottish Parliament had entered, for the marriage of their young Queen to King Edward VI. He entered Scotland at the head of a great army, attended by a fleet, and gained at Pinkiecleugh a victory, which proved more disastrous than any defeat to the policy he sought to further. He awakened the spirit of Bannockburn; and the whole Scottish nation, Catholic and Protestant,

Highlander and Lowlander, united to maintain the independence of their country against their "auld enemies" of England. They were thus thrown into the arms of France; and finally at the Convention of Haddington, when the Regent Arran had been bribed by the Duchy of Chatelherault and a pension of twelve thousand crowns, it was arranged that Mary should be at once transferred to France as the affianced bride of the Dauphin. It is of interest to note that the galley, of which Knox was one of the rowers, was in the fleet sent to support the besiegers of Haddington, but whose admiral, whenever the Convention was over, weighed anchor and, sailing by the Orkneys, came to Dumbarton, and taking Mary Stuart on board conveyed her to Brest; "and so," says Knox, "was she sold to go to France, to the end that in hir youth she should drink of that lycour, that should remane with hir all hir lyfetyme, for a plague to this realme, and for hir finall destructioun." This took place in June, 1548.

Early the following year Knox obtained his liberty; but the way not being open for his return to Scotland, he sought asylum in England and was appointed preacher at Berwick. There, and over all the North, in which till now the old doctrines had been comparatively undisturbed, it was speedily recognized that a man whose word was with power had appeared. Tonstall, Bishop of Durham, took alarm at his bold denunciation of the Mass, and summoned him before the Council of the North for Public Affairs in April, 1550. Knox at once obeyed the summons and delivered in presence of the Bishop and his doctors, with the whole Council, his famous "Vindication," beginning with the words, "This day I do appeir in your presence, Honourable Audience, to gif a reasone why so constantlie I do affirme the Mass to be, and at all times to haif been, Idolatrie, and abominatioun befoir God."[1] From the moment these words were spoken it was evident that a new force was about to make itself felt in the English Reformation. Till now, in the history of that movement, men had not been accustomed to so clear and unfaltering utterance. And the speaker, who maintained his thesis with keen logic, varied scholarship, scathing satire and deep-toned earnestness, was soon transferred to Newcastle, as a wider and more influential sphere.

At the close of the year 1551 he was appointed one of the chaplains to King Edward VI.; and in that high position he exercised large and enduring influence, not only as a royal preacher going from place to place kindling men's hearts by his burning words, but as one officially consulted in the revision of the Prayer Book and in the framing of the Articles of Belief. By his influence an important change was made in the Communion service, as it appeared in the revised edition of the Prayer Book which was issued in 1552, and a rubric was introduced explaining that by the act of kneeling no adoration of the bread or wine was meant, " for that were idolatory to be abhorred of all faithfull Christians." It was unquestionably to Knox that Dr. Weston alluded when, in his disputation with Latimer at Oxford in 1554, he said, " A runnagate Scot dyd take away the adoration or worshipping of Christ in the sacrament; by whose procurement that heresie was put into the last Communion Booke: so

[1] Works, vol. iii. p. 33.

much prevailed that one man's authority at that tyme."[1]

We have abundant evidence of "how painfullie and powerfully," as Calderwood expresses it, the Scottish Reformer laboured in England. It was arranged that in addition to their service at the Court, King Edward's chaplains should go among the churches in the various districts of the country. Accordingly we find Knox now a Court preacher and now an itinerating evangelist. In the former of those positions he was bold and fearless. He tells us that in his last sermon before the King, "and even to the faces of suche as of whom he ment," when preaching from the text, "He that eateth bread with me hath lifted up his heel against me," he "made this affirmacion, That commonlye it was sene, that the most godly princes hadde officers and chief counseilours most ungodlye, conjurned enemies to Goddes true religion and traitours to their princes." After illustrating his affirmation by reference to Achitophel and Shebna, who "had hyghe offices and promocions, with great authoritie, under the moste godly princes David and Ezechias," and to Judas, who "was purse-maister with Christ Jesus," he held the mirror up to three great officers of the State, by adding, "What wonder is it, then, that a yonge and innocent kinge be deceived by craftye, covetouse, wycked and ungodly counselours? I am greatly afrayd that Achitophel be counsailer, that Judas beare the purse, and that Sobna be scribe, comptroller, and treasurer." Knox has supplied us with the means of knowing that by "Sobna" he meant to indicate the

[1] Foxe's Acts and Monuments, vol. ii. p. 1388, ed. 1576, quoted by Laing. Knox's Works, vol. iii. p. 80.

Marquess of Winchester (Sir William Paulet), who was successively Comptroller, Secretary, and Lord Treasurer to Edward VI., and that by "Achitophel" he meant the Duke of Northumberland.[1] In looking back on his work in England from amid the gloom of his exile, Knox lamented that he had " in the begynnyng of this battell appeired to play the faynt-heartit and febill souldeour,"[2] and that he " was not so fervent in rebuking manifest iniquitie " as it became him to have been.[3] But if this be a fair specimen of his style of preaching it is difficult to see any good ground for the self-accusation.

In the passage we have last quoted he indicates one reason why he was dissatisfied with the retrospect of his work. He says: " In preaching Christes Gospel . . . . the love of frendes and carnal affection of some men with whom I was most familiar, allured me to make more residence in one place than in another, having more respect to the pleasure of a fewe than to the necessitie of many." It is probable that he here alludes to the fact that even after his appointment to the chaplaincy he spent much of his time in Newcastle, where his ministry was so powerful that large numbers of his fellow-countrymen were drawn across the Border.[4] This could not but be pleasing to the exiled Scot, and possibly kept him longer in the north than he would

---

[1] A Faythfull Admonition—Works, vol. iii. pp. 281-3, and Laing's Note. Froude's History, ch. 29.

[2] An Exposition of the Sixth Psalm. Works, vol. iii. p. 154.

[3] Faythfull Admonition, p. 270.

[4] It seems reasonable to recognize in the strength which the Presbyterian Church has always maintained in Newcastle a result of Knox's ministry there.

otherwise have remained. But the northern location had a yet stronger attraction. When he first visited England and was preaching in Berwick, he met Marjory Bowes, daughter of the Captain of Norham Castle, and grand-daughter of Sir Robert Bowes of Streatlam, and of Sir Rodger Aske of Aske. The motherly kindness of good Mrs. Bowes, and the maidenly love of her daughter, must have been peculiarly sweet to the liberated galley-slave, who for at least nineteen months had known no gentle ministry, and so Marjory won his heart. Newcastle was a convenient base of operations for prosecuting his suit; and in 1553, in spite of the opposition of her father, Marjory became his affianced bride.

Whatever was the secret of his preference for Newcastle, it was not pleasing to the great magnate of the northern shire. The Duke of Northumberland wrote a letter, dated 27th October, 1552, to Secretary Cecil, strongly recommending that Knox should be appointed to the vacant Bishopric of Rochester. While naïvely hinting " that he would not only be a whetstone to quicken and sharp the Bishop of Canterbury, whereof he hath need; but he would be a great confounder of the Anabaptists lately sprung up in Kent," the Duke was honest enough to assign as his second reason that "he should not continue the ministration in the North"; and for his third, that " the family of the Scots, now inhabiting in Newcastle chiefly for his fellowship, would not continue there, wherein many resorts unto them out of Scotland, which is not requisite."[1] It does not appear whether Knox was actually offered the vacant bishopric; it is certain that he would not have

[1] Tytler's Edward VI., etc., vol. ii. p. 142.

accepted it, for the Duke of Northumberland, who had an interview with him on the subject found him "neither grateful nor pleasable," but a little disposed to indicate an opinion which, as we have seen, he afterwards indicated more publicly, that the Duke was "a dissembler in religion." While gladly serving the Church of England as a preacher, he did not, on account of his objection to the polity and ritual of that Church, feel free to accept even of an ordinary benefice. He was not only offered the living of All-hallows in London, but summoned before the Privy Council and dealt with because he refused it. Among other difficulties in the way, kneeling at the Lord's table was discussed, and the interview between him and the Lords of Council had this characteristic ending: "They were sorry to know him of a contrary mind to the common Order. He answered that he was more sorry that a common Order should be contrary to Christ's institution."[1]

During the years of Knox's ministry in England the sweating sickness—the records of whose ravages mingle with all the history of the Reformation—was desolating the land. Its presence must have given peculiar power to the words of doom spoken by this Court preacher; the burden of whose message was the judgment surely coming. His keen grey eye had looked into the face of the young King, and had read the writing there which foretold an early death; it had looked into the characters of his chief councillors, and had seen that most of them were "dissemblers in religion," who, when Edward was gone, would transfer their allegiance to Mary and turn against the Refor-

[1] Calderwood's MS. History, quoted by Laing.

mation; and so he passed through the land like a prophet, calling on men to regard the time of their merciful visitation and to cast out the evil leaven which remained in the Church. He learnt to love the country which he served so faithfully, and after he was driven from it he writes thus: "My dailie praier is for the sore afflicted in those quarters. Somtyme I have thought that impossible it had bene, so to have removed my affection from the Realme of Scotland, that eny Realme or Nation coulde have been equall deare unto me. But God I take to recorde in my conscience, that the troubles present (and appearing to be) in the Realme of England are double more dolorous unto my hert than ever were the troubles of Scotland."[1]

Though he foresaw the changes which would inevitably follow the King's death, he still hoped the best. Edward died on 6th July, 1553, but the Reformer continued his labours till October, drawing large congregations, which he exhorted to steadfastness, and using a form of prayer in which these petitions occur: "Illuminate the harte off our Soveraigne Lady Quene Marie with pregnant giftes of thy Holy Ghoste. And inflame the hartes of her Counsayl with thy trew feare and love. Represse thou the pryde of those that wold rebelle; and remove from all hartes the contempte of thy Worde." This form was published, with a "Declaration of the true nature and object of Prayer,"[2] which gives a clear exposition of the Reformation doctrine on the subject, sounds the Protestant watchword that "the haill earthe creatit be God is equallie holie,"

[1] An Exposition of the Sixth Psalm. Works, vol. iii. p. 133.
[2] Works, vol. iii. p. 77.

and yet "condempneth all sic as contempneth the congregatioun gatherit in his name." At last the preacher was put to silence, and amid the increasing horrors of persecution the prayer for the Queen would have seemed a mockery. Early in 1554, Knox consented to seek a refuge abroad and landed at Dieppe, where he lingered for a month, writing his Exposition of the Sixth Psalm and his "Godlie Letter too the fayethfull in London, Newcastell, Barwyke, &c.," both of which had been begun in England. The former was addressed to his future mother-in-law, Mrs. Bowes. Of this good lady Knox says: "Her company to me was comfortable (yea, honorable and profitable, for she was to me and myne a mother); but yet it was not without some croce; for besydes trouble and fasherie of body susteyned for her, my mynde was seldome quyet, for doing somewhat for the comfort of her troubled conscience."[1] She was a woman of a sorrowful countenance. "Sathan did continually buffette her that remission of sinnes in Christ Jesus apperteyned nothing unto her."[2] She was haunted with fears that she had sinned the sin unto death for which there is no forgiveness;[3] and with suspicions lest Knox and others should judge her not to be one of their number.[4] The Reformer was constantly receiving letters from her, "the piteous complayntis whairof pierced his heart,"[5] but he was very sympathetic and rarely lost patience. He turned her case to good account for the help of others. He tells her on one occasion that the

[1] Preface to Letter published in 1572, with his Answer to Tyrie, Works, vol. vi. p. 514.
[2] Ibid.   [3] Letters—Works, vol. iii. p. 369.   [4] Ibid., p. 370.
[5] Ibid., p. 376.

very instant her letter came he was dealing with "thrie honest pure women" who were similarly afflicted, to whom it was a comfort to hear of her trouble.[1] It is very beautiful to see this man who chid rulers and moulded national histories occupying himself with the doubts and fears and spiritual sorrows of trembling souls.

The "Godlie Letter," which is subscribed as "From ane sore trubillit heart upon my departure from Dieppe whither God knaweth," is a most urgent appeal to resist the defections of the time and not to shrink from the sufferings involved in faithfulness. After writing it Knox visited Geneva and the Swiss churches, consulting the brethren there as to certain politico-religious questions,[2] of some of which we shall hear presently. His intercourse with like-minded men, and especially with the master-mind of Calvin, seems to have revived his heart, for the "Two Comfortable Epistles" which, after his return to Dieppe in May of the same year, he addressed to the sufferers in England, breathe a very different spirit from the gloom and sadness of the "Godlie Letter." They are full of light, and of anticipation of victory for the cause which was meanwhile passing through its baptism of blood and fire. These epistles were followed in July by the "Faythfull Admonition," which is based on the Gospel story of the Disciples in the storm and of Christ coming to them. It was written with the double object of strengthening the English Protestants and of protesting against the marriage of the Queen with Philip of Spain. Its

[1] Letters—Works, vol. iii. p. 379.
[2] Certain Questions concerning Obedience, etc.—Works, vol. iii. p. 217.

tone is uncompromising, and its language strong against Mary and her creatures, Gardiner, Bonner, and Tonstall; but its tenderness and its faith that all will come right are even more noteworthy than its invective, though that is so strong that it is said to have stung the Queen into frenzy, and thus to have hastened the death of Ridley and Latimer.

The most interesting feature of all these letters, epistles, and admonitions, is their application of ancient Scripture to the actual world of the writer's time. The long-sealed Book had been opened, no longer to furnish the tiny portions read in strange language and unnatural tone as part of a pompous ritual; but to be studied as a true guide of life, in which men may find their politics as well as their religion, and to be used as an armoury from which they may draw weapons for the battle of truth and righteousness in whatever land or age it has to be fought. This manner of using Scripture was characteristic of Knox to the close. In the pulpit of St. Giles, in his interviews with the Queen at Holyrood, and in his conferences with the Lords of her Council, he freely quoted the facts of Hebrew history and the burning words of Hebrew prophecy when denouncing Mary and her flatterers. "Thay wer singular motiounis of the Spirit of God," said Maitland of Lethington at one of the conferences, "and appertene nothing to this our aige." To whom Knox replied, "Then hes the Scriptour far dissavit me, for Sanct Paule teichis me that 'whatsoevir is wryttin within the Holie Scriptouris, the same is writtin for our instructioun.' And my Maister said, that 'everie learnit and wyise scribe bringis furth his tresour baith thingis auld and thingis new.'"

In October, 1554, Knox, who had in the interval gone back to Geneva, accepted an invitation to become the pastor of a congregation of English exiles in Frankfort. We cannot here enter on the details of the unhappy disputes between him and some zealous ritualists who insisted on the use of those forms which, as we have seen, were so distasteful to him. His opponents in this congregational dispute were so bitter against him that they denounced their pastor to the magistrates as having in his references to the royal marriage in the "Faythfull Admonition" cast reflections on the Emperor, the father of Philip of Spain. Knox was constrained to leave the city, and in March, 1555, he returned to Geneva.

Meanwhile the way was being opened for his visiting Scotland. Events, in themselves untoward, had been over-ruled for the furtherance of the cause of Reform in that country. The death of Edward, and the terrors of the Marian persecution had sent into the northern kingdom some of the English refugees, whose teaching, accompanied as it was by stories of the faithfulness of the martyrs and the cruelty of their persecutors, was influential in evoking sympathy with the Reformed doctrine. The elevation of Mary of Guise to the Regency was intended by the Cardinal of Lorraine to strengthen the French alliance, and in the end to crush the cause of Protestantism. This intention was clearly discerned by the Protestants. Knox, in recording how she had "a croune putt upone hir head," adds that it was "als seimlye a sight (yf men had eis), as to putt a sadill upoun the back of ane unrewly kow." But the first effect of her elevation was in the direction of religious liberty. The Duke of Chatelherault, whom she superseded, had been entirely under the influence of his infamous brother the Archbishop of St. Andrews; and it was Mary's policy to show herself to some extent independent of the clerical party. Knox, who never forgot the land of his birth, and in whom the desire to be more directly identified with the Church that was struggling into existence there, had probably been stirred by his experience of English ritualism at Frankfort, resolved to visit Scotland, and left Geneva in August, 1555.

In addition to the public motive which at this time drew him to his native country, he had the natural desire to see his affianced bride and, if circumstances proved favourable, have his marriage consummated. Indeed, in a letter to Mrs. Bowes, he acknowledges that God had made her the instrument to draw him "from the den" of his own ease. "Yow allane," he says, "did draw me from the rest of quyet studie, to contemplat and behald the fervent thrist of our brethrene, nyght and day sobbing and gronying for the breid of lyfe."[1] Accordingly, Berwick, which was still the home of Mrs. Bowes and her daughter, was his landing-place. He did not linger long there, but passed on to Edinburgh, where he put himself in communication with those who seemed best affected to the Reformed doctrines. Prominent among them were John Erskine of Dun, and William Maitland of Lethington, who, attracted by his discourse, brought their acquaintances in ever increasing numbers to his lodging, so that he had to address them in successive assemblies, and was occupied day and night in dealing with inquiries after truth.

[1] Works, vol. iv. p. 217.

He found that the adherents of the Reformation had hitherto deemed it expedient to attend the services of the Church of Rome. With this temporizing spirit Knox could have no sympathy, and he set himself " alsweall in privy conference as in doctrine, to schaw the impiete of the Messe, and how dangerous a thing it was to communicat in any sort with idolatrie." His remonstrances led to a discussion at a supper-party in Erskine's lodging, the result of which was that even Maitland said: " I see perfytlye that our schiftis will serve nothing before God, seing that thei stand us in so small stead befoir man." From that time Scottish Protestantism occupied a worthier attitude.

Knox's ministrations were not confined to the metropolis. He spent a month at Dun, in Forfarshire, as the guest of Mr. Erskine, and preached daily to the neighbouring gentry and their followers. He next resided at Calder, the seat of Sir James Sandilands, where such men as Lord Erskine, afterwards Earl of Mar; Lord Lorne, afterwards Earl of Argyle; and Lord James Stuart, afterwards Earl of Murray, waited on his instructions and approved his doctrine. In mid-winter he returned for a time to Edinburgh, and after Christmas passed to Kyle; a great comet, which men named " The fyrie boosome," all the while blazing in the heaven.[1] In the old seat of Lollardism Knox found a specially hearty welcome, and remained for several months, preaching in the town of Ayr and in the country houses of Barr, Carnell, Kingyeancleuch,

[1] History, vol. i. p. 254. We introduce the comet at this point on Knox's authority, though there seems to be some confusion in his notice of contemporaneous events; and it is possible that he assigns to this memorable winter a phenomenon which did not appear till a later date. *Vide* Laing's note.

Ochiltree, and Gadgirth. It seems to have been in Ayrshire that he first took the bold step of administering the Lord's Supper, according to the Genevan order, to those whom he had persuaded no longer to attend mass.

From Ayrshire he passed into Renfrewshire—the home of his ancestors—where he was the guest of the Earl of Glencairn at Finlayston. There, under the sombre shadow of a yew tree, amid woods bright with fresh buds—for it was " befoir the Pasche," which in that year fell on the 5th of April—he administered the Sacrament, giving to the laity the long-forbidden wine in silver cups, which in after years were used in the parish kirk of Kilmalcolm. Besides the Earl and his lady, who was a daughter of the late Regent, two of his sons and certain of his friends " war parttakaris." It is pleasant to realize the scene, and to picture the guise of that little company of Christ's Sacramental host, seated on the tender grass, with the motions of the spring around them, and the air filled with sounds of the green-leaved earth. We can well believe that the worn exile would be glad, and that as the Sacramental hymn was sung, " My saule praise thow the Lord alwyes,"[1] the words of another song would be making music in his heart, " Lo, the winter is past, the rain is over and gone ; the flowers appear on the earth ; the time of the singing of birds is come."

[1] This line does not correspond with any of the known versions of the 103rd Psalm—which, from the first, was the " hymn " they sung in Scotland before they went out from the table ; but it must have been in use in Knox's time, for in the account of the death of Elizabeth Adamson, which he gives in his History, the line is quoted as the beginning of the 103rd Psalm, which " a littil befoir hir departuyre" she desired her sister to sing.

Leaving Renfrewshire he returned to Calder, "whare diverse frome Edinburgh, and frome the countrey about, convened, asweall for the doctrin as for the rycht use of the Lordis Table which befoir thei had never practised." We find him next on a second visit to Dun, where "the moist parte of the gentilmen of the Mernse" whom he taught "in grettar libertie," having asked that they might enjoy the new privilege accorded to their brethren in the South, received the Lord's Supper at his hands. It was from one or other of these places that he wrote to Mrs. Bowes: "The trumpet blew the ald sound thrie dayis together, till privat houssis of indifferent largeness culd not conteane the voice of it. . . . O! sueit war the death that suld follow sic fourtie dayis in Edinburgh, as heir I have had thrie."[1]

The tidings of the work which the Reformer was doing, and of the welcome that was given him by high and low in all the districts to which he went, alarmed the bishops; and they summoned him to appear at their Convocation in the Church of the Greyfriars, on the 15th May, 1556. This assembly, if Knox had stood before it, would have at least equalled in interest any subsequent gathering of the clergy in the month of May at Edinburgh; and it was not his fault that the "dyet held nott." He welcomed the opportunity of bearing his testimony and prepared to appear. But the bishops took fright and, on the Saturday before the day appointed, cast their summons. Knox came to the metropolis notwithstanding, and for ten days taught morning and afternoon at the Bishop of Dunkeld's lodgings to larger audiences than on his former visit.

[1] Familiar Letters—Works, vol. iv. p. 218.

Among those who came to him was the Earl Marischal, introduced by the Earl of Glencairn. These two noblemen prevailed on the Reformer to address a letter to the Queen Regent, urging her, as she loved her own salvation, to regard and protect the true religion. The letter was written in courtlier style than Knox was wont to use, but in matter it was faithful, and in spirit deeply earnest. Lord Glencairn undertook the delivery of the letter, and it was probably he who reported to Knox that Mary, after running her eye contemptuously down its pages, handed it to the Archbishop of Glasgow, saying, "Please you, my lord, to read a pasquil." Who was this bold preacher who presumed to lecture her about her soul's salvation and her public policy ? Was she not the sister of a cardinal, and had she not her high officers whose duty it was to watch for her soul; and what had the latter subject to do with the former? She had not been studying the Hebrew prophets like Knox, and had not learned that the eternal destiny of rulers is affected by the manner in which they rule—that Tophet is ordained of old; yea, for the king it is prepared: He hath made it deep and large. It was not wonderful, therefore, that she hardly deemed the writing serious that spoke to her, on the one hand, of recompense for righteous government and for protection of the innocent, from Him "who pronounceth mercy to apperteyn to the mercifull, and promiseth that a cuppe of cold water geven for hys name's sake shall not lacke rewarde "; and on the other hand, of "dejection to torment and payn everlasting," as the result of a "regiment and using of power" after the manner of "the multitude of princes and head rulers." The writing seemed to her a pasquil. Her "woordis cuming to the earis of the said Johne," as he tells us in his History, "was the occasion that to his letter he made his additionis." Two years later, when, in Geneva, he had tidings which convinced him that she had not only sneered at, but utterly disregarded his warnings, he expanded and published his letter, kindling his old words as with burning fire.[1]

Yet another of his writings—an exposition of the Temptation of Christ—belongs to the period of this visit to Scotland. It had evidently done duty in some of his preachings, for it has all the vividness and life of his spoken utterance. It reveals dramatic power. The dialogues between our Lord and the Tempter are as life-like as his records of his own interviews with Queen Mary, or of his reasoning with the Abbot of Crossraguel.

Knox having received an urgent call to return to the English congregation at Geneva to which he had been ministering, and deeming it wiser to retire and let the leaven work, left Scotland in July, 1556, joining Marjory Bowes, to whom he was now married, and her mother, at Dieppe, whither he had sent them on before him. He left behind him a "Letter of wholesome counsel addressed to his brethren in Scotland."[2] No sooner had he gone than the bishops resumed proceedings against him. He was at a safe distance. In the unlikely event of his obeying their summons, it was open to them as before to execute a retreat on the eve of the conflict. If he did not appear, they could condemn

[1] Letter to the Queen Dowager, Regent of Scotland; and the same augmented and explained by the Author. Works, vol. iv. p. 69 and p. 423.
[2] Works, vol. iv. p. 129.

him as contumacious. It was this easy triumph they won. They pronounced sentence of excommunication, depriving him of his priest's orders, delivering his soul to damnation, and his body to the secular power for the punishment of death. The sham sentence was followed by a sham execution. His effigy was burned at the Cross of Edinburgh. Knox tells the story thus: "Me as an heretic and this doctrine as heretical, have your false bishops and ungodly clergy damned, pronouncing against me a sentence of death, in testification whereof they have burned a picture."

After this cowardly action of the clergy, Knox immediately addressed "An Appellation to the Nobilitie and Estates of Scotland," in which, having set forth the leading articles of the faith which the clergy had condemned, he urges, from manifold Scripture precept and example, the duty which lies upon rulers and magistrates to protect the upholders of the true faith, and to overturn the idolatrous system of the Papacy. He makes short work of the objections which he supposes may be advanced against this use of the secular arm. "Seing," he says, "that Moses was so far preferred to Aaron that the one commaunded and the other did obey; who dar esteme that the civile power is now becomed so prophane in God's eyes, that it is sequestred from all intromission with the matters of religion? The Holie Ghost in divers places declareth the contrarie." To Knox the fact that the kingdom from which he took his examples was a theocracy did not in the least diminish their practical value. He held it to be "evident that the Rulers, Magistrats, and Judges, now in Christes kingdome, are no lesse bound to obedience unto God than were those under the law."[1] The battle of freedom is fought bit by bit, and the full doctrine of civil and religious liberty is only spelled out through the experience of centuries.

Of that doctrine Knox laid the foundation. At the same time as he sent the Appellation to the Nobility and Estates, he addressed "A Letter to the Commonalty of Scotland,"[2] in which he pleads with them to realize their responsibility in relation to the work of reformation. His far-seeing instincts taught him that, argue as he might from Hebrew precedents of the duty of rulers to advance the truth by the power of the sword, it is to the sympathy of the people we must look for the furtherance of the righteous cause. It was Knox, as we shall see presently, who made the commons of Scotland a power in the land; and it was by that power that he defeated the machinations of the Court and saved the Reformation.[3]

In addition to those writings there are other two belonging to this period which specially refer to Scottish affairs—"A Letter to his Brethren,"[4] written in May, 1557, in answer to an invitation to return; and "A Letter to the Professors of the Truth,"[5] written in December of the same year, when he had found it expedient to prolong his absence, and exhorting to patience, courage, and obedience meanwhile to the constituted authority. During the same time of comparative rest he prepared a form of service for the

---

[1] The Appellation. Works, vol. iv. pp. 461-520.

[2] A Letter, etc., Ibid., pp. 521-538.

[3] The Influence of the Reformation on Scottish Character, in Froude's Short Studies, vol. i. p. 154.

[4] Works, vol. iv. p. 261.   [5] Ibid., p. 276.

English Church at Geneva. It became the model from which his Book of Common Order was framed for the Church of Scotland. Knox's fundamental principle with regard to ritual was that nothing should enter into divine service which has not the authority of Scripture. This principle is recognized in the Genevan Liturgy by the marginal references to Scripture texts in support of each successive clause in the various parts of the service. A translation, with a preface, of an Apology for imprisoned Protestants in France,[1] made when, towards the close of 1557, he had, in response to a letter from the Scottish Lords, gone to Dieppe on his way to Edinburgh, but was arrested by less favourable intelligence; a long treatise on Predestination;[2] an Epistle and Exhortation to the inhabitants of Newcastle and Berwick;[3] his share in the preparation of the Geneva version of the English Bible; and his world-famous First Blast of the Trumpet against the Monstrous Regiment of Women[4] —complete the catalogue of his literary labours during his Geneva pastorate.

We can only refer more particularly to the last-named of these works. It was written in support of the thesis that it is unnatural and unscriptural for a woman to reign. In none of Knox's writings is the style more vigorous, or the evidence clearer that the author's whole soul was in the doctrine he promulgated. The "Blast" was published early in 1558, and therefore it was probably written when he was in Dieppe at the close of the previous year. We can hardly wonder at the vehemence with which he maintains

[1] Works, vol. iv. p. 287. [2] Ibid., vol. v. p. 7. [3] Ibid., p. 469.
[4] Ibid., vol. iv. p. 349.

his thesis. His indignation was stirred by the tidings which reached him of the atrocious cruelties still perpetrated under Mary of England; and though the Queen Regent of Scotland was meanwhile restrained by considerations of policy from sanctioning severe persecution, yet her attitude was one of uncompromising hostility to the Reformed faith, and Knox knew well that she only bided her time. The massacre and imprisonment of French Protestants, in connection with which the Apology just referred to was written, had taken place under the royal house with which, through the marriage of Mary Stuart, Scotland had been brought into alliance. The risk of alien influence and foreign domination, to which the marriages of female sovereigns exposed the countries they ruled, was one of Knox's chief grounds of opposition to the "regiment" of women. And to a patriotic Protestant it was indeed galling that the liberties of England should be laid at the feet of the Spaniard, and the liberties of Scotland at the feet of the Frenchman. Knox wrote in no honied words, but spoke out in the bitterness of his soul against all "wicked Jesabels."

Yet withal the publication of the "Blast" was a serious blunder. Its argument is an example of too hasty generalization. For once the keen grey eyes that so often pierced the future were at fault. Knox could not have seen so far down the centuries as to forecast the liberty and peacefulness of the reign of Queen Victoria; but if he had been in more hopeful mood "the spacious times of Great Elizabeth" need not have been wholly hid. That Princess—a Protestant and a sufferer for her Protestantism—was the heir to the English throne, and circumstances made it even then not improbable that she would soon come to it. Had Knox been able to divine what was to be, and withheld his ill-timed "Blast," his subsequent work in Scotland would have been easier than it proved. As it was, he had to contend with Elizabeth's bitter resentment against himself, even when her clear judgment told her that the policy to which he exhorted her was wise. That resentment extended to his associates at Geneva. Calvin, in testimony of his joy at her accession, dedicated some of his Commentaries to the English Queen. He learned that the act of homage was not well received, and had to write to Sir William Cecil disavowing all sympathy with the Scottish Reformer's position. In his letter he naïvely admits that the government of women "was a deviation from the original and proper order of nature; it was to be ranked no less than slavery among the punishments consequent upon the fall of man."[1]

In December, 1557, at the very time when Knox was waiting in despondency at Dieppe, the Protestant Lords were subscribing a bond at Edinburgh, and renewing their invitation to the Reformer to come to their aid. The letter they addressed to him did not reach Geneva till November, 1558—the very month in which Mary of England died. Knox prepared to obey the summons. The times were hopeful. The great door and effectual had been gradually opening, and the many adversaries were more decidedly declaring their hostility. The Protestant Lords had adopted measures for establishing the purer worship in all parish churches, were taking the few available preachers of the Reformed doctrine under their direct pro-

[1] Zürich Letters, Second Series, p. 35, quoted by Laing.

tection, and were boldly laying their demands for reformation before the Government. On the other hand the Queen Regent was throwing off the mask and encouraging the Primate to do his worst against heretics. He was not slow to take advantage of her changing policy. Having failed to wrest a more prominent teacher from the hands of the Earl of Argyle, who had made him his chaplain, he took his revenge on an old priest named Walter Mill, who had been condemned for heresy in Beaton's time, but escaped execution. Discovering his retreat, the Primate had him arraigned before his Court at St. Andrews. He appeared there bowed with the burden of eighty-two years, and worn with a life of hardship and of fear; but his grey hairs moved no pity in the churchman's heart, and he was consigned alive to the flames on the 28th August, 1558. The "reik" of this old man's burning proved as infectious as that of young Patrick Hamilton. The whole nation was moved with horror, thousands crowded to the Reformed worship, and the preachers were emboldened to speak God's word and dispense the Sacraments with greater publicity than heretofore. The way was clearly open for the return of the man who alone was able to give coherence to the party of Reform and lead it on to victory.

Though Knox left Geneva in January, 1559, he did not reach Edinburgh till May. He waited at Dieppe for liberty to pass through England, which Elizabeth refused to the author of the "Blast." But the months he spent in France were not wasted. In troublous times men become quick of hearing, and birds of the air carry matters of highest import. Knox contrived somehow to inform himself thoroughly of the plots which were even then being laid to dethrone Elizabeth and destroy the Reformation, through the Scottish Queen who was heir presumptive of the English Crown. It is one of those strange coincidences of which history is full, that "the ship in which he crossed carried a seal to the Regent engraved with the arms of England, and carried with it also in himself the person who, above all others, baffled the conspiracy and saved Elizabeth and the Reformation." [1]

When the Reformer reached Edinburgh a council of Churchmen was in session. On the morning after his landing some one entered the monastery of the Greyfriars where they sat and announced that John Knox had come. It is said that the panic-stricken clergy stood not upon the order of their going, but dispersed in confusion. Even if this story be in the letter apocryphal,[2] it is in spirit historically true. The advent of this solitary man was at that crisis—and Churchmen knew it well—of more moment than if an English army had crossed the Border.

Immediately after he landed, Knox learned that the preachers Paul Methven, John Christison, William Harlaw, and John Willock were under summons to appear before the Justiciary Court at Stirling eight days later. He praised God that he had come "even in the brunt of the battell," and at once resolved to stand by the side of his brethren, "be life, be death, or els be both, to glorifie His godlie name, who thus mercifully hath heard my long cryes." [3]

After his coming, events, each one of which is a

[1] Froude's History, ch. 37.   [2] See M'Crie's note in loco.
[3] Letters—Works, vol. vi. p. 21.

landmark in the history, followed in rapid succession. At a conference in Dundee to which Knox hurried, it was resolved "that the whole multitude and number of of brethrein sould accompanie their preachers"[1] to Stirling, as before they had threatened to do when the summons was to St. Andrews. For that purpose they advanced to Perth: and the Laird of Dun went on before to apprise the Queen Regent that the object of their coming "was onlie to geve confessioun with thare preachearis, and to assist thame in thare just defence."[2] The crafty daughter of the House of Guise received him with her most winning smile, and gave promise that if the Congregation would remain in Perth the summons should be "continued till farther advisement." Though not without suspicion of guile, the leaders deemed it best to accept the assurance. They were shamefully deceived. When the 10th of May arrived and the preachers did not appear they were outlawed and put to the horn: and the gentlemen who had become sureties for their appearance were fined.

The tidings of the Regent's perfidy reached the Congregation the following day. We can well believe that Knox would be in his most fervid mood when he entered the pulpit and thundered forth God's curse against idolatry; but nothing unusual would have happened, for the greater part of the audience had quietly dispersed, had not a priest advanced to the high altar, and, as if in defiance of the doctrine which had just been proclaimed, begun to celebrate mass. A boy cried out, "This is intolerable, that when God by His Worde

---

[1] Letters—Works, vol. vi. p. 22.
[2] History, vol. i. p. 317.

hath planelie damned idolatrie, we shall stand and see it used in despyte." The priest struck the boy, who after the manner of his kind threw a stone at his assailant, which missing its mark shattered to pieces an image on the altar. The iconoclastic spirit is infectious, and in a few minutes all the madonnas and saints and angels and crucifixes in the building were lying on the floor broken into a thousand fragments. Some one having raised the cry, "To the Greyfriars," there was a rush from the dismantled church, and in a very short time, spite of gates and bars, the monasteries of the Grey and Blackfriars, and the Charter-house—the burial-place of the first of the Jameses—were completely wrecked; "the walles onlie did remane of all these great edificationis."

Though Knox is careful to exculpate the gentlemen and the "earnest professouris" from all share in this outrage, which he attributes to "the raschall multitude," yet it is not without touches of sympathetic glee that he tells, for example, of how "in verray deid the Grey Frieris was a place so weall provided, that oneles honest men had sein the same, we wold have feared to have reported what provisioun thei had. Thare scheittis, blancattis, beddis, and covertouris wer suche, as no Erle in Scotland hath the bettir. Thair naiprie was fyne. Thei wer bot awght personis in convent, and yitt had viii punscheonis of salt beaff (considder the tyme of the yeare, the ellevint day of Maii), wyne, beare, and aill, besydis stoare of victuallis effeiring thareto. The lyik haboundance was nott in the Blak Frearis; and yitt thare was more then becam men professing povertie."[1]

The Queen Regent saw in the riot an opportunity

[1] History, vol. i. pp. 322-3.

for carrying out more boldly than heretofore the French policy. She summoned the foreign troops garrisoned at Leith, and entirely disregarded the counsels of moderation addressed to her by Argyle and Lord James Stuart, who were still with her. The news of her determination to march on Perth spread like wildfire, and soon Glencairn, at the head of an army of two thousand five hundred Westland men, was on his way to the defence of the menaced city. The Regent was fain to secure its peaceable surrender by once more making promises which she never meant to keep.

It is at this point that Knox comes to the front as the avowed leader of the Congregation. We can trace his hand in the series of manifestoes issued from Perth, addressed to the Queen Regent, to the nobility of Scotland, and to "the generatioun of Antichrist, the pestilent Prelattis and thare schavellingis," which are in a firmer tone and show deeper insight into all the issues involved in the conflict, than the documents which had been drawn up before his return. Nor did he shrink from the responsibilities of leadership. He waited on Argyle, Lord James Stuart, and Lord Sempill, who had come as Commissioners from the Regent, and he sent to her by them two solemn warnings which, said he, "I require of yow, in the name of the eternall God, *as from my mouth*, to say unto hir Grace."

No sooner had the Regent obtained possession of Perth than the terms on which the Congregation had surrendered it were flagrantly violated. The mass was re-established. Knox, who failed not to see the humorous side of any incident, tells us that "becaus the altaris war nocht so easy to be repaired agane, thay provided tables, whairof sum befoir used to serve for drunkardis, dysaris, and carteris; bot thay war holy aneuch for the Preast and his padgean." A garrison, if not of French soldiers, at least of soldiers paid with French money, was placed in the city "to maynteane idolatrie, and to resist the Congregatioun."

The Earl of Argyle, Lord James Stuart, and others of the nobility who had till now been on the side of the Regent, in the interests, as they supposed, of good order, were so shocked by her violation of the word they had plighted in her name that they withdrew from her standard and joined the Congregation, which at their summons convened at St. Andrews. The Primate in alarm gathered as many followers as he could, and threatened the Lords that if John Knox were allowed to preach in his cathedral church, he should "be saluted with a dosane of culveringis, quherof the most part should lyght upoun his nose." The more timid counselled that some other preacher should occupy the pulpit, but the Reformer was resolute. In this place God had first called him to speak publicly in His name. He had been reft from it by the tyranny of France and by procurement of the bishops; when he was wasted and weary in the galleys he had seen the steeple of this church through the mist, and there had been given to him then an "assured houp" "in oppin audience, to preache in Sanctandrois befoir he depairted thys lyeff." Since God had brought him to the place, nothing should hinder him from doing his duty. Of what were they afraid? Is not his "lyef in the custody of Him whose gloric he seaks." Clearly this is not a man with whom counsels of prudence would much avail; and so he had his way, and "did entreat of the ejectioun of the byaris and the sellaris furth of the Tempill of Jerusalem" to such good purpose, that not by public tumult, but in an orderly manner, and under the sanction of the magistrates, "all monumentis of idolatrie" in the city were destroyed.

Then followed the muster on Cupar Moor, at which "men seemed rained from the clouds"; the withdrawal of the Regent, first to Edinburgh and then to Dunbar; the relief of Perth from the hated garrison; the sack of Scone; the march on Stirling and destruction of its abbeys, till at last the Congregation took possession of Edinburgh on the 29th of June. It was on the 2nd of May that Knox had landed at Leith. Within the space of two short months the battle had been fought and won; the mediæval Church of Scotland was already lying in ruins. Save for the blood of martyrs, it was up to this point an all but bloodless victory. It had cost, indeed, the sacrifice of many a fair abbey, the levelling of many a goodly pillar, and the shattering of many a storied window. We regret these accidents of the war, as in celebrating any triumph we fail not to mourn the thousands slain; but we venture to assert that the religious and political freedom of Scotland was in these months cheaply purchased. It is not at all certain that Knox ever said that "the best way to keep the rooks from returning was to pull down their nests"; but if he did he was probably right.

Before the work of destruction thus accomplished could be pronounced permanent and the work of reconstruction begun, costlier sacrifices had to be made. The Reformers were magnanimous in the hour of their triumph, and hastened to the Queen Regent with the assurance that in what they had done they meant no disloyalty to her Government. They found her in a conciliatory mood. She was ready to promise to recall the sentence of outlawry that had been pronounced against the preachers, and to concede almost any reasonable demand. All the while she was labouring to disunite the Congregation and to gain time till the multitude which had hurriedly gathered to the standard of Reform should have dispersed. Her device was so far successful that when at last she marched on Edinburgh, the remnant of the Congregation who held it were fain to come to terms, and give up the city on condition that the Reformed worship should not be disturbed. It was deemed expedient that Knox, who had been already elected minister of Edinburgh, should not remain when the surrender took effect. His place in St. Giles' was filled by John Willock, while he occupied himself by preaching in almost all the districts of the Lowlands, thus doing more to extend and consolidate the Reformation than if he had remained in the metropolis.

It soon became evident that the Congregation were not, if left unaided, equal to the task of overcoming the Regent. The unfortunate delay which followed their triumphant march to Edinburgh led not only to the dispersion of a large part of their forces, but to an accession of strength to the other side. The peace between France and England concluded at Cambray on March 12th, 1559, enabled the Regent to obtain re-inforcements of French troops, which entrenched themselves at Leith. The Castle of Edinburgh was held by Lord Erskine, and maintained a position of neutrality, which, however, might any day be changed into one of hostility to the Congregation. The deposition of the Regent, after consulting Knox and Willock, and obtaining from them a declaration that there was scriptural warrant for the deed, was in the circumstances an empty form. The Duke of Chatelherault was once more on the side of Protestantism, but what could he—a waverer at the best—do against the power of France, guarded by strong fortifications. He had at his back only an undisciplined and ill-armed host, consisting of the barons and their household retainers, with a motley company of civilians who had been attracted to their standard; and there was no money to provide food for his army, even if it had been otherwise hopeful for that army to attempt a siege.

All eyes were turned to England, whose Protestant Queen was the natural ally of the Scottish Congregation. But altogether apart from her dislike of Knox, and her queenly disinclination to interfere in behalf of subjects nominally in rebellion against their lawful sovereign, there were acknowledged difficulties in Elizabeth's way. She had just concluded a treaty of peace with France; and even if she had been disposed to risk the renewal of hostilities with that country, the attitude of Philip of Spain made it very doubtful whether he would not in that event ally himself with her enemies. If she interfered in Scotland she thus ran the risk, for the sake of a cause with which she only half sympathized—for the Scottish Reformation was taking a form that was not pleasing to her—of having all the Catholic powers arrayed against her. The best evidence that those dangers were not imaginary, is that even Knox—who of all men loved a straightforward policy—brought himself in the desperate case to suggest dissimulation. In a letter of 25th October, 1559, signed "John Sinclair," and addressed to Sir James Crofts, Governor of Berwick, he says: "If you list to craft with thame, the sending of a thousand or mo men to us can breake no league nor point of peace contracted betwix you and Fraunce: For it is free for your subjects to serve in warr any prence or nation for thare wages. And yf ye fear that such excusses shall not prevaile, you may declayr thame rebells to your Realme when ye shal be assured that thei be in our companye."[1]

On the other hand it would clearly be in the end fatal for Elizabeth to permit the Protestantism of Scotland to be stamped out under the heel of the Frenchman, and thus to give to those who sought to overturn her throne, and with it the English Reformation, the very fulcrum on which of all others they most wished to rest their lever. This the clear-eyed Cecil, who was in constant communication with Knox, saw well; but he was only able to obtain the consent of his mistress to unavowed and intermittent help. At length, after the wreck, by a storm as timely as that which scattered the Spanish Armada, of a French fleet which had sailed for Leith; after the death of Mary of Guise, which took from the French party the chief inspiration of their courage; and after Elizabeth had come to see that her devices to conceal the assistance she was rendering were too transparent, and that by half measures she was losing much and gaining little, the beleagured and half-starved Frenchmen in Leith were brought to terms and sent home in English transports. The treaty of peace was proclaimed at the Cross of Edinburgh on the 8th of July, 1560. The deliverance

[1] Letters, etc., Works, vol. vi. p. 90.

had come so suddenly at last that the Congregation were like men that dreamed. They gathered in St. Giles', and Knox rendered solemn thanks in their name. The words of thanksgiving, which he has preserved in his History, are simple, some may think them prosaic; but surely no Te Deum that ever pealed out the praises of a triumphant nation was the utterance of a more heartfelt gratitude. On August 1st the estates of Parliament that had been adjourned, re-assembled. It was remitted to Knox and his colleagues to prepare the Confession of Faith. They did their work in four days. Creed-making was easy then; when in revolt against the authority of Popes and Councils, men had laid hold of a few simple truths of Scripture, and the age of speculation had not yet come. It was specially easy in Scotland, where there was one master-mind to guide deliberation. On the 17th of August, all necessary preliminaries having been gone through, the Confession was ratified and the Reformation was established.

During the session of Parliament, Knox "taught publiclie the prophet Haggeus"—that part of him clearly in which he chides those who say the time is not come, the time that the Lord's house should be built. He spoke so vehemently of the duty which now devolved on the delivered nation to make provision for the maintenance of the Reformed Church, that Maitland of Lethington, the ablest, but not the most spiritual of the leaders of the Congregation, exclaimed, "We mon now forget our selffis, and beir the barrow to buyld the housses of God." The rest of Knox's life-work was a contention with the spirit which these words reveal, and which was more or less the spirit of all the barons who had joined the Congregation. With some of them the only motive, with many of them a chief motive, of their reforming zeal, was that they might share the spoil of the dispossessed monks. They were ready enough to ratify a Confession of Faith, but when it came to the Book of Discipline, with its provision for the superintendents, ministers, and readers, and its liberal arrangements for secondary and primary schools, they hesitated and delayed. With them, and with another who is now to come more directly on the scene, Knox had unresting conflict to the close.

That other was Mary Stuart, who, now a widow, returned to her native country to take the reins of government into her own hands. Knox specifies not only the day when she landed—the 19th August, 1561—but the hour, "betwix sevin and aught houris befoir noon," and adds, "The verray face of heavin, the time of hir arryvall, did manifestlie speak what confort was brought into this contry with hir, to wit, sorow, dolour, darknes and all impietie. . . . The sun was not seyn to schyne two dayis befoir nor two dayis after."[1] It was in no churlish spirit that he thus wrote. He did not grudge the cordiality of the welcome she received, or that the Protestants joined in it—"thairintill thai war not to be blamed." But it was his deliberate judgment as a historian—and the verdict of subsequent history has confirmed it—that it was a dark day for Scotland that 19th of August, 1561.

The collision between the preacher and the Queen came very soon. On the first Sunday after her landing, mass was privately celebrated at Holyrood. Great was the commotion among the Congregation at the setting up of "that idoll" which Parliament had so recently

[1] History, vol. ii. pp. 268-9.

banished, making its restoration a capital offence. Loud were the mutterings to the effect that "the idolater preast should dye the death"; but Lord James Stuart took his stand at the chapel door to secure for the Queen the liberty of worship he had promised her when he conveyed the invitation to return. One after another of the fiery lords came spurring up to Edinburgh as the tidings reached them; but like the riders forth from Jezreel at Jehu's advance, they had hardly put their indignant question when they submissively fell silent. Robert Campbell of Kingyeancleugh said to his Ayrshire neighbour, Lord Ochiltree, when the latter appeared upon the scene: "My Lord, now ye are come, and almost the last of all the rest; and I perceave by your anger that the fyre-edge is nott of you yit; but I fear that after that the holy watter of the Courte be sprinckled upoun you, that ye sall become als temperat as the rest: For I have been here now fyve dayis, and at the first I hard everie man say, 'Let us hang the Preast,' but after that had bene twyse or thrise in the Abbay all that fervency was past. I think thair be some inchantment whareby men ar bewitched."[1]

It was even so. The girl-widow of nineteen, with that peculiar beauty which so baffled painters that no two of them gave the same rendering of it, charmed the rough Lords of the Congregation, if not into approval of her ways, at least into sullen acquiescence. And those of them who had seen the world, and were withal too strong to be wheedled out of their principles by a woman's smile, were no less "bewitched" by the hope of making Mary the instrument of the policy

[1] History, vol. ii. pp. 275-6.

of union with England, which sad experience of the fruits of the French alliance had now taught them was the one true policy for Scotland. Some of them—Maitland notably—cared nothing for religion, deeming it "a bogle of the nursery," and only worthy the attention of grown men when it could be made an instrument of statecraft. Others of them, such as Lord James Stuart, who were sincere in their attachment to the principles of the Reformation, believed that by forbearance they could gain the political end they sought without sacrificing the liberties they had fought for—nay, they were not without hope that Mary might even be found willing to secure the English succession at the cost of sacrificing her Catholicism.

There was one man in the land who was proof against either witchery. His keen grey eye could look into Mary's face and not be blinded by her smile; it could see into her policy and divine the schemes which that smile was meant to conceal. And so, on the very first Sunday he mounted the pulpit of St. Giles', and "inveighing against idolatrie, schew what terrible plagues God had tacken upon realmes and nationis for the same;" and added, "That one messe (thair war no mair suffered at the first) was more fearful to him then gif ten thousand armed enemyes war landed in any pairte of the realme, of purpose to suppress the hoill religioun." These are not the words of ignorant fanaticism. They express the deliberate conviction of the most enlightened man in the Scotland of that day. Recent research into long-buried State papers has brought to light the fact that when Mary Stuart resolved to return to Scotland, it was of deliberate purpose to destroy the Reformation. From the day of her landing that purpose was avowed in letters to her uncle, Cardinal Lorraine, and the French ministers, to the Spanish King and the Duke of Alva, and to the Pope himself. At the very time, in 1566, when she issued a proclamation to her subjects assuring them of her determination to uphold the established religion and rebutting as calumnies all assertions to the contrary, we find her writing to Philip of Spain telling him that the hour had come for him to send assistance to restore Scotland to the Catholic Church.[1]

In the same letter she reveals that the ultimate design was on England as well. If that which the Lords of the Congregation, in their zeal for the union of the Crowns, joined with her in importunately asking—the formal recognition of her claim to the English succession—had been conceded, it does not admit of doubt that Elizabeth's throne would very soon have been vacant; that Mary would have ascended it over the ruins of both the Churches; and that the Smithfield fires would have been once more lighted. Bacon and Cecil saw this and laboured, with a majority of the English Council against them, to prevent even an interview between Elizabeth and the Scottish Queen. Knox alone on the north of the Border had his eyes open to the danger, and it was therefore that he reckoned one mass at Holyrood to be more fearful than ten thousand armed men.

The sermon in which the words were used led to the first of his famous interviews with the Queen. In

---

[1] Labanoff, referred to and quoted in an admirable lecture on the Influence of Knox and the Scottish Reformation on England, delivered in 1860 by the Right Honourable Lord Moncrieff, then the Lord-Advocate for Scotland. See also Froude's History, and Influence of the Reformation, in Short Studies, vol. i.

that long " ressoning," Mary Stuart heard from the lips of Knox, with an amazement which struck her dumb "more than the quarter of ane hour," words anent the rights of subjects on occasion to resist their princes " even by power "—words which were used in the next century to justify the action of those who brought her grandson to the scaffold. But all is spoken with the truest courtesy, and when they were parting he said, " I pray God, madam, that ye may be als blessed within the Commounwealth of Scotland, yf it be the pleasur of God, as ever Debora was in the Commounwealth of Israell." Though in subsequent interviews there were stronger words on his part and stormier behaviour on hers, he never forgot the respect due to her sex and to her office. But he, too, had an office which he deemed as sacred as hers. When she sent for him anent his sermon, preached when there had been dancing at the Court, after evil tidings had come from France of successes against the Huguenots, she proposed in conciliatory tone that if he had aught to complain of, he should come to herself and tell her. He replied courteously but firmly that he was " called to to ane publict function within the Kirk of God," that he was " appointed by God to rebuke the sinnes and vices of all." " I am not," said he, " appointed to cum to everie man in particular to schaw him his offense; for that laubour war infinite." If her Grace would come to the Kirk she would fully understand both what he likes and mislikes, " als weall in your Majistie as in all others." Finally, if she would assign him a day and hour when it would please her to hear "the forme and substance of doctrin " he was publicly teaching, he should wait upon her Grace. " But to waitt upon your chalmer-doore or ellis whair, and then to have no farther libertie but to whisper my mynd in your Grace's eare, or to tell you what others think and speak of you, neather will my conscience nor the vocatioun whairto God hath called me suffer it." It was at the close of this interview that he was going out "with a reasonable meary countenánce; whairat some Papistis offended said, 'He is not effrayed.' Which heard of him he answered, 'Why should the pleasing face of a gentill woman effray me? I have looked in the faces of many angrie men, and yet have nott been effrayed above measure.' "[1]

At another interview—that following his sermon against the Spanish marriage—when she asked him angrily, "What have ye to do with my mariage? or what ar ye within this Commounwealth?" he answered, and in his reply we seem to hear the far-off tread of the advancing democracy: "A subject borne within the same, madam. And albeit I be neather Erle, Lord, nor Barroun within it, yitt hes God maid me (how abject that ever I be in your eyes) a profitable member within the same." At the plain but still courteous words that followed she burst into passionate tears. Good John Erskine of Dun tried to comfort her, as one not over-wise might comfort a petulant child, by giving "unto hir many pleasing wordis of hir beautie, of hir excellence, and how that all the Princes of Europe wold be glaid to seak hir favouris." Not so the other John. It is a fine picture we have given us in the old chronicle. He "stood still, without any alteratioun of countenance for a long seasson, whill that the Quene gave place to hir in-

[1] History, vol. ii. p. 334.

ordinat passioun; and in the end he said; 'Madam, in Goddis presence I speak: I never delyted in the weaping of any of Goddis creatures; yea I can skarslie weill abyd the tearis of my awin boyes whome my awin hand correctis, much less can I rejoise in your Majestie's weaping. But seeing that I have offered unto you no just occasioun to be offended, but have spocken the trueth, as my vocatioun craves of me, I man sustean (albeit unwillinglie) your Majesties tearis, rather then I dar hurte my conscience, or betray my Commounwealth through my silence," I ask you to judge which of these two ways of speaking to the Queen was the more truly respectful?

But it was in St. Giles' that Knox's power was felt. He was the uncrowned, but real king of Scotland, and his pulpit was his throne. Around it he gathered the forces that saved the Reformation—the Commons of Scotland, whom he so taught to see with his own intelligence the issues of the conflict which he was waging against the Court, and so nerved with his own courage that they stood firm, when the Lords —even those of them who still remained true to Protestantism—were tempted to waver. Every one knows that picture drawn for us by James Melville,[1] of the old man " with a furring of martricks about his neck, a staff in the an hand, and guid godlie Richart Ballanden, his servand, halding upe the uther oxtar from the Abbey to the paroche kirk" of St. Andrews, "and be the said Richart and another servant lifted upe to the pulpit, whar he behovit to lean at his first entrie; bot or he haid done with his sermont, he

[1] Autobiography and Diary of Mr. James Melville (Woodrow Socy. ed.) p. 33.

was sa active and vigorus that he was lyk to ding that pulpit in blads, and fly out of it." It is not so well known that this was at an important crisis, when his voice, "like ten thousand trumpets braying in the ear of Scottish Protestantism," averted a disastrous policy.

Only one of his sermons has been preserved in full. Its subject is the first nine verses of the 26th chapter of Isaiah. The circumstances in which it was preached are memorable. Poor Darnley, finding that his attendance at the Queen's mass was exciting suspicion that he had abjured his Protestantism, resolved to appear at St. Giles' in state. He had a throne set up in the Church on which he sate himself down, doubtlsse expecting that the preacher would be duly grateful for this evidence of his loyalty to the established order in religion. Little did he know that preacher's character. No smooth words flattered the vanity of the poor kingling. Sharp arrows flew about his head—words quoted from the Geneva version of the prophet's oracle, concerning God's dealings with the land, "from whom he taketh away the strong man," and to whom he will appoint "children to be their princes, and babes shall rule over them. Children are extorcyoners of my people and women have rule over them."[1] We do not wonder that Darnley returned to the palace in great wrath, nor that it was deemed advisable that Knox should retire from Edinburgh for a little after this incident.

His labours were not confined to the capital, nor did he occupy himself only with politics. We find him in 1562, for example, answering a challenge sent him by

[1] A Sermon, etc., Works, vol. vi. p. 242.

JOHN KNOX. 467

Abbot Kennedy of Crossraguel, and "ressoning" for three days in the house of the Provost of the Collegiate Church at Maybole, on the doctrine of the Mass. The record of the "ressoning" has been preserved by Knox, and the house in which it took place is standing still, in a steep, narrow street of the old feudal town, so that we are able to realize the scene. In presence of the lords and gentry of the west, who, forty on either side, were crowded into an upper room, and looked on as at a tournament—for the age of chivalry has given place to the age of "ressoning," and the conflict of ideas has begun—the two combatants, the stern preacher on the one hand, the son of an Earl and of an Earl's daughter, the lordly Abbot on the other, enter the lists. There is all the fine courtesy of the old chivalry. Knox calls his opponent "My Lord," though he is careful to protest that he does so "by reason of blood and not of office." For three days the battle rages round one single point. The Abbot, who opens the debate, contends that Christ could not be a priest after the order of Melchizedek unless he offered a propitiatory sacrifice of bread and wine, inasmuch as Melchizedek offered such a sacrifice. Knox replies that there is no evidence that the bread and wine brought forth by Melchizedek were offered in propitiatory sacrifice. He suggests, but with true Scotch caution is careful to protest that the suggestion is in no wise essential to his arguments, that the bread and wine were brought forth for the refreshment of Abraham and his men. And so on from day to day the contention proceeds between two men who both understand the art of intellectual fencing. At the end of the third day Knox, always practical and always human, suggests that "the noblemen here assembled are altogether destitute of all provision both for hors and man," and that the reasoning might be adjourned to Ayr, "whair that better easment might be had for all estates." But to this Kennedy, who has probably had enough of it, will not agree, and so the battle ends.

In Knox's record of the debate we have a fine example of his humour, his grim, Semitic humour, as of Elijah mocking the priests of Baal, or Isaiah making mirth of idolaters. He says: "The poore god of bread is most miserable of all other idoles; for, according to there matter whereof thay are made, they will remane without corruption many yeares. But within one year this god will putrifie, and then he must be burnt; they can abyde the vehemencie of the wind, frost, rain, or snow. But the wind will blow that god to the sea, the rain or the snow will make it dagh again; yea, which is most of all to be feared, that god is a pray (if he be not wel kept) to rattes and mise; for they will desire no better denner than white rounde gods ynew. But O then, what becometh of Christes natural bodie? By myrackle, it flies to the heaven againe, if the Papists teach treulie; for how sone soever the mouse takes hold, so sone flieth Christ away, and letteth hir gnaw the bread. A bold and puissant mouse, but a feble and miserable god: yet wold I ask a question; whether hath the priest or the mouse greater power? By his words it is made a god: by hir teeth it ceaseth to be a god: let them avise, and then answer."[1] Humour such as this—and sometimes of a kindlier type—were an unfailing

[1] Works, vol. vi. pp. 172, 3.

characteristic of Knox. It served to keep him from becoming morbid amid the stern conflicts of his life. It saved him from being one-sided, and helped to preserve the balance of mind by virtue of which he united to the most burning earnestness, a Scotch caution, and a statesmanlike prudence.

His humour gives its peculiar charm to his History of the Reformation, with the preparation of which he occupied himself at intervals during the busy years of his Edinburgh ministry. His authorship of this work has been disputed, but the internal evidence that his hand and no other drew those graphic pictures seems to us conclusive. If Knox did not write the first four books of the History, then another man of apparently equal intellectual power, but of whose existence we have no other trace, lived in Scotland in the latter part of the sixteenth century.

But the time came when John Knox must lay down the burden of mortal life. We have pleasant pictures of the closing scenes in that old house in the Canongate, where he was lovingly ministered to by his young wife; for Marjory Bowes was dead, her poor mother had also gone out from among the shadows which encompassed her, and Knox had wedded a daughter of Lord Ochiltree. When some of his old friends came to see him he "caused peirce ane hoggeid of wine" which was in his cellar, that they and he might have happy fellowship before they parted. His dying request to his wife that she should read to him the 17th chapter of St. John, where he "first cast anchor," is very beautiful. That anchor he cast had held, though storms had been loud and long; and he would cast it anew that he might ride out the last storm of all. When the end was at hand, and the voice before which rulers had trembled had gone silent, they asked him to indicate that faith failed not, and he did so by lifting his hand upward. And thus on Monday, 24th November, 1572, he entered into rest, of whom Regent Morton said at his burial, that he never feared the face of man.

His grave in the courtyard of the Parliament House, under the shadow of his own St. Giles', is not desecrated though the busy crowds pass over it, and hardly note it as they hurry on:

> " Let the sound of those he wrought for,
> And the feet of those he fought for,
> Echo round his bones for evermore."

If our civil and religious liberties have made our nation great and strong, it is to him we owe them. He is the father of his country. He saw much that was hidden from his generation, and many things he indicated in his Book of Discipline are still unrealized. Shall we complain that the man who won for us our freedom often used rough words? The complaint is surely unreasonable—as unreasonable as it would be to detract from the glory of Bannockburn because the men who fought our battle there did not fight it with Armstrong guns and Martini rifles, but with the spears and the battle-axes that were laid to their hands. John Knox spoke the word that was given him to speak; he spoke it in the dialect of his time; and by speaking it he saved his land.

The Second Edition, in Crown 8vo., price 7s. 6d.

THE LIFE OF A SCOTTISH PROBATIONER;

Being the Memoir of THOMAS DAVIDSON.

With his POEMS and LETTERS.

BY JAMES BROWN, D.D., ST. JAMES'S, PAISLEY.

Dr. John Brown,
Author of "Rab and his Friends."

"A worthy record of a man of rare genius—dead ere his prime. His poems are as beautiful as flowers or birds, and the letters might have been written by a Scotch U.P. Charles Lamb."

Blackwood's Magazine.

"This life of an unknown Scotch probationer is equal in interest to anything of the kind we have had since Carlyle's 'Life of Sterling' was written. Thomas Davidson, as a poet, as a humourist, as a simple, loving, honest, reticent, valiant soul, demands adequate recognition at the hands of the critic—a career kind and unostentatious, glorified, however, in its uneventful homeliness by a rare vein of poetry and a rich vein of humour. The key-note of the character is its sound and healthy but modest manliness. The *mens sana* is a most precious possession. Davidson began to sicken of the disease of which he died before he was eight-and-twenty, but sickness did not unsteady the even balance of his mind. It is after he is laid aside from active work that his humour is at its best and brightest, and his lyrical faculty in its finest mood. The whole picture is pleasant, but the finishing touches make it nearly if not altogether unique.......... The poetry is genuine, the humour is genuine, and the character (that which underlies both) as genuine as the poetry and the humour—the humour, indeed, went deep into the life."

Spectator.

"A charming little biography. His was one of those rare natures which fascinates all who come in contact with it."

Nonconformist.

"It is an unspeakable pleasure to a reviewer weary of wading through piles of commonplace to come unexpectedly on a prize such as this."

Dundee Advertiser.

"Davidson's letters and poems prove him incomparably superior in genius, wit, and humour to any Border poet of this century, except, it may be, Thomas Aird. Apart from 'Ariadne,' with its exquisitely finished and classical pathos, and the 'Hobgoblinade,' which ranks with Burns's 'Death and Dr. Hornbook,' the lines on 'The Cheviots' are the finest descant on those famous hills we ever heard, and passes over them like the most delicious and spiritual gleam of a dying autumn day, giving them a lustre not of this earth."

GLASGOW: JAMES MACLEHOSE & SONS, Publishers to the University.

LONDON: MACMILLAN & CO.

SCOTTISH HISTORY AND LITERATURE,
TO THE
PERIOD OF THE REFORMATION.

By JOHN M. ROSS, LL.D.

Edited, with Memoir, by JAMES BROWN, D.D.

Demy 8vo, 450 pp., 14s.

Times.

"Dr. Ross was deeply versed in Old Scotch Literature; his patriotic enthusiasm is intense, but duly controlled in expression by a sufficient sense of humour. His book is not a dry compendium of facts, but a vivid account of the national life of Scotland viewed now from the political and now from the literary point of view."

Athenæum.

"This volume is 'thorough and honest,' is written in an engaging style, and forms a masterly and complete survey of the periods and subjects with which it deals. The whole work is characterized by a fulness of knowledge, a closeness of study, a breadth of vision, a firmness of grasp, and a shrewdness of observation, together with an elegance and sometimes eloquence of expression that will make it at once pleasant to the common reader and satisfactory to the exacting critic."

Scotsman.

"Dr. Ross's volume must be pronounced to be a work of quite exceptional literary and historical value. It fills a place of its own at once in the literary history and in the historical literature of Scotland."

Academy.

"There is no trace in this volume of mental weariness or perfunctory cram. It is nothing short of masterly. The style is full, nervous, perspicuous, vitalized by an enthusiasm always kept on the safe side by humour and good sense. In the warmth of his patriotic and moral enthusiasm, in his thorough mastery of details, as well as in the glowing energy of his style, he reminds us of Mr. Green."

Spectator.

"This is the best manual of the two subjects of which it treats at present in existence. Dr. Ross has evidently had a passion for his subject, and has gone straight to the ancient records, both Scotch and English, as the fountain head of all available knowledge. Dr. Ross is seen at his best when dealing with the legends that have grown round the memories of Scotland's national heroes. He separates the wheat from the chaff in Barbour's Brus; and we have never seen a more masterly exposition than that which he gives of the brutalities and chronological absurdities of Blind Harry's Wallace. . . . . Nothing in northern literature shows the intensity of the Scotch national spirit more clearly than this book."

British Quarterly Review.

"The volume is at once popular and descriptive, critical and philosophical."

www.ingramcontent.com/pod-product-compliance
Lightning Source LLC
Chambersburg PA
CBHW051856300426
44117CB00006B/413